RSAC

JUN   2002

D0072840

In *The Cambridge Companion to Keats*, leading scholars discuss Keats's work in several fascinating contexts: literary history and key predecessors; Keats's life in London's intellectual, aesthetic and literary culture; the relation of his poetry to the visual arts; the critical traditions and theoretical contexts within which Keats's life and achievements have been assessed. These specially commissioned essays examine Keats's specific poetic endeavours, his striking way with language, and his lively letters as well as his engagement with contemporary cultures and literary traditions, his place in criticism, from his day to ours, including the challenge he poses to gender criticism. The contributions are sophisticated but accessible, challenging but lucid, and are complemented by an introduction to Keats's life, a chronology, a descriptive list of contemporary people and periodicals, a source-reference for famous phrases and ideas articulated in Keats's letters, a glossary of literary terms and a guide to further reading.

CAMBRIDGE COMPANIONS TO LITERATURE

CAMBRIDGE COMPANIONS TO CULTURE

THE CAMBRIDGE
COMPANION TO
KEATS

EDITED BY
SUSAN J. WOLFSON
Princeton University

CAMBRIDGE
UNIVERSITY PRESS

PUBLISHED BY THE PRESS SYNDICATE OF THE UNIVERSITY OF CAMBRIDGE
The Pitt Building, Trumpington Street, Cambridge, United Kingdom

CAMBRIDGE UNIVERSITY PRESS
The Edinburgh Building, Cambridge CB2 2RU, UK
40 West 20th Street, New York, NY 10011-4211, USA
10 Stamford Road, Oakleigh, VIC 3166, Australia
Ruiz de Alarcón 13, 28014 Madrid, Spain
Dock House, The Waterfront, Cape Town 8001, South Africa

http://www.cambridge.org

© Cambridge University Press 2001

This book is in copyright. Subject to statutory exception
and to the provisions of relevant collective licensing agreements,
no reproduction of any part may take place without
the written permission of Cambridge University Press.

First published 2001

Printed in the United Kingdom at the University Press, Cambridge

Typeface Adobe Sabon 10/13pt   *System* QuarkXpress®   [SE]

A catalogue record for this book is available from the British Library

Library of Congress Cataloguing in Publication data
The Cambridge companion to Keats / edited by Susan J. Wolfson.
p.   cm.
Includes bibliographical references and index.
ISBN 0 521 65126 3 (hardback) – ISBN 0 521 65839 X (paperback)
1. Keats, John, 1795–1821 – Criticism and interpretation.   I. Wolfson, Susan J., 1948–

PR4837.C27 2001
821′.7–dc21

ISBN 0 521 65126 3 hardback
ISBN 0 521 65839 X paperback

821.7 K226zw 2001
The Cambridge companion to
Keats

To the memory of Stuart M. Sperry, Jr.,
our companion to John Keats

CONTENTS

NOTES ON CONTRIBUTORS

JOHN BARNARD, Professor of English Literature at the School of English in the University of Leeds, is the author of *John Keats* (1987) and the editor of *John Keats: The Complete Poems* (1973). In addition to still other work on the Romantics, he has written on seventeenth-century literature and book history.

JEFFREY N. COX, Professor of Comparative Literature and Director of the Center for Humanities and the Arts at the University of Colorado, Boulder, is the author of *Poetry and Politics in the Cockney School: Keats, Shelley, Hunt and their Circle* (1998). His work on Keats also includes essays in *Studies in Romanticism, Texas Studies in Literature and Language*, and *Romanticism on the Net*.

JOHN KANDL, Associate Professor of English and Director of the Honors Program at Walsh University, has published articles and reviews on Keats and Romanticism, and is editing *Keats's Selected Poems* for Broadview Press.

WILLIAM C. KEACH, Professor of English at Brown University, is the author of *Shelley's Style* (1984), and "Cockney Couplets: Keats and the Politics of Style" (1986). He has edited *Coleridge: The Complete Poems* (1997), and is completing a book about language and politics in the Romantic period.

THERESA M. KELLEY, Professor of English at the University of Wisconsin, is the author of *Wordsworth's Revisionary Aesthetics* (1988) and *Reinventing Allegory* (1997), as well as articles on Keats: "Keats, Ekphrasis, and History" (1994) and "Poetics and the Politics of Reception: Keats's 'La Belle Dame sans Merci'" (1987).

GREG KUCICH, Associate Professor of English at the University of Notre Dame and and co-editor of *Nineteenth-Century Contexts: An*

Interdisciplinary Journal, is the author of *Keats, Shelley and Romantic Spenserianism* (1991), "John Keats," in *Literature of the Romantic Period: A Bibliographic Guide* (1998), and essays on women writers of the Romantic era. He is also editing a collection of essays on nineteenth-century British women writers and developing a book tentatively titled *Romanticism and the Re-Engendering of History*.

ANNE K. MELLOR, Distinguished Professor of English and Women's Studies at University of California, Los Angeles, is the author of *Blake's Human Form Divine* (1974), *English Romantic Irony* (1980), *Mary Shelley: Her Life, Her Fiction, Her Monsters* (1988), *Romanticism and Gender* (1993), and *Mothers of the Nation: Women's Political Writing in England 1780–1830* (2000). She edited *Romanticism and Feminism* (1988), and co-edited *The Other Mary Shelley* (1993), *British Literature 1780–1830* (1996), and *Passionate Encounters in a Time of Sensibility* (2000).

VINCENT NEWEY is Professor of English at the University of Leicester, joint editor of *The Byron Journal*, and Past President of the British Association for Romantic Studies. He is the author of "Keats, History, and the Poets" (*Keats and History*, 1994). Other publications include *Cowper's Poetry: A Critical Study and Reassessment* (1982), *Centring the Self: Subjectivity, Society and Reading from Thomas Gray to Thomas Hardy* (1995), and (coeditor) *Mortal Pages, Literary Lives: Studies in Nineteenth-Century Autobiography* (1996).

ALAN RICHARDSON is Professor of English at Boston College. His books include *Literature, Education, and Romanticism: Reading as Social Practice* (1994), *British Romanticism and the Science of the Mind* (forthcoming), and (co-editor) *Romanticism, Race, and Imperial Culture 1780–1834* (1996). He has also published numerous essays on Romantic-era literature and culture, particularly in relation to gender, childhood and education, colonialism, and early neuroscience.

CHRISTOPHER RICKS is Warren Professor of the Humanities and co-director of the Editorial Institute at Boston University. His publications include *Milton's Grand Style* (1963), *Keats and Embarrassment* (1974), *The Force of Poetry* (1987), *Essays in Appreciation* (1996), and *The Oxford Book of English Verse* (ed., 1999). He is a member of the Association of Literary Scholars and Critics.

PAUL SHEATS teaches romantic literature at University of California, Los Angeles. He is the author of "Stylistic Discipline in *The Fall of Hyperion*" (1968), *The Making of Wordsworth's Poetry 1785–1798* (1973), and "Keats, the Greater Ode, and the Trial of Imagination" (1990), as well as revised editions of Wordsworth and Keats. He is currently working on a study of poetic form in the romantic age.

GARRETT STEWART, James O. Freedman Professor of Letters at the University of Iowa, is the author, most recently, of *Reading Voices: Literature and the Phonotext* (1990), *Dear Reader: The Conscripted Audience in Nineteenth-Century British Fiction* (1996), and *Between Film and Screen: Modernism's Photo Synthesis* (2000).

JACK STILLINGER, Advanced Study Professor of English at the University of Illinois, has been writing on Keats for more than forty years. He is the author of *"The Hoodwinking of Madeline" and Other Essays on Keats's Poems* (1971) and "John Keats," in *The English Romantic Poets: A Review of Research and Criticism* (1985). His editions include *The Poems of John Keats* (1978), *John Keats: Poetry Manuscripts at Harvard: A Facsimile Edition* (1990), and the works of Keats in *The Manuscripts of the Younger Romantics: A Facsimile Edition* (1985–1989). His most recent books are a trilogy on literary transaction: *Multiple Authorship and the Myth of Solitary Genius* (1991), *Coleridge and Textual Instability: The Multiple Versions of the Major Poems* (1994), *Reading "The Eve of St. Agnes": The Multiples of Complex Literary Transaction* (1999).

KAREN SWANN, Professor of English at Williams College, has published essays on Wordsworth, Coleridge, and on Keats, the last including "Harassing the Muse" (1988) and "The Strange Time of Reading" (1998). She is developing a study of the posthumous celebrity of Romantic poets, *Lives of the Dead Poets*.

SUSAN J. WOLFSON, Professor of English at Princeton University, is co-editor of "The Romantics and Their Contemporary Writers," *Longman Anthology of British Literature* (1997) and the author of *Formal Charges: The Shaping of Poetry in British Romanticism* (1997), *The Questioning Presence: Wordsworth, Keats, and the Interrogative Mode in Romantic Poetry* (1986), and numerous essays on Romantic-era writers, including Keats: "Keats and the Manhood of the Poet" (1995), "Keats Enters History: Autopsy, *Adonais*, and the Fame of Keats" (1994), "Feminizing Keats" (1990), and "Keats the Letter-Writer" (1982).

DUNCAN WU, Professor of English Literature at St. Catherine's College, Oxford University, is the author of *Wordsworth's Reading 1770–1815* (2 vols., 1993–1995), and editor of *Romanticism: An Anthology* (2nd edn., 1997), *Romantic Women Poets: An Anthology* (1996), and *Selected Writings of William Hazlitt* (9 vols., 1998). He is currently working on *Keats: Interviews and Recollections*.

ACKNOWLEDGMENTS

The Cambridge Companion to John Keats owes much to the scholarship that has produced the editions of the poems and letters we cite throughout the volume, and to the remarkable body of scholarship, criticism, and related writing on which we draw. I thank all the contributors for their generous intelligence, their expertise, and their patience with their editor. I also thank the Department of English at Princeton University for substantial material support.

Susan J. Wolfson

TEXTS AND ABBREVIATIONS

References are to these editions (full information is in the Bibliography):

The Poems of John Keats, ed. Jack Stillinger (unless otherwise specified).
Keats's own titles (*Sleep and Poetry*) are in italics; untitled poems conventionally known by opening phrase or line are titled with quotation marks ("I stood tip-toe").

The Letters of John Keats, ed. H. E. Rollins; cited *KL* by volume and page.
Spelling, punctuation, etc. are original; our insertions for comprehension appear [in square brackets]; Rollins's suppositions about missing letters from tears in the mss. are {in curly braces}

Keats's prose, other than letters, follows *John Keats*, ed. Elizabeth Cook.

The Keats Circle, ed. Rollins (writing by Keats's friends, family &c); cited *KC* by volume and page.

Keats: The Critical Heritage, ed. G. M. Matthews (reviews and reactions); cited as *KCH*

KSJ: *Keats–Shelley Journal*

Works of well-known writers such as Spenser, Shakespeare, Milton, Pope, Wordsworth, Shelley, and Byron are not referred to any specific edition, unless there is a textual issue.

The bibliography supplies full publication information for items cited by title only in the notes and lists for further reading.

GLOSSARY
(all examples are from Keats's poetry)

Alliteration: a repetition of consonants: "beaded bubbles winking at the brim"; "the fever and the fret."

Anagram: a word made of letters rearranged from another word: Keats takes steak; stakes Kate's skate. In "Those lips, O slippery blisses," *lips* is anagrammatically figured in the descriptive, *slip*pery.

Anaphora: the repetition of a word or phrase at the beginning of a series of poetic lines or sentences. "Faded the flower and all its budded charms, / Faded the sight of beauty from my eyes, / Faded the flower and all its budded charms, / Faded the sight of beauty from my eyes, / Faded the shape of beauty from my arms, / Faded the voice . . ."

Apollo: in Greek and Roman mythology, the god of poetry, medicine, and the sun – and so allegorically (of light), of learning, knowledge, and the arts. Keats wrote early odes of dedication to Apollo, and intended this god to be the hero of his epic, *Hyperion*.

Apostrophe: an address to a figure, usually not present, or to an object or idea, *personified* for the sake of being subject to address: "O golden-tongued Romance!"; "O Melancholy, linger here awhile! / O Music, Music, breathe despondingly!"; "O Goddess! hear these tuneless numbers"; "O attic shape! Fair attitude!"

Blank verse: unrhymed; usually referring to iambic pentameter: "Anon rush'd by the bright Hyperion; / His flaming robes stream'd out beyond his heels, / And gave a roar, as if of earthly fire."

Chiasmus: (from "chi" the Greek letter X), describing a mirrored crossing of words or syntactic units. "Beauty is truth, truth beauty" is almost a perfect chiasmus.

Couplet: two lines of rhymed verse. The *Shakespearean sonnet* ends with a couplet. The *heroic couplet* (so named for its use in epics featuring heroic deeds) is in rhymed iambic pentameter, usually containing a complete syntax, often with punctuated internal pauses, at the end of the first line, and / or the middle of the lines. Keats parodies this form when he writes

"There flowers have no scent, birds no sweet song, / And great unerring Nature once seems wrong." The *romance* or *open couplet* conspicuously violates this neoclassical form with *enjambment* and *feminine rhymes* that weaken the chime of line-endings: "And many a verse from so strange influence / That we must ever wonder how, and whence / It came. Also imaginings will hover / Round my fire-side, and haply there discover / Vistas of solemn beauty, where I'd wander / In happy silence, like the clear meander / Through its lone vales."

Ekphrasis, ekphrastic: a genre of writing that describes visual art – such as a painting or a sculpture. *On Seeing the Elgin Marbles* (about sculptural fragments from the Athenian Parthenon) and *Ode on a Grecian Urn* are famous instances of this tradition.

Ellipsis: grammatical matter that is dropped from (elided within) a sentence, but tacitly understood, often by syntactic parallelism: "Beauty is truth, truth beauty" implies a second "is."

Embedded sonnet: a paragraph, stanza, or unit within a longer verse form that has definition as a fourteen-line section, often with thematic significance. The opening paragraph of *Hyperion* is a sonnet-stanza, and similar forms appear in *Lamia*.

Enjambment: French for "striding over." The forward push of syntax from one poetic line to the next, sometimes from one stanza to the next. This effect can be *mimetic*, as when, for example, the subject of the poetry is about flowing over a boundary: "a voice will run / From hedge to hedge." The grammatical sentence of "It keeps eternal whisperings around / Desolate shores, and with its mighty swell / Gluts twice ten thousand caverns; till the spell / Of Hecate leaves them their old shadowy sound" (*On the Sea*) does not end until "sound," and it gets there by washing over all the line boundaries, with only a brief pause, like the cresting of a wave, at "caverns." Sometimes enjambment makes metaphoric use of the blank page-space at the end of the line: in "imaginings will hover / Round my fire-side," *hover* hovers at the end of the line, as if on an open space for imaginings to flicker, before the line rounds to *Round*.

End-stopped line: the opposite of *enjambment*, where a syntactic pause or close coincides with the termination of the poetic line, sometimes with *mimetic* effect: "Write on my tablets all that was permitted, / All that was for our human senses fitted" uses endstopped lines and endlocked rhymes to mimic the controls of permitting and fitting.

Eponym: a character whose name is given to a title – La Belle Dame, Lamia, Hyperion – or a name associated with an object or event: the Elgin Marbles, named for Lord Elgin who took them from Greece to England; the Pindaric ode, named for Pindar.

Euphony: ("good sound"): mellifluous verse sounds, often with *mimetic* effects: "O soothest Sleep! if so it please thee close" and "shade to shade will come too drowsily, / And drown" evoke in sound the soothing drowsiness described.

Field rhyme: rhymes that chime across a field beyond the local rhyme scheme. The word that concludes stanza four of *Ode on a Grecian Urn* ("not a soul to tell / Why thou art desolate, can e'er *return*") is such a rhyme with the last word of the ode's title (especially since *return*'s rhyme partner in stanza four, *morn*, is a non-demanding *slant rhyme*). That this ode follows right after *Ode to a Nightingale* in the 1820 volume allows a further afield rhyme (between the poems) of *Urn*'s "tell" with an end-word that chimes a related moment of recognition in *Nightingale*: "Forlorn! the very word is like a bell."

Homophone: "same sound": "*Here* were men sit and *hear* each other groan."

Internal rhyme (or echo): a consonance within a line: "Aye, *by* that *kiss, I* vow an end*less bliss.*" In "not to the sensual ear, but, more endear'd," *ear* (with *mimetic* suggestion) gets an internal echo in "end*ear*'d"; in "At tender *eye*-dawn of aurorean love: / The winged boy *I* knew," the awakened *eye* rhymes internally with the cognizant *I*; in "E'en like the passage of an angel's *tear* / That falls through the *clear* ether silently," the *enjambment*, the internal link of *tear* and *clear*, and the fall of the *ear*-sound into a faint echo in *ether* all convey the sense of the simile ("like . . ."), of a silent passing through the air.

Inversion: a reversal of normal syntactic order: "Oft of one wide expanse had I been told"; "Then felt I"; "Fled is that music"; "Of all its wreathed pearls her hair she frees."

Liaison: a sliding of sound from one word or syllable to the next: "leaden-ey*ed de*spairs"; "lea*f-f*ring'd"; "dos*t t*ease." This effect can be intensified with *sibilance*: "perilou*s s*eas" "the wheel*s s*weep / Around"; "incen*se* sweet"; "end*less s*leep." In "Tho*se l*ips, O *sl*ippery blisses," a liaison of *s* and *l* slips into the sound of "those lips."

Mimetic effects: words or their arrangement enacting what they describe. Sound, for example may imitate ("mime") sense ("Those lips, O slippery blisses"). Meter can be mimetic: as one says "Thou *foster child* of *silence and slow time*," the iambic tempo is forced into slow time by three stressed syllables of "*and slow time*." See *spondee*.

Neologism: a "new word," sometimes coined by joining known words ("worldwind" in *On a Dream*; in *The Fall of Hyperion*, "fault" and "failure" joined to make "faulture"); sometimes by giving new forms (in *The Fall*, "realmless," "nerveless," "unsceptered"), or new uses (in *The Fall*, "mourn" as a noun).

Octave: an eight-line unit of verse, most often describing the first unit of a sonnet's fourteen lines. In the *Italian* or *Petrarchan* form, the octave is identified by a distinct rhyme scheme (such as *abba, abba*), sometimes a separate stanza. It articulates a phase of thought or description to which the second part of the sonnet, the *sestet* reacts or responds.

Ode: a verse form dating from classical times, when it was sung by a chorus at public events, with three basic movements, a *strophe* (sung while the chorus moves in one direction), an *antistrophe* (sung while it moves in the opposite direction) and an *epode* (sung while it stands still); often these movements correspond to motions of thought or feeling. In the *Pindaric* or regular ode, from Greek poet Pindar (fifth-century BC), the strophes and antistrophes have the same stanza form, the epode another. The regular or *Horatian* ode, named for Roman poet Horace, uses stanzas of the same length and rhyme scheme (Keats's odes favor this form). In the irregular ode, popular in seventeenth- and eighteenth-century English poetry, regular stanza forms are dispensed with, to give the illusion of verse being shaped by intense or sublimely inspired feeling.

Pentameter: a verse line with "five measures" (metrical feet), the most common being *iambic* (a "foot" with an unstressed followed by a stressed syllable): "The *day* is *gone*, and *all* its *sweets* are *gone*!"; "*Away*! a*way*! for *I* will *fly* to *thee*."

Personification: the representation of an idea or an object as if a person, such as addressing a Grecian Urn as a "bride of quietness", or a "sylvan historian," or Autumn as a harvester.

Petrarchan: derived from fourteenth-century Italian poet Francesco Petrarcha, the adjective names a *sonnet* form he made famous and an attendant set of conventions and conceits (images) for love poetry: the beloved lady as beautiful, enchanting, and cruel; the poet-lover as devoted, enthralled, in torment. She is a goddess; he is a stricken deer. She shines afar; he burns.

Quatrain: a four-line stanza or a verse unit with a distinct rhyme pattern, such as *abab, abba, abaa*. The first twelve lines of a *Shakespearean sonnet* are patterned as three quatrains, usually rhymed *abab, cdcd, efef*.

Rhyme, feminine: the pairing of metrically unstressed syllables (sometimes muted further by *enjambment*) that orthodox principles of prosody tend to regard as weak: "Lo! I must tell a tale of chival*ry*; / For while I muse, the lance points slanting*ly* / Athwart the morning air."

    masculine: a chime of metrically stressed syllables: "O that our dreamings all of sleep or *wake* / Would all their colours from the sunset *take*."

    slant (also called "off" or "sight"): an internal or end rhyme in which the vowel sounds (even when, as is "form" / "worm," the letters line up) are slightly off. The *quatrain* that opens stanza two of *Ode on a Grecian Urn* makes poetic capital out of rhymes dissonant to the ear: "Heard melodies are sweet, but those *unheard* / Are sweeter; therefore, ye soft pipes, play *on*; / Not to the sensual ear, but, more *endear'd*, / Pipe to the spirit ditties of no *tone*."

Sometimes, as in this case, rhyme may be *semantic*, making a point about the principles of rhyming or their frustration. What isn't heard may play to the eye: in the *slant*-rhyme above, the *ear* within both "unh*ear*d" and "end*ear*'d" and the "tone" that gets no sound-rhyme are the point. The eye, furthermore, may play on the letters to enjoy the *chiasmus* of "on / No[t]" and the *liaison* of "Not to . . . no tone." Or a couplet may be about echoes, pairings, matchings that echo, pair, or match. In "'Fool!' said the sophist, in an under-tone / Gruff with contempt; which a death-nighing moan / From Lycius answer'd," the word "moan" answers in sound and sense the sophist's "under-tone." In "And the stars they glisten, glisten, / Seeming with bright eyes to listen" the rhyme asks our eyes to look and our ears to listen in order to see "listen" inside "glisten."

Sestet: a six-line verse unit, and in a *Petrarchan sonnet*, the last six lines, in a rhyme pattern distinct from that of the first eight (the *octave*).

Sibilance: The hissing of *s* sounds: "the airy stress / Of music's kiss." "His silent sandals swept the mossy green."

Sonnet: There are two main traditions for this fourteen-line poem, as well as a genre of writing meta-sonnets (sonnets on "the sonnet"). The Italian or *Petrarchan* (from Italian poet Francesco Petrarcha) sonnet has an *octave* (*abba abba*) and a *sestet* (*cdcdcd* and *cdecde* are the most common) and sometimes a stanza break. *On First Looking into Chapman's Homer* and *On Seeing the Elgin Marbles* are *Petrarchan*. This structure often involves a two-part drama, the octave posing a question or dilemma, or describing a situation, to which the sestet responds. A *Shakespearean* sonnet deploys three *quatrains* (sometimes with a hint of the Petrarch *octave* in the first two) and a *couplet*, usually a pithy summation of a situation unfolded across the quatrains. A common rhyme scheme is *abab cdcd efef gg*. "When I have fears," "The day is gone," and "I cry your mercy" are in this form.

Spondee: a stressed syllable substituted into a metrical pattern where an unstressed one would occur – often to enhance sense with sound effects: "And *no birds sing*"; "thou *foster child* of silence *and slow time*"; "But *where* the *dead leaf fell, there did it rest*"; "And *feed deep, deep* upon her peerless eyes" (a feeding of sound that persists into *peer*less).

Substantive: a noun, or noun form of a word familiar as another part of speech. When Endymion calls to his dream goddess, "Speak, delicious fair!" *fair*, normally an adjective, is made a substantive, as if to convey the sense of real being that Endymion has felt in his dream.

Synaethesia: evoking one kind of sensory experience with another. "What soft incense hangs upon the boughs" images smell as tactile (soft) and substantive (with material weight). In *Lamia* the disordering of senses is part of the serpent-woman's seduction of her prey: "delicious were the words she sung" blends the pleasures of hearing and tasting; "soon his eyes had drunk her beauty up" matches the seduction, blending sight into tasting.

Tetrameter: a "four-measure" line: "She *found* me *roots* of *relish sweet, / And honey wild*, and *manna dew*."

Trimeter: a "three-measure" line: "Up*on* the *mid*night *hours*."

Trochee: a metrical unit formed of a stressed then an unstressed syllable. Trochaic variations often appear at the start of an iambic pentameter line: "*Forest* on *forest hung* a*bove* his *head*"; "*Full* on this *case*ment *shone* the *win*try *moon*"; "*Thou* wast not *born* for *death*, im*mor*tal *Bird!*"

A BIOGRAPHICAL NOTE

Keats's poetry is so familiar that it seems to have a life of its own, decorating the walls of the world's most prestigious libraries and reading rooms, endowing book titles and popular songs: "A thing of beauty is a joy for ever"; "tender is the night"; "Beauty is truth; truth Beauty." This cultural presence is all the more remarkable, given the short career of its poet, and his decidedly local, though enthusiastic recognition during his lifetime. Keats's life as a poet was brief. He wrote his first poem, as a medical student, in 1814; his last effort may have been his revision of his sonnet "Bright Star" in September 1820, while he was on board a ship to Italy, where he would die early the next year. "Oh, for ten years, that I may overwhelm / Myself in poesy," he prayed in 1816 (*Sleep and Poetry*). Not even claiming a decade, Keats's life as a writer had come to a close by his twenty-fifth birthday. At the same age, Chaucer and Spenser had yet to write anything, and if Shakespeare had died at twenty-four, he would be known only (if at all) by a few early works. Victorian sage Thomas Carlyle was born the same year as Keats. What if Keats had been given the same span, of tens and tens of years, not dying until 1881? The fascination of Keats is still deeply involved in this poignancy of genius nipped in the bud, of unknown potential. Would he have stayed with poetry, having hit his stride with the 1820 volume – *Lamia, Isabella, The Eve of St. Agnes, Ode to a Nightingale, Ode on a Grecian Urn, Ode on Melancholy, To Autumn*, and the spectacular fragment of *Hyperion*? Would he have followed his dream to write modern drama? Might he, as his lively letters suggest, have developed a talent for the personal essay, or even the novel? Would he have become a political journalist (also a possibility he entertained)?

Keats's origins were relatively inauspicious. He was the eldest of four children, their father an ostler who married the owner's daughter of a livery-stabler, then inherited the suburban London business. Just after Keats began his studies at the progressive Enfield Academy, his father died in a riding accident, then his mother quickly remarried. Her affection for her children was as erratic as it was doting, and Keats was devastated when, apparently miserable in her second hasty marriage, she disappeared, abandoning the children to their grandmother. When she returned four years later, sick and consumptive, Keats devoted himself to her care; she died when he was fourteen. The shocks of this bewildering flux of events would be perpetually registered in the series of adored and adoring but inconstant women in his later poetry. Keats found solace and escape in the excitements of his education. At Enfield he was tutored and befriended by Charles Cowden Clarke, the headmaster's son, who introduced him to literature, music, the theater – and eventually to the London and suburban literary culture in which Keats's aspirations as a poet took root and flourished.

After Keats's mother died, the children were remanded to the legal guardianship of a practical businessman whose chief concern was to apprentice the boys to some viable trade and to keep their young sister from their influence. He apprenticed Keats to a surgeon in the grim days before anesthesia. Keats was soon enrolled as a student at one of the progressive London hospitals and stayed with his medical training long enough to earn his license as an apothecary (a kind of general practitioner), but he did not let go of the love of literature developed at Enfield, and frequently escaped his medical studies to read and to write poetry. The poets that mattered most to him were Spenser (his first poem, written in 1814, is a deft *Imitation of Spenser* in Spenserian stanzas), Chaucer, Shakespeare, Milton, and Chatterton, and among his contemporaries, Leigh Hunt, Wordsworth, and Byron. When he came of age in 1817, he gave up medicine to seek a career as a poet. By this point, Keats was already enjoying the society of Clarke and his circle of politically progressive thinkers, artists, poets, journalists, and publishers, many of whom became close friends. One of the hubs of this culture was radical journalist and poet Leigh Hunt, who launched Keats's career, publishing his first sonnets in his weekly paper, *The Examiner*, and advertising him in a critical essay as one of the age's rising "Young Poets." It was through him that Keats met some of the chief non-establishment writers of the day – Wordsworth, William Hazlitt, Charles Lamb, Percy Shelley – and the controversial painter Benjamin Robert Haydon.

In 1817 Keats's first volume, simply titled *Poems*, was published. Its themes – great poets and poetic greatness; political values; views of imagination; an enthusiasm for classical mythology – were advanced in a performance of poetic skill and versatility. In addition to twenty sonnets (many previously in *The Examiner*) there were Spenserian stanzas, odes, verse epistles, romance fragments, and meditative long poems. Keats warmly dedicated the volume to Hunt, and in its long concluding piece, a poetic essay titled *Sleep and Poetry*, he boldly took to task "the foppery and barbarism," "musty laws," and "wretched rule" of a still prestigious eighteenth-century neoclassical poetry. Byron despised Keats for this tirade, and it made him a ready target for the conservative literary critics of the Tory journals, only too eager to jab at their enemy Hunt through his protégé. Appearing in a year when civil rights were weakened and radical publisher William Hone was brought to trial, *Poems* was ridiculed in terms marked by social snobbery and political prejudice: Keats was one of Hunt's tribe of "Cockney Poets" – vulgar suburban upstarts, enemies of Church and State. Though he had anticipated this reception, he was still stung.

Yet he was determined to persevere, and immediately took on a major challenge, its genesis a contest with Hunt and Shelley to see who could finish a 4,000-line poem by the end of 1817. Keats was the only one to succeed, with *Endymion: A Poetic Romance*, which he regarded as "a test" or "trial" of his talents, his chance to advance his career with a strong credential. "A thing of beauty is a joy for ever" begins this tale of a shepherd-prince who dreams of a goddess, and on waking is profoundly alienated from ordinary life in the world. In the 4,000-plus lines of this romance epic – the longest poem Keats ever wrote – the hero, after several ordeals, finally gets the girl and they seem destined to live happily ever after. By the time Keats was readying the poem for press, however, he had lost confidence in its fable, and said so in his Preface, describing the poem as a work of "inexperience, immaturity," indeed a "failure" that made him "regret" its publication. Whether this Preface was an honest confession or a tactic to forestall another round of ridicule, the same reviewers who had hooted at Keats's debut were waiting to savage *Endymion*. But the effect was less to discourage Keats than to confirm what he called "my own domestic criticism." He thought the poem "slipshod," and was convinced the most powerful poets did not write escapist, "golden-tongued Romance" but embraced the "fierce dispute" of life in the world – terms he used as he was rereading Shakespeare's *King Lear*. His curriculum in 1818 included not only this tragedy but also Hazlitt's lectures on English poetry, *Paradise Lost*, *Hamlet* (Keats once said he thought he had read this play forty times), and Dante's *Divine Comedy* in Henry Cary's recent translation. He was still irritated by Wordsworth's didacticism and egotism, but he also recognized that Wordsworth was working out a profoundly modern sense of the "dark Passages" of life – the pains, heartbreaks, and oppression that no simple romance (such as *Endymion*) nor any simplistic moral philosophy (so Keats understood *Paradise Lost*) could argue away.

It was in this temper that Keats began a second epic, a deliberate revision of Milton. The intended hero of *Hyperion* was Apollo, the god of knowledge, poetry, and medicine – a linkage dear to Keats. The most powerful and most deeply felt poetry he wrote, however – in the two books completed – described the painful bewilderment of the fallen Titan clan and Hyperion's incipient anxiety about his impending fate. When Keats started to write of Hyperion's designated successor, Apollo, he lost inspiration. Could the "Knowledge enormous" that the god of poetry claimed to gain "all at once" be reconciled with the poet's own acute sympathy with the very mortal pain of his beloved brother Tom, dying of tuberculosis, the disease that had killed their mother and that would claim Keats himself three years later (already he was suffering from a chronically sore throat)? Tom died at the end of 1818, and Keats, almost instinctively by now, again sought relief in his poetry, but put aside *Hyperion*. In a burst of inspiration that lasted well into the fall of 1819 (when he returned to *Hyperion*), he produced his most admired work: *The Eve of St. Agnes, La Belle Dame, Lamia*, all the Great Odes, and a clutch of brilliant sonnets including "Bright Star." Unlike most of his contemporaries, he wrote no theoretical prefaces and defenses, no self-promoting polemics, no critical essays, but he did write letters, ones that reflect a critical intelligence as brilliant as the poetic talent. A number of Keats's formulations therein – among them, "Negative Capability," "the egotistical sublime," truth "proved upon our pulses" – have entered the syntax of literary criticism and theory. From their first publication (several in 1848), Keats's letters have been admired for their wit and playfulness, their generosity and candor, and their insight and critical penetration.

Just as Keats's poetic talents were generating this incredible body of work, his health went into decline, and he suffered a major pulmonary hemorrhage early in 1820. With the force of his medical training, he read his "death warrant" and was devastated about lost prospects. Despite the shaky reception of his first two volumes, he was (understandably) optimistic about the forthcoming one and full of enthusiasm for new writing (journalism or plays). He was also in love with the girl next door, Fanny Brawne, whom he hoped to marry once he was financially capable. But his doctors told him he could not survive another English winter, and so in September 1820 he sailed for Italy. He died at the end of the next February, four months after his twenty-fifth birthday – far from Fanny Brawne, far from his friends, and in such despair of what he had accomplished that he asked his tombstone to read "Here lies one whose name was writ in water." He did live long enough to see some favorable reviews of his 1820 volume. The mythology Shelley sympathetically advanced in *Adonais*, of a young sensitive poet slain by hostile reviews, though it would often be retold as if the truth, could not have been further from it. "This is a mere matter of the moment," Keats assured his brother George after his first reviews, adding, "I think I shall be among the English Poets after my death."

CHRONOLOGY

JK: John Keats   FK: Fanny Keats

GK: George Keats   TK: Tom Keats

1795   John Keats born, 31 October to Frances Jennings Keats and Thomas Keats, chief ostler at the Swan and Hoop inn, owned by Frances's father.
      Famine in England (high prices, scarcity); Napoleon's army moves into Italy.

1796   M. Lewis, *The Monk*; M. Robinson, *Sappho and Phaon*. Death of Robert Burns.

1797   George Keats born. H. F. Cary, *Ode to General Kosciusko*.

1798   Battle of the Nile; Irish Rebellion; *Lyrical Ballads* (Wordsworth and Coleridge).

1799   Tom Keats born. Napoleon returns to France and in a coup d'etat becomes first consul; Religious Tract Society formed; Six Acts against the formation of political societies, anti-union Combination Acts.

1800   *Lyrical Ballads* 2nd edn (with Preface); first collected edition of Burns. Union of England and Ireland; Alessandro Volta produces electricity from a cell.

1801   Edward Keats born, dies before his fourth birthday. First census; Pitt resigns after George III refuses Catholic Emancipation. Thomas Moore, *The Wreath and the Chain*.

1802   Founded: Cobbett's *Weekly Political Register*; *Edinburgh Review*; the Society for the Suppression of Vice. Peace of Amiens between England and France; France reoccupies Switzerland; Napoleon made First Consul for life.
      Scott, *Minstrelsy of the Scottish Border*.

1803   Fanny Keats born; GK and JK enroll at John Clarke's Enfield Academy.
      England declares war on France; British capture Delhi, India. Lord

Elgin brings sculptural fragments from the Athenian parthenon to England.

1804　April: JK's father dies; June: mother remarries. The children go to live with their mother's parents, the Jenningses.

Pitt becomes Prime Minister; Napoleon crowned Emperor and prepares to invade England; Britain declares war on Spain. First Corn Laws (protective taxation of imported grain); Beethoven's *Eroica*.

1805　Grandfather Jennings dies.

Scott, *Lay of the Last Minstrel*. Hazlitt, *Essay on the Principles of Human Action*. Nelson dies in the naval battle with France at Trafalgar; French victory over Austria and Russia.

1806　Scott, *Ballads and Lyrical Pieces*; Bowles' edition of Pope. End of the Holy Roman Empire; deaths of Pitt and Fox; Napoleon closes Continental ports to British ships and defeats Prussia at Jena.

1807　Wordsworth, *Poems, in Two Volumes*; Moore, *Irish Melodies*; Byron, *Hours of Idleness*. French invasion of Spain and Portugal. Peninsular Campaign begins. Abolition of slave trade in England.

1808　*Edinburgh Review* ridicules Byron's *Hours of Idleness*. Leigh Hunt becomes editor of *The Examiner*. Charles Lamb, *Specimens of English Dramatic Poets*. Spanish uprising (May); Convention of Cintra (August).

1809　Byron, *English Bards and Scotch Reviewers*. Gifford becomes editor of *The Quarterly Review*. Peninsular war in Spain. Napoleon beaten by the Austrians.

1810　JK's mother dies from tuberculosis; grandmother Jennings appoints John Sandall and Richard Abbey as the children's guardians. Leigh Hunt edits *The Reflector*.

1811　JK leaves Enfield and is apprenticed to Edmonton surgeon and apothecary Thomas Hammond; GK becomes a clerk at Abbey's counting-house.

Prince of Wales becomes Regent, after George III deemed incompetent. Luddite riots against the weaving frames. National Society for the Education of the Poor founded. Lord Elgin offers to sell the British government his Greek Marbles, and public debate ensues, about their acquisition, their value, and the prospect of costly purchase. Shelley, *The Necessity of Atheism*; Mary Tighe, *Psyche; or the Legend of Love* (privately printed, 1805); Leigh Hunt, *The Feast of the Poets*, in *The Reflector*.

1812　Byron's "maiden" speech in the House of Lords opposes the Frame-Breaking Bill, which prescribed the death penalty; his epic romance,

Childe Harold's Pilgrimage, is an overnight sensation; Canto II opens with a diatribe against Lord Elgin as a thief and pirate. Britain declares war on US; Napoleon invades Russia in June and retreats from Moscow at the end of the year, with catastrophic losses.

1813 Byron becomes a celebrity in London society, has major commercial successes with his poetic romances *The Giaour* and *The Bride of Abydos*. Coleridge's play *Remorse* is a success. Southey publishes *Life of Nelson*, becomes Poet Laureate; Wordsworth gets a government patronage position; Leigh Hunt publishes *The Prince of Wales v. The Examiner* (defending *The Examiner*'s attacks on the policies of the Prince Regent) and is imprisoned for libel. Lamb, *Recollections of Christ's Hospital*; Shelley, *Queen Mab*.

Austria joins the Alliance against France; Napoleon defeated at Leipzig.

1814 JK writes his first poems, including *Imitation of Spenser*, a sonnet *On Peace* (to celebrate the end of war with France), and a sonnet *To Lord Byron*. After grandmother Jennings dies in December, FK goes to live with the Abbeys.

Byron's *The Corsair* sells 10,000 on the day of publication. H. F. Cary's translation of *The Divine Comedy*; Wordsworth, *The Excursion* (criticized by Hazlitt in *The Examiner* for "egotism"); Reynolds, *Safie, An Eastern Tale, The Eden of Imagination*; Hunt, new version of *The Feast of the Poets*; Shelley, *A Refutation of Deism*. Edmund Kean's debut at Covent Garden; Charles Brown's *Narensky* a success at Drury Lane theater.

The Allies invade France; Napoleon abdicates and is exiled; the Bourbons restored. P. B. Shelley elopes to the Continent with Mary Wollstonecraft Godwin.

1815 2 February: *Written on the Day that Mr. Leigh Hunt left Prison*; also February: *To Hope, Ode to Apollo*. October: Guy's Hospital as a student and becomes a surgeon's dresser (assistant); November: verse epistle to George Felton Mathew.

Four-volume edition of Byron's poems; Wordsworth's collected poems, including the fully titled version of *Ode, Intimations of Immortality from Recollections of Early Childhood*; Hunt, *The Descent of Liberty, a Mask*.

Napoleon escapes from Elba; battle of Waterloo; Napoleon exiled; restoration of the French monarchy. Corn Bill passed, with enormous benefits to landlords. Resumption of agitation for Parliamentary reform. Parliamentary debates about Britain's purchase of the Elgin Marbles (from the Athenian Parthenon).

1816   JK meets Haydon and Reynolds; June: sonnet, "To one who has been long in city pent"; July: passes exam qualifying him for practice as apothecary, physician, surgeon; July–August: vacations with TK at the coastal village of Margate; writes sonnet and verse-epistle to GK; September: verse-epistle *To Charles Cowden Clarke*; JK, TK, and GK living together in Hampstead; October: JK meets Leigh Hunt, who puts *O Solitude* (written late 1815) in *The Examiner*, JK's first publication; writes *On First Looking into Chapman's Homer*; November: visits Haydon's studio and writes a sonnet "Great Spirits"; October–December: *Sleep and Poetry*; December: "I stood tip-toe"; Hunt features him, Shelley, and Reynolds in his "Young Poets" article in *Examiner*, where he quotes the sonnet on Chapman's Homer entire; sonnet-writing contest with Hunt produces "The poetry of the earth is never dead." Abbey becomes the Keats children's sole guardian.

      In *The Examiner*: Haydon's defense of the Elgin Marbles (March); Hazlitt, *On Gusto* (May) and defense of the Marbles (June); Hunt's verse-epistles to Moore and Hazlitt (June–July); Wordsworth's *To B. R. Haydon* (also in *The Champion*); Hunt, *The Story of Rimini*; Hazlitt, *Memoirs of the Late Thomas Holcroft*; Shelley, *Alastor &c*; Reynolds, *The Naiad*; Coleridge, *Christabel* and *Kubla Khan*. Byron leaves England amidst the scandal over his separation from Lady Byron. Byron, *The Prisoner of Chillon & c* and *Childe Harold's Pilgrimage III*; at a bookseller's dinner, publisher Murray sells 7,000 copies of each volume. Elgin Marbles are purchased by the government and displayed in the British Museum; prosecution of William Hone (tried in 1817); Spa Field Riots.

1817   JK meets Charles Brown and Richard Woodhouse. January: dines at Horace Smith's, with P. Shelley, Hunt, and Haydon. February: socializes with the Shelleys and the Hunts; Hunt shows some of JK's poetry to Shelley, Hazlitt, and Godwin, and publishes sonnets *To Kosciusko* and "After dark vapours" in *The Examiner*. March: JK and TK move to Hampstead, north of London; Haydon takes JK to see the Elgin Marbles; JK's two sonnets on the occasion are published *The Champion* and *The Examiner* (also the sonnet, "This pleasant tale"); *Poems* published by the Ollier brothers, warmly reviewed by Reynolds in *The Champion*. April–November: writing *Endymion*. April: visits Isle of Wight, studies Shakespeare, writes *On the Sea* (in *The Champion* in August). June–July: Hunt's review of *Poems* in *The Examiner*; August: finishes *Endymion II*; September: with Bailey at Oxford, working on *Endymion III*, reading Katherine Phillips's poetry and *The Round Table*; TK and GK in Paris; October: visits Stratford-on-Avon with Bailey, *Monthly Repository* publishes his and Hunt's "grasshopper and cricket" sonnets; sees Shelley again; taking mercury, perhaps for venereal disease. November: reads Coleridge's *Sibylline Leaves* (1817), finishes *Endymion*; December: at Drury Lane sees Kean in Shakespeare's *Richard III* and writes a review for the *Champion*; sees Benjamin West's paintings at the Royal Academy; discusses "Negative Capability"; Haydon's "immortal dinner" where JK and Lamb drink a toast against Isaac Newton; meets Wordsworth.

Byron, *Manfred*; Hazlitt, *Characters of Shakespear's Plays*; Hazlitt and Hunt, *The Round Table*; Southey, *Wat Tyler* (written in the 1790s), published by his enemies to embarrass the Poet Laureate with his revolutionary work. *Blackwood's Edinburgh Magazine* founded; in October it prints Z.'s first "Cockney School" paper, attacking Hunt, and targeting JK.

Habeas Corpus suspended; Hone tried for blasphemous libel for parodies of the liturgy. Death of Princess Charlotte from complications in the delivery of a stillborn child; death of Polish patriot Kosciusko, who also fought in US Revolutionary War.

1818 January: JK visits Wordsworth and recites the "Hymn to Pan" from *Endymion*; goes to theater, and dines often with Haydon; writes sonnet on re-reading *King Lear*, attends (–February) Hazlitt's lectures on English Poetry, published later this year; corrects proof for *Endymion* (–February); February: begins *Isabella; or The Pot of Basil*; writes "Time's sea" and *To the Nile*; at Hunt's, sees the Shelleys, and meets Peacock, Hogg, and Byron's erstwhile mistress Claire Claremont; reading Voltaire and Gibbon; March: writes preface to *Endymion* and returns proofs; verse-epistle to Reynolds. March–April: at Teignmouth (resort) with TK, who had a bad haemorrhage in March. April: Reynolds and his publishers (Taylor and Hessey) reject the preface to *Endymion*; the two sonnets on the Elgin Marbles are reprinted in *Annals of the Fine Arts*; *Endymion* (with new preface) published; April: finishes *Isabella*; May: writes "Mother of Hermes" (sonnet-ode), and a long and revealing letter to Reynolds (comparing Wordsworth and Milton, describing life as a "Mansion of Many Apartments"), *Hymn to Pan* published in *The Yellow Dwarf*, dines with Hazlitt at Haydon's; GK marries Georgiana Wylie and they leave for America (they would make JK an uncle twice in his lifetime); *Blackwood's* sharpens its aim on JK as a target. June: nasty review of *Poems* in *The British Critic*;

June–August: walking tour of the Lake District and Scotland with Brown, visiting Wordsworth's home and Burns's tomb, climbing Ben Nevis; JK reading Cary's translation of *The Divine Comedy*; describes his "gordian complication" of feelings about women to Bailey; a sore throat and chills force his return to London, where he finds TK very ill; meets Fanny Brawne. September: Z.'s attack on Keats ("Cockney Paper" IV) in *Blackwood's*; *The Quarterly Review* ridicules *Endymion*; JK trying to write *Hyperion* while nursing TK and thinking of Fanny Brawne. October: Reynolds praises *Endymion* in a minor journal (Hunt republishes it in *Examiner*) and urges JK to publish *Isabella* to show his progress; JK formulates his notion of "the camelion Poet" as distinguished from the poet of the "wordsworthian or egotistical sublime," along with a notion of poetry as "speculation" rather than the statements of a "virtuous philosopher"; to Keats's embarrassment, Hunt prints *The Human Seasons* and *To Ailsa Rock* in *Literary Pocket-Book*, an annual he edited. December: TK dies; JK, exhausted and suffering from a bad sore throat, accepts Brown's invitation to live with him at Wentworth Place, Hampstead; the Brawnes rent Brown's half for the summer. By December, JK and Fanny Brawne are in love.

Byron, *Childe Harold IV*; P. Shelley; *The Revolt of Islam*; Scott, *Rob Roy*; Hunt, *Foliage, or Poems Original and Translated*; Hazlitt, *Lectures on the English Poets* and *A Letter to William Gifford, Esq*, in *The Examiner*. Radical publisher Richard Carlile tried and imprisoned. Habeas Corpus restored.

1819   Throughout the year, JK is beset with financial problems; Haydon continues to pester him for loans. January: *The Eve of St. Agnes*; February: *The Eve of St. Mark*; April: the Brawnes move into Dilke's half of Wentworth place, becoming next-door neighbors. March: JK visits the British Museum with Joseph Severn; reads Hazlitt's attack on Gifford, *The Quarterly's* editor; also reading Thomas Moore, Beaumont and Fletcher. March: gets a black eye playing cricket; Severn's miniature of him exhibited at the Royal Academy. April: meets Coleridge and they talk of nightingales; *La Belle Dame*, *Ode to Psyche*, "If by dull rhymes." May: *Ode to a Nightingale*, *Ode on a Grecian Urn*, *Ode on Melancholy*, *Ode on Indolence*; sets aside *Hyperion*, describes the world as "a vale of Soul-making," a more satisfying existential vision than the Christian one, JK says; burns old letters and returns all books he has borrowed. July: *Ode to a Nightingale* in *Annals of the Fine Arts*. July–August: JK at Isle of Wight with Brown, working on *Otho the Great* with him; writing

Lamia and *The Fall of Hyperion*, a revision and recasting of the poem set aside earlier this year. September: at Winchester; writes *To Autumn*, and "give[s] up" on *Hyperion*; reads Burton's *Anatomy of Melancholy*. October: sonnet "The day is gone." November: reading Holinshed's *Chronicles*, decides not to publish anything he has written. November: *King Stephen*; "I cry your mercy" (sonnet), reworking *Hyperion*. December: *Otho* accepted by Drury Lane for the next season; worsening sore throat; engagement to Fanny Brawne.

Hazlitt, *Lectures on the English Comic Writers*; Cary's translation of Dante republished by Taylor and Hessey; Byron, *Don Juan I–II*; *Childe Harold's Pilgrimage I–IV*; Wordsworth, *Peter Bell* and *The Waggoner*; Reynolds's satire, *Peter Bell, A Lyrical Ballad*, appears in advance of the poem itself. Hunt edits *The Indicator*. Scathing review of Shelley's *The Revolt of Islam* in *The Quarterly*, with a vicious attack on Shelley's character; Shelley also publishes *The Cenci* to outraged reviews (blasphemy, incest).

August: "Peterloo Massacre" – a militia charge on a peaceful worker's demonstration for fairer Parliamentary representation, at which Henry "Orator" Hunt, the champion of reform, is arrested; the controversy plays for weeks afterwards in the London papers; September: H. Hunt's triumphant entry into London, witnessed by JK; December: the Six Acts (abridging freedom of assembly, speech, and print). William Parry's Arctic expedition.

1820　January: GK in London to raise funds from Tom's estate, and probably compromises JK's claim; this is the last time JK sees GK, and he stops writing to him after he leaves; *Ode on a Grecian Urn* in *Annals of the Fine Arts*; sends *Otho* to Covent Garden. February: JK suffers severe haemorrhage, reads his "death warrant," is housebound for weeks. March: revises *Lamia*; Haydon exhibits *Christ's Entry into Jerusalem*, with Keats depicted in the crowd. April: *London Magazine* praises *Endymion*. May: when Brown rents out his half of Wentworth place, JK has to move; Hunt publishes *La Belle Dame sans Mercy* in *The Indicator*. June: JK has an attack of blood-coughing, and moves to Leigh Hunt's home for care; Hunt published *On a Dream* in *Indicator*.

July: JK's last lifetime volume, *Lamia, Isabella, The Eve of St. Agnes and other Poems* (including the fragment of *Hyperion*, the odes of spring 1919, *To Autumn*). *Ode To a Nightingale*, *To Autumn*, and other poems published in *Literary Gazette*; *To Autumn* also in the London *Chronicle;* Lamb's praise of *Lamia &c* in *New Times* is reprinted by Hunt in *The Examiner*. August: Francis Jeffrey, emerging over Z. and *The Quarterly's* Croker as the leading reviewer of the day, gives favorable notice to *Endymion* and the *Lamia* volume in *The Edinburgh Review*; Hunt praises the volume in *The Indicator* and also prints an excerpt from *The Cap and Bells*; JK returns to Wentworth place, where his health worsens; he is cared for by Fanny Brawne and her mother; when Shelley invites him to stay with him in Italy JK declines, and commenting on *The Cenci*, tells Shelley to "be more of an artist," less of a polemicist. JK's friends raise money for him to spend the winter in Italy; JK, hoping Brown will accompany him, writes his will and assigns his copyright to Taylor and Hessey for £200.

September: *New Monthly Magazine* and *The British Critic* praise *Lamia & c*; with Joseph Severn, JK sails for Italy (Hunt publishes an affectionate farewell in the *Indicator*); after a very rocky, uncomfortable voyage, they arrive in Naples in late October, where the ship is quarantined in the harbor for ten days; able to disembark on JK's twenty-fifth birthday, they leave for Rome. November: lodgings with Severn at the foot of the Spanish Steps, in the English district of Rome; JK writes his last known letter, to Brown. December: serious relapse.

Murray publishes an eight-volume edition of Byron's poems (1818–20). *London Magazine* and *John Bull* founded. Shelley, *Prometheus Unbound*; Clare, *Poems Descriptive of Rural Life*.

1821 23 February: JK dies in Severn's arms; 26 February, buried in the Protestant Cemetery at Rome. 17 March: the news reaches London. In Pisa, Shelley publishes *Adonais*, an elegy for Keats with a preface that sets the fable of the sensitive poet driven to fatal illness by hostile reviewers. Though not published in England, it is generously quoted in several journals that reviewed it, and is ridiculed in *Blackwood's*.

Posthumous events

1821 When Byron's *Don Juan III–V* is published in August, Murray's premises are mobbed by booksellers' messengers. The "Bowles controversy" erupts (Rev. Bowles's edition of Alexander Pope's poetry had a preface attacking Pope's character, and a heated exchange of public letters ensued); Byron writes two letters defending Pope and attacking his detractors among the Lake poets and the Cockneys, with nasty remarks about JK which he asks publisher Murray to strike when he learns of JK's death from Shelley. Taylor and Hessey buy *London Magazine*.

1822 Death of P. B. Shelley.

1823 Byron's *Don Juan* (now published by John Hunt instead of Murray): VI–VIII in July, IX–XI in August, and XII–XIV in December. Canto XI contains the soon to be famous line about Keats being "snuffed out by an article."

1824 Death of Byron in Greece.

1826 Fanny Keats marries novelist Valentin Llanos, born just weeks after JK.

1828 *Adonais* published in England. Leigh Hunt, *Lord Byron and Some of His Contemporaries*, with a chapter on Keats.

1829 *The Poetical Works of Coleridge, Shelley and Keats* published by A. and W. Galignani in Paris; it includes all the lifetime volumes plus "In drear-nighted December," "Four seasons fill," *On a Leander Gem*, and *To Ailsa Rock*, along with a memoir of Keats based on Hunt's in *Lord Byron*; Thomas Hood, editing the gift-book annual, *The Gem*, is the first to publish *On a Leander Gem*.

1833 Fanny Brawne marries Louis Lindo (later Lindon).

1834 Woodhouse dies from tuberculosis, which had beset him in 1829.

1835 Hunt writes about JK in *Leigh Hunt's London Journal*.

1836 Brown gives a public lecture on JK.

1841 Brown gives all his JK manuscripts to R. M. Milnes; GK dies on Christmas eve.

1842 Brown dies in New Zealand.

1843 Georgiana Keats marries John Jeffrey.

1844 Hunt's *Imagination and Fancy*, its first chapter on JK.

1845 Taylor sells his rights to Keats's poems and letters to Edward Moxon, R. M. Milnes's publisher. John Jeffrey transcribes JK's poems and letters for Milnes.

1846 Haydon kills himself.

1848 Milnes, *Life, Letters, and Literary Remains of John Keats* includes the first publication of many of JK's letters and of poems not published in his lifetime.

1854 Milnes's edition of *The Poetical Works of John Keats*.

1856 *The Fall of Hyperion* published; it is assumed to be the first version.

1863 Severn's "The Vicissitudes of Keats's Fame" in *Atlantic Monthly*.

1865 Death of Fanny Brawne.

1867 New edition of Milnes's *Life, Letters, and Literary Remains*.

1874 Charles Cowden Clarke's "Recollections of John Keats," *Gentleman's Magazine*.

1876 Milnes's (Lord Houghton), edition of *The Poetical Works of John Keats*.

1878   Fanny Brawne's identity made public with *Letters of John Keats to Fanny Brawne*, ed. H. B. Forman. These letters disgusted many, Arnold and Swinburne among them.

1883   H. B. Forman's four-volume edition of *The Poetic Works and other Writing of John Keats*. The indisputable sign of Keats's canonical status.

1887   *Keats*, by Sidney Colvin, added to "The English Men of Letters" series.

1889   Death of Fanny Keats.

Benjamin Bailey (1791–1853). In October 1816 Bailey entered Oxford as a divinity student and met Keats the next spring through J. H. Reynolds. They became close friends, and in September Keats stayed with Bailey at Oxford while he worked on *Endymion* Book III. Bailey valiantly defended Keats against early negative reviews, but the friendship cooled early in 1819 when Bailey, seeming to have been courting Reynolds's sister, suddenly married the daughter of an important official in the Scots Episcopal Church. Keats's last letter to him was a strained congratulation.

Blackwood's Edinburgh Magazine **and Z.** A monthly, founded by publisher William Blackwood in 1817 to counter the influence of the London-based, Tory, High Church *Quarterly Review*; popularly known as "Maga" but cited now as *Blackwood's*. Its reviewer Z. coined the term "Cockney" to smear and ridicule new, reform-minded (politically and stylistically) writers, first using it against Leigh Hunt in 1817 with a nod at Keats; the article on Keats appeared in August 1818. The signatory was probably John Gibson Lockhart, friend and later son-in-law of Walter Scott, and a year younger than Keats. Loathed by his targets, Z. was thought a "scorpion" even by his colleagues at Maga.

The Brawnes. Fanny (Frances) Brawne (1800–65) was the girl next door with whom Keats fell in love and to whom he wrote several letters, alternately adoring and vexed with jealousy and suspicion. Her identity was not publicly known until 1878. In the summer of 1818, when Keats and Charles Brown were touring the North, the Brawne family rented Brown's half of Wentworth Place in Hampstead. Keats met Fanny on his return and they seem to have reached some understanding by Christmas, certainly by the next October, planning to marry once Keats was able to support them. From April 1819 to 1829, the family rented Dilke's half of Wentworth Place, with Keats and Brown their first neighbors. Fanny and her (widowed) mother cared for Keats when he fell seriously ill in 1820, and he saw Fanny for the last time in September before parting for Italy, where he could not bear writing to or reading letters from her.

Charles Brown (1787–1842), about eight years Keats's senior, was an impetuous traveler and playwright (a successful comic opera in 1814); he met Keats in the summer of 1817, and Keats toured the northern British isles with him in summer 1818. After Tom's death at the end of this year, Brown invited Keats to reside with him at Wentworth Place. They spent several weeks together in summer of 1819 on the Isle of Wight, while they worked on *Otho the Great* and Keats wrote *Lamia*. Brown adored Keats and cared for him assiduously in February 1820 after his first major haemorrhage, but ever restless and independent, he left for his usual summer holiday. Keats hoped he would accompany him to Italy, but the two never saw each other again. His last known letter was to Brown.

Charles Cowden Clarke (1787–1877), about the same age as Brown, was the son of the headmaster of Enfield Academy, where the Keats brothers were educated. As teacher and friend, Clarke helped shape Keats's taste in music and literature, and introduced him to Leigh Hunt and Charles Lamb. The friendship drifted apart by early 1819.

Charles Wentworth Dilke (1789–1864), six years Keats's senior, was a civil servant and amateur scholar, publishing a six-volume edition of *Old English Plays* (1814–16). He and Keats became friends some time before September 1817. With schoolfellow Brown he built Wentworth Place, a double house in Hampstead, where all the Keatses were frequent guests. Dilke's disapproval of Keats's engagement to Fanny Brawne attenuated their friendship, but he remained loyal to the family after Keats's death, keeping in touch with George and supervising the financial affairs of Fanny Keats and Fanny Brawne.

William Gifford (1756–1826) became editor of *The Quarterly Review* in 1809, and was widely thought the author of its attack on Keats in 1818 (it was actually John Wilson Croker). Nearly forty years Keats's senior, he was born into poor circumstances, working as a shoemaker's apprentice until a benefactor enabled his education. Culturally and politically conservative, he edited *The Antijacobin Review* in the late 1790s, and was famed for bitingly satirical poetry. Hazlitt's attack on him in *Letter to William Gifford* (1819) so delighted Keats that he copied out a large part of it for George and Georgiana; Hunt also attacked him after Keats's death, in *Ultra-Crepidarius; a Satire of William Gifford* (1823).

Benjamin Robert Haydon (1786–1846), champion of the Elgin Marbles, painter of portraits and of historical subjects on an epic scale. His huge *Christ's Entry into Jerusalem* has Keats, Wordsworth, Hazlitt, and other luminaries in the crowd. Keats met him in 1816 (though Hunt) and was frequently a guest at his studio; Haydon introduced him to the Marbles. As he kept borrowing money from a financially strapped Keats without repaying but still nagging him for more, their friendship cooled.

Leigh Hunt (1784–1859), fearless editor of the radical-reformist weekly, *The Examiner*. In 1813 he and his brother John Hunt were sentenced to two years in prison for libeling the Prince Regent. He met Keats though Clarke in 1816, and the same year published a number of his poems, introducing Keats as one of the new "Young Poets," and showing his poetry to critic William Hazlitt. Keats celebrated Hunt as an opponent of tyranny ("Libertas") and was influenced by his politics and poetic style, an allegiance that would incur the wrath of Tory critics. Hunt remained a generous, if sometimes overbearing supporter of Keats, even after Keats grew ambivalent about his aesthetic self-fashioning.

The Keatses. Fanny (1803–89), the sister, was the only one to survive into old age. After their grandmother died, she was kept away, unhappily, from her brothers by her legal guardian. **Tom** (1799–1818), whom everyone adored, fell seriously ill from tuberculosis in 1818 and died at the end of the year. Keats wrote him long letters from his tour in the summer, nursed him, with care and devotion, throughout the fall. All the brothers lived together from 1816, until **George** (1797–1841) married **Georgiana Wylie**, and the couple left for a new life in America in June 1818. Keats composed long journal-letters to them, filled with news and views, and poems on which he was working. Always more adept at worldly matters than the poet, George returned briefly to London in 1820 to raise funds from Tom's estate. Not knowing of Keats's engagement to Fanny Brawne, he pressed his claims, at Keats's expense; Keats's letters to him ceased after this visit. George, too, died of tuberculosis, but not until his forties.

The Quarterly Review, edited in Keats's day by William Gifford, had an emphatic conservative, Tory, establishment orientation. Its large circulation made it the most influential review of the day; although its review of Keats was not as nasty as *Blackwood's*, it had more impact. It was *The Quarterly* that Shelley blamed (in *Adonais*) and Byron mocked for killing Keats ("snuffed out by an article," in Byron's unkind phrase) – a fable that belied Keats's own resilience and equanimity. Founder and publisher **John Murray** (1778–1843) was a leading publisher and bookseller, on his list Coleridge, Byron, Scott, Southey, Crabbe, Moore, Campbell, Austen, de Staël, Hemans, and even radical Leigh Hunt. Murray's home and offices were celebrated centers of literary society and cultural interaction.

John Hamilton Reynolds (1794–1852), of all Keats's friends, one of his dearest, and the one closest to his own age. Poet and reviewer, Reynolds met Keats through Hunt in 1817, and in turn introduced him to Bailey,

Brown, Dilke, and publishers Taylor and Hessey. Keats's letters to him are animated by intimate, candid discussions of poets and poetry, with Reynolds helping Keats achieve some critical distance from Hunt. He defended Keats against *The Quarterly*'s attack.

Joseph Severn (1793–1879), friend of Hunt, Reynolds, and Brown, was only casually acquainted with Keats, whom he met in 1816. He was persuaded to accompany him to Italy in 1820, hoping for benefits to his career as a painter, but Keats's health dramatically deteriorated and Severn nursed him, with complete devotion, until his death (Keats died in his arms). His several portraits of Keats include some on his deathbed. Severn remained in Rome, and at his own request he was buried beside Keats in its Protestant Cemetery.

John Taylor (1781–1864) and **James Hessey** (1785–1870), London publishers, whose list included Coleridge, Hazlitt, DeQuincey, Clare, Carlyle, added Keats after the Ollier brothers, cross about the sales and critical reception of the *Poems* of 1817, rudely concluded their association with him. They published *Endymion* and the 1820 volume, and were personally kind to Keats, extending hospitality and introductions, defending him against hostile reviews, lending him books and money and raising the funds to send him to Italy. Taylor edited *London Magazine* from 1821, which gave appreciative notices to Keats's poetry.

Richard Woodhouse (1788–1834), scholar, linguist, and lawyer, Taylor and Hessey's legal and literary advisor, an enthusiastic admirer of Keats's poetry and of Keats himself. With a serious, dedicated interest, he collected and copied Keats's letters, poem manuscripts, proofsheets, and assembled anecdotes. Convinced of Keats's greatness and his deserving of all support, he lent him books and journals, advised him about his poetry, debated ideas, and introduced him to the London literary scene – and finally, arranged the financing for his journey to Italy. One of the small band to see him and Severn off, he devoted himself after Keats's death to collecting Keatsiana and establishing Keats's fame.

WHERE DID KEATS SAY THAT?

Sources for some famous phrases and comments (with references to *KL*)

"Men of Genius" and "Men of Power"
"the holiness of the Heart's affections and the truth of Imagination – What
  the imagination seizes as Beauty must be truth"
"the Imagination may be compared to Adam's Dream – he awoke and found
  it truth"
"O for a Life of Sensations rather than of Thoughts!"
"we shall enjoy ourselves here after by having what we called happiness on
  Earth repeated in a finer tone"
to Benjamin Bailey, 22 November 1817 (1.183–85)

"the excellence of every Art is its intensity, capable of making all disagree-
  ables evaporate, from their being in close relationship with Beauty &
  Truth"
"Negative Capability, that is when man is capable of being in uncertainties,
  Mysteries, doubts, without any irritable reaching after fact & reason"
to his brothers, December 1817 (1.192–93)

"the gradations of Happiness [are] like a kind of Pleasure Thermometer"
to John Taylor, 30 January 1818 (1.218–19)

"are we to be bullied into a certain Philosophy engendered in the whims of
  an Egotist [. . .] We hate poetry that has a palpable design upon us"
to John Hamilton Reynolds about Wordsworth,
3 February 1818 (1.223–24)

"delicious diligent Indolence"
to Reynolds, 19 February 1818 (1.223–24)

"I have a few Axioms": "Poetry should surprise by a fine excess"; "its touches of Beauty should never be half way"; "if Poetry comes not as naturally as the leaves to a tree it had better not come at all"
to Taylor, 27 February 1818 (1.238–39)

"every mental pursuit takes its reality and worth from the ardour of the pursuer – being in itself a nothing [. . .] Nothings which are made Great and dignified by an ardent pursuit"
to Bailey, 13 March 1818 (1.242–43)

"the material sublime"
verse letter to Reynolds, 25 March 1818 (1.261–62)

"The innumerable compositions and decompositions which take place between the intellect and its thousand materials before it arrives at that trembling delicate and snail-horn perception of Beauty"
to Benjamin Robert Haydon, 8 April 1818 (1.264–65)

"the most unhappy hours in our lives are those in which we recollect times past to our own blushing – If we are immortal that must be the Hell"
to Reynolds, 27 April 1818 (1.273)

"axioms in philosophy are not axioms until they are proved upon our pulses"
"human life [as] a large mansion of Many Apartments": "the infant or thoughtless Chamber"; "the Chamber of Maiden-Thought"; "dark passages" where "We see not the ballance of good and evil."
because "his Genius is explorative of those dark Passages [. . .] Wordsworth is deeper than Milton," who had "resting places and seeming sure points of Reasoning – [. . .] He did not think into the human heart, as Wordsworth has done"
"there is a grand march of intellect – "
to Reynolds, 3 May 1818 (1.279–82)

"I have not a right feeling towards Women [. . .] When among Men I have no evil thoughts, no malice, no spleen [. . .] I must absolutely get over this – but how? [. . .] an obstinate Prejudice can seldom be produced but from a gordian complication of feelings"
to Bailey, 22 July 1818 (1.341–42)

"the attacks made on me in Blackwood's magazine and the Quarterly Review . . . [are] a mere matter of the moment – I think I shall be among the English Poets after my death"

to George and Georgiana Keats, 14 October 1818 (1.393–94)

"As to the poetical Character itself, (I mean that sort of which, if I am any thing, I am a member; that sort distinguished from the wordsworthian or egotistical sublime [. . .]) it is not itself – it has no self – it is every thing and nothing – It has no character – [. . .] it lives in gusto, be it foul or fair [. . .] the camelion Poet. [. . .] has no Identity – he is continually in for – and filling some other Body"

to Richard Woodhouse, 27 October 1818 (1.386–87)

"I never can feel certain of any truth but from a clear perception of its Beauty"

to George and Georgiana, 31 December 1818 (2.19)

"they are very shallow people who take every thing literal A Man's life of any worth is a continual allegory – and very few eyes can see Mystery of his life – a life like the scriptures, figurative – [. . .] Lord Byron cuts a figure – but he is not figurative – Shakspeare led a life of Allegory; his works are the comments on it – "

to George and Georgiana, 19 February 1819 (2.67)

"the history of [Jesus] was written and revised by Men interested in the pious frauds of Religion. Yet through all this I see his splendour."
"Though a quarrel in the streets is a thing to be hated, the energies displayed in it are fine; the commonest Man shows a grace in his quarrel – By a superior being our reasoning[s] may take the same tone – though errone-ous they may be fine – This is the very thing in which consists poetry; and if so it is not so fine a thing as philosophy – For the same reason that an eagle is not so fine a thing as a truth."

to George and Georgiana, 19 March 1819 (2.80–81)

"The vale of Soul-making": "how then are Souls to be made? [. . .] How, but by the medium of a world like this? [. . .] a grander system of salvation than the chrystain [. . . .] Do you not see how necessary a World of pains and troubles is to school an Intelligence and make it a soul? A Place where the heart must feel and suffer in a thousand diverse ways! [. . .] a system of Salvation which does not affront our reason and humanity"

to George and Georgiana, 21 April 1819 (2.102–3)

"I must take my stand upon some vantage ground and begin to fight – I must choose between despair & Energy – I choose the latter"
                                        to Miss Jeffrey, 31 May 1819 (2.113)

"I have two luxuries to brood over in my walk, your Loveliness and the hour of my death. O that I could have possession of them both in the same minute."
                                        to Fanny Brawne, 25 July 1819 (2.133)

"I am convinced more and more every day that (excepting the human friend Philosopher) a fine writer is the most genuine Being in the World – Shakspeare and the paradise Lost every day become greater wonders to me – I look upon fine Phrases like a Lover"
                                        to Bailey, 14 August 1819 (2.139)

"the false beauty proceeding from art" vs. "the true voice of feeling"
                                        to Reynolds, 21 September 1819 (2.167)

"Talking of Pleasure, this moment I was writing with one hand, and with the other holding to my Mouth a Nectarine – good god how fine – It went down soft pulpy, slushy, oozy"
                                        to C. W. Dilke, 22 September 1819 (2.179)

"I have but lately stood on my guard against Milton. Life to him would be death to me."
"The only means of strengthening one's intellect is to make up ones mind about nothing – to let the mind be a thoroughfare for all thoughts. Not a select party."
                                        to George and Georgiana, 24 September 1819 (2.213)

"an artist must serve Mammon – he must have 'self concentration' selfishness perhaps. You [. . .] might curb your magnanimity and be more of an artist, and 'load every rift' of your subject with ore"
                                        to Percy Bysshe Shelley, 16 August 1820 (2.322–23)

"the knowledge of contrast, feeling for light and shade, all that information (primitive sense) necessary for a poem are great enemies to the recovery of the stomach."
"I always made an awkward bow"
                                        to Charles Brown, 30 November 1819 (2.360; probably his last letter)

I

JOHN KANDL

The politics of Keats's early poetry
"Delight" with "liberty"

To read the public dimension of Keats's early poetry, particularly the pieces published in periodicals such as Leigh Hunt's *Examiner* and then gathered into the 1817 *Poems*, is not only to experience the stirrings of power unleashed in the poems of 1819–20 but also to recover a more pronounced public and political register than some later works would suggest. This chapter, without promoting public or political over personal and aesthetic intentions, shows how brilliantly Keats could join these interests.

Keats in *The Examiner*

Keats's public career begins with Leigh Hunt's essay, "Young Poets," in his weekly reform-minded newspaper, *The Examiner*, which quoted in full the sonnet *On First Looking into Chapman's Homer* (1 December 1816). Hunt, the editor, injected Keats (along with Shelley and J. H. Reynolds) into an arena of political controversy: fresh from two years in prison for "libeling" the Prince Regent, he was undaunted in his attacks on Tory corruption, and not shy about enlisting his literary enthusiasms to the cause.[1] In the language of a manifesto, Hunt promotes this new "school of poetry" to "extinguish the French one that has prevailed among us since the time of Charles the 2nd": the neoclassical "school" of order and decorum favored by the Tory establishment and epitomized by Alexander Pope (1688–1744), whose poetry was virtually synonymous with the well measured "heroic couplet," whose recurring models of style and decorum were the court and aristocratic culture, and whose brilliance, wit, and range of accomplishment were such that the first half of the eighteenth century was regarded as the "Age of Pope." Paradoxically but pointedly, Hunt's "new school" returns to older, truer values, meaning "to restore the same love of Nature, and of *thinking* instead of mere *talking*, which formerly rendered us real poets, and not merely versifying wits, and bead rollers of couplets" (as if poetry were written with an abacus). This critique is of a piece with Hunt's political rhetoric, in which a

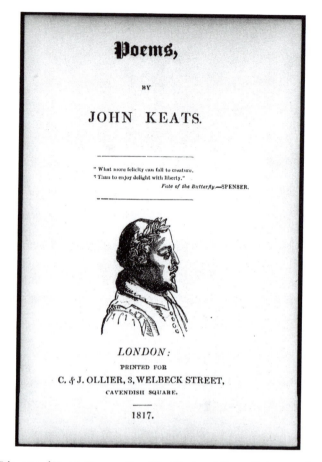

Figure 1. Title page of Keats's *Poems*, 1817. The identity of the profile has sustained a debate. Gregory Kucich reports that most of the early reviewers, noting the motto from Spenser, also took the head to be his, featured to announce Keats's reverence (*Keats, Shelley, & Romantic Spenserianism*, 145). Following this tradition, W. J. Bate still concedes some ambiguity: it "looks like a head of Shakespeare but is doubtless intended to be Spenser" (*John Keats*, 141). Stuart M. Sperry, Jr. means to resolve doubt, arguing that a "close inspection leaves no doubt [. . .] that the portrait was engraved after the Stratford monument bust of Shakespeare; and Woodhouse's underlined notation 'Shakespeare,' directly beneath the head on the title page of his copy shows that he, at least, was under no misapprehension as to its identity" ("Richard Woodhouse's Interleaved and Annotated Copy of Keats's *Poems* [1817]," *Literary Monographs* 1, ed. Eric Rothstein and Thomas K. Dunseath [Madison: University of Wisconsin Press, 1967], 120–21, referring to the title page of Woodhouse's copy of *Poems* [plate, facing 128]) – a view endorsed by Jack Stillinger in *John Keats: Volume I: A Facsimile of Richard Woodhouse's Annotated Copy in the Huntington Library* (New York and London: Garland, 1985), 245. Even so, Woodhouse's apparent need to inscribe an identification, perhaps in reaction to the first reviews, confirms the informing ambiguity. Photograph by Jim Dusen.

more democratic and "Constitutionally" valid national past – pre-Restoration, usually read into the Elizabethan age or in figures such as Alfred the Great – is wielded against present corruptions. Although these ages were still monarchical, Hunt saw them as more populist-minded than the present Tory oligarchy. His "new school" issued more than an aesthetic challenge, then. It was a challenge to modern political authority, fronted in aesthetic terms.

Hunt prints *On First Looking into Chapman's Homer* as an illustration of his argument, and Keats returns the gesture, celebrating Chapman's Elizabethan translation of Homer, himself a touchstone of literary authority. Because it was Pope's Augustan translation, in tidy couplets, that was the celebrated standard, the political implication of arguing for Chapman's rougher, less courtly verse would be clear, as Hunt well knew. When Keats revised line seven for *Poems*, he strengthened the implication. In *The Examiner* this reads: "Yet could I never judge what men could mean"[2] – The occasion of the only fault Hunt could name, an awkward rhyme of "demesne" and "mean." Keats's revision, "Yet did I never breathe its pure serene," is not only an improvement, but one wrung and rung at the expense of a line from Pope's Homer – "When not a breath – disturbs the deep serene" – satirized by Hunt in *The Feast of the Poets* (1814).[3] To describe the new line as mere "translator-ese" (as Marjorie Levinson does)[4] is to miss this significance, for the translator-ese is originally Pope's, and Keats's revision (possibly Hunt's suggestion) is a sly parody, juxtaposing Pope's self-consciously "literary" diction against Chapman's more "natural" expression. Keats emphasizes the parody in shifting the verse from the patently literary metaphor, "breathing" (with its latinate punning on inspiration), to the more direct experiential language of hearing and speaking, conveyed as the high thin vowels of "breathe" and "serene" drop to sonorous "o"s in "loud" and "bold": "Yet did I never breathe its pure serene / Till I heard Chapman speak out loud and bold" (7–8).

Hunt's polemic for older values is matched by the way the ensuing sestet promotes images of discovery by pointing not to "new" realities, but to a newly gained consciousness of ancient and sublime "natural" wonders: "a new planet," "the Pacific" – geological equivalents of Homer, experienced through the ken of Chapman. Keats may even have intended "Cortez" as his beholder of "the Pacific" (11–12), which was already known by other explorers. Tennyson, in a schoolmasterly mood, thought this an error for Balboa (the first European to see the Pacific), but it is Cortez's "first looking" and not Balboa's unprecedented (from a Eurocentric view) discovery that shapes Keats's analogy. "Cortez," moreover, gilds the image with historical connotation – the imperialist power of the Spanish conquistador stalled in the Homeric sublime.[5]

The emphasis on who is surveying what "realms" – whether Pacific or Homeric – evokes a debate about political authority. Directly following "Young Poets" in *The Examiner*, Hunt placed an article by William Hazlitt (759) berating arguments in the Tory press for Royal "Legitimacy": "this most barefaced of all impostures, this idiot sophism, this poor pettifogging pretext of arbitrary power, this bastard interpretation of divine right, – Legitimacy." In the aftermath of the Napoleonic wars, with the impending restoration of monarchies throughout Europe, the question of "legitimate" poetic authority was inextricable from the political question. Both Hunt's "new school" and Keats's poem are situated within and thickened by this debate. Keats's sonnet involves the question of political legitimation with his own most intense personal concern in 1816, his quest for poetic legitimation. Composed in a burst during a late night walk after reading Chapman with Charles Cowden Clarke, the poem must have felt like a revelation – a discovery of his own potential as a poet. Yet having made its debut in *The Examiner*, it was read less for this narrative than for its language of cultural and political reform.

"Young Poets" was the spur that goaded *Blackwood's Edinburgh Magazine* to a series of articles titled "On the Cockney School of Poetry," attacking first Hunt and then Keats, Hazlitt, Haydon (even, at times, Shelley and Byron, in so far as their poetry criticized or satirized the Tory regime). In the opening paragraph of its first "Cockney School" paper (October 1817), the author, signing himself "Z.," "christens" Hunt's "new school":

> It is strange that no one seems to think it at all necessary to say a single word about [a] new school of poetry which has of late sprung up among us. The school has not, I believe, as yet received a name, but if I may be permitted to have the honor of christening it, it may henceforth be referred to by the description of The Cockney School. Its chief Doctor and Professor is Mr. Leigh Hunt. [. . .] a man of little education. (38)

The slurs upon the Cockney lack of education, "vulgarity," "effeminacy," immorality, and inferior social class, are key moves in the Tory campaign to discredit the new school's bid for cultural authority. As Z. would remind his readers in a later paper, "Keats belongs to the Cockney school of Politics as well as the Cockney School of Poetry" (August 1818, 524).

Before Z.'s first paper appeared, Keats was fueling Tory ire with other poems in *The Examiner*, also cast in the vocabulary of reform. His sonnet *To Kosciusko* (*Examiner* 16 February 1817) celebrates this Polish freedom-fighter in terms akin to those in Hunt's "Political Examiner" editorials, which iconized Kosciusko as reformism in action, an antidote to political apostasy. In an article a few weeks before (12 January 1817), Hunt celebrated Kosciusko as the "head" of the "old lovers of freedom," whom "We may expect [. . .] to speak and act again, if the world go on as it promises" (18). Keats's linking of Kosciusko to "Alfred" sustains Hunt's discourse of "old" liberties – his rant, for example in *The Examiner* of 2 March 1817, that "to have our liberties at the mercy of mere courtiers and official automatons, with not an idea in their heads, is too humiliating to a nation that has had an ALFRED for a king, SHAKESPEARES and MILTONS for its poets, and SYDNEYS, MARVELLS and STEELES for its race of gentlemen" (129). Hunt derives political authority from poetic models, and Keats complements this by elevating political heroes with the language of poetic vision, treating them as a race of celestial sublimity:

> Good Kosciusko! thy great name alone
> Is a full harvest whence to reap high feeling:
> It comes upon us like the glorious pealing
> Of the wide spheres – an everlasting tone:
> And now it tells me that in worlds unknown
> The names of Heroes, burst from clouds concealing,
> Are changed to harmonies, for ever stealing
> Through cloudless blue, around each silver throne.

To present these names "stealing" around a "throne" is more than celestial sublimity, however; it is political provocation. The final lines underscore the point:

> Thy name with ALFRED'S, and the great of yore,
> Gently commingling, gives tremendous birth
> To a loud hymn, that sounds far, far away,
> To where the great God lives for evermore.

By this "commingling," Keats consolidates a massive historical "authority" on behalf of the reform movement and gives it a sublime status. Invoking the music of the spheres and the "tremendous birth" of a "loud hymn" that reaches the ears of God – receding infinitely and eternally into the distance – Keats's roster not only steals a silver throne but more potently steals the thunder of the current "divine right" rhetoric. In this "tremendous birth," the aesthetic sublime is inseparable from a political sublime.

Poems, 1817

Published in advance of Z.'s first "Cockney School" paper, Keats's debut volume not only allies him with Hunt but also consolidates the claims Hunt made for him in "Young Poets." Its construction is loosely symmetrical: two lengthy discursive poems bracket the volume, the untitled poem beginning

"I stood tip-toe upon a little hill" at the opening, and at the end (with a separate title-page), *Sleep and Poetry*, both in decisively non-Popian, "open" couplets.[6] In between are three sections: a set of poems invoking Spenserian romance and chivalry, a set of "Epistles" (announced by another internal title-page), then with another title-page, a sequence of "Sonnets" (some of these previously published in *The Examiner* and elsewhere). The opening and closing poems invoke and direct interpretive possibilities in these internal sections, even as they refer the collection as a whole to the aesthetic, erotic, and political heat of Hunt's *Story of Rimini* and the liberal-reformist editorials in *The Examiner* and *Champion*.[7]

The title-page and its sonnet of "Dedication" are the immediate public gestures and the most critically significant. "Practically every idea and motif in *Poems* of 1817," Jack Stillinger remarks, "can be seen as following from the opening proposition of the dedicatory sonnet 'To Leigh Hunt, Esq.'"[8] Stillinger notes the stylistic and ideological commitments of the opening line, "Glory and loveliness have passed away"; there is also political significance, of a piece with the title-page epigraph from Spenser (an early locus of glory and loveliness). This is from *Muiopotmos; or the Fate of the Butterfly*, a protest in behalf of "liberty," a political idea joined to a Huntian politics of "delight":

> What more felicity can fall to creature,
> Than to enjoy delight with liberty.[9]

In *Muiopotmos*, these lines (209–10) voice a real question, for a "thousand perils lie in close awaite / About us dailie, to worke our decay" (221–22); indeed, in the last stanza, this free-ranging butterfly falls prey to a "tyrant" spider. Spenser's poem has been read as a political allegory, and Keats's epigraph pulls the potential references into Regency politics. But where Spenser was also concerned with constraints on liberty, morally desired and politically imposed, Keats was tweaking a Tory press all too ready to translate any brief for a "liberty" joined to sensuous "delight" as a front for licentiousness. "*License*," *The Quarterly* contended in reviewing Hunt's tale of adultery *Rimini*, is really what Hunt means when he "cries *liberty*" (January 1816; 474). Keats enlists Shakespeare in refuting the charge by placing an engraving of the laureled bard on the title-page just below Spenser's lines, blazoning the two Elizabethan poets against Tory aesthetic and political authority. The epigraph carried an additional political force in using Spenser to critique Wordsworth, now a political conservative, whose "Intimations" *Ode* (its revised version published in 1815) was ready to relinquish "Delight and liberty" as the "simple creed of Childhood," left behind in the growth of a "philosophic mind" (137–38) – a maturity that had given up political reform in favor of spiritual equanimity. In retreat from the ideals of liberty and republicanism to which he was committed in the early 1790s, this "Wordsworth" was also in *The Examiner*'s sights: Hunt often seemed to define his "new" school not just as a renaissance of the Renaissance but also, and more immediately, as a kind of pre-apostasy Lake School.

Keats's dedicatory sonnet not only trumpets Hunt's patronage but also his aesthetic and political objectives, infusing nature with classical mythology, the world of "Flora, and old Pan." The opening line, "Glory and loveliness have passed away," augments the title-page epigraph's potential reference to Wordsworth's *Ode*, which had lamented the passing of a metaphysical "glory" sensed only in earliest childhood. Keats's lament for lost "glory" is more publicly tuned, affiliated with a specific historical past and with the reform movement's rhetoric of a return to earlier Constitutional values. Any sounding of past glory, moreover – Keats's or Wordsworth's – would evoke the "Glorious" Revolution of 1688 and its summoning as a prime point of reference in the debates over the French Revolution in the 1790s.[10] Wordsworth philosophically mourns; Keats would reconstruct. His octave, ostensibly lamenting a death, revives as poetic personification the very ideals it misses:

> GLORY and loveliness have passed away;
> For if we wander out in early morn,
> No wreathed incense do we see upborne
> Into the east, to meet the smiling day:
> No crowd of nymphs soft voic'd and young, and gay,
> In woven baskets bringing ears of corn,
> Roses, and pinks, and violets, to adorn
> The shrine of Flora in her early May.

Keats recreates what is "passed away" with a lushly imagined pagan relig-ious offering, and in his sestet performs such an offering to Hunt:

> But there are delights as high as these,
> And I shall ever bless my destiny,
> That in a time, when under pleasant trees
> Pan is no longer sought, I feel a free
> A leafy luxury, seeing I could please
> With these poor offerings, a man like thee.

For the lost world of glory and loveliness, Keats substitutes a modern frater-nity of "free" aesthetics, inscribed in the enjambment of "free," the very syntax of liberty and delight. Keats's modest offering "To Leigh Hunt, Esq." is not just this poem but the "leafy luxury" of *Poems* itself. Such are the com-pensatory modern "delights" for which the poet blesses his "destiny," including the "delight with liberty" emblazoned on the title-page. Involving as well the libertarian associations of "Pan," Keats's "free" luxury combines reformist, erotic, and poetic implications.[11] Even his key words, "free" and "thee," evoke a subtle field-rhyme with "Leigh" – indeed, all these associations concentrate in the signature "Leigh Hunt," the Regency emblem of aesthetic, moral, and political liberty, and the name of the reformist values to which Keats eagerly dedicates his "destiny" and his book.

He makes good on these preliminaries with a host of Huntian stylistic practices that would soon be scorned as "Cockney" and that were conspicuously "modern."[12] Keats does not employ these stylistics in a subtle manner but militantly out-Hunts Hunt. "A principle characteristic" of Keats's early writing, stresses W. J. Bate, "is the extent to which he tries to exploit one device after another in order to depart from the various eighteenth-century norms of style. He does almost everything Hunt does, but he carries it further."[13] Bate gives the inventory of Hunt's signature style: Spenserian tropes of chivalry, open (non-Popian) couplets, "sentiment" conveyed with "easy sprightliness":

> Hence the coy terms ("a clipsome waist," "with tip-toe looks," "with thousand tiny hushings"); the distinctive way [Hunt] makes adjectives of verbs ("scattery light"), or adjectives of nouns ("flamy heart's-ease," "One of thy hills gleams bright and bosomy"); adverbs made of participles ("crushingly," "tremblingly"); and the other mannerisms that Keats took over and used far more excessively than Hunt. There are also the stock words, usually nouns ("luxury") or adjectives ("The birds to the *delicious* time are singing"). Finally there is what one can only call a certain would-be smartness that comes in the attempt to be colloquial, and is most glaring when the subject is serious.
>
> (Bate, *John Keats*, 80)

The Huntian effects were palpable. Keats writes, "there crept / A little noiseless noise among the leaves, / Born of the very sigh that silence heaves" ("I stood tip-toe" 10–12). *The Quarterly* had nabbed "heaves" as one of Hunt's favorites, citing twelve instances in *Rimini*. Critics then and now have lamented Hunt's influence, or noted a few brilliantly original moments (the sonnets on Chapman's Homer and on the Elgin Marbles), then moved quickly on to the later work, sometimes not even commenting on *Endymion* (1818).[14] While the association with Hunt made the conservative ridicule predictable, Keats's style proved a strain even to favorably disposed readers: *Edinburgh Magazine* admired some of the *Poems*, but also regretted moments that seemed "perverse," "common," and "contemptuous."[15]

Yet as Jerome McGann observes (noting this review), some of Keats's contemporaries saw this poetry as "smart, witty, changeful, sparkling, and learned – full of bright points and flashy expressions that strike and even seem to please by a sudden boldness of novelty." What later readers tended to despise as cloying sentimentality, Keats's contemporaries found innovative, even jarring.[16] For Keats, "experimental" meant a bold revision of traditional imagery, involving classical mythology, romance, and chivalry – all with Huntian connotations. As his dedicatory sonnet made clear, he shared Hunt's polemic for classical myth, not only for its sensual delight but also as a challenge to the authority of the Church of England. Keats and others knew that Hunt's sensual imagery of pagan nature worship (Hunt's religion of "chearfulness") was also intended as "a battering ram against Christianity" – so he wrote to Hunt himself in May 1817, referring to his editorial in *The Examiner* on 4 May (*KL* 1.137). In his "war with established power," Robert Ryan points out, Hunt matched his political attacks by fighting "with equal vigor, and sometimes with apparently greater relish, on the religious front"; "The *Examiner* regularly used 'Greek Religion' as a touchstone to suggest the moral and theological flaws in England's national religion."[17]

The other champion of classical mythology during the Regency was Wordsworth, and although he was no advocate of reform politics, his nostalgia for the imaginative vitality of the old myths impressed Keats, whose love of relevant passages in *The Excursion* prompted him to greet the poem (which had not been well reviewed when it appeared in 1814) as one of the three things to marvel at in the age (*KL* 1.203). What he admired and echoed in his own poetry were the passages of pagan enthusiasm for a "nature" informed with divine presences, an ancient pastoral realm in which humans communed with nature:

> The nightly Hunter, lifting up his eyes
> Towards the crescent Moon, with grateful heart
> Called on the lovely wanderer who bestowed
> That timely light, to share his joyous sport:
> And hence, a beaming Goddess with her nymphs,
> Across the lawn and through the darksome grove,
> (Not unaccompanied with tuneful notes
> By echo multiplied from rock or cave)
> Swept in the storm of chase, as Moon and Stars
> Glance rapidly along the clouded heavens,
> When winds are blowing strong . . .   (1814 text, 4.878–88)

What Keats didn't admire and was at pains to resist was Wordsworth's *modern* religion, a spiritual quietism too easily joined to political conservatism, if not an outright retreat.

The mythology of "I stood tip-toe" emerges from this ambivalence. It is at once nostalgically pagan but also pointedly modern and pointedly anti-Tory.

After an erotically charged recounting of mythological love affairs (Cupid and Psyche, Pan and Syrinx, Narcissus and Echo), Keats focuses intently upon the poetic intercourse of Endymion and Cynthia. This Endymion (not yet the hero of Keats's 4,000-line romance) is richly ambiguous. Keats presents him as a creation of poetry, born of a pagan poet's empathy for the lonely longings of the moon-goddess and a shepherd, but he is also a double for the modern poet – "He was a poet, sure a lover too" (193) – whose inspiration is the lovers' lack of liberty:

> The Poet wept at her so piteous fate,
> Wept that such beauty should be desolate:
> So in fine wrath some golden sounds he won,
> And gave meek Cynthia her Endymion.   (201–4)

The union of Endymion and Cynthia is poetically engendered, reflecting a poet's romance with the (natural) source of his inspiration. The action is also revolutionary: wrathfully breaking the Jovian edict that would keep Cynthia eternally chaste, this "Poet" releases not just these two but liberates a host of lovers from their states of isolation, oppression, or the repression that renders them the "languid sick" (223). The lovers awaken, gazing "clear eyed"

> To see brightness in each others' eyes;
> And so they stood, fill'd with a sweet surprise,
> Until their tongues were loos'd in poesy   (233–35)

This loosening inspires "poesy" with erotic liberty, while poetry itself is returned to its source in pagan myth, then projected as a communal emancipatory force:

> Therefore, no lover did of anguish die:
> But the soft numbers, in that moment spoken,
> Made silken ties, that never may be broken.   (236–38)

Keats's mythology is serenely earthbound; it is the healing, amatory, and generative powers of poetry and nature that he celebrates – with dramatically sexual resonances – imagining a kind of new millennium for lovers, healed through the bond of natural and imaginative forces. This is Hunt's poetry of cheerfulness in a Keatsian narrative of liberation from oppression.

In the final lines, wittily playing upon the erotic liberation of these "loos'd" lovers, Keats decorously acknowledges that he has taken Endymion and Cynthia as close to the actual sexual act as he prudently can: "Cynthia! I cannot tell the greater blisses, / That follow'd thine, and thy dear shepherd's kisses" (239–40). The immediately ensuing and often debated question – "Was there a Poet born?" (241) – puts a teasingly humorous emphasis on the possible issue of the sexual union of this mortal and goddess, while seriously emphasizing the generative and regenerative potential of their symbolic fusion. The imaginative power of poetry is argued as transformative and implicitly revolutionary. Commenting on the Keatsian signature in this projection of love as a "communal bond," Paul de Man notes how "the union of Cynthia and Endymion spontaneously turns into a public feast, [a] kind of Rousseauistic brotherhood" of love widening into "a communal spirit of friendship with social and political overtones; something of the spirit of the French Revolution."[18]

Keats's final lines, however, shade these optimistic public resonances with anxiety over personal, poetic legitimacy. Its question – "Was there a Poet born?" – implicates Keats himself, as a poet potentially born of his own imagination. Yet "asked both *in* and *of* the tale," it is left open, suspended – "as a subject of speculation for reader and poet alike":[19] "Was there a Poet born? – but now no more, / My wand'ring spirit must no further soar. – " (241–42). One answer is spelled by the rest of the volume, which shows a poet at work and play. Moving from a sexually electrified classical mythology into poems of chivalry and romance, Keats summons another generic register. But it is no less contentious, for it also stamped by Hunt. The titles, *Specimen of an Induction to a Poem* and *Calidore. A Fragment*, advertise an experimental intent. Promising a revival of chivalric romance, Keats's poems are no "specimens" or "fragments" of medieval poetics; they are imitations of Spenserian romance in modern Huntian style. This is "Spenser" reconfigured for reformist purposes, shorn of his royalism and Christianity (still anti-Popian – only for this "Spenser" the Pope is Alexander).

Keats's "Spenser" is a talisman of "delight with liberty" – and as such his name becomes a public "crest" for the brotherhood defined by Keats and Hunt. In *Specimen*, Keats casts Hunt as Spenser's disciple, his "lov'd Libertas" (61) – the chivalric name honoring Hunt's courage in imprisonment and his status as a political prisoner and martyr of his political conscience.[20] As in the dedication and title-page, Spenser and Hunt are interfused with contemporary values of "liberty." Keats's *Imitation of Spenser* (in this same section) is also an imitation of Hunt. Huntian stylistics mark such phrases as "lawny crest" (3), "jetty eyes" (16), and "clouds of fleecy white" (27). As Andrew Motion points out, moreover, the peaceful Spenserian bower depicted is a political vision as well as a poetic retreat, "a miniature England that belongs to a specific historical context [. . .] the Peace between England and France, which was signed in Paris at the time it was written, and which Hunt also celebrated in an 'Ode to Spring' published in the *Examiner* in April 1814."[21]

Keats was aware that some of the poems of this section risked confusing chivalric idealism with a mawkish sentimentality, especially *To Some Ladies*; *On receiving a curious Shell, and a Copy of Verses, from the same Ladies*; *To ****; and *To Hope*. Hence the disclaimer he inserts on the page after the dedicatory sonnet to Hunt: "The Short Pieces in the middle of this Book, as well as some of the Sonnets, were written at an earlier period than the rest of the Poems." Even so, these poems, too, resonate with public issues. *To Hope* (which Keats dates at its end "February, 1815") begins with a poet's private, Coleridgean ruminations "by my solitary hearth," but modulates into a public and political register:

> In the long vista of the years to roll,
>   Let me not see our country's honour fade:
> O let me see our land retain its soul,
>   Her pride, her freedom; and not freedom's shade.   (31–34)

This broad view is politically specified in the next stanza:

> Let me not see the patriot's high bequest,
>   Great Liberty! how great in plain attire!
> With the base purple of the court oppress'd,
>   Bowing her head, and ready to expire:
>   But let me see thee stoop from heaven on wings
>   That fill the skies with silver glitterings!   (37–42)

The apostrophe to "Hope" that is the poem itself turns from private gloom and despondency with a burst of patriotic "Liberty," fueled, as the stanza above shows, with an attack on the court – the plain attire of the patriots elevated over the the debased purple of an oppressive regime. In 1817, Keats knew his call to Hope would be heard as the voice of reform politics, a language in which private and public, aesthetic and political visions coalesce.

This interrelation is developed in the next section, the "Epistles." Each is framed as a personal address to a friend about a shared concern with poetry and poetics; but "Epistle" is also a public genre, here addressed to the readers of *Poems*, construed as friends. Each epistle turns the personal letter at some point into a statement of a political commitment, privately validated. The first, *To George Felton Mathew*, celebrates a friendship between poets as a "brotherhood in song" (2), "brotherhood" evoking reform, indeed, revolutionary politics ("Liberty, Brotherhood, Equality" was the English translation of the French Revolutionary slogan). Keats does not amplify this implication but presents a battery of Italian, classical, and English pastoral associations, then modulates into a celebration of key poetic influences (Chatterton, Shakespeare, Milton), then a declaration of public poetic purpose:

> We next could tell
> Of those who in the cause of freedom fell;
> Of our own Alfred, of Helvetian Tell;
> Of him whose name to ev'ry heart's a solace,
> High-minded and unbending William Wallace.
> While to the rugged north our musing turns
> We well might drop a tear for him, and Burns.   (65–71)

The "brotherhood in song" publicizes its devotion to "the cause of freedom," celebrating the Swiss and Scottish freedom fighters William Tell and William Wallace, as well as (again) Alfred the Great, and finally, Robert Burns, Scots patriot and champion of the French Revolution. Keats relates these inspiring figures to his courtship of the "Muse" and his pastoral fantasies, shaped with the early mythologies of "chaste Diana" and Apollo (72ff). This mythological turn is not a retreat from the political landscape, but a continuation of it in an aesthetic desire that artfully blends personal epistle into public declaration. The ideal of a "brotherhood in song" joins an intimately shared enthusiasm for poetry to a broad public purpose – underwritten by the sincere bonds of friendship.

This trope of privacy-in-public inhabits the next section, a set of sonnets, several cast as brief personal epistles, but by force of keeping company with the *Examiner* sonnets such as *Chapman's Homer* and *To Kosciusko*, acquiring some of this public energy. Some, moreover, have overt public reference and a political point. Sonnet III, *Written on the day that Mr. Leigh Hunt left Prison*, praises Hunt's attack on the Regent, the cause of his prison sentence. Keats renames the crime officially called "libel" as Hunt's daring "for showing truth to flatter'd state" (1), and he stresses the liberty of spirit that abided in the insulted state's apparatus of imprisonment. Hunt, like a modern-day Lovelace (for whom stone walls could "not a prison make"), has "In his immortal spirit, been as free / As the sky-searching lark, and as elate" (3–4). Hunt found in Spenser a way to enter "bowers fair, / Culling enchanted flowers," and "he flew / With daring Milton through the fields of air" (9–11). Invoking Hunt's affection for and prison-reading of Milton and Spenser, the sonnet celebrates Hunt as a genius in their line and of their spirit: "To regions of his own his genius true / Took happy flights" (12–13). The State, Keats implies, might as well have (indeed, might have) imprisoned Spenser or Milton, and he closes with a direct, Huntian attack upon Hunt's appointed prosecutor: "Who shall his fame impair / When thou art dead, and all thy wretched crew?" (13–14). Addressing the Regent himself, the captain of that "wretched crew," as "Minion of Grandeur" (5), and with Habeas Corpus just recently suspended (allowing indefinite imprisonment without trial), this is a bold charge for any young poet. It is as if Keats were courting Huntian prosecution, Huntian punishment. The figurative joining of Milton and Spenser with Hunt, all "Culling enchanted flowers," could be (and was) read by the Tory press only with disdain, as a Cockney attempt to claim these historical greats as honorary "Cockneys."

To this visionary company, Sonnets XIII and XIV – *Addressed to Haydon* and *Addressed to the Same* – add the volatile Haydon, and even staid Wordsworth. Any poem naming Haydon would evoke his championing of the "Elgin Marbles" (the sculptural fragments Lord Elgin had removed earlier in the century from the Athenian acropolis, and which he wanted the state to purchase, at a considerable sum, for its "national" art collection). Byron had already attacked Elgin and Britain as pirates, robbing Greece of its treasures (*Childe Harold's Pilgrimage*, Canto II), but others felt that Elgin deserved praise, the Greeks being unable to protect their treasures from Turkish vandalism, or worse, Napoleonic spoil. Others focused on the aesthetic (and relatedly, monetary) value: were these coarse refuse, or relics of former grandeur bearing the aura of ancient Greek Liberty? Keats joined the debate with two sonnets, not published in *Poems*, but concurrently in the journals, including *The Examiner*. His sonnets in *Poems* praise Haydon's devotion to the Marbles, as well as his commitment as an artist to heroic subjects and heroic canvases. Keats celebrates him as "a stout unbending champion," who "awes / Envy, and Malice to their native sty" (*Addressed to Haydon* 11–12) – "Envy" and "Malice" are epithets for Haydon's opponents, derived from a current article in *The Quarterly*.[22] Keats reads Haydon's triumph as a national plebeian victory: Haydon is the champion not only of the "Highmindedness" of "the great man's fame" but also of its dwelling in "people of no name, / In noisome alley, and in pathless wood" (1–4) – those "Unnumber'd souls" who "breathe out a still applause, / Proud to behold him in his country's eye" (13–14).

To make this point Keats quotes the phrase "singleness of aim" from Wordsworth's *Character of the Happy Warrior* (*Poems*, 1815), subtly interpolating Wordsworth into this argument by reinforcing a public link between Haydon and Wordsworth recently forged by Wordsworth himself in his sonnet *To B. R. Haydon, Esq.* (*Champion*, 1 April 1816). This link is strengthened in the companion sonnet, its first line, "Great spirits now on earth are sojourning," not only echoing Wordsworth's "Great men have been among us," but also directly enlisting Wordsworth to first place on Keats's roster:

> He of the cloud, the cataract, the lake,
> Who on Helvellyn's summit, wide awake,
> Catches his freshness from Archangel's wing. (2–4)

Keats reclaims Tory Wordsworth for cultural reform. The next honoree is Hunt, "He of of the rose, the violet, the spring, / The social smile, the chain for Freedom's sake" (5–6), then Haydon, "whose stedfastness would never take / A meaner sound than Raphael's whispering" (7–8). Wordsworth's quasi-Miltonic visionary power, Haydon's defense of the Elgin Marbles, and Hunt's political martyrdom spell Keats's commitments, his ideology of greatness.

The name of Wordsworth was in play among both Tories and reformists. The *Quarterly* and *Edinburgh* reviewers, as well as Hunt, Hazlitt, and Shelley, alternately criticized and praised him; Haydon and Reynolds, Keats's most recent influences, worshipped him. Keats summons "Wordsworth" as validation for his project, closing "Great spirits" with the unlikely trio of him, Hunt, and Haydon as agents of change in what could be seen, in 1817, as a cultural and political challenge to a public sphere alive with discussions of "Secret Committee Reports" and the suspension of Habeas Corpus. All "Upon the forehead of the age to come," the trio is ready, Keats suggests, to advance aesthetic and political reform – and in the process, Britain's international prestige:

> These, these will give the world another heart,
> And other pulses. Hear ye not the hum
> Of mighty workings? – –
> Listen awhile ye nations . . .   (11–14)

As with the conclusion of *Written on the Day that Leigh Hunt Left Prison*, a call such as this was a taunt to Tory reviewers – and it is to the challenge of Keats's Cockney "hum" that they brutally responded.

Keats amplifies and brings to a climax the "hum / Of mighty workings" in *Sleep and Poetry*. From a stance of neophyte modesty, "O Poesy! for thee I hold my pen / That am not yet a glorious denizen / Of thy wide heaven" (47–49), Keats outlines his poetic project, passing first through the pastoral "realm of Flora, and old Pan" (deities he invoked in his dedication), then to the epic realm of "the agonies, the strife / Of human hearts" (124–25). Keats laments the passing of the classical spirit, with a nod toward the Elizabethan bards, "The fervid choir that lifted up a noise / Of harmony" (173–74). "Ay," Keats complains, "in those days the Muses were nigh cloy'd / With honors" (178–79) and then, hitting his stride, he contrasts this lost glory to the present regime:

> Could all this be forgotten? Yes a scism
> Nurtured by foppery and barbarism,
> Made great Apollo blush for this his land.

> Men were thought wise who could not understand
> His glories: with a puling infant's force
> They sway'd about upon a rocking horse,
> And thought it Pegasus. (181–87)

These lines became infamous in no small part because they reiterate Hunt's polemic, in "Young Poets" and elsewhere, for a return to truer values, and Keats is not shy about echoing Hunt's and Hazlitt's several criticisms of the school of Pope.[23] He sees hope in modern poetry, and its name is the Lake School. "Now 'tis a fairer season" (221):

> for sweet music has been heard
> In many places; – some has been upstirr'd
> From out its crystal dwelling in a lake,
> By a swan's ebon bill; from a thick brake,
> Nested and quiet in a valley mild,
> Bubbles a pipe; fine sounds are floating wild
> About the earth: happy are ye and glad. (223–29)

Echoing the sentiments of Sonnet XIV ("Great Spirits"), these lines present the Huntian project as, once again, validated by Wordsworthian poetics.

Keats is also alert to the critiques of the Lake School, whose darker poems, along with Byron's, were heard as "strange thunders from the potency of song" (231), the product (as Hunt himself suggested) of "morbidities, as well as mistaken theories" (*Examiner*, 1 June 1817). To correct the error, Keats applies a Huntian view:

> A drainless shower
> Of light is poesy; 'tis the supreme of power;
> 'Tis might half slumb'ring on its own right arm.
> The very arching of her eye-lids charm
> A thousand willing agents to obey,
> And still she governs with the mildest sway. (235–40)

Terms such as "supreme of power," "might," and all of 239–40, give a vision of politics as well as poetry: "the great end / Of poesy, that it should be a friend / To sooth the cares, and lift the thoughts of man" (245–47). Here is the most direct justification of the Keats's stylistic commitments. This is a poetry of health, cheer, and sensuous freedom: "delight with liberty." The image of potency in reserve ("might half-slumb'ring on its own right arm") employs the figure just as Haydon and Hazlitt had suggested – as a model for artists and statesmen.

Keats rejoices in Lake School poetics but does not want the increasingly reactionary politics associated with Wordsworth, Coleridge and, most vehemently, Poet Laureate Southey. The problem was to redeem the poetics and counter the politics. His gesture is to transume Wordsworth's *Tintern Abbey* into his own poetic credo. As critics often note, the stages of development Wordsworth describes (65–111) are echoed in *Sleep and Poetry* (85–162). What has not received sufficient attention is Keats's turning Wordsworth's "sense sublime / Of something far more deeply interfused" away from egotistical sublimity and into a general "idea" of "liberty," at once political and poetic:

> yet there ever rolls
> A vast idea before me, and I glean
> Therefrom my liberty; thence too I've seen
> The end and aim of Poesy.   (290–93)

At this point in his career, the "end and aim" is not the Wordsworthian solace of private, scarcely recoverable memory, but a present endeavor: the aesthetic, social, and political project associated with Hunt and *The Examiner*. Hence this summary poem honors Huntian imagery and stylistics, coming to rest in Hunt's home, "a poet's house who keeps the keys / Of pleasure's temple" (354ff). The final lines take the inventory: Huntian-rococo and pastoral influences, combined with classical imagery and Huntian diction in an extended ekphrastic depiction of Hunt's room, especially its icons, "Sappho," "Great Alfred," and patriot Kosciusko's face "worn / By horrid sufferance – mightily forlorn" (381–88).

The reviews of *Poems*

Although *Poems* was a commercial failure, it did attract the notice of several major periodicals, and since most quoted extensively, Keats's poetry found audience here, too. But the payoff was divided. The liberal, reformist publications, such as *Champion*, and *Monthly Magazine*, without emphasizing political concerns, praised the poems, often commending the very features condemned by the Tory press. More moderate reviews, such as the *Edinburgh Magazine*'s, struggle, without partisan points to make, with the "newness" of the poetry. The *European Magazine*'s review, though mainly unsympathetic, tries to balance a concern for the moral, political, and religious resonances of this poetry with an appreciation of Keats's potential as a poet. But the Tory press, emphatically *Blackwood's* Z., attacked Keats and the Cockneys personally – characterizing them as "low-born," "immoral," "uneducated," and using this discourse strategically to elide the kind of open, objective discussion evident in less partisan reviews. The Tory agenda was to dictate taste and values, not engage debate. What irritated *Blackwood's* and the Tory press in general was Keats's bold vocabulary of

political, aesthetic, and cultural reform, in the arena of the reformist press –
this upstart graduate of Hunt's new school issuing a liberal challenge to the
prevailing social, political, and moral order. In the first actual review of Keats
in *Blackwood's*, Z. was exactly right, if not exactly appreciative, when he
warned readers that Keats belongs to the "Cockney school of versification,
morality, and politics."[24]

NOTES

1 Hunt's prison term was earned by his derision of the Prince Regent as "a violator
of his word, a libertine over head and ears in debt" (*Examiner*, 24 February
1812).
2 Quotations, here and following, are from the first published versions – either in
The Examiner or in *Poems*; line numbers correspond to Stillinger's edition.
3 *The Feast of the Poets, with Notes, and Other Pieces in Verse, by the Editor of
the Examiner* (London, 1814), 35.
4 Marjorie Levinson, *Keats's Life of Allegory: The Origins of a Style*, 13.
5 Tennyson's comment is in Palgrave's *Golden Treasury* (1861), 320. For a case for
"Cortez," see Susan J. Wolfson, *The Questioning Presence: Wordsworth, Keats,
and the Interrogative Mode in Romantic Poetry*, 221 and her note on precedents.
For the political implications of Cortez, see Daniel Watkins, *Keats's Poetry and
the Politics of the Imagination*, 26–31.
6 See William Keach, "Cockney Couplets: Keats and the Politics of Style."
7 *The Story of Rimini* (1816) told of the "incest" of Paulo and Francesca, the lovers
damned in Dante's *Inferno. Rimini* was popular, and reviled as immoral and stylistically vulgar by *The Quarterly* and *Blackwood's*. Like "Young Poets," Hunt's
"Preface" to *Rimini* attacked Popian poetics and urged a return to the poetics of
earlier eras. Keats repeats the attack in *Sleep and Poetry*, 181–206, and takes a
line from *Rimini* ("Places of nestling green for Poets made") as his epigraph for
"I stood tip-toe." These poems, as well as *Specimen of an Induction to a Poem*
and *Calidore*, boldly echo *Rimini's* non-Popian couplets, with Huntian style
apparent throughout Keats's volume.
8 Jack Stillinger, *"The Hoodwinking of Madeline" and Other Essays on Keats's
Poems*, 5.
9 For a further discussion of the politics of "liberty and delight" see Nicholas Roe,
John Keats and the Culture of Dissent, 203–29. For a darker reading of the lines
from Spenser, emphasizing a conflict between liberty and governance, see Gregory
Kucich, *Keats, Shelley, and Romantic Spenserianism*, 164–65.
10 Richard Price's *Discourse on the Love of Our Country* (1789) celebrates the 1688
revolution, polemically linking it to the American and French Revolutions, "both
glorious." For the imagery of "glory" and "light" in revolution-debates, see
Ronald Paulson, *Representations of Revolution (1789–1820)* (New Haven: Yale
University Press, 1983), 38, 57–58.
11 On the politics of pagan myth and Pan-worship, see Roe, *Culture of Dissent*,
74–87, 208–12.
12 Recent evaluations have been more appreciative of Keats's risks. Rodney Stenning
Edgecombe calls the style Huntian "rococo" (*Leigh Hunt and the Poetry of Fancy*

[Madison: Farleigh Dickinson University Press, 1994], 63–87); Jerome McGann sees Keats making a case for the "authority of sentimentality" (*The Poetics of Sensibility* [Oxford: Clarendon, 1996], 120–25); Richard Cronin and Elizabeth Jones describe a "poetics of suburbia" (Cronin, "Peter Bell, Peterloo, and the Politics of Cockney Poetry," *Essays and Studies*, ed. Kelvin Everest [Cambridge: D. S. Brewer, 1992]; Jones, "Keats in the Suburbs," *KSJ* (1996), 23–43).

13 Walter Jackson Bate, *John Keats*, 77.

14 See, for example, Jack Stillinger's unit on Keats for *The English Romantic Poets*, 4th edn. (New York: MLA, 1985), which devotes just two paragraphs to Keats's first volume and *Endymion*, while later works warrant seven closely printed pages.

15 *Edinburgh Magazine*, October 1817, 236.

16 Jerome J. McGann, *The Beauty of Inflections: Literary Investigations in Historical Method & Theory*, 30–31.

17 Robert Ryan, *The Romantic Reformation: Religious Politics in English Literature, 1789–1824* (Cambridge: Cambridge University Press, 1997), 154–55.

18 Paul de Man, *John Keats: Selected Poetry*, xviii.

19 Wolfson, *Questioning Presence*, 219–20.

20 See also *To My Brother George* (24) and *To Cowden Clarke* (44–45).

21 Andrew Motion, *Keats*, 63.

22 The article states that Elgin had been "traduced by ignorance, envy and malice." "Lord Elgin's *Collection of Sculptured Marbles*," *Quarterly Review*, January 1816, 514.

23 For Hazlitt, see *Examiner*, 20 August 1815.

24 "Cockney School of Poetry, No. IV" (August 1818), 521.

2

KAREN SWANN

Endymion's beautiful dreamers

We read *Endymion* with a sharp awareness of its role in the fashioning of Keats. He himself described it as a rite of passage: a "test, a trial of my Powers of Imagination and chiefly of my invention [. . .] by which I must make 4000 Lines of one bare circumstance and fill them with Poetry"; a "[leap] headlong into the Sea" (*KL* 1.169–70, 374). For most readers, the thrill and tedium of reading *Endymion* – and the mixture of affection and irritation one feels for it – are linked to this sense of it as a young poet's testing ground: the biographical figure seems revealed in his preciosity, his ambition, his absorption, his overweening love of "fine Phrases" (*KL* 2.139), and his trying lapses of taste and judgment. The most influential analyses have acknowledged its critical place in Keats's poetic development: "In working out the destiny of his hero," writes Stuart Sperry, Keats "was in fact working out his own."[1]

But the poet of *Endymion* also attempts to make himself in more entrepreneurial terms: as Marjorie Levinson puts it, this is "the pastoral epic that would, literally, *make* [Keats]."[2] Of all the projects the poet takes up, the most concertedly pursued is arguably one of self-commodification. *Endymion* proliferates images of the poet as a glamorous, arrested youth: these include Endymion himself but also Adonis, Glaucus, Hyacinth, Ganymede, Narcissus, the fevered author of the Preface, halted in a "space of life between" boyhood and manhood (p. 103), and his dedicatee Thomas Chatterton – all abstracted dreamers, all piercingly beautiful, all singled out by the gods, all marvelous fated boys, all destined for celebrity.

This dimension of the poem pointed its most scandalized contemporary responses. Yet paradoxically, and despite *Endymion*'s almost perfect failure *as* a commodity, the early battles around Keats's reputation suggest an almost uncanny success of the poem's strategy to "make" its youthful author. Both detractors and supporters remained caught in the poem's image-making machinery. Those who reviled Keats for "Cockney" aspirations, for his wishful, self-exposing, and ultimately *failed* efforts at self-fashioning, nonetheless cast him in the image of *Endymion*'s image of the poet. In the virulent attacks of *Blackwood's Edinburgh Magazine* and Byron's letters to his publisher John Murray, "Johnny Keats" appeared as an abject version of his own Endymion or Adonis: a self-absorbed, self-glamorizing "Cockney rhymester, dreaming a phantastic dream at the full of the moon" (*Blackwood's* "Z."), producing "a sort of mental masturbation," "the very *Onanism* of poetry" (Byron).[3] Conversely, the poet's defenders characterized him as a youth chosen by the gods, fatally wounded, and ultimately destined for immortality: one in a series that included Endymion, Adonis, Glaucus, Chatterton and Kirke White, and, with Keats's death but months before theirs, Shelley and Byron.[4]

Endymion's project of image-making begins but does not end with the poem. Until recently, Romanticists and other friends of Keats have viewed *Endymion* and its reviews as a moment in a life-story that takes a swerve from this point: after, and as a result of his work on *Endymion*, Keats finds his poetic voice, leaves his "Cockney" origins behind, and becomes canonical Keats, the poet of "Negative Capability," the "poetical Character" who "has no character" (*KL* 1.193, 386–87).[5] Critics have recently returned to Keats's Cockney context, in part to expose the idealizing, decontextualizing gestures of these assessments.[6] Yet "Cockney" and "canonical" Keats are less discontinuous than either approach assumes: the "Cockney" poem and its scandalized responses produced the Keats that even cool modernism came to love – the Keats who continues to move us as we find and lose ourselves in *Endymion*.

I

What is the poet? In the 1800 Preface to *Lyrical Ballads*, Wordsworth's famous answer is "a man speaking to men." Keats's answer would seem to be, "a youth singled out by the gods." Such a youth draws every gaze and every maiden's sigh most effectively when he doesn't speak at all, when he gives the impression of having vacated this world:

> Now indeed
> His senses had swoon'd off: he did not heed
> The sudden silence, or the whispers low,
> Or the old eyes dissolving at his woe,
> Or anxious calls, or close of trembling palms,
> Or maiden's sigh, that grief itself embalms:
> But in the self-same fixed trance he kept,
> Like one who on the earth had never stept –
> Aye, even as dead-still as a marble man,
> Frozen in that old tale Arabian.　　　　(1.397–406)

Earlier, Endymion was legible in the Byronic way, a "lurking trouble in his nether lip" (1.179); later, he confesses to his concerned sister Peona his ardent attachment to a lost high object. But here, he is fascinating for his opacity, as an excess of melancholic consciousness topples over into unconsciousness and he acquires the sharp loveliness of one lost to the present scene, transported to some other place. As the youth becomes aestheticized, "alchemiz'd" (780) into a figure from story, an image of himself, the culture of which he has been a part becomes reoriented into a circle, onlookers dissolved into the traces of affective responses – tears, voices, sighs – that attest to but also become his radiance or charisma.

Endymion suffers from an embarrassment of riches and, especially, from a surfeit of such youths, whose exquisite beauty emerges, not when they are thinking too much, but when we have no route to what they are thinking, when they become "abstracted." Although their lapsedness can appear as an effect of having been loved and left by immortals, it is also the quality that smites the gods in the first place. Think, for instance, of the ravishing Adonis, adored by Venus and kept by her in suspended animation until her periodic returns. Endymion comes upon the slumbering youth and, for an instant, sees as a god sees:

> After a thousand mazes overgone,
> At last, with sudden step, he came upon
> A chamber, myrtle wall'd, embowered high,
> Full of light, incense, tender minstrelsy,
> And more of beautiful and strange beside:
> For on a silken couch of rosy pride,
> In midst of all, there lay a sleeping youth
> Of fondest beauty; fonder, in fair sooth,
> Than sighs could fathom, or contentment reach:
> And coverlids gold-tinted like the peach,
> Or ripe October's faded marigolds,
> Fell sleek about him in a thousand folds –
> Not hiding up an Apollonian curve
> Of neck and shoulder, nor the tenting swerve
> Of knee from knee, nor ankles pointing light;
> But rather, giving them to the filled sight
> Officiously. Sideway his face repos'd
> On one white arm, and tenderly unclos'd,
> By tenderest pressure, a faint damask mouth
> To slumbery pout; just as the morning south
> Disparts a dew-lipp'd rose.   (2.387–407)

This filling vision is a structuring motif of the poem: Endymion comes upon the sleeping Adonis just as Venus had earlier come upon Adonis and fallen in love with him, just as Diana had come upon the beautiful dreaming Endymion and fallen in love with him, just as, in the story Glaucus tells to Endymion, Circe had come upon the sleeping boy Glaucus and fallen in love with him. Adonis is one is a series of boys, boys, boys – mute, self-enclosed, and infinitely seductive, all officiously displayed to the filled sight.

Endymion's beautiful dreamers pose an answer to that old question: what does the Other want? Predictably, like most desiring subjects, the gods want a youth who eludes their desire – who doesn't present himself to them but upon whom they must stumble, by chance, when he is asleep or lost in thought. Like his earlier avatars, known for their audacious indifference to Venus, Adonis answers to the other's desire by not answering: when Venus appears he doesn't *want* to be wakened and forego onanistic delights (the dew from Venus's car, falling on his shoulders, "made him still / Nestle and turn uneasily about" [2.521–22]). The problem is that he overplays the role: or some hand, anyway, knowing there's nothing so desirable as withholding-ness, too officiously displays to view his retentive charms.

This is a richly mortifying scene, but I would disagree with Christopher Ricks that we are "embarrassed" for Adonis's sake, for his unwitting vulner-ability to our gaze.[7] It is the oversolicitation of the image that disconcerts. Adonis is framed and framed again – by the suddenly opening chamber, by the delicately tinted couch and coverlids, by the cupids that surround him and dispense the dew, rain, and hushed music that are his aura, by the arrested, gazing Endymion. "In midst of all," "officiously" displayed to the "filled sight," is Keats's gorgeous, perfectly superficial youth – an ostenta-tiously froufrou confection, a flagrantly material boy, wrapped in silk and damask, and brought to seductive, slumbery pout. Adonis's Apollonian looks evoke no tragic gap between immortal and mortal, but simply his status as simulacrum, while the seamless packaging of his "coverlids" func-tions only to draw attention to his surfaces, to suggest that there is nothing beneath the covers – no phallus, no provocative deficiency. In the manner of the radically abstracted and self-absorbed model or commodified image, he seems at once hollow and too full of himself, completely occulted and too ostentatiously promoted.

Keats's scene, then, exposes more than just Adonis. It stages the awkward erotic bind of "playing hard to get," in which one must figure out how to perform indifference in a way that captures the other's attention and regard. "Playing hard to get," moreover, is arguably *the* characteristic predicament of a broad range of situations peculiar to modern commercial society and its cultivation of the image. Especially germane are the emergent, prestigious constructions of poetic identity associated primarily with Wordsworth and Byron – of the poet as "chosen" or fated, in rapt communication with his own high soul, indifferent to public applause, and so on. Keats's staging of Adonis punctures the mystique that accrues to these representations by highlighting their iconic, produced, and commodified character: the scene flagrantly promotes a self-image whose glamor is wholly dependent on its flagged disregard for market concerns. In thus aggressively presenting the poet as a youth careless of his reception, the scene more generally exposes a potentially embarrassing impasse of consumer culture: how *does* one promote an image whose surplus value necessarily derives from its appearance of unattainability, its identity as more than can be priced and bought?

But what is most scandalous about this scene – and also most precociously modern and Keatsian – is its suggestion that these impasses may only enhance the provocation of the image. The god's belief in the object's valuable reserve, if face-saving, may not be structurally necessary. Exposed as one whose power to fascinate derives from positioning rather than from intrinsic qualities, Adonis would seem to puncture the illusions upon which we imagine charm to depend. But his charm is to fascinate anyway: to enthrall us even as we see through his magic. Keats's tableau exposes and exploits this charm: the eye moves giddily over the boy's luscious and unfathomable surfaces, knowing all the while that there's nothing behind the screen of this fantasy – knowledge that makes the situation only more arresting.

It's hard to resist gathering these mortification effects back to the youthful author, who here seems to expose him*self* through his oversolicitous, self-reflexive framing of the scene. But is it possible to say in what spirit Keats tips his hand? Is he perfectly, naively absorbed in this construction – so rapt in this desirable image of his own wished-for desirability that he has forgotten his vulnerability to our perspective? (Is he, as Z. claims, just "a young Cockney rhymester, dreaming phantastic dreams"?) Or is he a supremely *self*-conscious framer of his own activity – busily, aggressively working this image, the most potent one a poet of his class and age could claim, in the hope of some return? Could he be engaged in a witty and even cynical exposé of an embarrassingly solicitous Cockney style – one that promises depths and delivers surfaces, and that happens to be the style of this poem? Is he cockily involved in a grander exposé – of the gods, who get exactly what they want in this bonbon of a boy, or, more grandly still, of an emergent scene of the production and consumption of cultural images? Or could he see through the scene and, nonetheless, be perfectly absorbed in it?

All these possibilities seem credible, most have legitimacy even within recent Keats criticism, and some are capable of producing striking and salutary accounts of the early Keats. Yet taken together, such efforts to locate a Keats and a determining context beyond the figure of Adonis are troubled by an impossible logic: the Keats so constructed seems at once, or undecidably, utterly lost and too officiously present in the scene. I am reminded of the tentative but striking account of the unsettlingness of reading *Endymion* offered by its first and friendly reviewer. "The secret of the success of our modern poets, is their universal presence in their poems," he suggests; they are "the shewmen of their own pictures, and point out its beauties." In contrast, "Mr Keats goes out of himself into a world of abstractions." Like Shakespeare's *Venus and Adonis*, his is "a *representation* and not a *description* of passion": "Both these poems would, we think, be more generally admired had the poets been only veiled instead of concealed from us."[8] The poet is completely instantiated in his represented "abstractions," and he is nowhere to be found in them.

Endymion precipitates an early version of the Keatsian "poetical Character," an endlessly fascinating youth of "no character." Suspended between biography and poetry, this poetical character is one of a series of youths who together reproduce the perfection of the alluring Adonis: each is absorbed by (another like) himself, to lose himself and/or to see himself there.[9] Yet however provocatively this gallery suggests the degree to which even our most prestigious accounts of Keats derive their lineage from "Cockney" poetry and partake of that poetry's concern with the image, it fails to account for the volatile images of Keats that emerged in the first reviews, which presented an abject, failed version of the seductively self-enclosed figure.

II

Like Adonis, Endymion is possessed of a certain stagey dreaminess. But whereas the eternally embowered Adonis is a figure without a trajectory, Endymion's entrance onto the scenes that await him produces the effect of destiny and the shape of a project. This, anyway, is the story adumbrated in Book III, a kind of allegory of the poet's progress. As it opens, Endymion, who has been wandering around on the ocean floor, strays by fate or chance into the place where it is prophesied a youth will one day appear, and is hailed by Glaucus: "Thou art the man!" (234); "Thou art commissioned to this fated spot / For great enfranchisement" (297–99). Stepping into the "fated spot," Endymion takes on the role of the messianic youth who was fated to appear just here, "elect[ed]" (710) to accomplish the task of restoring antiquity's beautiful dead lovers to life.

Endymion, who has been suffering under the weight of the past, needs some such rescue. Just prior, he had been experiencing the ocean as a repository of weighty, inscrutable objects "more dead than Morpheus' imaginings" (3.122) – a cultural detritus that gestures toward the grandeur of lost

civilizations and lost stories and strikes him with a "cold leaden awe" (136).
He had almost become a dead thing himself, Keats's narrator tells us, had he
not been warmed by Diana's light, which "kiss[es] dead things to life" (57)
and stirs conflicted thoughts of his mysterious love. An old man (later identified as Glaucus) bracingly interrupts these drifting authorial anxieties.
Conning in a book when Endymion first sees him, his cloak the ground of
figures that become magically animated under an observer's gaze, his ante-
cedents the Glaucus of myth, but also, Wordsworth's Leech-Gatherer,
Coleridge's Ancient Mariner, Milton's Lycidas, and Spenser's Archimago,
Glaucus is a patently poetic figure: a figure for the poet and the charm of
poetry. As literary predecessor to the belated Endymion, his first act is to
anoint the youth as his successor, "the man" who has come to complete and
redeem his work.

Endymion, however, initially resists the call. In the manner of Keats, who
declares of Milton, "Life to him would be death to me" (*KL* 2.212), he can
imagine his encounter with the elder poet only as a sacrificial exchange:

> What lonely death am I to die
> In this cold region? Will he let me freeze,
> And float my brittle limbs o'er polar seas?
> Or will he touch me with his searing hand,
> And leave a black memorial on the sand?
> Or tear me piece-meal with a bony saw . . .? (3.258–63)

The calling, however, works in mysterious ways. Endymion's bristly refusal
of poetic agon – of a battle for self-definition against his precursors – only
allows and confirms his election. Glaucus weeps at his obduracy, Endymion
pities, and Glaucus relates the story of his own youth, of "distemper'd longings" (375), a plunge into the sea, a goddess's overcloying and destructive
desire. He reveals the terms of Circe's curse and the promise of its remission
that he has read in a book delivered to him by an "old man's hand" (669):
if over thousands of years he assiduously gathers and "deposits" all drowned
"lovers tempest tost" (703–5) and masters certain spells, a "youth elect"
(710) will come along and free him. This crazily self-reflexive narrative
circuit provokes Endymion's recognition of himself in Glaucus's story and as
the "youth elect" of the prophecy. "We are twin brothers in this destiny!"
(713) he cries, recognizing Glaucus at last as a "young soul in age's mask"
(310), merely antiqued rather than truly archaic. With this shift of heart, the
relation of predecessor and newcomer is magically divested of all weight,
their mutual task of all difficulty. The work is all in the preparation and
belongs entirely to the older figure; its success requires merely the ease of the

fated youth – his pure heart, his unconsciousness of gravity, his willing participation in the "charm" that restores the dead to life.

And his ability to "work through": to move out of a paralyzingly hierarchical, competitive model of poetic influence and toward a fraternal one. Endymion's shift of heart corresponds to the expressed philosophy of the poem, which consistently celebrates eros over agon (see 2.1–43 and 3.1–40). Such emphasis, as Jeffrey Cox points out, is in keeping with the self-conscious political and aesthetic values of the Hunt circle, whose members consistently performed, against hierarchical, patriarchal models of governmental power and Tory aesthetics, gentler, more democratic ideals of community and fraternity.[10] The episode is also "Cockney" in spirit, a Cockney solution to a Cockney predicament, which is less that of the belated poet than of the *arriviste*. The insouciant casting of one's alter ego as a messianic character who rescues the calcified progenitor from his crustiness by, simply, refusing his weight is of a piece with "Cockney" practices that infuriated *Blackwood's* and Byron – most immediately, the presumption of easy familiarity with the classical poetic tradition.[11] In the terms of Levinson's less celebratory account of Cockney aesthetics (16–17), the archaic text reappears in the Cockney poem as a commodified sign – an object that has shed its context, its particular history, the labor of its production and the work of its reappropriation, to appear "new-born" (2.554) like Keats's glamorous, impervious Adonis.[12] The Cockney poet peers back through time and sees, in the predecessor poet, a youth like himself, an erotically wayward friend to love, a "twin brother" – just as Keats does when, in the Preface to this ambitious Ovidian, Spenserian, Shakespearian poem, he claims his lineage from the antiqued, arrested Chatterton, the young forger of old poetry who committed suicide at age seventeen, and to whom Keats dedicated the poem: "*Endymion: A Poetic Romance* // 'The stretched metre of an antique song' // INSCRIBED TO THE MEMORY OF THOMAS CHATTERTON" (*Poems* 102).

This, then, is one way to read Book III – as an allegory of "Cockney" aesthetic production that magically "makes" poet, precursor, and poem in the form of the commodity. But there is a significant slip between story and product: unlike Hunt's *Story of Rimini*, *Endymion* was not remotely successful in attaching to itself the factitious glamor of the new born, antiqued object. *Endymion*, its critics agreed, "outhunted Hunt" with an excess that readers found hard to assimilate to pleasure, or even to understanding.[13] It may even, as P. G. Patmore astutely speculated, be *sui generis* (in a class unto itself), not least for the way *any* account of its plot seems only to misrepresent the experience of reading it.[14] Reading *Endymion* we are lost, but not, primarily, to a captivating figure that halts and then mirrors our own absorption across a temporal gap. Rather, we find ourselves adrift in the poetic medium.

Recall, for instance, the recognition scene that initiates the drama of the calling. When the abstracted Endymion first spies Glaucus, he "starts": "At this a surpris'd start / Frosted the springing verdure of his heart" (3.187–88). Glaucus is himself "lifeless" (220) until he views Endymion. Then he in turn starts:

> Suddenly
> He woke as from a trance; his snow-white brows
> Went arching up, and like two magic ploughs
> Furrow'd deep wrinkles in his forehead large.   (3.220–23)

The "start" – a coming to life and, simultaneously, an arrest – moves from figure to figure (Endymion to Glaucus), and of ground (Glaucus) to surface (Glaucus's forehead) to figure (the "magic ploughs") – a refractive transference effect that continues to the author, whose brows arched up when he read the passage to his friend Bailey, and to us, if we are "startled" by the showy image. It is possible to account for these starts in psychological terms, as, say, jolts of shame or mortification that come of being caught out in a moment of equivocal self-absorption. (Endymion has been day-dreaming, Glaucus is conning in a book that happens to refer to his own story.) But the upshot is to empty the moment of its particular emotional and dramatic content for the sake of effects, however striking, that feel unrelated to the story, or even its possible allegories.

This virtuoso, clamorous working of the figure exemplifies the insubordination that Hunt and others criticized in Keats's style and attributed to the exuberance of youthful genius, or, less indulgently, to adolescent self-display, or even, to idiocy brought on by self-abuse; Levinson characterizes such effects as the early poetry's fetishistic "badness" (24–25). "Character" – and everything else that lends drama and depth to narrative – is voided into the arresting "fine phrase." Once convulsively reanimated, Glaucus exclaims, "I shall be young again, be young!" (3.237). But in becoming young, he is merely alchemized into yet another showy poetic figure – "a youthful wight / Smiling beneath a coral diadem, / Outsparkling sudden like an upturn'd gem" (775–77) – his life metonymically suggested by and eclipsed into the "outsparkling" diadem. The outsparkling, rejuvenated Glaucus is an image of the flashy, Keatsian image, which catches the light – comes to life – at the very moment it takes on its occulted, fetishistic character. Or, shifting figures, and thinking now of the way "life" continually and fitfully rushes to the surface of the poem, we could say (with debts to Ricks) that the text blushes.

Speculating about the eroticism of *Endymion*, Sperry astutely comments of the love scenes, "The imagery [. . .] suggests not so much the physical passion of real lovers as the communion of the poet with the vital springs of his imaginative life": "the poet explore[s], through the metaphor of carnal knowledge, his own relation to the hidden springs of inspiration" (102–3). "Carnal love" is linked to "love of poetry," he suggests, in a relation of analogy. Yet the connection feels more like metamorphosis than metaphor: the poem's startling effect on the reader has to do with its performance of an erotics that takes the form of a relationship between blushing bodies and poetic images. Eros in this poem is interspecies romance: romance across the bar that divides mortal from immortal, or more precisely, the human organism from the figures of the poetic medium.

This is perhaps just another way of saying that *Endymion* explores what it is to "look upon fine Phrases like a Lover" (*KL* 2.139) – and, conversely, what it is for a phrase to behave as a "love." If so, this dimension of *Endymion* is not in itself out of keeping with the Cockney aesthetic values associated with the Hunt coterie. Later in Book III, the poet explicitly directs us to an image of the text as a "crystal place" housing "line by line" such perpetually blushing loves:

> Turn to some level plain where haughty Mars
> Has legion'd all his battle; and behold
> How every soldier, with firm foot, doth hold
> His even breast: see, many steeled squares,
> And rigid ranks of iron – whence who dares
> One step? Imagine further, line by line,
> These warrior thousands on the field supine: –
> So in that crystal place, in silent rows,
> Poor lovers lay at rest from joys and woes. –
> The stranger from the mountains, breathless, trac'd
> Such thousands of shut eyes in order plac'd;
> Such ranges of white feet, and patient lips
> All ruddy, – for here death no blossom nips.
> He mark'd their brows and foreheads; saw their hair
> Put sleekly on one side with nicest care;
> And each one's gentle wrists, with reverence,
> Put cross-wise to its heart.   (728–44)

The passage casts the work as a repository of poetic "beauties" (to draw on the language of nineteenth-century reviewing), and our reading experience as a string of breathless encounters with rows on rows of the alluring, docile dead, each with the face of an Adonis, a Hyacinth, a Ganymede, an Endymion, each poised in anticipation of our animating backward glance.

But Glaucus, who arranged these beauties, has a bit of the overnice "Sir

Dainty" about him (570); implicit in Circe's taunt is the suggestion that he likes his erotic pleasures sanitized. The text he constructs is not the one we experience, although the latter, too, is stuffed full of pretty things. Taken as the aggregate of its 4,000 clamorous loves, however, *Endymion* is less a shimmering, architecturally coherent "crystal place" than a promiscuous, riven, violently blushing body. Its beauties do not passively await our advent, but ambush us: they start to life suddenly and anarchically, officiously obtruding their charm – the magic by which they shed their work, their context, their history – and invoking, in their Glaucus-like outsparkling, the scenes that had to vanish in order for them to appear in just this "fated spot." The result is a product that incites in the reader, not the cool gaze elicited by the self-enclosed form of the commodity, but the full range and volatility of affect that can befall the true "lover" – besottedness, agitation, oversatedness, impatience, fury, exhaustion, tedium, and, of course, mortification.

The scene of Adonis disconcerts because of the excessiveness of its framing, which imprisons us in our own self-reflexive fascination with Adonis, and at the same time reminds us of the power of frames to work this way. The poem repeatedly stages such encounters, in which a wandering subject is theatrically halted and twinned across a temporal divide by the sudden advent of the lovely, suspended dead. In a sense, these recognition scenes allegorically render the reader's experience, which consists of repeated encounters with its officiously staged, outsparkling phrases. Yet if each fine phrase captivates and frames us, the poem as a whole proliferates frames to the point where we lose our bearings. It is less like Glaucus's crystal place than like his cloak, marked with characters that, coming to life when one looks at them, produce a vertiginous relation between figure and ground: "the gulphing whale was like a dot in the spell, / Yet look upon it, and 'twould size and swell / To its huge self" (3.205–7). Every line, every "love" we encounter is like a dot on this cloak, one bare but potentially illimitable circumstance capable of swelling to 4,000 lines, a figure capable of engulphing its ground. More unsettling than our framing encounter with the poetic image is a sense of becoming absorbed into and overwhelmed by the medium itself.

In the Glaucus episode the poet comes into his calling, stepping into his awaited place. The poem's Cockney allegory suggests that this is an election without sacrifice. Keats's practice, however, suggests that the scene of calling entails a prior, more equivocal, even fatal call. Glaucus describes how, in his "distemper'd longing" for the sea, he crossed the bar between mortal and immortal, becoming "full alchemiz'd" (to use Endymion's own adjective [1.780]) into a denizen:

> Long in misery
> I wasted, ere in one extremest fit
> I plung'd for life or death. To interknit
> One's senses with so dense a breathing stuff
> Might seem a work of pain; so not enough
> Can I admire how crystal-smooth it felt
> And buoyant round my limbs. (3.378–84)

Before his charged encounters with Scylla and Circe, before his redemption by the youth who twins him, comes the sharp pleasure of sense and skin meeting and interknitting with the medium. He becomes truly "absorbed," taking his place among the other stuff suspended and preserved in Poseidon's chambers. Like the drowned loves he preserves, he can start to hectic life when he comes into the theater of a lover's revivifying regard, but he will never again leave the sea. He remains there still, arrested, forever lost to the world he left behind.

Glaucus's career begins in his riotous, exhilarating testing of the medium, and ends with his outsparkling into a gem-like point of light – into a glamorous sign that magically absorbs everything into itself. Keats's poem, a leap headlong into the sea, also begins in riot. Increasingly, however, it becomes a search less for a particular high object than for some impediment capable of resisting the magical machinery of a style that transforms all lost things into antiqued versions of themselves – a quest for some loss that is irrecuperable and thus capable of bringing this potentially limitless production to a halt. This is the muse behind the increasingly overt designation of "sorrow" as the thing Endymion pursues. Yet ultimately the poem conveys the pathos of the commodity form itself – the thing that briefly and gloriously outsparkles into its image and then takes its place among the detritus that a too-efficient aesthetic machinery produces.

Endymion's "Cockney" tactics and values offend. But the poem scandalizes when it outhunts Hunt to the point where a whole magical system of production collapses. Out of this collapse emerges the figure of the poet. In the first reviews, some dubbed this figure "Johnny Keats" – promiscuously eroticized, precociously arrested, at once too full of himself and completely lost to his medium. At the same moment a variant of this poetical character began to emerge: a "Keats" at once supremely self-conscious and so absorbed in the medium that he can seem lost to us. This precocious, fated genius already possesses the pathos of the ever-youthful antique characters of *Endymion*, who seem to look out at us through the medium that preserves them, unconscious of their coming death, their posthumous celebrity, and our reanimating look:

Fair creatures! whose young children's children bred
Thermopylae its heroes – not yet dead,
But in old marbles ever beautiful.
High genitors, unconscious did they cull
Time's sweet first-fruits.   (3.317–20)

III

Like his own Endymion, Keats stepped by fate or chance into a place waiting for him. Most obviously, his "fated spot" was the issue *Blackwood's* had reserved for him in its "Cockney School" papers, its articles on Hunt indicating, well before *Endymion* reached print, that a piece on Keats was in the wings. Keats's Preface, composed with this anticipated reception in mind, invites "men who are competent to look, and do look with a zealous eye, to the honour of English literature" to read as friends or lovers: friends both to love and to youths like the author. The poet (depicted in a "space of life between" boyhood and manhood, "in which the soul is in a ferment, the character undecided, the way of life uncertain, the ambitions thick-sighted"), the poem ("It is just that this youngster should die away"), and Chatterton all have a whiff of fatality about them.

The reception was notoriously otherwise, short on love and friendship, killing in its hostility. *Blackwood's* and *The Quarterly* responded to the poem with attacks that were furiously *ad hominem*, even in the context of other reviews of the Hunt circle. The "Keats" they attacked is an abject version of *Endymion's* glamorous, arrested youths: mortally ill (with the "*Metromanie*") and scandalously eroticized ("vulgar," "prurient," exhibitionist, and, by implication, onanistic). Both reviews decry a kind of systemic disorder: the unbinding of people from their stations (Z. claims the "*Metromanie*" is suddenly afflicting "we know not how many farm servants and unmarried ladies"), of poetry from classical education and even from "sense," and, one suspects, of literary culture from the control of a certain class of men. "Keats" could be said to operate symptomatically – at once figuring the ills of modernity, and allowing the rebinding of certain anxieties to himself.

We know how much of this response was generated by perceived allegiances to the "Cockney" politics and aesthetics of the Hunt circle. I want to suggest that the reviews also mark the beginning of a new formation – "The Keats Circle" – that derives from the constructions of the reviews themselves, and before that, from the poem's image-making project, its articulation of boy-dreamers as the primary vehicle of imaginative idealism. Reading the first reviews, Levinson argues that their erotic opprobrium, especially the charges of onanism, were ways "to isolate Keats without agonizing him" (16) – without, that is, conferring on him the dignity of heroic struggle. At the same time, however, these attacks placed the poet in the position of the transfixing, self-absorbed youth. The critics' antagonism took the form of discipline rather than of agon: "back to the shop Mr John," advised Z. (524), while *The Quarterly* claimed justification from the poet having "told us that he is of an age and temper which imperiously require mental discipline" (205). This vigorous disciplining of the masturbating boy by a circle of gentlemen has its own perverse charge, as Byron well knew and did not forebear to convey to Murray in November 1820: "No more Keats I entreat – flay him alive – if some of you don't I must skin him myself [;] there is no bearing the drivelling idiotism of the Mankin" (*BLJ* 7.225). The onanism of which Keats is accused structures the scene of his disciplining, in which a circle of entitled men belabor a little phallic guy – Byron's (flaccid and drivelling) Mankin, Z.'s diminutive (and also drivelling) "boy of pretty abilities"(522) – and betray (in Byron's case, with a wink and a nod) both the pleasure that invoking and rebuffing Keats's provocation can bring to a circle of literary gentlemen. If "Keats" is symptomatic of the decline of literary culture, he also reinvigorates its dynamics.

The reviews thus isolated Keats, but also positioned him in a certain "fated" – and fatal – "spot." So thought the men who became "the Keats circle" at this time. It is at this point – long before the symptoms of consumption appeared – that Keats's friends gathered around the poet they understood to have suffered a mortal wound. They began to refer to him as "poor Keats" and, in ways that would strike us as prescient were they not so weirdly overt and entrepreneurial, started preparing for the fame-to-be of the dead poet: Woodhouse's collecting of "Keatsiana" began at this time, and it was now that Keats first entered the ranks of poets who died young of the public's neglect, as protests about the reviews began linking him to Chatterton and Kirke White.[15] Thus the *Endymion* reviewers killed Keats, just as Shelley claimed in the preface to *Adonais*, and they also anticipated the form his posthumous life would take. For the reviewers – who close ranks around the arrested, magnetizing body of a boy and derive unseemly pleasure from the spectacle of his abjection – prefigure, even in the management of their discipline, the Keats circle they bring into being and, finally, the dynamics of Keats's posthumous life, when, once again, a circle of literary men would avidly pass among themselves and ultimately into a broader public sphere Severn's transfixed and transfixing wash drawings and accounts of the beautiful, haunting, lost youth.[16] Keats's attackers and defenders thus collude to move the poet onto center stage, transforming him into a "sensation," and "making" him in the image of his own beautiful youths and, in the process, making his readers into friends of Keats.

At least since the publication of Milnes's biography in 1848, this scandalous, sentimentalized figure has had to be repeatedly killed off by Keats's critics and biographers, in order for the virile poet to emerge. Yet the most prestigious accounts of Keats trail behind them the Adonis effect, nowhere more than in Keats's famous account of the poetical character in a letter to Woodhouse of October 1818, about six months after the publication of *Endymion*, and in the wake of the first reviews:

> As to the poetical Character itself, (I mean that sort of which, if I am any thing, I am a Member [. . .]) it is not itself – it has no self – it is every thing and nothing – It has no character [. . .] A Poet is the most unpoetical of any thing in existence; because he has no Identity – he is continually in for – and filling some other Body [. . .] When I am in a room with People if I ever am free from speculating on creations of my own brain, then not myself goes home to myself: but the identity of every one in the room begins to press upon me that, I am in a very little time an[ni]hilated – not only among Men; it would be the same in a Nursery of children[.]
> (*KL* 1.386–87)

The capacity, or propensity, to be annihilated can itself be a great resource. This is the point of another letter, written the same month, that again describes the "poetical Character" in his social role. Here, Keats explains, some social effects are "with [his] will":

> Th[i]nk of my Pleasure in Solitude, in comparison of my commerce with the world – there I am a child – there they do not know me not even my most intimate acquaintance – I give into their feelings as though I were refraining from irritating {a} little child – Some think me middling, others silly, others foolish – every one thinks he sees my weak side against my will; when in truth it is with my will – I am content to be thought all this because I have in my own breast so great a resource. This is one great reason why they like me so; because they can all show to advantage in a room, and eclipse from a certain tact one who is reckoned to be a good Poet –
> (*KL* 1.404)

Like that famous narcissist "His Majesty the Baby," his apparent weakness more than counterbalanced by his plentiful reserves, the eclipsed "Poet" is also the point around which everything else revolves.[17] In society – and first of all, in the circle that made him – he occupies the magic place of the occulted center, the absence that holds the whole fabric together.

Like Adonis's, Keats's charisma derives from a potent structural effect, particularly when his young death answers the symbolic demands of this early project of image-making. The glamor of *any* image created for the marketplace of desire can be described in this way. What distinguishes Keats –

and makes him at once peculiarly volatile, "literary," and modern – is the way the Keatsian image lays bare the mechanism of such a commodity without becoming dissociated from its effects. Keats's project of self-commodification exposes the image of the poet as a commodity like any other. Yet what is a commodity that sees through its own hollowness, that recognizes its own pathos, that shows its own hand, but Genius? Thus the Cockney rhymester reflecting on his own image is only a turn away from the Keatsian "poetical Character" – that supremely indifferent locus of not-thereness, that charged empty place around which an entire culture revolves. Both are "twin brothers" pursuing the destiny of the POET in a commodity culture and a material world.

NOTES

1 Stuart M. Sperry, *Keats the Poet*, 97; for the longer history of the poem's criticism, see 90–97, and Walter Jackson Bate, *John Keats*, 172–74.

2 Marjorie Levinson, *Keats's Life of Allegory: the Origins of a Style*, 7.

3 "Z.," *Blackwood's* 3 (August 1818), 522, cited hereafter by page number; Byron to Murray, November 1820, *Byron's Letters and Journals*, ed. Leslie Marchand (London: John Murray, 1977), 7.217, 7.225; cited hereafter as *BLJ*.

4 See especially the letter from "J. S." to the Editor of the *Morning Chronicle*, 3 October 1818; J. H. Reynolds's unsigned review in *The Examiner* (11 October), 648–49; P. G. Patmore's unsigned review, Baldwin's *London Magazine* (April 1820), 2.380–89; and the obituary notice by "L" ("Barry Cornwall" [Bryan Waller Procter]), Baldwin's *London Magazine* (April 1821), 3.426–27, in which he links Keats to Byron and Shelley as poets who were forced to live abroad: "[Keats] was the youngest, but the first to leave us." All are in *KCH*.

5 This, for instance, is the trajectory of Bate's *John Keats*; see especially 233–35. For accounts of the durable power of this narrative see Levinson, *Keats's Life of Allegory*, 1–44, and Jeffrey N. Cox, *Poetry and Politics in the Cockney School: Keats, Shelley, Hunt and their Circle*, 82–85.

6 In particular, see Jerome McGann, "Keats and the Historical Method in Literary Criticism," Levinson, *Keats's Life of Allegory*, 1–44, and Cox, *Poetry and Politics*.

7 Christopher Ricks, *Keats and Embarrassment*, 12–14.

8 Unsigned review, *Champion* (8 June 1818), 363 (*KCH* 89); Reynolds is commonly thought the author, but Matthews makes a case for Woodhouse (*KCH* 87).

9 Each youth (and the whole series) seems to figure the allure that Jean Baudrillard attributes to the commodity form, which fascinates to the degree that it "radically excludes us in the name of its internal logic or perfection," and is exemplified by "a smooth body, without orifices, doubled and redoubled by a mirror, devoted to perverse autosatisfaction" ("Fetishism and Ideology," *For a Critique of the Political Economy of the Sign*, trans. Charles Levin [St Louis, MO: Telos Press, 1981], 96). Baudrillard's formulation could almost have been written about Keats's staging of Adonis.

10 See Cox, *Poetry and Politics*, especially chapter 2, "The Hunt Era," 38–81.

11 For accounts of Keats's "Cockney classicism," see Cox, *Poetry and Politics*, 101–22 and 146–186. Z.'s mocking response is, "John Keats has acquired a sort of vague idea, that the Greeks were a most tasteful people, and that no mythology can be so finely adapted for the purposes of poetry as theirs" (522; *KCH* 103). Byron's description of "Cockney" verse as "shabby-genteel" is also directed at the ostentatiously casual way it wears its learning; "A Second Letter to John Murray, Esq., on the Rev. W. L. Bowles's Strictures on the Life & Writings of Pope" (*KCH* 130).

12 See also Baudrillard, "Fetishism and Ideology": "Thus, fetishism is actually attached to the sign object, the object eviscerated of its substance and history, and reduced to a state of marking a difference, epitomizing a whole system of differences" (93).

13 *Blackwood's* 18 (January 1826), xxvi.

14 Patmore, Baldwin's *London Magazine* 1 (April 1820): "Endymion is totally unlike [. . .] all other poems" (381; see *KCH* 136).

15 For early references to "poor Keats" around the time of the first *Endymion* reviews, see *KC* 1.35, 37. For an account of Woodhouse's "Keatsiana," see *KC* 1.cxlvi.

16 See *KC* 1.145–252 for evidence of the circulation of Keats's and then Severn's letters. Severn's drawing of the dying Keats is reproduced in Bate, *John Keats*, plate 32, Allott's edition of the poems, facing 677, and Motion's biography, plate 70.

17 Sigmund Freud uses the phrase in quotation in "On Narcissism: An Introduction" (1914); reprinted in *General Psychological Theory*, ed. Philip Reiff (New York: Collier Books, 1963), 72.

3

DUNCAN WU

Keats and the "Cockney School"

In October 1817 *Blackwood's* "Z." launched a notorious attack on what he christened "The Cockney School of Poetry." "Cockney" was (and still is) a name for anyone born within the sound of Bow Bells in the City of London, but Z. expanded the definition:

> Its chief Doctor and Professor is Mr Leigh Hunt, a man certainly of some talents, of extravagant pretensions both in wit, poetry, and politics, and withal of exquisitely bad taste, and extremely vulgar modes of thinking and manners in all respects. He is a man of little education. He knows absolutely nothing of Greek, almost nothing of Latin, and his knowledge of Italian literature is confined to a few of the most popular of Petrarch's sonnets, and an imperfect acquaintance with Ariosto, through the medium of Mr Hoole.[1]

In Z.'s anatomy, a "Cockney" lacked taste and education but was full of "vulgar" pretension. The term was a class slur by which the well-educated Tories portrayed their liberal counterparts as ill-bred social climbers. Its most important aspect by far, especially in the case of Keats, was poetic manner.[2] This essay examines "Cockney style" and traces Keats's shifting, and problematic, relation to it.

It will help, first, to look more closely and objectively than Z. has at Hunt's poetry, with particular attention to its wavering indebtedness to Wordsworth, sometimes praising his sensibility, sometimes criticizing it. Keats would become involved in these motions. It was convenient for Hunt's enemies to pretend either that he had no idea what poetry was, or that his standards were debased. Yet Hunt's poetics were clear and consistent. In "An Answer to the Question 'What Is Poetry?'" (1844), he summarized his principles:

> Poetry is a passion,* because it seeks the deepest impressions; and because it must undergo, in order to convey, them. [. . .] Poetry is imaginative passion. [. . .] He who has thought, feeling, expression, imagination, action, character, and continuity, all in the largest amount and highest degree, is the greatest poet.

Passio, suffering in a good sense, – ardent subjection of one's-self to emotion.[3]

Hunt knowingly echoes Wordsworth, who insisted in a note in the 1800 *Lyrical Ballads* that "the Reader cannot be too often reminded that Poetry is passion: it is the history or science of feelings," and whose Preface stated his "deep impression of certain inherent and indestructible qualities of the human mind, and likewise of certain powers in the great and permanent objects that act upon it which are equally inherent and indestructible."[4] Although these ideas were established by 1844, Hunt's admiration of Wordsworth dated from long before, in the years immediately preceding his first encounter with Keats.

Reading Wordsworth was as crucial to Hunt's definition of poetic principles as it would be for Keats. Hunt admired his poetic achievement but was also critical, even of Wordsworth himself. As early as 1811, he was allying himself with the detractors when, in *The Feast of the Poets* (first published in *The Reflector*), he refused Wordsworth a seat at the table of Apollo. Wordsworth always followed his reviews and reception, and probably read Hunt's poem shortly after publication.[5] Hunt soon modified his view, reflecting this in an extensive footnote in the second edition (1814) of *The Feast*, about which Wordsworth learned when his patron Sir George Beaumont, also an acquaintance of Hunt, wrote to him on 2 June 1814: "Leigh Hunt no great favorite of mine – after some severe sarcasms in verse has thought proper to do you some justice in a note which follows."[6] On 23 June Wordsworth replied:

> Mr Lee Hunt whose "amende honorable" you mention had not read a word of my Poems, at the time he wrote his sarcasms. This I know from an acquaintance of his; so that neither the censure nor the praise of such people is in *itself* of any value. It however affects the immediate sale of works, and authors who are tender of their own reputation would be glad to secure Mr Hunt's commendations. For my own part, my *dignity* absolutely requires an indifference upon this point.[7]

While this frigid indifference hardly seems a basis for friendship, relations between the two thawed. Wordsworth knew that Hunt had been in Surrey Jail since February 1813 for libeling the Prince Regent. When he happened to meet his defense counsel, Henry Brougham, in September 1814, he learned from him that Hunt "valued" his writing.[8] In a gesture of friendship and solidarity, Wordsworth sent Hunt a copy of his collected *Poems* (1815) the following February, just a few days after Hunt's release from prison.

There was a potential strain that summer, when Hunt's weekly, *The Examiner*, carried a piece by Hazlitt vilifying Wordsworth for political apostasy, citing his sonnet celebrating George III's "regal fortitude."[9] Wordsworth (in London on business) felt it worth visiting Hunt at his home to talk the matter over. Hunt labored to pacify him, going even so far as to "disclaim" the article, and their mutual regard survived. When Hunt's *Descent of Liberty: A Mask* was reprinted in October, he presented an inscribed copy to Wordsworth. In December, B. R. Haydon (who had yet to meet Keats, but was by then Wordsworth's principal informant on matters Huntian) told Wordsworth that "Leigh Hunt's respect for you seems to encrease daily – His Brother it is who has had your bust made."[10] Not only was this quite a compliment, coming from *The Examiner*'s radical publisher (John Hunt), it was also a gesture Wordsworth would have welcomed in the wake of a series of hostile reviews of his volumes from 1798 onward, in *The Edinburgh Review* and other leading periodicals. The amity of the Hunts and Wordsworth seems to have taken, for by the next spring, 1816, Wordsworth was publishing sonnets in *The Examiner*, remarking on 9 April, "I have great respect for the *Talents* of its Editor" (*MY* 2.299) – no small praise from one known for a scrupulous meanness with compliments. Keats met Leigh Hunt later that year, on 9 October 1816.[11]

Keats must have been impressed by the amity of Hunt and Wordsworth, but this did not erase some crucial distinctions between Wordsworthian and Huntian style, on which Hunt himself insists. In his extensive notes to the 1814 *Feast of the Poets*, he commends "the greatness of Mr. Wordsworth's genius" (p. 89), but then chides him for "solitary morbidities":

> we get up, accompany the poet into his walks, and acknowledge them to be the best and most beautiful; but what do we meet there? Idiot Boys, Mad Mothers, Wandering Jews, Visitations of Ague, and Frenzied Mariners, who are fated to accost us with tales that almost make one's faculties topple over. [. . .] Let the reader observe that I am not objecting to these subjects in behalf of that cowardly self-love falsely called sensibility, or merely because they are of what is termed a distressing description, but because they are carried to an excess that defeats the poet's intention, and distresses to no purpose. (94–95)

Coming from a political radical, this is surprising criticism, yet what bothers Hunt is not Wordsworth's concern with social and political ills but his means of representing their embodiments. Hunt liked *The Female Vagrant*, and *The Examiner* was friendly to political poetry, including such sonnets by Keats in 1816–17, as John Kandl's chapter shows. What offended Hunt in 1814 was Wordsworth's tendency to combine social realism and spiritual aspiration with an "excess" that defeated the poetry's apparent purposes. To elaborate this critique, he enlists Wordsworth's own criticism of fashionable gothic chillers. Modern literary taste, he complained in the 1800 Preface to *Lyrical Ballads*, was too eager to satisfy "a craving for extraordinary incident" and the "rapid communication of intelligence." Alluding to this complaint and its answering by the poems of *Lyrical Ballads*, Hunt says that Wordsworth

> wishes to turn aside our thirst for extraordinary intelligence to more genial sources of interest, and he gives us accounts of mothers who have gone mad at the loss of their children, of others who have killed their's in the most horrible manner, and of hard-hearted masters whose imaginations have revenged upon them the curses of the poor. In like manner, he would clear up and simplicize our thoughts; and he tells us tales of children that have no notion of death, of boys who would halloo to a landscape nobody knew why, and of an hundred inexpressible sensations, intended by nature no doubt to affect us, and even pleasurably so in the general feeling, but only calculated to perplex and sadden us in our attempts at analysis. (96)

Far from effecting political reflection, such poetry, Hunt suggests, "turns our thoughts away from society and men altogether, and nourishes that eremitical vagueness of sensation, – that making a business of reverie, – that despair of getting to any conclusion to any purpose, which is the next step to melancholy or indifference" (97).

I quote Hunt's critique of Wordsworth at such length because it was Hunt's counter-aesthetic of "delight and liberty" that first attracted Keats and was reflected in the poetry of 1816–17, much of which Hunt encouraged, published, and reviewed and praised. By late 1817, however, Keats was outgrowing some excesses evident in Hunt himself and growing into those very Wordsworthian themes that Hunt had lamented – "Misery and Heartbreak, Pain, Sickness and oppression," so he describes his admiration of *Tintern Abbey* (in *Lyrical Ballads*) to fellow poet Reynolds in May 1818: Wordsworth's "Genius is explorative of those dark Passages," he declares (*KL* 1.281). Keats also had a critique of Wordsworth, but it was not Hunt's. Quite to the contrary, it focused on the ways Wordsworth could be compounded with Hunt unattractively, as a figure of egotism and vanity. "I will have no more of Wordsworth or Hunt in particular," he vows to Reynolds in February 1818, complaining of being "bullied" by "the whims of an Egotist" (1.223–24). Just weeks after coining the phrase "the wordsworthian or egotistical sublime" later that year (1.387), he describes Hunt to his brother and sister-in-law as "vain, egotistical" (2.11).[12]

These were complicated resistances, however. As Keats sensed, Wordsworth's Genius may not just be the rival of his egotism, but was wrought up with it – as was Hunt's irritating egotism with his endearing idealism. Few men of his time were as preoccupied with the need for political change as Hunt; but Hunt wanted to keep poetry for "pleasure," summing the case in "What is Poetry?": "Poetry [. . .] is the utterance of a passion for truth, beauty, and power," and "its ends, pleasure and exaltation" are the "keeping alive among us the enjoyment of the external and the spiritual world" (*Imagination and Fancy*, 1). In the Preface to *Foliage* (1818), he insisted that "a delight in rural luxury" (love of the natural world) was "within the reach of every one, and much more beautiful in reality, than people's fondness for considering all poetry as fiction would imply. The poets only do with their imaginations what all might do with their practice, – live at as cheap, natural, easy, and truly pleasurable a rate as possible" (18–19). This was as egalitarian in aim as the millenarian brotherhood Wordsworth and Coleridge envisaged in the 1790s, but Hunt did not share their belief that poetry was an instrument of reform: "We should consider ourselves as what we really are, – creatures made to enjoy more than to know" (Preface to *Foliage*, 16). This conviction not only informed his criticism but also his own poetry, even his politics: "I do not write, I confess, for the sake of a moral only, nor even for that purpose principally: – I write to enjoy myself" (18). Wordsworth's career, whatever his wavering, was underwritten by a philosophy and a political commitment that stemmed from his first-hand experiences of the French Revolution, while Hunt (the precursor of *fin de siècle* decadents and aesthetes) was devoted to literature as decoration, as the effect of beauty. He begins his review of Wordsworth's *Peter Bell*, "This is another didactic little horror of Mr. Wordsworth's" (*Examiner*, 2 May 1819, p. 282).

The aesthetics of "little horror" linked to didacticism could not have been more opposite to Hunt's poetics of delight and pleasure, the very values that Z. glossed as Cockney vulgarity, first in Hunt, then in Keats. By 1816, Keats had enough horror at Guy's Hospital, where he was training as an apothecary. Hunt gave needed encouragement and support, against his unsympathetic guardian Richard Abbey, to entertain and embark on a literary career. Their intimacy in autumn of 1816 "was altogether intoxicating" (Bate, *John Keats*, 111). Keats often spent the night at Hunt's new home in the Vale of Health. Commenting on *Sleep and Poetry*, Hunt proudly recalled that this – "the last and longest" and "certainly" the "best" of the 1817 *Poems* – had "originated in [Keats's] sleeping in a room adorned with busts and pictures," Hunt's library (*Examiner*, 13 July 1817, p. 443).[13] As the poem's opening shows, the atmosphere had infused Keats with Hunt's ideas and idiom:

> What is more gentle than a wind in summer?
> What is more soothing than the pretty hummer
> That stays one moment in an open flower,
> And buzzes cheerily from bower to bower? (1–4)

The poem as a whole reflects Hunt's influence at its strongest, and (some think) Keats's talents at their feeblest. Ornamental imagery, feminine rhyme-endings, affected sensuousness, and lame posturing ("gentle," "pretty," "cheerily") – such a lexicon promises no banging of political drums, just pleasurable sensation. At one climax, Keats proclaims:

> All hail delightful hopes!
> As she was wont, th'imagination
> Into most lovely labyrinths will be gone,
> And they shall be accounted poet kings
> Who simply tell the most heart-easing things.   (264–68)

Who but Hunt could be thus accounted?

Hunt's tireless promotion of Keats and his related claims to decisive influence on his talents were launched with the "Young Poets" essay in *The Examiner* in December 1816, and began in earnest with a three-part review of Keats's 1817 *Poems*, in *The Examiner* in the summer of 1817. The first installment (1 June, 345) beams praise on Keats in its opening paragraph, but is chiefly devoted to a critique of eighteenth-century poetry and then of "the Lake Poets." On the former, Hunt sounds (oddly) like what Z. would say of him, a few months on (was Z. turning Hunt's critique on Hunt himself?):

> Pope distilled as much real poetry as could be got from the drawing-room world in which the art then lived – from the flowers and luxuries of artificial life [. . .] But there was little imagination, of a higher order, no intense feeling of nature, no sentiment, no real music or variety. Even the writers who gave evidences meanwhile of a truer poetical faculty, Gray, Thomson, Akenside, and Collins [. . .] were content with a great deal of second-hand workmanship, and with false styles made up of other languages and a certain kind of inverted cant.

Hunt then praises the Lake Poets as "the first to revive a true taste for nature," but not without a familiar complaint: "they went to an extreme, calculated [. . .] to make the readers of poetry disgusted." Wordsworth survives this indictment: "in spite of some morbidities as well as mistaken theories in other respects," he "has opened upon us a fund of thinking and imagination, that ranks him as the successor of the true and abundant poets of the older time" – i. e., Spenser and Milton.

Hunt's next installment, on 6 July, seeks credit for its praise of Keats's "sensitiveness of temperament" (428) by first observing some "faults." These amount to excesses that compromise the Huntian standard of poetic pleasure (their statement and examples taking up about half the review): Keats's "passion for beauties, and a young impatience to vindicate them" inspire "a tendency to notice every thing too indiscriminately and without an eye to natural proportion and effect" and a tendency to "variety of versification without a due consideration of its principles" (429). When Hunt praises Keats, he links him to Wordsworth, noting that the mythology of "I stood tip-toe" is played "on the ground suggested by Mr. Wordsworth in a beautiful passage of his *Excursion*. Here, and the other largest poem, which closes the book [*Sleep and Poetry*], Mr. Keats is seen to his best advantage" (429).[14] So far, so good; but in the third installment (13 July), Hunt enlists Keats in his own criticism of Wordsworth:

> Mr. Keats takes an opportunity [. . .] to object to the morbidity that taints the productions of the Lake Poets. They might answer perhaps, generally, that they chuse to grapple with what is unavoidable, rather than pretend to be blind to it; but the more smiling Muse may reply, that half of the evils alluded to are produced by brooding over them. (43)

Then, under the title "*Happy Poetry Preferred*" – a headline so recognizably Huntian that it could be a Cockney-School slogan – Hunt quotes the verse paragraph from *Sleep and Poetry* that begins, "These things are doubtless . . ." (230–47). In these lines, Keats issues his complaint about modern poetry:

> in truth we've had
> Strange thunders from the potency of song;
> Mingled indeed with what is sweet and strong,
> From majesty: but in clear truth the themes
> Are ugly clubs, the Poets Polyphemes
>
> .   .   .
>
> forgetting the great end
> Of poesy, that it should be a friend
> To soothe the cares, and lift the thoughts of man.
>
> (Hunt's transcription, changing Keats's "sooth" to "soothe"; cf. 246–47)

Yet if such sentiments sound Huntian, Hunt was wrong to read into them his own attack on Wordsworth.[15] Had Keats been the glib poetaster portrayed by his hostile critics, he might have welcomed, or at least acquiesced in, being discerned a disciple of Hunt's school, in all its courses. But his resistance to Hunt's instruction is as central to his development as was as his early delight to Huntian ideas. Hunt himself said (in the second installment) that he admired Keats's "strength" of resistance to "the lingering enticements" of the "former system" (eighteenth-century neoclassicism), which found enforcement in the "self-love" (self-interest) of other poets (428). It is a mark of Keats's superior intellect that he resisted Hunt's critique of Wordsworth, and as other passages of the 1817 *Poems* make clear, as even parts of *Sleep and Poetry* make clear, he was always a greater admirer of Wordsworth's poetry. "I am convinced that there are three things to rejoice at in this Age," he told Haydon early in 1818: "The Excursion Your Pictures, and Hazlitt's depth of Taste" (*KL* 1.203). Keats aligned these praises, despite the fact that Hazlitt's depth of taste (Keats was thinking immediately of *Characters of Shakespear's Plays*) included his published impatience with *The Excursion* in 1814 (Keats had similar complaints about Wordsworth's egotism).

Hunt meanwhile tried to keep Keats in line, subjecting *Endymion*, which Keats was completing in the autumn of 1817, to ham-fisted editing. What Hunt did, or attempted to do, with Keats's draft, is not clear, but it provoked an indignant reaction. Writing to Bailey on 8 October, Keats says, "I am quite disgusted with literary Men and will never know another except Wordsworth":[16]

> Haydon says to me Keats dont show your Lines to Hunt on any account or he will have done half for you – so it appears Hunt wishes it to be thought. When he met Reynolds in the Theatre John told him that I was getting on to the completion of 4000 lines. Ah! says Hunt, had it not been for me they would have been 7000! If he will say this to Reynolds what would he to other People?
>
> (*KL* 1.169)

Bristling at Hunt's appropriation of him, Keats rehearses the aspirations he indulged with *Endymion*, "a test, a trial of *my* Powers of Imagination and chiefly of *my* invention. [. . .] this is a great task" (169–70, emphasis added). He concludes with regret over his affiliation with Hunt: "I hope Apollo is {not} angered at my having made a Mockery at him at Hunt's" (170), he cringes, referring to an evening the past April when, primed by after-dinner wine, a "whim seized them to crown themselves with laurel after the fashion of the elder Bards."[17] Keats insists his composition of *Endymion* has been "independant" of Hunt, but

> Hunts dissuasion was of no avail – I refused to visit Shelley, that I might have my own unfetterd scope – and after all I shall have the Reputation of Hunt's elevé – His corrections and amputations will by the knowing ones be trased in the Poem – This is to be sure the vexation of a day – nor would I say so many Words about it to any but those whom I know to have my wellfare and Reputation at Heart – (*KL* 1.170)

Keats's irritation at how "the knowing ones" will read *Endymion*, as the work of Hunt's "elevé" (punning on the French for "pupil" and the past participle of "elevated"), was almost certainly inspired by the attack on *Poems* (1817) just published in *Eclectic Review*:

> Mr. Keats dedicates his volume to Mr. Leigh Hunt, in a sonnet which, as possibly originating in the warmth of gratitude, may be pardoned its extravagance; and he has obviously been seduced by the same partiality, to take him as his model in the subsequent poem, to which is affixed a motto from the

"Story of Rimini." To Mr. Hunt's poetical genius we have repeatedly borne testimony, but the affectation which vitiates his style must needs be aggravated to a ridiculous excess in the copyist. Mr. Hunt is sometimes a successful imitator of the manner of our elder poets, but this imitation will not do at second hand, for ceasing then to remind us of those originals, it becomes simply unpleasing.

The "strange assay" entitled Sleep and Poetry, if its forming the closing poem indicates that it is to be taken as the result of the Author's latest efforts, would seem to shew that he is indeed far gone, beyond the reach of the efficacy of either praise or censure, in affectation and absurdity.

(*Eclectic*, September 1817, pp. 270, 272)

Though partisan, this is also level-headed. Unlike *Blackwood's* Z., this reviewer (Josiah Conder) does not make an issue of Keats's social origins but concentrates on his poetic ability. To sustain his judgment, he quotes *Sleep and Poetry* 270–93: "Will not some say that I presumptuously / Have spoken? . . . / . . . yet there ever rolls / A vast idea before me, and . . . / . . . I've seen / The end and aim of Poesy . . .". And he notes some of Keats's more extravagant rhymes, finding them ridiculous: "Our Author is a very facetious rhymer. We have *Wallace* and *solace*, *tenderness* and *slenderness*, *burrs* and *sepulchres*, *favours* and *behaviours*, *livers* and *rivers*; – and [. . .] *put on*, / . . . *Chatterton*" (273). *Blackwood's* Z. would make a similar point: "Mr Keats has adopted the loose, nerveless versification, and Cockney rhymes of the poet of Rimini" (August 1818, 522). Keats was stung by much of what he read in the reviews, but it is telling that he didn't argue the point of rhyme and that, moreover, his rhymes henceforth would never be so Cockney. The *Eclectic*'s penultimate remark carried a sting that found its mark: "the patronage of the friend he is content to please, places him wholly out of the danger of adding to the number of those who are lost to the public for want of the smile of praise" (275). Keats seemed not so independent after all. The reviewer attempts to help him out by closing with a full quotation of "Happy is England!" (the last of the Sonnet-section of *Poems*) as evidence of Keats's capacity for "simple and pleasing" poetry, when he was not constrained by patron-pleasing. Keats's response, as his letter to Bailey indicates, was to despise himself for having thrived on the tutelage and praise of someone whose own abilities were so clearly suspect.

Keats learned much from Hunt, but he resisted appropriation to all of Hunt's enthusiasms, and did not share his critique of Wordsworth. At the heart of Keats's earliest "Cockney" writings one may detect Wordsworthian influence. Take, for instance, the two slight sonnets on the grasshopper and cricket, which Keats and Hunt composed on 30 December 1816 during one of their quarter-hour sonnet-writing contests.[18] Keats's appeared in *Poems*; then, six months on, Hunt published the pair side by side in *The Examiner*,

21 September 1817 (599), perhaps, among other motives, to advertise Keats's affiliation with him and to remind Keats himself of his indebtedness.

TWO SONNETS ON THE GRASSHOPPER AND CRICKET.

I.

[FROM POEMS BY JOHN KEATS.]

THE poetry of earth is never dead:
    When all the birds are faint with the hot sun,
And hide in cooling trees, a voice will run
From hedge to hedge about the new-mown mead;
That is the Grasshopper's; – he takes the lead
    In summer luxury, – he has never done
With his delights; for when tired out with fun,
He rests at ease beneath some pleasant weed.
The poetry of earth is ceasing never:
    On a lone winter evening, when the frost
        Has wrought a silence, from the stove there shrills
The Cricket's song, in warmth increasing ever,
    And seems to one, in drowsiness half lost,
        The Grasshopper's among some grassy hills.
December 30, 1816.

II.

BY LEIGH HUNT; – NEVER BEFORE PUBLISHED.

GREEN little vaulter in the sunny grass,
    Catching your heart up at the feel of June,
    Sole voice left stirring midst the lazy noon,
When ev'n the bees lag at the summoning brass; –
And you, warm little housekeeper, who class
    With those who think the candles come too soon,
    Loving the fire, and with your tricksome tune
Nick the glad silent moments as they pass; –
O sweet and tiny cousins, that belong,
    One to the fields, the other to the hearth,
Both have your sunshine; both though small are strong
    At your clear hearts; and both were sent on earth
To ring in thoughtful ears this natural song,
    – In doors and out, – summer and winter, – Mirth.
December 30, 1816.

Keats's phrase "summer luxury" (6) is distinctly Huntian, but his sonnet resolves differently from his mentor's. Hunt's suggestion that both insects sing of "sunshine" and "Mirth" turns them into models of the poet himself, and concentrates our attention on the underlying principle of his poetry. As Rodney

Stenning Edgecombe has observed, the sonnet offers "a covert philosophical proposition – his philosophy of cheer."[19] Hunt puts both singers within a poet's direct hearing; Keats is more measured and meditative: his cricket-song transports the listener from the dead of winter into high summer, as the half-dreaming poet imagines he hears the song of the grasshopper. Instead of a scene of direct hearing, Keats represents a poet's imagination involved in memory and fantasy. The distinction is akin to that between hearing music and straining to hear it. Keats's grasshopper plays to a mind that may well ask, "Do I wake or sleep?" – the self-same that would give ear to how a nightingale's

> plaintive anthem fades
> Past the near meadows, over the still stream,
> Up the hill-side; and now 'tis buried deep
> In the next valley-glades.
>
> (*Ode to a Nightingale* 75–78)

Even at the height of his Cockney phase, Keats's attenuation of present mirth signals an emerging independence of Hunt. When Keats's poet only "seems" to hear the cricket's song, there is more of a Wordsworthian than Huntian echo. In the Essay supplementary to the Preface to his collected *Poems* of 1815, Wordsworth insisted that "the appropriate business of poetry" is "to treat of things [. . .] not as they exist in themselves, but as they *seem* to exist to the *senses*, and to the *passions*."[20] Wordsworth-wise, Keats's "seems" brings imagination into play, blending the cricket's song into grasshopper's, winter into summer, and lone silence into tuneful companionship.

As Keats's "seems" also softly reminds us, the sensation is apparent rather than actual: the cricket is not a grasshopper; "in warmth increasing ever" may describe the cricket's song, but the syntax also allows a grammatical relation to "the stove," and in this syntax, the singing cricket is in peril of destruction by the very circumstance that warms his song into expression. This was Keats's aesthetic. The satisfactions enjoyed in the odes of 1819 are notably attenuated: Psyche's bower exists only in shadowy thought; the nightingale's song fades away; the Grecian urn will always remain inscrutable. Keats followed his sense of complicated enjoyments – of mirth never being unalloyed. This is not Hunt's teaching. *The Eclectic*'s sharp comments in September 1817, as more than one of Keats's letters suggest, set him questioning Hunt's influence and thinking more intently about Wordsworth's poetry. Z.'s first assault on Huntian poetics, hereafter known as "the Cockney School" (*Blackwood's*, October 1817), can only have encouraged this turn. Z. shamed Hunt with Wordsworth:

How such a profligate creature as Mr Hunt can pretend to be an admirer of Mr Wordsworth, is to us a thing altogether inexplicable. One great charm of

Wordsworth's noble compositions consists in the dignified purity of thought, and the patriarchal simplicity of feeling, with which they are throughout penetrated and imbued. We can conceive a vicious man admiring with distant awe the spectacle of virtue and purity; but if he does so sincerely, he must also do so with the profoundest feeling of the error of his own ways, and the resolution to amend them. (40)[21]

Could Keats read himself here, and be shamed to do better by his admiration of Wordsworth? Keats certainly noticed the damning link in Z.'s epigraph (38) for this and subsequent Cockney-School papers, verse credited to Cornelius Webb, a regular at Hunt's:

> Our talk shall be (a theme we never tire on)
> Of Chaucer, Spenser, Shakespeare, Milton, Byron,
> (Our England's Dante) – Wordsworth – HUNT, and KEATS,
> The Muses' son of promise; and of what feats
> He yet may do.[22]

Within a few short weeks, Keats was writing to Bailey with attention to the future tense:

> There has been a flaming attack upon Hunt [. . .] – These Philipics are to come out in Numbers – calld 'the Cockney School of Poetry' There has been but one Number published – that on Hunt to which they have prefixed a Motto from one Cornelius Webb Poetaster – [. . .] they have put Hunt and Keats in large Letters. [. . .] I dont mind the thing much – but if he should go to such leng[th]s with me as he has done with Hunt I mu[s]t infalibly call him to an account – if he be a human being and appears in Squares and Theatres where we might possibly meet – I dont relish his abuse (3 November 1817; *KL* 1.179–80)

Repeated attempts were made to uncover the man in the mask of "Z." but they were not successful, and Keats never got to challenge John Gibson Lockhart to a duel. That was left to John Scott (editor of the *London Magazine*), who was mortally wounded in "an account" with Lockhart's associate Jonathan Christie in 1821.

With a calmer view of "the World's Quarrels" (*KL* 1.184), Keats wrote to Bailey again later that month. He meant quarrels among his friends, but his impulse to generalize suggests that he was also thinking of his own with Z. He went on to entertain a series of several remarkable speculations (Men of Genius vs. Men of Power; the holiness of the Heart's affections; the truth of Imagination; a life of Sensations rather than of Thoughts; the repetition of earthly experience in a finer tone hereafter), then exclaimed,

> What a time! I am continually running away from the subject – sure this cannot be exactly the case with a complex Mind – one that is imaginative and at the same time careful of its fruits – who would exist partly on sensation partly on

thought – to whom it is necessary that years should bring the philosophic Mind
– such an one I consider your's.   (*KL* 1.185–86)

As the knowing allusion to Wordsworth makes clear, the "complex Mind" Keats attributes to Bailey, one given to thought as well as sensation, is essentially Wordsworthian. The allusion is to a line in Wordsworth's strenuous resolution of lament in his great Ode, recently retitled in the *Poems* of 1815 as *Ode: Intimations of Immortality*:

> Though nothing can bring back the hour
> Of splendour in the grass, of glory in the flower;
> We will grieve not, rather find
> Strength in what remains behind,
> In the primal sympathy
> Which having been must ever be,
> In the soothing thoughts that spring
> Out of human suffering,
> In the faith that looks through death,
> In years that bring the philosophic mind.   (180–89)

For Wordsworth, a "philosophic mind" is gained from "suffering" and the "faith that looks through death" – the very intensities outlawed by Hunt's creed of pleasure. Keats aspires to this complexity.

More than thirty years later, Bailey wrote of Keats's sense of the ode, recalling that he "deeply felt" the lines about the poet's "obstinate questionings / Of sense and outward things" (144–45) but noting that Keats seemed "to value this great Poet rather in particular passages than in the full length portrait, as it were, of the great imaginative & philosophic Christian Poet, which he really is," adding perhaps wistfully, "& which Keats obviously, not long afterwards, felt him to be" (*KC* 2.274–75). But the poet that Keats was responding to, from 1816 to 1819, was attuned to the vitality of the old, pre-Christian religions. It was these imaginations in *The Excursion*, and not those of Christian philosophy, that Keats most audibly echoed. And most deeply felt of all was the Wordsworth of obstinate questionings, of the burden of the Mystery, of the complex philosophical mind, rather than the didactic poet of "certain Philosophy."[23] But as he had with Hunt, Keats asserts his independence. Wordsworth's *Ode* advanced an essentialist soul, pre-existing and eternally destined. Keats emphasized the existential trials that Wordsworth named in his *Ode*, and (with a refutation of the cult of the exalted souls of children) he articulated, in April 1819, an idea of "Soul-making" as an event of life in the world: "Do you not see how necessary a World of Pains and troubles is to school an Intelligence and make it a soul? A Place where the heart must feel and suffer in a thousand diverse ways!"

(*KL* 2.102). If the Huntian poet would cry, "No!" Keats's last great endeavor, *The Fall of Hyperion*, suggests that he was coming to agree with Wordsworth that "Suffering is permanent, obscure, and dark, / And has the nature of infinity."[24]

Keats's death became a legend not of this kind of noble Wordsworthian suffering, but of nerveless Huntian suffering. Though promoted sympathetically, Shelley fixed the fable of Keats's collapse from savage reviews, most notably in the Preface to *Adonais* (Pisa, 1821):[25]

> The savage criticism on his Endymion, which appeared in the Quarterly Review, produced the most violent effect on his susceptible mind; the agitation thus originated ended in the rupture of a blood-vessel in the lungs; a rapid consumption ensued, and the succeeding acknowledgements from more candid critics, of the true greatness of his powers, were ineffectual to heal the wound thus wantonly inflicted.

Byron presented this fable more succinctly in *Don Juan* XI (1823), in a couplet destined for fame: "'Tis strange the mind, that very fiery particle, / Should let itself be snuffed out by an Article" (stanza 60). Byron's wry skepticism was ignored and the myth embellished. Yet far from being snuffed out by an article or two, Keats learned from his critics, emerging rapidly from "The Cockney School." If his most adversarial readers were small-minded, politically motivated and class biased, their remarks about his affiliation with Hunt's poetic tastes and technique were sufficiently near the mark to confirm Keats's own misgivings and to prompt him to discover his own voice. Far from being his assassins, these critics played a vital role in nurturing Keats's early promise.

NOTES

1 "On the Cockney School of Poetry No.1," *Blackwood's Edinburgh Magazine* 2 (1817), 38. Hoole was a translator.

2 For recent treatments of "Cockney" issues, see Jeffrey Cox, *Poetry and Politics in the Cockney School: Keats, Shelley, Hunt and their Circle*; Marjorie Levinson on reviewers' class antipathy, *Keats's Life of Allegory: The Origins of a Style*, 3–4; and on Cockney opposition, Nicholas Roe, *John Keats and the Culture of Dissent*, 61–62, 226–27.

3 Leigh Hunt, *Imagination and Fancy; or, Selections from the English Poets, Illustrative of Those First Requisites of their Art; With Markings of the Best Passages, Critical Notices of the Writers, and an Essay in Answer to the Question "What is Poetry?"* (London: Smith, Elder, 1844), 2–3, Hunt's note.

4 Quotations follow William Wordsworth, *"Lyrical Ballads," and Other Poems, 1797–1800*, ed. James Butler and Karen Green (Ithaca: Cornell University Press, 1992), 351 and 747.

5 Hunt edited *The Reflector*, a more strictly literary publication than *The Examiner*,

from 1810 to 1812. Wordsworth's home at Rydal Mount had a copy, probably acquired by June 1814; see my *Wordsworth's Reading, 1800–1815* (Cambridge: Cambridge University Press, 1995), 114. In 1814, the year *The Excursion* was published, Wordsworth was known primarily by *Lyrical Ballads* (1798–1805) and *Poems, in Two Volumes* (1807).

6 I thank the Chairman and Trustees of the Wordsworth Library, Grasmere for permission to quote from this letter.

7 *The Letters of William and Dorothy Wordsworth: A Supplement of New Letters*, ed. Alan G. Hill (Oxford: Clarendon Press, 1993), 144–45; Wordsworth's emphases.

8 *The Letters [. . .] Middle Years, 1806–20*, ed. Ernest de Selincourt, rev. Mary Moorman and Alan G. Hill, 2 vols. (Oxford: Clarendon Press, 1969–70), 2.195; cited *MY* hereafter.

9 Hazlitt, *Examiner* (11 June 1815), 382; see my *Wordsworth's Reading*, 106.

10 For Hunt's *Descent*, see Edmund Blunden, *Leigh Hunt: A Biography* (London: Cobden-Sanderson, 1930), 94; Chester L. and Alice C. Shaver, *Wordsworth's Library* (New York: Garland Press, 1979), 133; and *MY* 2.273. Haydon's letter, 29 December 1815, is at the Wordsworth Library, Grasmere.

11 Walter Jackson Bate, *John Keats*, 90.

12 For similar terms of alliance, see Keats's letters to Haydon, May 1817: Hunt's "self delusions are very lamentable" (*KL* 1.143); and to his brothers: Hunt's writing is "mixed up with so much egotism of that drivelling nature that pleasure is entirely lost" (December 1817; *KL* 1.191).

13 Charles Cowden Clarke recalled the circumstance; *Recollections of Writers* (London, 1878; facsimile rpt. Sussex: Centaur Press, 1969), 133–34.

14 Keats admired passages in *Excursion* IV (1814 text: 735–80; 864–900); see Bailey, *KC* 2.276, as well as the many echoes in *Poems* and later poetry.

15 The more likely targets were Byron and Coleridge. See the note by Woodhouse (always a careful reader of Keats); Stuart M. Sperry, Jr., "Richard Woodhouse's Interleaved and Annotated Copy of Keats's *Poems* (1817)," *Literary Monographs* I, ed. Eric Rothstein and Thomas K. Dunseath (Madison: University of Wisconsin Press, 1967), 155.

16 I thus question Beth Lau's sense that Keats at this time shared "Hunt's opinion of Wordsworth's faults" (*Keats's Reading of the Romantic Poets*, 21).

17 Woodhouse's report, cited in Miriam Allott's edition of *Poems*; Keats and Hunt wrote poems on the occasion, Keats withholding his from publication.

18 For accounts of the contest, see Woodhouse's note (Sperry's "Woodhouse," 151) and Clarke's *Recollections*, 135–36.

19 Rodney Stenning Edgecombe, *Leigh Hunt and the Poetry of Fancy* (London: Associated University Presses, 1994), 210.

20 *The Prose Works of William Wordsworth*, ed. W. J. B. Owen and Jane Worthington Smyser, 3 vols. (Oxford: Clarendon Press, 1974), 3.63.

21 When the monthly issues were bound in 1818 as "Volume II," the first phrase was revised to "How such an indelicate writer . . ." Z. would work this vein in his review of Keats himself (*Blackwood's*, August 1818), provoked by the sonnet "Great Spirits" (1817 *Poems*), which praised Hunt and Wordsworth in one breath. "Wordsworth and Hunt!" Z. exclaims; "what a juxta-position! The purest, the loftiest, and, we do not fear to say it, the most classical of living English

poets, joined together in the same compliment with the meanest, the filthiest, and the most vulgar of Cockney poetasters" (520).

22 In September 1817 Webb sent an *Epistle to a Friend* to Blackwood, who may have shown it to Lockhart for advice or amusement; Blackwood did not publish it (except, possibly, the verse of Z.'s epigraphs) and the ms. has disappeared (Roe, *Culture of Dissent*, 129n54).

23 See *KL* 1.281–82. For Keats's mixed and divided response to Wordsworth, see Susan J. Wolfson, *The Questioning Presence: Wordsworth, Keats, and the Interrogative Mode in Romantic Poetry*, esp. 191–98.

24 William Wordsworth, *The Borderers* 3.5.64–5 (1797–99), ed. Robert Osborn (Ithaca: Cornell University Press, 1982). Keats may have known these very lines (unpublished) via Hazlitt, who having heard Wordsworth recite them in 1803, quoted them frequently in his lectures and essays. See *The Selected Writings of William Hazlitt*, ed. Duncan Wu, 9 vols. (London: Pickering and Chatto, 1998), 5.407. For a fine treatment of the Miltonic and Wordsworthian elements in these works, see John Barnard, *John Keats*.

25 See James Heffernan, "*Adonais*: Shelley's Consumption of Keats," *Studies in Romanticism* 23 (1984); rpt. *Romanticism: A Critical Reader*, ed. Duncan Wu (Oxford: Blackwell, 1994), 173–91; and Wolfson, "Keats Enters History: Autopsy, *Adonais*, and the Fame of Keats."

4

JEFFREY N. COX

Lamia, Isabella, and The Eve of St. Agnes

Eros and "romance"

Keats's final lifetime volume of poetry, published in the summer of 1820, is named for its three romances – *Lamia, Isabella, The Eve of St. Agnes, and Other Poems* – and the title page identifies the poet as "Author of *Endymion*," his longest romance of all. Keats and his publishers sought to present him as a narrative poet on a literary scene dominated by popular writers of romances, such as Scott and Byron. This is remarkable, not only because *Endymion* had been ridiculed, but also because Keats himself had seemed intent to secure his name, like Homer or Milton, through epic. In *Sleep and Poetry*, the finale to *Poems* (1817), he imagined bidding farewell to the poetry of delight, "the realm . . . / Of Flora, and old Pan" (101–2), in order to treat "the agonies, the strife / Of human hearts" (124–25), matter for epic or tragedy. This pivot is most revealing, however, in projecting the way Keats's farewells to romance stay dialectically engaged with it. Even his last attempt at epic, *The Fall of Hyperion* (late 1819), begins in a romance setting, amid the remnants of an Edenic feast, and takes the form of a Dantean dream-vision, a motif from quest-romance. From the 1817 *Poems*, with its various gestures of romance ("Lo! I must tell a tale of chivalry," begins *Specimen of an Induction to a Poem*), through *Endymion*, to the 1820 volume and after, Keats seems always on a quest to write a few fine quest romances.

Romanticism, as this retrospective labeling of the era suggests, owed much to the eighteenth-century revival of medieval romance, which brought old texts back into circulation, spurring their positive evaluation in new literary histories and inspiring a large body of new works shaped with romance conventions, such as Southey's *Thalaba* (1801), Scott's *The Bridal of Triermain* (1813), and Thomas Moore's *Lalla Rookh, An Oriental Romance* (1817). Drawing upon the conventional quest romance ("nearest of all literary forms to the wish-fulfillment dream," says Northrop Frye), Romantic-era writers subjected "old romance" (as Keats called it in *Isabella*) to modern critiques and new purposes.[1]

Isabella, composed in early 1818, has been taken as the harbinger of these newer modes. Yet Keats balked at publishing it, even though his friends praised it: Charles Lamb thought it the "finest thing" in the 1820 volume (*New Times,* 19 July 1820), and John Hamilton Reynolds hoped its "simplicity and quiet pathos" would "answer" and "annul" the negative criticism Keats had received in conservative journals for his "Cockney" innovations (*KL* 1.376). Keats was still concerned that it was "mawkish" and sentimental (*KL* 2.162) and gave Woodhouse "a few reasons why I shall persist in not publishing The Pot of Basil":

> It is too smokeable [. . .] There is too much inexperience of live, and simplicity of knowledge in it [. . .] I intend to use more finesse with the Public. It is possible to write fine things which cannot be laugh'd at in any way. Isabella is what I should call were I a reviewer 'A weak-sided Poem' with an amusing sober-sadness about it. [. . .] this will not do to be public – If I may so say, in my dramatic capacity I enter fully into the feeling: but in Propria Persona I should be apt to quiz it myself – There is no objection of this kind to Lamia – A good deal to S\ Agnes Eve – only not so glaring –   (*KL* 2.174)

As Keats's misgivings about *Isabella* make clear, romance, a mode of enchantment linked to wish-fulfillment, was prone to being seen as a weak indulgence, incapable of sterner stuff – in Keats's summary term, "too smokeable." This adjective, usually taken to mean "easily exposed in its faults," carried a more precise sense of "too easily made fun of" – as Keats himself was in the conservative reviews.[2] If *Isabella* might seem to show the "inexperience of li[f]e" of an adolescent naively embracing the idealizations of romance, would its author risk finding himself the object rather than the master of humor?[3] Particularly after Byron's *Beppo* (published the month Keats began *Isabella*) and *Don Juan* (Cantos I–II, 1819) had demonstrated the sensational popularity of an ironic treatment of romance and romantic love, Keats may well have worried that his romances would court a defensive ridicule from readers intent to deny their susceptibility to the wish-fulfilling enchantments of the genre. Although Keats was finally persuaded that *Isabella* was worth publishing, his private judgment has been repeated in modern critical tradition, which has preferred the complexities of *St. Agnes Eve* and the blend of sophisticated irony and dramatic power in *Lamia.*

These judgments, together with the prospectus in *Sleep and Poetry* and the compositional order of the narrative poems of 1818–19, have encouraged assessments of Keats's romances on a developmental model: *Isabella* is "early" apprentice-work, paving the way for the "mature" *Eve of St. Agnes,* and then *Lamia,* the characteristic work of the "late" Keats who takes up earlier forms and ideas only to ironize and to deconstruct them.[4] But the fourteen months between late April 1818, when Keats completed *Isabella*, to late June 1819, when he began *Lamia*, is a very short term for the logic of such a narrative (even for a poet who in three years could move from *Calidore*, a romance fragment about knights and ladies, to the "Great Odes"). A deeper motive for the developmental model is to privilege a "post-Cockney" Keats, the great poet who becomes the true heir of Shakespeare, Milton, and Wordsworth by outgrowing the so-called aesthetic weaknesses of the Hunt school and developing his mature art. *Blackwood's* put Keats in the "Cockney School of Politics, as well as the Cockney School of Poetry" (3 [August 1818], 524), and so Keats's "development" can seem to have a political arc, too. Jerome McGann, for instance, reads the 1820 volume as a "great and (politically) reactionary book," the "whole point" of which was "to dissolve social and political conflicts in the mediations of art and beauty."[5] Whether the story is maturation or reaction, the developmental model suppresses the many ways in which the romances of the 1820 volume still reflect the ideological vision and poetic practices of the Cockney School – the intellectuals and artists of the Hunt circle that included, when Keats joined them in the fall of 1816, the Shelleys, Hazlitt, Godwin, Reynolds, Haydon, Vincent Novello, Peacock, and many more, with Byron as a kind of corresponding member.

The romances of the 1820 volume are not just documents of individual aesthetic development. They continue the Cockney campaign to reform poetry, culture, and politics.[6] All embrace collective Cockney experiments. *Isabella* was planned as part of a collaborative project with Reynolds – who produced *The Garden of Florence* and *The Ladye of Provence* (*The Garden of Florence and Other Poems* [1821]) – to offer modern adaptations of Boccaccio's *Decameron*, an idea urged by Hunt and Hazlitt, with Hazlitt's *Lectures on the English Poets* (1818) recommending the tale of Isabella in particular.[7] *Isabella* and *The Eve of St. Agnes* join the Cockney project of using traditional Italian literature to underwrite innovative English creations: hence Hunt's infamous adaptation of the tale of adulterous love between Paolo and Francesca, related in the fifth canto of Dante's *Inferno*, in *The Story of Rimini* (the first Cockney School paper saw it celebrating incestuous love)[8] and Shelley's Dantesque *Epipsychidion*, which argues for free love beyond patriarchal controls. *The Eve of St. Agnes*, owing some of its luxurious sensuousness to Hunt's romance, joins *Rimini* and *Epipsychidion* in sympathizing with lovers in revolt against restrictive societies. *Lamia*, akin to Peacock's *Rhododaphne* (1818) and Hunt's classical romances, *Hero and Leander* and *Bacchus and Ariadne* (1819), advances another Cockney theme, the turn to classical myths and forms as embodying a pre-Christian vision found in works from Hunt's *Nymphs* (1818) to Horace Smith's

Amarynthus the Nympholept (1821); as Marilyn Butler remarks, Lycius's attack on Apollonius (2.277–90) is "a call on behalf of the pagan and against the Christian approach to the life of the senses."[9] The triangular relationship between Lycius, his tutor Apollonius, and his exotic love, Lamia, resonates with other works produced within the circle, such as Reynolds's *Romance of Youth*, in which a mysterious "Queen of the Fairies" enchants a young man who is destroyed when he follows an Apollonius-like counselor, who turns him from enchantments to "reality."

Pursuing Cockney themes, Keats's romances also engage a Cockney style. While critics in our century have tended to see Hunt's new school through Keats's language of disenchantment ("mawkish"), contemporary reviewers, as McGann notes (31), recognized the experimentalism. This "new fangled" poetry (as Gold's *London Magazine* [1820] called it) was patently urban, chic and cheeky. It could be "vivacious, smart, witty, changeful, sparkling, and learned," said Scot's *Edinburgh Magazine* (1817) – but maybe seem "too full of conceits and sparkling points." With the *Lamia* volume in its sights, *Monthly Review* (1820) described a "laboriously obscure" style, full of "strange intricacies of thought, and peculiarities of expression," "continually shocking our ideas of poetical decorum."[10] Flashing a Cockney style, Keats's romances advertise their modernity. In these lights, the seeming sentimentalities of *Isabella* appear as controlled by wit: opening with "Fair Isabel, poor simple Isabel," Keats tweaks "simple" to suggest the naivete which will fall, with black humor, to "wormy circumstance" (385). Scot's *Edinburgh Magazine* discerned the Cockney style of *Endymion* even in *Lamia*, where Keats flaunts Cockney coinages and compounds such as "psalterian" (114) and "cirque-couchant" (46), indulges a cocky humor unusual in romance, and happily risks a sensuality that often embarrasses.[11] Keats stayed a poet of romance but he did so through the ironizing he explained to Woodhouse: "in my dramatic capacity I enter fully into the feeling: but in Propria Person I should be apt to quiz it myself" (*KL* 2.174). Woodhouse discerned a tone of Byronic quizzing in the last stanza of *The Eve of St. Agnes* (*KL* 2.163), and such tones are quite audible at the opening of *Lamia* Part II. At the same time, the order of the romances in the 1820 volume also makes an argument for full feeling: the movement from *Lamia* to *Isabella* to *The Eve of St. Agnes* produces the enchantments of the last romance beyond irony, beyond the self-smoking procedures of *Lamia*'s distancing effects, beyond even *Isabella*'s "amusing sober-sadness."

Read in the volume's sequence, the poems also offer, as Stuart Curran points out, an experiment with the modes of "Greek (in couplets), Italian (in ottava rima), and British (in Spenserian stanzas)" romance, as Keats plots a cultural movement from the classical past through the Christian middle ages to the present.[12] Keats could have learned how to use traditional materials for contemporary purposes from his model, Dryden's *Fables* (see Woodhouse; *KL* 2.165), for Dryden also modernizes classical (Ovid), Italian (Boccaccio), and English (Chaucer) romances. Moreover, by engaging Milton's *Paradise Lost* but shifting from his epic ground to romance, Dryden showed Keats how to "translate" the generic and cultural power of epic to another form, the "epic as cento."[13] As a sequence, the three romances of the 1820 volume offer a modern equivalent to the synoptic vision of epic.

Lamia opens the volume with an evocation of the past cultures these poems will move beyond:

> Upon a time, before the faery broods
> Drove Nymph and Satyr from the prosperous woods,
> Before King Oberon's bright diadem,
> Sceptre, and mantle, clasp'd with dewy gem,
> Frighted away the Dryads and the Fauns . . .   (1–5)

The realm of romance is already marked by the politics of dynastic struggle. Keats places his romance within slow time, particularly the time of cultural history, as he explores the "pastness of the past," the experience of a difference between our moment and earlier cultural systems.[14]

As many note, Keats is concerned in *Hyperion* with the historical movement between cultural periods, defined as the shift from the Titans to the Olympians. *Ode to Psyche* – closer to *Lamia*, which echoes it (1.66, 2.22–25) – moves from the classical period of "antique vows," when "holy were the haunted forest boughs, / Holy the air, the water, and fire" (36–39), through the period when the "faint Olympians" (42) were replaced by the Christian God, the vanquisher of paganism celebrated in Milton's *Nativity Ode* (echoed throughout the middle section of *Psyche* [Allott, 518]), then to Keats's own day, beyond these earlier belief systems. The modern poet must turn for inspiration to Psyche, the self, and to "warm Love," the hope for connection with the other – even though he knows that the "shadowy thought" of modern poetic fancy may only "feign" where others could believe (58–67).

The opening of *Lamia*, "Upon a time," and the distancing close of *St. Agnes* ("And they are gone: ay, ages long ago"; 370) call attention to the outmoded beliefs and fictions of "old Romance." So, too, *Isabella*'s authorial interruptions: these are not (as sometimes argued) a Keatsian affectation; they are a Cockney tactic. Keats describes *Isabella* as an attempt to "make old prose in modern rhyme more sweet" (156) for an age that may yearn "for the gentleness of old romance" (387); Reynolds makes the same point in *Ladye of Provence* when he notes that his tale offers the "old Italian"

Boccaccio "tamed into Northern verse" (p. 156); and Hunt justifies his intrusions in the *The Florentine Lovers* by arguing that a writer seeking to revive "the good faith and simplicity in the old romances" cannot forget that he writes in a modern time marked by an "accursed critical spirit" (*Liberal* 1 [1822], 70). The authorial asides in *Isabella* are tuned to the Cockney consciousness of their critical, ironic, self-conscious times, an age in which not even romance can avoid romantic irony.

Yet Keats moves beyond irony, including the historicizing irony that distances the beliefs of "old Romance." His impulse, indeed his devotion, is to discover a new eroticized romance, with *eros* not as a power of dubious enchantment but as a means of connecting with the physical world. The quest of Keats's lovers is not for any world of wish-fulfillment (Frye), nor for the powers of the wishing self (Harold Bloom), but for an erotic reality that fulfills even as one strips away the self's illusions. As Porphyro proclaims to Madeline in *The Eve of St. Agnes* after they make love, "This is no dream, my bride, my Madeline!" (326).

To win such consummation, Keats insists, one must confront and dispel the illusions surrounding the erotic. His advertised source for *Lamia* (excerpted in an endnote to the poem), Burton's *Anatomy of Melancholy* (1621), places the story of Lycius and Lamia within an analysis of "Heroical Love causing Melancholy." *Lamia*, too, explores the vicissitudes of desire, as love easily shades into jealousy, possessiveness, and violence in a world dominated by what René Girard calls the "triangulation" of desire. By this, Girard means that desire is not straightforward, but always vectored through other factors: through dreams formed by literary romance ("I want a love just like the ones I have read about"), through the desires of others ("I want her/him because my rivals want her/him"), through displacement onto a mediator (I really desire X, but – for whatever reasons – I cannot admit it, so I desire Y who is desired by X).[15] Keats's "ever-smitten Hermes," "bent warm on amorous theft" (*Lamia* 1.7–8), burns in "celestial heat" for a nymph because "a world of love was at her feet" (21–22). In heat for the nymph because this world of others desires her, Hermes is appropriately marked by "jealous curls" (26); he is "full of painful jealousies / Of the Wood-Gods, and even the very trees" (33–34). The "pleasures" of the "long immortal dream" that Keats's narrator tells us Hermes eventually finds with his nymph (127–28) depend upon their escape from the economy of triangulated desire and its travails of competitive love. Secured by Lamia where she is "unaffronted, unassail'd / By the love-glances of unlovely eyes" (101–2), the nymph can fulfill one Hermetic desire, a male dream of a fully erotic relation that is fulfilling only because the woman is aware of no one but her lover.

Lamia entices Lycius as a similarly unmediated object of desire. The narrator calls him happy, for Lamia is a "virgin purest lipp'd, yet in the lore / Of love deep learned to the red heart's core" (1.189–90); though "still unshent" (untouched), Lamia has the aura of a "lovely graduate" of "Cupid's college" (197–8). A virginal "full-born beauty new and exquisite" (172), she is a kind of erotic Athena born from the desirer's mind into the art of love. Coming to her first erotic contact seemingly with no prior life, Lamia can evoke no jealousy. Forging a paradise, the lovers form "so complete a pair" (2.12) that they need no one else. They seemingly escape the triangulation of desire. Except that their love is beset from both within and without. If Lamia appears to Lycius as a "new" beauty, we know she has been a serpent (described in a set-piece of Keatsian sensuous verse; 1.47–67). This duplicity is part of what dooms their romance, but Lycius, too, is a flawed lover, now the gullible youth, now a tyrant over Lamia, now "senseless Lycius" (2.147). We first meet him when, after a visit to the temple of Jove to pray for a happy marriage (1.226–29; Allott, 626), he has turned from his comrades, "wearied of their Corinth talk" (1.232). The implication is that he has rejected Corinth's preoccupation with pleasures of the flesh (its Temple of Venus, Burton notes, was a famous whorehouse). Lycius is "lost" in a "phantasy" of "Platonic shades" (235–36), of love free of sensuality. Like Madeline in *The Eve of St. Agnes*, Lycius prays to a supernatural force for a dream-mate. Appearing as if a gift from above, Lamia plays right into this dream.

Even as the pair would secure a love completely apart from society, the cynical lines that open Part II (1–6) remind us that love – whether in a hut or a palace – must face limits imposed by social context. The external world invades the erotic retreat as Lycius (like Antony recalled from Cleopatra's arms) is awakened from dreams of eternal passion by "a thrill / Of trumpets" (27–28). His "golden bourn" now seems a "purple-lined palace of sweet sin," condemned by the "noisy world almost forsworn" (30–33). As if renewing his loyalty to this world, Lycius turns from his harbor of "bliss" (9) and starts to think of Lamia as his "prize":

> My thoughts! Shall I unveil them? Listen then!
> What mortal hath a prize, that other men
> May be confound and abash'd withal,
> But lets it sometime pace abroad majestical,
> And triumph, as in thee I should rejoice
> Amid the hoarse alarm of Corinth's voice.
> Let my foes choke, and my friends shout afar,
> While through the thronged streets your bridal car
> Wheels round its dazzling spokes.   (2.57–64)

Returning Lamia to desire's triangulations, Lycius finds enjoyment in domination:

> Perverse, with stronger fancy to reclaim
> Her wild and timid nature to his aim:
> Besides, for all his love, in self despite,
> Against his better self, he took delight
> Luxurious in her sorrows, soft and new,
> His passion, cruel grown, took on a hue
> Fierce and sanguineous. (2.70–76)

As pleasure shifts from otherworldly bliss to worldly boasting, eros turns to violence, creating an unequal though still powerful relationship: "She burnt, she lov'd the tyranny" (2.81).

It is an irony of Lycius's sensation of imminent social and erotic victory in a world of triangulating desires that Lamia is most threatened by the cold stare of his mentor, Apollonius. As he announces the "truth" about her life as a snake, his "sophist's eye / Like a sharp spear, went through her utterly, / Keen, cruel, perceant, stinging" (2.299–301). The historical Apollonius, half Pythagorean philosopher, half magician, lived in the early Christian era, and his presence in Keats's poem signals the shift from Classical to Christian culture found in the opening lines. In Keats's day, Apollonius was a charged figure, with Edward Gibbon slyly paralleling him with Jesus (his disciples credited him with many of the same miracles), and with Edward Berwick's translation of the *Life of Apollonius of Tyana* (1809) challenging such connections, in order to protect Christianity from a corrosive comparative mythology.[16] Keats's Apollonius – kin to Apollo with his vision of rational order and a Jesus wannabe – also epitomizes the "cold philosophy" (science) that dispels "all charms," reduces the sublime rainbow to "the dull catalogue of common things," and conquers "all mysteries by rule and line" (2.229–35). Apollonius embodies what Nietzsche would later call the great error in Western thought: the belief in a transcendent truth that renders the "mere" appearances of lived life false. In "How the 'True World' Finally Became a Fable: The History of an Error" (*The Twilight of the Idols*), Nietzsche traces this denigration from Plato's claim that the "true world" is attainable only by the virtuous sage (i.e. Plato), through the Christian version of the "true world" as the afterlife won by "the sinner who repents," to modern science's faith in its will to truth. With ties to the Greek philosophical quest, to Christianity, and to science, Apollonius is the *ne plus ultra* (supreme instance) of triangulation: everything has value only insofar as it is mediated through the ultimate Other – the Ideal, God, the Truth. No pleasure, whether the passing experience of the rainbow, a fluctuating desire, or what Keats called "a fine isolated verisimilitude caught from the Penetralium of mystery" (*KL* 1.193–94) can survive such triangulation. Keats appropriately has Apollonius preside over the destruction of erotic life at the poem's close.

If *Lamia* stages the threat posed by the triangulation of desire, *Isabella* uses its "amusing sober-sadness" to expose what happens when even unviolent love is caught up in what Hunt called the "spirit of money-getting." From Baldwin's *London Magazine* (1820), with its complaint that Keats's description of the brothers as "money-bags" is "no better than extravagant school-boy vituperation of trade and traders," through George Bernard Shaw's praise of these same stanzas (14–18) as a "prophecy" of Marx, to the best recent work on the poem, critics have recognized Keats's attack upon a money-mad society.[17] Lorenzo and Isabella are implicated in the economic oppression that is central to their world, however much their romance seems opposed to "money-getting." What the lovers share in "private" has links to "private enterprise": they and the merchant-brethren are ensnared in the same isolating social configuration, with the economics of desire mimicking mundane economics. The brothers are involved in a global, imperial capitalism whose grasp extends from Ceylon to the arctic, from the depths of the seas to the depths of mines, from the gathering of raw materials to the manufacture of goods in "noisy factories" (105–20). Yet for all their worldly reach, these consummate capitalists are isolated, distanced from the reality of the suffering that is their main product: "Half-ignorant, they turn'd an easy wheel, / That set sharp racks at work, to pinch and peel" (119–20). Keats's narrator intrudes just after these lines to ask, repeatedly in stanza sixteen, "Why were they proud?" Quizzing the brothers' pride – their public arrogance, a boastful "glory" socially defined in contrast with the misery of others – this stanza sets up the sharp turn of the next stanza:

> *Yet* were these Florentines as self-retired
> In hungry pride and gainful cowardice,
> As two close Hebrews in that land inspired,
> Paled in and vineyarded from beggar-spies.
>
> (129–32; my emphasis)

For all their economic and political power, the brothers are utterly cut off from human contact, encamped within an estate built and "Enriched from ancestral merchandise" (106). In his draft, Keats added that these Florentines may have seemed "Two young Orlandos far away," but "on a near inspect their vapid Miens" showed these venture capitalists to be anything but venturesome. Playing on the myth that a child's features reflect a mother's thoughts during pregnancy, Keats imagines that the brothers' mother "dream'd / In the longing time of Units . . . / Of proudly-bas'd addition and of net – / And both their backs were mark'd with tare and tret" (Stillinger, *Poems*, 250). These human "Units" were marked from birth for self-enclosed, isolated commerce.

Coming together in love, Isabella and Lorenzo would seem a stark contrast to these "money-bags" (145), these "ledger-men" (137); but the language with which Keats surrounds the lovers places them within the same world of private enterprising. Everything about their love – except their sexual contact – suggests more solitude than sociality. Their secrecy is, in part, enforced by class strictures, in which Isabella should wed "some high noble and his olive-trees," rather than the "servant" of her brothers' "trade designs" (165–68). But it is also a seclusion built upon illusions, for the lovers are every bit as "self-retired" as the brothers, first so isolated from one another that they cannot speak except alone, to their pillows, and then, after they have consummated their love, retreating like Lamia and Lycius into a society of two. Keats repeatedly describes their union as "close" ("All close they," "Close in a bower"; 81, 85), and he applies the same word to the brothers: "self-retired . . . / As two close Hebrews" (129–31). Just as these money-bags seem sick in their "hungry pride and gainful cowardice" (130), so Isabella and Lorenzo experience love as an illness, "some malady" (in the very opening stanza, 4), a "sick longing" (23) that makes Isabella actually ill. When Lorenzo disappears, she pursues an even more internalized love or, rather, "instead of love, O misery! / She brooded o'er the luxury alone" (235–36), as "Selfishness, Love's cousin," (241) holds vigil. She fixates upon his severed head in the basil pot as an emblem of her totally private emotion. The pot, for which she asks "amorously" (490), is her perfect love object, for hers has always been a narcissistic love, happiest perhaps with the dead "prize" (402), a "jewel, safely casketed" (431). Wolfson, Heinzelman, and Everest have drawn attention to the language of riches that defines Isabella's relation to the dead Lorenzo: she and her brothers are secret sharers in a world of private enterprise, privatized emotion, and isolation, even in love. Appropriately, the brothers end in exile, and Isabella dies alone.

The Eve of St. Agnes is set in another flawed world, divided between the otherworldly aspirations of an Apollonius and the crass materialism of the sensual Corinthians or Isabella's brothers. The Beadsman (employed to pray for his patrons) dreams so strongly of a better world that he neglects this one. Depicted in a freezing landscape (1–4), he seems dead to this life: "his frosted breath . . . Seem'd taking flight for heaven, without a death" (6–8); "already had his deathbell rung; / The joys of all his life were said and sung" (22–23). Yet the next life seems only to repeat the sorrows of this one: as he passes by the tombs of the dead, he imagines how they "seem to freeze, / . . . how they may ache in icy hoods and mails" (14–18). He divides this world with those for whom he prays, the selfish, violent revelers, prideful (32) and "blood-thirsty" (99). With their "argent revelry" and "rich array" (37–38), they are rapacious predators, "barbarian hordes, / Hyena foeman, and hot-blooded lords" (85–86). This bifurcated world, turned now to the life-denying spirit, now to the violently physical, is set against the lovers: like Romeo and Juliet, like Lorenzo and Isabella, even a little like Lycius and Lamia, Porphyro and Madeline find their love opposed by families and mentors.

Coming in the 1820 volume after *Lamia*'s satire on the triangulation of desire and after *Isabella*'s ironic investigation of privatized emotion, *The Eve of St. Agnes* can offer a celebration of the erotic that is not "smokeable," because Keats has already demonstrated his ironic credentials. In much the way that *Don Juan* can embrace eros while lampooning various canting attitudes towards the erotic, so Keats, having produced ironic versions of classical and medieval Italian romance, can offer a modern British return to erotic romance. This is not a sudden shift. The narrator of *Lamia* allowed some sympathy with Lamia's love-longing, sympathy even with Lycius's sudden enchantment. Refusing the myth of unhappy love, the narrator of *Isabella* asks of its lovers, "Were they unhappy?" (89), and then proceeds to answer that the only truly unhappy lovers are those such as Ariadne and Dido, abandoned by men with worldly ambitions. All others reap, in "the general reward of love, / The little sweet [that] doth kill much bitterness" (97–98); the "richest juice" of sexual pleasures is found even in "poison-flowers" (104). Even so, in *Lamia* and *Isabella*, the general reward of love cannot forestall disaster and death.

In *The Eve of St. Agnes*, though this fate haunts the poem's similes and allusions, eros remains liberated and liberating. At first, Madeline, like Isabella, shares in her world's errors. Kept from Porphyro by a family feud, she ignores the courting of "many a tiptoe, amorous cavalier" (60), cherishing the "whim" (55) of the Eve's rituals, which promise "visions of delight" (47) in dreams. Like Lycius, she is enchanted by fantasy, so "Hoodwink'd by faery fancy" that she seems "all amort" (70), as dead to earthly life as the Beadsman in his spiritual "flight for heaven" (8). Pursuing his spellbound lover, Porphyro is a strategizing date-rapist, argued Jack Stillinger in a once controversial reading ("The Hoodwinking of Madeline") that has gained considerable support. Yet the poem's dramatic, ironic distance also allows Porphyro to appear as Keats's most straightforward lover, questing his way through a household of dangers in order to rescue and release Madeline from "those enchantments cold," as she lies "asleep in lap of legends old" (134–35). Keats's skill in keeping open a number of perspectives is an ironic negative capability essential to the poem's revival of romance, for it protects

Keats from being "smoked."[18] Yet what permeates Keats's poetry, early and late, is the strain that endorses Porphyro's stance against the dangers of cold fairy-fancy. In *Sleep and Poetry*, despair follows when an enchantingly ideal vision evaporates: "The visions all are fled," and a "sense of real things comes doubly strong, / And, like a muddy stream, would bear along / [the] soul to nothingness" (157–59). In his verse epistle to Reynolds, Keats wonders if the aspiring "Imagination" courts the fate of being "Lost in a sort of Purgatory blind," cut off from "any standard law / Of either earth or heaven," and poisoning the pleasures with a false ideal: "It forces us in Summer skies to mourn: / It spoils the singing of the nightingale" (*KL* 1.262). Desiring heaven (as do those who pursue Nietzsche's error), Imagination may belittle earthly life, the life that is all we know and all we need to know. To wish for an idealized dream-lover may be (as Porphyro fears) to miss the vitality of warm, breathing human love.

Porphyro lures Madeline back from her dreams to a reality that he hopes to show her is as rich as any ideal she might imagine. To reveal the wonderful depth of physical reality and the glorious abundance of lived life, he presents a sensuous feast of luscious fruits, spices, and sweets "From silken Samarcand to cedar'd Lebanon" (270). When, however, she finally stirs from her "woofed phantasies (287), Porphyro's fears prove sound. She sees her real lover only as a pale imitation of her dream lover:

> " . . . those sad eyes were spiritual and clear:
> How chang'd thou art! How pallid, chill, and drear!
> Give me that voice again, my Porphyro,
> Those looks immortal, those complainings dear!
> Oh leave me not in this eternal woe,
> For if thou diest, my love, I know not where to go."   (310–15)

Preferring the "spiritual" Porphyro of her dreams, Madeline would protect love from death. But for Keats, this is simply a denial of life. Keatsian romance rejects the quest for the immortal in order to endorse a romance of reality.

Faced with a Madeline who cannot return to life from her dreams, Porphyro offers her the one thing her dream lover cannot: sex, embodied love. He may not be immortal, but,

> Beyond a mortal man impassion'd far
> At these voluptuous accents, he arose,
> Ethereal, flush'd, and like a throbbing star
> Seen mid the sapphire heaven's deep repose;
> Into her dream he melted, as the rose
> Blendeth its odour with the violet, –
> Solution sweet . . .   (316–22)

"This is no dream, my bride, my Madeline!" he assures her (326).

The sexuality was not lost on the publisher's advisor, Woodhouse, who was particularly bothered by a revision Keats fervently wanted:

> See, while she speaks his arms encroaching slow,
> Have zoned her, heart to heart . . .
>
> .   .   .
>
> More sooth, for that his quick rejoinder flows
> Into her burning ear . . .
>
> .   .   .
>
> With her wild dream he mingled, as a rose
> Marrieth its odour to a violet.
> Still, still she dreams   (Stillinger, *Poems*, 314)

Woodhouse read these lines with dismay, and transmitted a report to John Taylor:

> As the Poem was orig[y] written, <u>we</u> innocent ones (ladies & myself) might very well have supposed that Porphyro, when acquainted with Madeline's love for him, & when "he arose, Etherial flush[d] &c &c (turn to it) set himself at once to persuade her to go off with him, & succeeded & went [. . .] to be married, in right honest chaste & sober wise. But, as it is now altered, as soon as M. has confessed her love, P. winds by degrees his arm round her, presses breast to breast, and acts all the acts of a bonâ fide husband, while she fancies she is only playing the part of a Wife in a dream.   (*KL* 2.163)

Taylor was prepared to tell Keats to take this sexually explicit tale elsewhere (*KL* 2.183), despite the "Keats-like rhodomontade" (so Woodhouse reported) that "he sh[d] despise a man who would be such an eunuch in sentiment as to leave a maid, with that Character about her, in such a situation" (2.163).

Keats's insistence suggests that he sought something in this scene beyond titillation, "flying in the face of all Decency & discretion" as Taylor thought (*KL* 2.183). Sexuality offers Porphyro and Madeline a way to heal the splits in their world, "saved by miracle" (339). Having framed their erotic romance in opposition to life-denying religion (the Beadsman), to the riots of the merely material (the foemen), and to fairy-fancy "all amort," Keats wants his lovers to discover a physical reality that has the value of an ideal, that offers earth as heaven. The lovers escape to another realm – "o'er the southern moors I have a home for thee," Porphyro promises Madeline (51) – leaving this cloven world to collapse into nightmares and death. Keats closes his romance both on this grotesque note of "ashes cold" (378) and with a sudden historicizing distancing – "And they are gone: ay, ages long ago"(370) – that assigns erotic success to remote legend. Both gestures protect *The Eve of St. Agnes* from being "smoked" out, and thus preserve the powerful sensuousness at its center: the rejection of a world turned against eros, the celebration of fulfilled lovers, the narrative climax as sexual climax.

Together, *Lamia*, *Isabella*, and *The Eve of St. Agnes* combine a critique of society's mishandling of desire with an argument for the erotic as a power of social transformation. Beyond *Lamia*'s triangulation of desire and *Isabella*'s privatized emotion, *The Eve of St. Agnes* reclaims the immediacy and power of erotic pleasure, fulfilling, on the far side of irony, the liberatory, salvific promise suggested in the preceding poems. As McGann writes of Shelley, "Eroticism [. . .] is the imagination's last line of human resistance against [. . .] political despotism and moral righteousness on the one hand, and on the other selfishness, calculation, and social indifference."[19] The conservative opponents of Keats and the Cockneys did not miss the political point, and they counterattacked vigorously, especially against the leader Hunt, "the most irresistible knight-errant erotic extant," as *Blackwood's* called him in 1822. In 1818, the *Gazette* attacked Hunt's politics as "a noxious and disgusting mixture of libertinism and jacobinism." *Eclectic Review* found the Cockneys' use of mythology particularly suspect, arguing in 1818 that Hunt's was the "creed of the heathen," and suggesting in a review of Keats's 1820 volume that the turn to myth by "Mr. Keats, and Mr. Leigh Hunt, and Mr. Percy Bysshe Shelley, and some of the poets about town" panders to a taste for "grossness – its alliance to the sensitive pleasures which belong to the animal." In 1818, *The Quarterly Review*, objecting to a poem addressed to Shelley in Hunt's *Foliage* (*On the Degrading Notion of the Deity*), argued that the Hunt circle was conspiring to bring about a "systematic revival of Epicureanism. [. . .] Lucretius is the philosopher whom these men profess most to admire; and their leading tenet is, that the enjoyment of the pleasures of intellect and sense is not to be considered as the permitted, and regulated use of God's blessing, but the great object, and duty of life."[20]

The Cockneys' critics got it right. Keats does embrace intellectual and sensual pleasure – the joys of the ironic intellect and of the sensuous body – as the goal of life. Together with his fellow Cockneys, he evokes a Lucretian vision in which life can have meaning without relying upon any degrading notion of a deity, without resort to "vulgar superstition" (*Written in Disgust of Vulgar Superstition*; 1816). The three romances that title the 1820 volume trace a path beyond the great explanatory systems of classical and Christian cultures, in search of what Keats calls (in a letter to divinity-student Bailey) "a recourse somewhat human independent of the great Consolations of

Religion and undepraved Sensations. of the Beautiful. the poetical in all things" (*KL* 1.179). Through the ironizing turn of historicism, Keats not only leaves behind the consolations of earlier belief systems but also turns a satirical eye on the ways contemporary society organizes desires in various fantasies of escape and retreat. When we read these poems chronologically and biographically, our tendency is to see the opposition of Lamia's beauty and Apollonius's truth as unraveling or deconstructing the more positive vision of earlier poems such as *The Eve of St. Agnes*. Read in the volume's sequence, however, the poems move through various forms of quest romance to discover, beyond irony and the unmasking of our erotic illusions, an eroticism that is no dream.

NOTES

1 Northrop Frye, *Anatomy of Criticism* (Princeton: Princeton University Press, 1957), 186–87. Recent evaluations include: Harold Bloom, who sees Romantic-era romance "internalizing" the old external quest as modern psychic journey ("The Internalization of Quest Romance," in *Romanticism and Consciousness*, ed. Harold Bloom [New York: Norton, 1970], 3–24); Jack Stillinger, who sees Keats creating a kind of "anti-romance" genre, tuned to the sorrows of life beyond wish-fulfilling enchantments (*"The Hoodwinking of Madeline" and Other Essays on Keats's Poems*, 31–45); Tilottama Rajan, who reads Keatsian romance as a deconstructive mode, both engaging and turning from its conventions (*Dark Interpreter: The Discourse of Romanticism*, 97–142); and Susan J. Wolfson, who sees Keatsian "new romance" as "meta-romance," a reading of the genre itself (*The Questioning Presence: Wordsworth, Keats, and the Interrogative Mode in Romantic Poetry*, 270–300, 333–43). For a comprehensive account of the genre in the age, see Stuart Curran, *Poetic Form and British Romanticism*, 128–57.

2 K. Everest, *"Isabella* in the Market-Place: Keats and Feminism," in Roe, ed., *Keats and History*, 109–10.

3 See Wolfson, *Questioning Presence*, 285–86.

4 See Paul de Man, "Introduction," xxvi–xxvii, and Stuart Sperry: *"Lamia* is a work written by a poet against his better self" (*Keats the Poet*, 292).

5 Jerome J. McGann, "Keats and the Historical Method," *The Beauty of Inflections*, 53.

6 See the essays by John Kandl and Duncan Wu in this volume, as well as work in the bibliography by William Keach, Greg Kucich, Nicholas Roe, and myself.

7 Keats and Reynolds drew from the fourth day of the *Decameron*, as did another member of their circle, Bryan Waller Proctor ("Barry Cornwall") who adapted, like Keats, the fifth tale in his *Sicilian Story* as well as two others (in *A Sicilian Story, with Diego Montilla & c* [1820] and *Dramatic Scenes & c* [1819]).

8 Hunt's mind "seems absolutely to gloat over all the details of adultery and incest," said Z. ("On the Cockney School of Poetry. No. I," *Blackwood's Edinburgh Magazine* 2 [October 1817], 42).

9 Marilyn Butler, *Romantics, Rebels, and Reactionaries* (Oxford: Oxford University Press, 1982), 134–35; cf. Miriam Allott, *Poems*, 614.

10 Gold's *London Magazine* 1 (April 1820), 401; Scot's *Edinburgh Magazine* 1 (October 1817), 254–57; *Monthly Review* n.s. 92 (July 1820), 305–10.

11 *Edinburgh [Scots] Magazine* 7 [August 1820], 107–10. For the embarrassments of sensuality, see Ricks, *Keats and Embarrassment*. For the poem's new tones, see Georgia S. Dunbar, "The Significance of the Humor in 'Lamia,'" *KSJ* 8 (1959), 17–26; similarly, Sperry, *Keats the Poet*, 297.

12 Curran, *Poetic Form*, 150. For a case for reading the 1820 poems as a sequenced volume, see Neil Fraistat, *The Poem and the Book: Interpreting Collections of Romantic Poetry* (Chapel Hill: University of North Carolina Press, 1985), 95–140.

13 See Earl Miner, "Dryden's Admired Acquaintance, Mr. Milton," *Milton Studies* 11 (1978), 3–27.

14 See Terence Hoagwood, "Keats and Social Context: *Lamia*," *Studies in English Literature* 29 (1989), 689–90; Daniel Watkins, *Keats's Poetry and the Politics of the Imagination*, 140–42.

15 René Girard, *Deceit, Desire, and the Novel*, trans. Yvonne Freccero (Baltimore: Johns Hopkins University Press, 1965). See Marjorie Levinson, *Keats's Life of Allegory: The Origins of a Style*, 296n.10; and Martin Aske, "Keats, the Critics, and the Politics of Envy," in Roe, ed., *Keats and History*, 46–64.

16 See Maneck H. Daruwala, "Strange Bedfellows: Keats and Wollstonecraft, Lamia and Berwick," *Keats–Shelley Review* 11 (1997), 83–132.

17 Baldwin's *London Magazine* 2 (September 1820), 315–21; George Bernard Shaw, "Keats," in *The John Keats Memorial Volume*, ed. George C. Williamson (London: John Lane, 1921), 173–76; Wolfson, *Questioning Presence*, 280–83; Kurt Heinzelman, "Self-Interest and the Politics of Composition in Keats's *Isabella*," *ELH* 55 (1988), 159–93; Everest, "Isabella in the Market-Place"; Michael J. Sider, *The Dialogic Keats: Time and History in the Major Poems* (Washington, D.C.: Catholic University of America Press, 1998).

18 See Sperry, *Keats the Poet*, 199–200; Anne Mellor, *English Romantic Irony*, 89–92; Wolfson, *Questioning Presence*, 291–94.

19 Jerome J. McGann, *The Romantic Ideology: A Critical Investigation* (Chicago: University of Chicago Press, 1983), 118.

20 *Blackwood's* 12 (December 1822), 775; *Gazette* 4 (25 May 1880), 49; *Eclectic* 2nd ser. 10 (November 1818), 485, and 14 (September 1820), 169; *Quarterly* 18 (January 1818), 327.

5

VINCENT NEWEY

Hyperion, The Fall of Hyperion, and Keats's epic ambitions

Epic ambitions are dear to the poetical character. Milton, preoccupied with his election for great purpose, laments in *Lycidas* not only the death of a friend but also the compulsion the "sad occasion" places upon him to make trial of his powers before "season due" (1–7). In *The Prelude*, Wordsworth, another chief forebear to Keats's *Hyperion* project, relates his casting round for heroic matter, "some British theme, some old / Romantic tale by Milton left unsung," and his settling at last on a "philosophic Song / Of Truth that cherishes our daily life" (1805 text; 1.179–80; 230–31). He was planning a three-part epic, *The Recluse*, to which this autobiography was a "prelude," but he completed and published only one part (in nine books) in his lifetime: *The Excursion* (1814), which Keats knew and absorbed. It was *The Prelude*, begun in 1798 and published just after his death in 1850, that became Wordsworth's true epic, unfolding the core subject of modernity, the drama of self-consciousness. Citing the precedent of Milton elevating the subject of *Paradise Lost* above those of classical epics ("argument / Not less but more heroic than the wrath / Of stern Achilles" [9.13–15]), Wordsworth credits his autobiographical "theme" as at least equal: "What pass'd within me" is, "in truth, heroic argument" (*Prel.* 3.173–74, 182). Keats's involvement with *Hyperion* would ultimately propel a journey "within," *The Fall of Hyperion: A Dream*, but with far less certain claims.

From the outset Keats aspired to high seriousness, poetry on a grand scale. In *Sleep and Poetry* (late 1816, published 1817), he pledged to pass the "realm . . . / Of Flora, and old Pan" (101–2) for the "nobler life" of writing of "the agonies, the strife / Of human hearts" (123–25). The ensuing vision, of a "charioteer" looking "out upon the winds with glorious fear" (127–28), was aptly glossed by one of his most attentive readers, Richard Woodhouse, as a "Personification of the Epic poet, when the enthusiasm of inspiration is upon him."[1] Yet the charioteer's sight of shapes of "delight" as well as "mystery" (138) and the narrowing of this array to a "lovely wreath of girls" (149) point to a devotion that Keats, for all his commitment to "nobler life," never casts off, and it involves his inability to finish the *Hyperion* project.

This tension between ambition and static introversion is anticipated in another poem of expectation, *On First Looking into Chapman's Homer* (1816). Long admired as a harbinger of Keats's poetic powers, this sonnet has recently been read as the bid of a young parvenu poet, relatively lowborn, for a stake in literary tradition, eyeing, like a conquistador or a fortune-hunter, "the realms of gold . . . many goodly states and kingdoms . . . many western islands" (1–3) held by the established devotees of Apollo, god of poetry.[2] Marjorie Levinson (13–14) even sees in Keats's final simile for his sensation on reading Chapman's translation –

> Or like stout Cortez when with eagle eyes
> He star'd at the Pacific – and all his men
> Look'd at each other with a wild surmise –
> Silent, upon a peak in Darien.   (11–14)

– a sympathy for the subordinate men. Yet not only does Keats's overall syntax ("Then felt I like . . .") propose a primary identification with Cortez, but also the image of conquest and command, of discovery and possession, is usurped by a final effect of suspended animation, a mental "high" with no reference to values or purposes beyond itself: "wild surmise – / Silent." This is the "end-stopped" quality that John Jones (*John Keats's Dream of Truth*) sees as Keats's peculiar gift and, in certain respects, his problem.

The *Hyperion* project would become end-stopped composition on an epic scale, fully testing Keats's ambitions, with triumph and ultimately frustration. His purposes were already formulated by January 1818. Answering Haydon's request for a passage from *Endymion* for illustration (Keats's publisher wanted it for a frontispiece), he advises him to wait for *Hyperion*, "the nature of [which] will lead me to treat it in a more naked and grecian Manner – and the march of passion and endeavour will be undeviating" (*KL* 1.207). Keats's march would not be undeviating, but it would span virtually the whole of his great creative period (from *Isabella*, *The Eve of St. Agnes*, *La Belle Dame*, all the major odes, to *Lamia*). This was also a time of intense intellectual activity. He was reading and carefully annotating *Paradise Lost* from late 1817 on, and took Cary's translation of Dante's *Divine Comedy* with him on his Northern tour of summer 1818. This literary study was part of a sustained effort of exploration and insight that embraced wider aesthetic issues, current events, and the course of human affairs. Keats began *Hyperion* in fall 1818, abandoned it in mid-sentence by April 1819, began a reconstruction as *The Fall of Hyperion. A Dream* in July, completed most of all he would ever write of it by 21 September, and tinkered until the end of the year. During these years his personal life involved the lingering illness and death of his beloved brother Tom (1 December 1818), a budding romance with Fanny Brawne (with whom he reached an "understanding" the same month), and the progression of his own eventually fatal illness.

While all these forces press on the composition of *Hyperion*, Keats's idiom is ancient (pre-Christian) myth on the stage of history and politics. His scene is the interval between the fall of most of the Titan gods and the impending fall of Hyperion in his confrontation with the Olympian successor, Apollo. The poem's opening is dominated by Saturn's "fallen divinity": "His old right hand lay nerveless, listless, dead, / Unsceptred; and his realmless eyes were closed" (1.18–19). Keats coined "realmless" for this verse; when Saturn finally summons the power to speak, it is only to say as much:

> – I am gone
> Away from my own bosom: I have left
> My strong identity, my real self,
> Somewhere between the throne, and where I sit
> Here on this spot of earth. Search, Thea, search!
>
> .   .   .   .
>
> Search, Thea, search! and tell me, if thou seest
> A certain shape or shadow, making way
> With wings or chariot fierce to repossess
> A heaven he lost erewhile: it must
> Be of ripe progress – Saturn must be King.
> Yes, there must be golden victory.   (1.112–16, 121–26)

Saturn's plight, proposes Morris Dickstein, draws "political resonance" from the virtual dethronement of "mad" George III (the prince became Regent in 1811) and the dawning of an era of civil unrest and agitation for parliamentary reform, reaching a climax in a militia attack on a peaceful demonstration at St. Peter's Fields, Manchester, August 1819 – a debacle dubbed "the Peterloo Massacre" by the reform press.[3] Yet Keats's fallen gods, especially Hyperion, are not so much prospective as sunset figures – evoking Napoleon's escape from Elba, the Hundred Days of his restored reign, and his downfall at Waterloo in 1815.

Keats criticized Napoleon on the grounds that his aggressive militarism had spawned the reactionary forces which in 1815 were able to reinstate the old, pre-Revolutionary monarchies across Europe: "Notwithstand[ing] the part which the Liberals take in the Cause of Napoleon," he writes to George and Georgiana, "I cannot but think he has done more harm to the life of Liberty than any one else could have done: not that the divine right Gentlemen have done or intend to do any good [. . .] he has taught them how to organize their monstrous armies" (14 October 1818; *KL* 1.397). Keats's critical regard of those he calls "Men of Power" (22 November 1817; *KL* 1.184) does not prevent an imaginative engagement. Saturn is a study of position coterminous with being: dead because "unsceptred"; bereft of "identity" because "realmless." Like Shakespeare's Lear, he must be King or he is nothing. Keats does gives him an aura of grand pathos, but he emphasizes limitation and dangerous delusion. Saturn, like Napoleon on the road to Waterloo, can conceive of redemption only in the ironic form of renewed conflict and a return to domination, another "golden victory." Men of Power are unable to change inwardly or to understand progress in the world outside.

Over against Men of Power, Keats sets "Men of Genius," who influence humankind subtly and profoundly, dispensing enlightenment like "ethereal Chemicals operating on the Mass of neutral intellect" (*KL* 1.184). Keats uses similar terms of praise in his letter to Reynolds, 3 May 1818, in which he offers an idea of advance different from and more valuable than military conquest (1.281–82). This is "a grand march of intellect," in which Milton and Wordsworth are leaders. Milton tried to assess vice and virtue for a people "just emancipated from a great superstition" (Roman Catholicism), but Wordsworth, the pioneer of modernity, shows a "Genius" for exploring the "dark passages" of individual human experience – for "think[ing] into the human heart" with no discernible "ballance of good and evil" but rather, a feel for the "burden of the Mystery" (a phrase Keats echoes from *Tintern Abbey*). Neither Wordsworth nor Milton operates with entire free will, however: "a mighty providence subdues the mightiest Minds to the service of the time being, whether it be in human Knowledge or Religion" (1.282). Keats's anatomy of Power in the posture and utterance of Saturn is one way he himself serves "the time being." Another is the voice he writes for Oceanus, who gives the council of fallen Titans a doctrine of progress meant to console them amid the ravages of violent change:[4]

> We fall by Nature's law, not force
> Of thunder, or of Jove . . .
>
> .   .   .
>
> . . . to bear all naked truths,
> And to envisage circumstance, all calm,
> That is the top of sovereignty . . .
>
> .   .   .
>
> 'tis the eternal law
> That first in beauty should be first in might:

> Yea, by that law, another race may drive
> Our conquerors to mourn as we do now
>
> (2.181–82, 203–5, 228–31)

Characterizing Saturn as "only blind from sheer supremacy," Oceanus offers a far-seeing wisdom that makes comforting sense of revolution and war (mythic or European) in terms of evolutionary design: Nature's law, "purer life" leading on to "fresh perfection" (2.211–12). This is not the only "truth" Keats auditions in *Hyperion,* but it does reflect a sense of history he himself expressed, reflecting on the Peterloo crisis, just before he abandoned the *Hyperion* project. Convinced anew that "All civiled countries become gradually more enlighten'd and there should be a continual change for the better" (*KL* 2.193), he rehearses the gains and reversals over the centuries in the efforts of the "Multitude" to throw off the "Tyranny" of kings and nobles. The restoration of "despotism" in the aftermath of the French Revolution, he suggests, is a only a temporary setback, the distress of which may rouse the cause of freedom:

> our Courts [. . .] spread a horrid superstition against all innovation and improvement – The present struggle in England of the people is to destroy this superstition. What has rous'd them to do it is their distresses – Per[h]aps on this account the pres[ent] distresses of this nation are a fortunate thing – tho so horrid in the[i]r experience. You will see I mean that the french Revolution put a tempor[a]ry stop to this third change, the change for the better – Now it is in progress again and I thin[k] in an effectual one. This is no contest b[e]tween whig and tory – but between right and wrong.
>
> (letter to George and Georgiana, 18 September 1819; *KL* 2.193–94)

Keats stood firmly on "the Liberal side of the Question" (22 September 1819; *KL* 2.180) – a Republican, anti-Monarchal view that subtends the arguments in *Hyperion* (voiced by Oceanus and figured in Apollo) that change is irresistible, beneficent, very much "for the better."

In reviewing the grand march of intellect (*KL* 1.281–82), Keats took pains to praise Wordsworth's poetic "Genius" over Milton's "Philosophy." Oceanus's philosophy is decidedly un-Miltonic, because un-theological. Questions of good and evil, of vice and virtue, of moral action, of damnation or redemption from sin, do not figure in his account of universal destiny to progressive "perfection." Take, for example, his key analogy:

> Shall the tree be envious of the dove
> Because it cooeth, and hath snowy wings
> To wander wherewithal and find its joys?
> We are such forest-trees, and our fair boughs
> Have bred forth, not pale solitary doves,

> But eagles golden-feather'd, who do tower
> Above us in their beauty, and must reign
> In right thereof.   (2.221–28)

In a Christian lexicon, the snowy dove, a symbol of purity and reconcilia-
tion, is superior to imperious, golden eagles. But in Oceanus's lore, there is
only the claim of towering "beauty." If Keats got this notion of progress
from anywhere, it was not from Milton but from Wordsworth's Wanderer,
in *The Excursion*, Book 7:

> The vast Frame
> Of social nature changes evermore
> Her organs and her members, with decay
> Restless, and restless generation, powers
> And functions dying and produced at need, –
> And by this law the mighty Whole subsists:
> With an ascent and progress in the main.
> Yet oh! how disproportioned to the hopes
> Of self-flattering minds.   (1814 text; 1033–41)

In the Oceanic conception, the Wanderer's "vast Frame / Of social nature"
has been stretched to "Nature," but the theory is the same. Oceanus does
not deny the suffering that progress or generation entails, still less *Hyperion*
as a whole. What Keats most values in Wordsworth is his recognition "that
the World is full of Misery and Heartbreak, Pain, Sickness, and oppression,"
a weight of knowledge leaving us shrouded "in a Mist," feeling but not easily
explaining "the burden of the Mystery" (*KL* 1.281).

Keats's preoccupation with suffering is reflected in other texts of the
period. The sonnet he transcribed for his brothers on 23 January 1818, "On
sitting Down to King Lear once Again," reports a drama of fate and desire,
a "fierce dispute, / Betwixt Hell torment & impassioned Clay" (*KL* 1.215).
In April 1819 he describes the world as a "vale of Soul-making": "how necessary a World of Pains and troubles is to school an Intelligence and make
it a soul" (*KL* 2.102). *Hyperion* is a veritable gallery of studies in pain.
Enceladus disputes Oceanus's philosophy not only by advocating a counter-
revolution against the Olympians, but also by expressing a burden of feeling
that cannot be simply rationalized or consoled: "Much pain have I for more
than loss of realms: / The days of peace and slumberous calm are fled"
(2.334–35). For the goddess Clymene, it is not the loss of the old and familiar that is unsettling, but the strangeness of the new: sensing the coming dis-
pensation of Apollo, she hears in his "golden melody" a "living death in
each gush of sounds," and so is "sick / Of joy and grief at once" (2.279–89).
Keats sets all the Titans in a "nest of woe," unreduced in physical stature
but, in pain, evacuated of dignity and the flow of life itself: "Instead of

thrones, hard flint they sat upon, / . . . / Their clenched teeth still clench'd, and all their limbs / Lock'd up like veins of metal, crampt and screw'd" (2.14–15, 24–25). The epic landscape is invested with this presence of absence – starkly in the opening, a sonnet-stanza that situates us *in medias res*, Saturn's desolate paralysis imaged by the "shady sadness" of the "vale" that encloses him, his burden of grief by "Forest on forest hung above his head" (1.1–6). The vast scene telescopes to the detail of how "the Naiad 'mid her reeds / Press'd her cold finger closer to her lips" (13–14); elsewhere such fateful suspense is conveyed by long-distance shots, such as the dying splendor of Hyperion portrayed as "a vast shade / In midst of his own brightness" (2.372–73).

The theater of "giant agony" counters the force of Oceanus's philosophy, exposing the latter as an "over-wise" (as Enceladus thinks [2.309]) cerebral detachment from ordeal and tribulation. What the Oceanic argument for progress through "first in beauty" lacks in comparison with other epics (the founding of Rome in Vergil's *Aeneid*, the spiritual quests of Spenser's *Faerie Queene*, Milton's account of the Fall, Wordsworth's story of the growth of a Poet's mind) is the element of narrative progression. In *Hyperion* the action is either over (the Olympian revolt) or to come (the confrontation of Apollo and Hyperion). Keats's poem is an interval of arrested reactions – soliloquy (Saturn), anxiety (Hyperion), and oration (Oceanus, Enceladus) – and emblematic posture or topography, often approximating statuary or painting. Thea evokes a "Memphian sphinx, / Pedestal'd haply in a palace court" (1.31–32); she and Saturn are "postured motionless, / Like natural sculpture in cathedral cavern" (1.85–86). What Keats achieves above all in *Hyperion* is the aestheticization of suffering.

This twilight of the early gods dramatizes feeling rather than action – and feeling takes a human form. Of Thea, Keats writes,

> One hand she press'd upon that aching spot
> Where beats the human heart, as if just there,
> Though an immortal, she felt cruel pain. (1.42–44)

Keats's analogical syntax, "as if," conveys her from immortal to mortal sensations.[5] So, too, the old patriarch Cœlus observes his children's "fall" into the state of mortals:

> Now I behold in you fear, hope, and wrath;
> Actions of rage and passion; even as
> I see them, on the mortal world beneath,
> In men who die. (1.332–35)

Yet even as Keats's myth evoked the mortal world, it allowed him to transmute it and set it at a distance (just as historical circumstance is both reflected and deflected). By these means, he finds a way to make "Sorrow more beautiful than Beauty's self" (1.36).

Keats worried about this detachment. It becomes a direct question in his revision, *The Fall of Hyperion*, and already stirs in *Hyperion*, by force of Keats's nursing his dying brother as he was writing a poem whose title character has seen his brother-gods die, yet whose beautiful hero would emerge as a superior god of medicine and poetry. The image of Apollo at the end, just before Keats gave up, seems less a god being born than a man dying:

> Soon wild commotions shook him, and made flush
> All the immortal fairness of his limbs;
> Most like the struggle at the gate of death;
> Or liker still to one who should take leave
> Of pale immortal death, and with a pang
> As hot as death's is chill, with fierce convulse
> Die into life: so young Apollo anguish'd. (3.124–30)

Tom's "identity presses upon me so all day that I am obliged to go out" or "obliged to write, and plunge into abstract images to ease myself of his countenance his voice and feebleness – so that I live now in a continual fever," Keats confesses to Dilke on 21 September 1818, adding "it must be poisonous to life although I feel well" (*KL* 1.369). The next day, writing to Reynolds, he tries to forgive himself for "the relief, the feverous relief of Poetry": "This morning Poetry has conquered – I have relapsed into those abstractions which are my only life – I feel escaped from a new strange and threatening sorrow. – And I am thankful for it – There is an awful warmth about my heart like a load of Immortality" (370).

Poetry was therapy, Geoffrey Hartman suggests; "translat[ing] the mortal facts into the sublimity and impersonality of myth."[6] Yet "relapsed," "fever," and "poisonous" expose an incomplete avoidance: is "Poetry" release or burden? glory or ruin? life or more hectic dis-ease? The sensation of "a load of Immortality" implies that writing *Hyperion* may overwhelm him, too. *Hyperion*, argues Stuart Sperry, is most deeply a projection of Keats's turmoil and insecurity.[7] Hyperion's cry –

> "O dreams of day and night!
> O monstrous forms! O effigies of pain!
> O spectres busy in a cold, cold gloom!
>
> .   .   .
>
> Why do I know ye? why have I seen ye? why
> Is my eternal essence thus distraught
> To see and to behold these horrors new?" (1.227–29, 231–33)

– is a poet's vision into the dark underside of the imagination. Poetry may put specters at bay, but it also gives them substance to bear down, and in *The Fall of Hyperion* they do so on the poet himself. The letters Keats wrote while he was nursing Tom haunt Moneta's interrogation of the poet-vision-ary:

> What benefit canst thou do, or all thy tribe,
> To the great world? Thou art a dreaming thing;
> A fever of thyself –   (*Fall of Hyperion* 1.167–69)

Yet if *Hyperion* does not directly confront this challenge, it still has cou-rageous objectives. Keats's attempt to revivify the epic subjects of divinity and the war in heaven fronts a powerful, if unconscious, urge to allegorize, and induce, the supersession of one kind of poetry by another. Saturn bears marks of fallen dynasts Napoleon and Lear, but he is also a poetic figure, a personification of Wordsworth in the aspect in which Keats did not warm to him: "the wordsworthian or egotistical sublime" (27 October 1818; *KL* 1.386–87). Transfixed by "my strong identity, my real self" (1.114), Saturn embodies the sublime egotism that for Keats was the antitype of "the poet-ical Character" of which he declared himself "a Member" as he was writing *Hyperion*: "A Poet [. . .] has no Identity – he is continually in for – and filling some other Body" (*KL* 1.387). Another egotist is Byron, the likely referent of the poet-dreamer's attack in *The Fall* on "all mock lyricists, large self wor-shippers" (1.207). In both poems, Keats implicitly displaces the poetic titans of his own age, arguing, through the deification of Apollo, for a Shakespearean "*Negative Capability,*" a notion formulated in late 1817 (*KL* 1.193) of disinterested poetic consciousness.

Yet in Apollo's voice at the breaking-off point of *Hyperion*, this language sounds attenuated, or merely theoretical:

> Knowledge enormous makes a God of me.
> Names, deeds, gray legends, dire events, rebellions,
> Majesties, sovran voices, agonies,
> Creations and destroyings, all at once
> Pour into the wide hollows of my brain,
> And deify me, as if some blithe wine
> Or bright elixir peerless I had drunk,
> And so become immortal.   (3.113–19)

The climactic language of Apollo's dying-into-life bears visionary promise, but it cannot support the weight of significance placed upon it. And what of its basis, the scene of Apollo's generation at the opening of Book III? This is a paradise of intense rose-glow, voluptuous fleecy clouds, breathing Zephyrs, blushing maids, and bubbling wine (15ff), where "pain and pleasure" blend in an atmosphere of "tuneful wonder" (66–67) – and where, to quote Keats on the "intensity" of art, "all disagreeables evaporate, from their being in close relationship with Beauty" (*KL* 1.192). How convincing is the sunrise sensibility that is being heralded?

The question is partly one of aesthetic force: in Books I and II, Keats's poetry had empathized richly and powerfully with the fallen gods, as if they were bearing his feeling for "the overpowering idea of our dead poets" (9 June 1819; *KL* 2.116), and more particularly, for his dying brother. Breaking off *Hyperion* less than twenty lines after Apollo's declaration of his immortality, Keats seems to have recognized that this poetry was not producing any "mighty poet of the human Heart" (*KL* 2.115) – especially compared to the poetry he had written for Saturn and Hyperion. More than a few readers have seen Book III as a regression to earlier idioms. Recall the problem with the charioteer's vision in *Sleep and Poetry*, where epic inspirations dissolve into figures of sensuous delight. The supposed transformation of Apollo from "ignorance" into "power" does not escape this idiom: "wild commotions shook him, and made flush / All the immortal fairness of his limbs," and "His very hair, his golden tresses famed, / Kept undulation round his eager neck" (3.124–25, 131–32). When Keats wrote to Reynolds on 22 September 1818, he named two pressures that gripped him as he worked on *Hyperion*: "Poor Tom – that woman": "I never was in love – Yet the voice and the shape of a woman has haunted me these two days" (*KL* 1.370). Apollo enacts both the suffering of a dying body and a fascination with a woman, as his "enkindled eyes . . . / . . . steadfast kept / Trembling" upon the beautiful goddess, Mnemosyne. If this moment is supposed to convey a turning-point in the progress of poesy and the cultural history of humankind, it also seems orgasmic fantasy. Climax vies with anticlimax, transcendence with banal embodiment.

No wonder that Keats's re-vision, *The Fall of Hyperion*, becomes a psychomachia, or mind-debate, about the function and value of poetry. It is frankly cast as *A Dream* (the subtitle), the very mode of disordered logic and progression. In the first paragraph (the induction), the poet argues that poetry alone "can save / Imagination from the sable charm / And dumb enchantment" (1.9–11). Anyone with "soul" can have "visions," but only those with command of language, who have "lov'd / And been well nurtured in [their] mother tongue" (14–15), may tell them into poetry. Yet for all this, Keats's dreamer-poet will soon concede the greater power of practical philanthropists, "Who love their fellows even to the death; /. . . / And more, like slaves to poor humanity, / Labour for mortal good" (156–59). While "less than they" (166), poets are still superior to (if not happier than) the "thoughtless," who "sleep away their days" in ignorance (150–51). Indeed, the reason this dreamer-poet has been permitted to approach Moneta's shrine and share her anguished visions of the fall of the Titans is that poets are ones for whom "the miseries of the world / Are misery, and will not let them rest" (149–50). Poets are priest-kings, bearing the ills of the tribe, suffering in the service of a collective well-being.

This must be what Keats has in mind when the protagonist talks of his "sickness not ignoble" (176) and Moneta addresses him as one carrying "more woe than all his sins deserve" (184). In this image we glimpse a figure at once Christ-like and scapegoat. Throughout the new, preliminary verse, the conception of the poetical character and its station swings between positive and negative poles. Moneta voices Keats's misgivings. Is the gift of imagination more truly a curse, a "fever" (1.169) of the self? How are genuine poets to be known from pseudo-poets or futile "dreamers"?

> – "Art thou not of the dreamer tribe?
> The poet and the dreamer are distinct,
> Diverse, sheer opposite, antipodes.
> The one pours out a balm upon the world,
> The other vexes it."   (1.198–202)

There may be something to be said for "vexing" the world, for unsettling it, being the irritant in the oyster – but only as part of therapy or cure. Keats's poet-protagonist wishes to be a bearer of wisdom, beneficence, and healing, arguing in advance of Moneta's challenge (above):

> sure a poet is a sage;
> A humanist, physician to all men.
> That I am none I feel, as vultures feel
> They are no birds when eagles are abroad.   (1.189–92)

This self-deprecation signifies no impotent surrender, but a reach for a fresh start, perhaps even at the expense of the status quo. Eagles are predators; vultures are carrion-feeders: do these images expose aggressive poetic ambition? (Recall Cortez's "eagle eyes.") Keats's argument for the poet as humanist finds some tension with this vehicle of expression.

How far does *The Fall of Hyperion* keep with its own picture of the ideal poet? The issue at stake is a serious, and pervasive (male) Romantic preoccupation, and as Paul Sheats has shown, Keats sought to train his sensuousness of style to "an artistic self-discipline that was ethical and philosophic in its authority."[8] Such discipline pervades *The Fall* and invests the religious aura of its rites of initiation, which take place in an "old sanctuary" before an "altar" spread with "lofty sacrificial fire" (1.62, 93, 103). The birth of poetic power that had been rendered in *Hyperion* as the agony of Apollo is now recast as the human poet-dreamer's trial by agony, as he experiences, in advance of seeing gods die, the sensation, on his pulses, of his own death. Challenged to ascend Moneta's altar-steps, he finds "hard task" and "prodigious toil" (120–21). Apollo's orgasmic transformation is now a human poet's entry into a new order of perception, taking him upwards from the earthly to the divine plane:

> I shriek'd; and the sharp anguish of my shriek
> Stung my own ears – I strove hard to escape
> The numbness; strove to gain the lowest step.
> Slow, heavy, deadly was my pace: the cold
> Grew stifling, suffocating, at the heart;
> And when I clasp'd my hands I felt them not.
> One minute before death, my iced foot touch'd
> The lowest stair; and as it touch'd, life seem'd
> To pour in at the toes: I mounted up,
> As once fair angels on the ladder flew
> From the green turf to heaven. –   (1.126–36)

In this drama of life recovered from near death, we see what Sheats means by Keats's effort to draw the "intensity" of "concrete particulars" into "logical, thematic, or moral significance" (235). Having survived this ordeal, the poet is immediately rewarded, or cursed, when Moneta unveils her face to him:

>   Then saw I a wan face,
> Not pin'd by human sorrows, but bright blanch'd
> By an immortal sickness which kills not;
> It works a constant change, which happy death
> Can put no end to; deathwards progressing
> To no death was that visage; it had pass'd
> The lily and the snow; and beyond these
> I must not think now, though I saw that face –
> But for her eyes I should have fled away.
> They held me back, with a benignant light,
>
>   .   .   .   .
>
>   they saw me not,
> But in blank splendour beam'd like the mild moon,
> Who comforts those she sees not . . . knows not.
>   (1.256–56, 268–70)

This iconography is etched with dying Tom, Christ, King of Sorrows, and the Madonna, eternally mourning, forever the compassionate intercessor. Keats's imagery permeates the literal with the spiritual, but it does not console or spread a "balm" upon the world. Eternally suffering, with no cure and no release, the "high tragedy" of the Titans' fall forever plays in the wide hollows of Moneta's brain (276–77). It is this realm of suffering (her eternal vale of soul-making), and not Milton's Christian structures of understanding, into which Keats's dreamer-poet steps – back into the "giant agony" (157) of the Titans.

This greater and deeper purpose is the antithesis of any story of progress. Having entered Moneta's vision, the poet-dreamer's imagination is arrested by, and absorbed by, his subject. He beholds Saturn and Thea:

> Long, long, these two were postured motionless,
> Like sculpture builded up upon the grave
> Of their own power. A long awful time
> I look'd upon them; still they were the same;
> The frozen God still bending to the earth,
> And the sad Goddess weeping at his feet;
> Moneta silent. Without stay or prop,
> But my own weak mortality, I bore
> The load of this eternal quietude,
> The unchanging gloom and the three fixed shapes
> Ponderous upon my senses, a whole moon.
> For by my burning brain I measured sure
> Her silver seasons shedded on the night,
> And ever day by day methought I grew
> More gaunt and ghostly. Oftentimes I pray'd
> Intense, that death would take me from the vale
> And all its burthens. Gasping with despair
> Of change, hour after hour I curs'd myself:
> Until old Saturn rais'd his faded eyes, ...   (1.382–400)

Is this a poet's vale of soul-making, or its impossibility? As an appositive to the "three fixed shapes," "the whole moon," suggests Hartman (9), marks both a temporal cycle and the totality of the numinous trinity. Keats is arrested in the moonlight zone of more-than-human forms, able to bear their weight for a while, but fated, "ever day by day," to be crushed, as the load of immortality becomes overload. How ironic that the young poet whose chosen task is, at one level, to revivify the old deities, to make the sculptures live, is repaid with the threat of extinction, or something worse – a lingering non-existence, "spectre-thin" (*Ode to a Nightingale* 25), "gaunt and ghostly," from which death is a release devoutly to be wished.

Does Keats's problem lie with the effort of trying to release what is ineluctably turned to stone or with the power of the mythic to refuse, and thereby overwhelm, his authority? Either way, the effect is the same: unmediated (Moneta herself falls silent as a stone), the supernatural will squeeze the life out of you. Entering the realm of myth in *The Fall*, the poet is confident of his command, claiming the disposition of "an eagle's watch" and the Apollonian endowment of "enormous ken, / To see as a God sees" (1.303–5). Here Keats retrieves the text of *Hyperion* (1.310ff), yet not to see as a God sees, but as a human being. At the beginning of Canto II, a voice (the poet's or Moneta's?) offers to mediate to this end:

> Mortal, that thou may'st understand aright,
> I humanize my sayings to thine ear,
> Making comparisons of earthly things . . .   (2.1–3)

But this is to get things the wrong way round. Only through turning the epic of gods into a drama of human feelings can Keats make headway.

To humanize the supernatural is to give it relevance and to put a curb upon it – ultimately, to return it to rest. Keats's revisions point in this direction. He tones down the epic similes, writes in a style less Miltonic, more Shakespearean. Saturn's speech is now "psychologically [. . .] truer," says Kenneth Muir; "Saturn is humanized, because [. . .] his sorrows are a reflection of the sorrows of humanity" (228). Muir approves of Keats's excision of Saturn's hope for success in a second war ("it must / Be of ripe progress – Saturn must be King" [*Hyperion* 1.125–26]), since "it is the new gods alone that stand for progress" (228). Yet Saturn was psychologically true in the self-enclosed desperation of the original outburst, which Keats's revision retains. Raging, "There is no death in all the universe, / . . . there shall be death," the Saturn of *The Fall* confesses impotence: "I have no strength left" (1.423–27). The revision is a more direct expression of inward desolation, its human witness imagining he has heard "some old man of the earth / Bewailing earthly loss" (440–41).

The suggestion at the beginning of Canto II, that "comparisons of earthly things" exist for the sake of rendering comprehensible a "legend-laden" noise (2.3–5), sits uneasily with Keats's strong interest in the human itself, and perhaps betrays in him an uncertain position between dedication to the natural and the supernatural, drama and myth. This quandary may have contributed to his abandoning the poem.

Muir and others think he stopped writing because he had already used up his climax in Canto I: a human poet preempting the agonizing transformation reserved for Apollo in *Hyperion*. Yet Keats's own explanation was that *The Fall* was still too Miltonic: "there were too many Miltonic inversions in it," he wrote to Reynolds on 21 September 1819, referring to the Latinate syntax that he thought interfered with "the true voice of feeling." "Miltonic verse cannot be written but in an artful or artist's humour," he concluded, adding, "I wish to give myself up to other sensations. English ought to be kept up" (*KL* 2.167). Three days later, he wrote in a similar vein to George and Georgiana Keats:

The Paradise lost though so fine in itself is a curruption of our Language – it should be kept as it is unique – a curiosity. a beautiful and grand Curiosity. The most remarkable Production of the world – A northern dialect accommodating itself to greek and latin inversions and intonations. [. . .] I have but lately stood on my guard against Milton. Life to him would be death to me. Miltonic verse cannot be written but i[n] the vein of art – I wish to devote myself to another sensation –   (*KL* 2.212)

There is more at issue here than Latinate constructions. The reference to stylistic manner screens a deeper anxiety: the specter of belatedness and mere imitative posturing, and therefore of defeat, in relation to his rival forebear – the phrase "on my guard" letting slip both the fact of a contest and Keats's defensiveness. Battling on Milton's ground, Keats stares "death" in the face. It is no coincidence that the poet's dream in *The Fall* begins in the leftovers of the repast enjoyed by Adam, Eve, and Raphael in Milton's Paradise: "refuse of a meal / By angel tasted, or our mother Eve," "empty shells," "remnants" – "whose *pure kinds* I could not know" (1.30–34, my italics; cf. *Paradise Lost* 5.341–49).

At the same time, death to Milton releases Keatsian poetic life. One of its pulses is Keats's zeal for "keeping up" English, a devotion he elaborates with reference to Chatterton, "the purest writer in the English Language [. . .] genuine English Idiom in English words" (*KL* 2.167, cf. 2.212). Another is an embrace of "other sensations." Keats set aside the *Hyperion* project not only in defeat but for these purposes as well. He was conscious of having achieved them in another poem, about a fall with a difference. The letter to Reynolds of 21 September is the same that mentions some recent lines on the seasonal landscape of England. This was *To Autumn*, a pursuit of unadulterated English, with echoes not only of Chatterton but also of Thomson and Coleridge, and words such as "oozings" or "plump." The "sensations" aspire to perfect transcendence. One strain is a subsuming of the Peterloo crisis (the month before), so that, for example, the images of "conspiring," "cells," laboring "bees" are at once the trace and the forgetting of politics and history; while in the same way, the absence of an "*I*" or the genderless figure of Autumn imply the artist's conquest of subjectivity (even as the poet himself was agonizing over Fanny Brawne). *To Autumn* affirms the abundance and unfailing beauty of nature, where transience and death join a perpetual cycle; it is a redemptive "fiction," a myth of naturalness that has become a cultural icon.[9] It is here, if anywhere, that Keats fulfils his ideal poetic function – a physician, pouring a balm upon the world. *To Autumn* stands at the opposite Romantic pole from *Hyperion* and *The Fall*. It is a triumph of lyrical completeness, organically unified, "in midst of other woe . . . a friend to man," as Keats wrote of the power of art in *Ode on a Grecian*

Urn (47–48). Yet if the *Hyperion* project would remain a fragment, baffled and baffling, it was also a monumental, and deeply honest, failure whose abandonment can paradoxically be seen, in D. G. James's words, as "the greatest achievement of Romanticism; in it the Romantic mind beheld its own perplexity and condemned itself."[10]

NOTES

1 See Stuart M. Sperry, Jr., "Richard Woodhouse's Interleaved and Annotated Copy of Keats's *Poems* (1817)," *Literary Monographs I*, ed. Eric Rothstein and Thomas K. Dunseath (Madison: University of Wisconsin Press, 1967), 154.

2 See Marjorie Levinson, *Keats's Life of Allegory: The Origins of a Style*, 11–15; and my "Keats, History, and the Poets," 183–85.

3 Morris Dickstein, "Keats and Politics," 180. See also Alan Bewell's essay, in the same forum.

4 See, for example, Kenneth Muir, "The Meaning of *Hyperion*" (1958); rpt. John Spencer Hill, ed., *Keats: Narrative Poems*, 213; Marilyn Butler, *Romantics, Rebels and Reactionaries* (Oxford: Oxford University Press, 1981), 151–54; my "Keats, History," 179–82. For views of Keats's ironic or dramatic distance on this voice of reasoned consolation, see Stuart M. Sperry, *Keats the Poet*, 184–86, and Susan J. Wolfson, *The Questioning Presence: Wordsworth, Keats, and the Interrogative Mode in Romantic Poetry*, 256–59.

5 See Stuart Ende's discussion of this effect throughout the poem (108–9, 158–9).

6 Geoffrey Hartman, "Spectral Symbolism and the Authorial Self: An Approach to *Hyperion*," *Essays in Criticism* 24 (1974), 6.

7 Sperry, *Keats the Poet*, 187–93; cf. Keats's own confessions: to Fanny Brawne he described his mind (after his own first serious hemorrhage) as "the most discontented and restless" (March [?] 1820; *KL* 2.275) and to James Rice as a melting-pot of "haunting [. . .] thoughts and feelings" (14, 16 February 1820; *KL* 2.259).

8 Sheats, "Stylistic Discipline in *The Fall of Hyperion*" (1968), 76; rpt. Hill, *Narrative Poems*, 234.

9 Geoffrey Hartman, "Poem and Ideology: A Study of Keats's 'To Autumn,'" *The Fate of Reading*; see also John Barnard, *John Keats*, 140. For the poem's qualified traces of politics and history, see my "Keats, History," 185–90. For the poem's more precarious perfections, see Wolfson, *Questioning Presence*, 362–67.

10 D. G. James, *The Romantic Comedy* (London: Oxford University Press, 1948), 126.

RECOMMENDED READING FOR THE HYPERION PROJECT

Allott, Miriam, ed. *The Poems of John Keats*, 394–441, 655–685.

Baker, Jeffrey. *Keats and Symbolism*. Brighton: Harvester Press, 1986, 77–133.

Barnard, John. *John Keats*, 56–67, 129–37.

Bate, Walter Jackson. *John Keats*, 88–417, 562–605.

Bewell, Alan J. "The Political Implication of Keats's Classical Aesthetics."

Butler, Marilyn. *Romantics, Rebels and Reactionaries*. Oxford: Oxford University Press, 1981, 151–54.

Dickstein, Morris. "Keats and Politics."

Ende, Stuart. *Keats and the Sublime*, 98–115, 145–59.

Evert, Walter H. *Aesthetic and Myth in the Poetry of Keats*. Princeton: Princeton University Press, 1965, 225–43, 287–99.

Hartman, Geoffrey. "Spectral Symbolism and the Authorial Self: An Approach to *Hyperion*."

Hill, John Spencer, ed. *Keats: Narrative Poems*. London: Macmillan, 1983.

James, D. G. *The Romantic Comedy*. London: Oxford University Press, 1948, 134–51.

Jones, John. *John Keats's Dream of Truth*, 74–104.

Levinson, Marjorie. *Keats's Life of Allegory*, 191–226.

Muir, Kenneth. "The Meaning of *Hyperion*," *John Keats: A Reassessment*, ed. Kenneth Muir. 1958; Liverpool: Liverpool University Press, 1969, 103–23; rpt. Hill, 209–32.

Newey, Vincent. "'Alternate uproar and sad peace': Keats, Politics, and the Idea of Revolution," *Yearbook of English Studies* 19 (1989), 265–89.

"Keats, History, and the Poets."

O'Neill, Michael. "'When this warm scribe my hand': Writing and History in *Hyperion* and *The Fall of Hyperion*," *Keats and History*, ed. Roe, 143–64.

Rajan, Balachandra. "The Two *Hyperions*: Compositions and Decompositions," *The Form of the Unfinished*. Princeton: Princeton University Press, 1985, 211–49.

Sheats, Paul D. "Stylistic Discipline in *The Fall of Hyperion*" (1968); rpt. Hill, 233–48.

Sperry, Stuart M. *Keats the Poet*, 155–97, 310–35.

Watkins, Daniel P. *Keats's Poetry and the Politics of Imagination*, 85–103, 156–76.

Wicker, Brian. "The Disputed Lines in *The Fall of Hyperion*," *Essays in Criticism* 7 (1957), 28–41.

Wilkie, Brian. "Keats and the Mortal Taste," *Romantic Poets and Epic Tradition*. Madison: University of Wisconsin Press, 1965, 145–87.

Wittreich, Joseph Anthony, Jr. *The Romantics on Milton*, 545–65.

Wolfson, Susan J. *The Questioning Presence*, 253–69, 344–61.

6

PAUL D. SHEATS

Keats and the ode

Keats composed his first ode early in 1815, while an apprentice surgeon-apothecary. Addressed to Apollo, it imagines bards singing in the western sky, Shakespeare and Milton among them, their lyres strung with the rays of the setting sun. In the next five years he wrote eleven more, of which five, the so-called "Great Odes" of 1819, stand among the most celebrated in English: *Ode to a Nightingale, Ode on a Grecian Urn, Ode to Psyche, Ode on Melancholy,* and *To Autumn.*[1] But what is – and was – an "ode"?

"I'd like all suchlike odes there've ever been, binned by a truly democratic nation."[2] This reaction to the possibility, in 1999, of a Poet-Laureate ode should be compared with John Aikin's claim, in 1772, that the "modern ode" displays "the boldest flights of poetical enthusiasm, and the wildest creations of the imagination, and requires the assistance of every figure that can adorn language and raise it above its ordinary pitch."[3] Both comments, political and aesthetic, apply to the ode as Keats knew it, a contradictory genre that came, like the ancient artifact it is, not only with a distinct "attitude" but also, as Stuart Curran reminds us, a "fully realized literary history."[4] Its principal formal variants (the strict Pindaric, the stanzaic Horatian, and the irregular) had been mastered by Wordsworth, Coleridge, and others; all remained working options for Keats and his generation. And yet the inherent paradoxes of the form were particularly obvious at this point in its history. Traditionally dedicated to the celebration of an external object, the ode and its characteristic figures, apostrophe and personification, were frequently read self-reflexively, as bravura displays of visionary imagination. And as the loftiest of lyric kinds – the equivalent of the heroic epic, in the fading neoclassic hierarchy of genres – the "greater" or "sublime" ode predictably attracted satire. A lively genre of mock odes, many aimed at the much despised Laureate odes, flourished throughout the period. In the slang of Keats's letters, the ode was easily "smoked."

In the five odes Keats wrote before 1819 (none a "major" effort, none he wanted to publish), his technical and thematic choices are suggestive.[5]

Instead of abstractions or natural objects, he invokes mythological or literary figures as "Presider[s]" over his maturation (so he denominates
Shakespeare; *KL* 1.142): Apollo (three poems), Maia, and Milton. Avoiding
the extremes of the visionary sublime and the comic, self-parodic ode, he
employs the ode as a site of apprenticeship, as well as of generic retreat from
the burdens of his first "endeavour after a long Poem," *Endymion* (*KL*
1.170). In the last of these early odes, the fragmentary but splendid ode to
Maia ("Mother of Hermes!"), composed May-day 1818, he constructs an
ideal audience, a "little clan" (8), utterly unlike the "Enemy" public he had
just addressed in the Preface to *Endymion* (so he called it in April; *KL* 1.266).
His attitude toward formal discipline often seems similarly contrarian. With
a prescribed form such as the iambic-pentameter couplet, Keats rebels enthusiastically ("I stood tip-toe"; *Sleep and Poetry*; *Endymion*). With the culti-
vated rebellion of the irregular ode, he seeks formal and thematic discipline
(the ode to Maia is patterned on the sonnet). "In my walk to day," he told
Reynolds just after he had composed *To Autumn*, "I stoop'd under a rail way
that lay across my path, and ask'd myself 'Why I did not get over' Because,
answered I, 'no one wanted to force you under'" (*KL* 2.168).

If Keats's early minor odes provided respite from *Endymion*, the great
odes of 1819 were shadowed by another challenge, the epic *Hyperion*
project, which by spring 1819 was going nowhere. In early January, Keats
was already projecting a volume of "minor poems," intended for "those
people [. . .] who cannot bear the burthen of a long poem" (*KL* 2.26), and
in subsequent letters he joked about writing an "ode to darkness" (2.43),
and began exploring the themes, and sometimes the terms, of odes to come.
"Nightingales, Poetry" were subjects of conversation during a walk on April
11 with Coleridge (2.88). A decision to abandon *Hyperion* later that month
precipitated a burst of lyric composition: a ballad, *La Belle Dame*, a choral
Song of Four Fairies, and *Ode to Psyche*, which Keats copied out on the last
day of April, almost a year to the day since the ode to Maia. When and in
what order he composed the other odes is partly guesswork, but the best
guess is that he composed *Nightingale* in early May 1819, a few days after
Psyche, and that *Urn*, *Melancholy*, and *Indolence* followed in May and early
June. *To Autumn* was composed in September (*KL* 2.167). The first published, both in the quarterly *Annals of the Fine Arts*, were *Nightingale* (July
1819) and *Urn* (January 1820). The *Lamia* volume (1820) had all but
Indolence, which first appeared in the *Literary Remains* of 1848.

The craft that produced these poems is visible in facsimile editions
(Stillinger, Gittings) and plates of manuscripts (Motion, Allott, and elsewhere), where we can trace Keats's cancellations and fresh starts. A fine short
appreciation of this craft is Leigh Hunt's, in response to Byron's claim not to

understand a bold metaphor from *Nightingale*, "a beaker full of the warm South" (15). Byron's "sort of poetry," Hunt observed, was "not accustomed to these poetical *concentrations*" (*KCH* 254, my emphasis). In writing odes, Keats concentrates and intensifies techniques he had mastered in other genres, especially a characteristic, slow-moving, orchestration of sound, versification, and sensuous imagery. Nowhere do we sense more keenly his trust, shared with Wordsworth, in the power of imagery to arouse pain and pleasure, especially when it draws on the "knowledge of contrast" Keats thought necessary for a poem (*KL* 2.360). Yet the surface of these poems frequently bristles with other sorts of linguistic activity – puns, internal echoes, apparently fortuitous aberrations of decorum – as well as an unparalleled density of links, intentional or not, to other literary texts and the fine arts.

An inventory of themes can mislead, not only because the odes resist the eighteenth-century practice of self-summary at a high level of abstraction (even or especially when Keats sounds this voice), but also because their art frustrates paraphrase. All are concerned with poetry, its power over the passions and imagination, its moral bearings. The twenty-three-year-old who portrayed himself "writing at random – straining at particles of light in the midst of a great darkness" (*KL* 2.80) did not welcome moral dogmatism in any form. His odes, unlike the character of his "Godwin-methodist" friend Charles Dilke, are not "preresolved" with respect to their subject-matter (2.213); they do not flesh out abstract proposition with relevant imagery. When he wrote poetry, he told Woodhouse, "thoughts come about him in troops," from which "he culls [. . .] the best"; his poems could seem even "to come by chance or magic – to be [. . .] something given to him" (*KC* 1.128–29). The result is a poetry that does not so much pre-resolve thematic issues as represent them in ways that invite resolution, and completion, by the reader. In Susan Wolfson's apt phrase, this is a "poetics of cooperation," which predicates its art on the reciprocal activity of an imagining, desiring reader, and which ideally embodies an ethic of openness and generosity toward both reader and subject.[6] In the Great Odes, we see the paradoxical but fruitful encounter between a form that fostered self-display and a poet who frequently deplored it: "Poetry," Keats wrote to Reynolds early in 1818, "should be great & unobtrusive, a thing which enters into one's soul, and does not startle it or amaze it with itself but with its subject" (*KL* 1.224).

The happiest and yet the most deliberate of the odes, about soul itself, is *Psyche*, written "leisurely" and with "moderate pains," Keats said (*KL* 2.105–6). Often seen as a preview of the odes to come, it was also conceived in the mold of earlier odes: an irregular form; an address to a classical deity; and the large theme of *Maia*, the renewal of modern poetry. Psyche herself plays multiple roles. Most obviously, as Keats emphasized (*KL* 2.106), she is a victim of historical process, a neglected late Roman goddess whom the poet redeems by becoming her modern "priest" (50). Her name invites a second, allegorical, sense: "soul" or "mind," as in traditional Neoplatonic readings of the classical tale by Apuleius, or in the modern notion of life as a "vale of Soul-making" that Keats worked out just days before composing the ode (*KL* 2.102). He embodies these possibilities in a palpably present erotic love-goddess, whom we see, in the splendidly pictorial tableau of the first stanza, in intercoital slumber with her immortal lover (7–23) and, in the final lines, awaiting him with "a bright torch, and a casement ope at night" (66). Both scenes emphasize light, implying that the dark, secret love of Psyche's past has ended, and that, after many trials and long separation, she has been reunited with Cupid. Both scenes cast the poem as a love or marriage ode, celebrating not only the classical pair but also (no doubt) their modern counterparts at Wentworth Place, Keats and Fanny Brawne.

Within this frame, Keats redefines the modern poet's relation to classical myth. Released from the demand to represent the "large utterance of the early Gods" (so the poet of *Hyperion* laments; 1.51), Keats asserts the authority of the poet who commands the present: "I see, and sing, by my own eyes inspired" (43). The elaborate conceit of the last section even charts the future revision of *Hyperion* by relocating myth in the poet's imagination and the anatomy of his material body, the "working brain" (60) and its "branched" thoughts (52).[7] The poem-flowers bred by "gardener Fancy" (62) function reflexively, accounting not only for the ode's genesis but also (we now realize) for the lovers' bower of "leaves and trembled blossoms" (11) in the opening section:

> 'Mid hush'd, cool-rooted flowers, fragrant-eyed,
>   Blue, silver-white, and budded Tyrian,
>   They lay calm-breathing on the bedded grass.   (13–15)

Line thirteen alone addresses four senses, in a sequence rising to the tactile empathy of "cool-rooted," an image that disciplines the erotic touch ("a dream accompanied by a sense of touch" was one of Coleridge's topics two weeks earlier).[8] "Fragrant-eyed" then reaffirms the dominant sense-mode, sight, imaging the object seen as the organ that sees.

Such highly wrought local effects support the central argument: flowers such as these grow only in the garden that is the poet's brain. Like Wordsworth, Keats affirms that modern poetry no longer requires a "faded" classical mythology.[9] Yet even more than for Wordsworth, this stance entails loss. Greeting his goddess with "tuneless numbers, wrung / By sweet enforcement and remembrance dear" (1–2), Keats's poet echoes not only Mary Tighe's popular modern account of Psyche's wanderings (in her Spenserian epic

Psyche, or the Legend of Love) but also the opening of Milton's elegy, *Lycidas*.[10] For all her beauty and pathos, the historical goddess is ultimately irrelevant to the poet's authority, and it is not surprising that in the remaining odes Keats draws subjects not from the "beautiful mythology of Greece" (so he described *Endymion* in his Preface) but from the world of immediate experience.

Unlike *Psyche*, *Ode to a Nightingale* was written easily and quickly, completed, according to Brown, in "two or three hours" (*KC* 2.65), as if one of those somethings "given" of which Woodhouse speaks. Within a new and auspicious form, Keats arranges a host of themes, images, and practices from the work of the previous three years. Crucial to this success was his decision to abandon the irregular in favor of the stanzaic form. The great technical challenge of the irregular, met only partially by *Psyche*, is the need to invent a constantly changing principle of formal structure. The stanzaic form subscribes to a metrical "contract" (Wordsworth's term in the Preface to *Lyrical Ballads*), against which a contrarian poet such as Keats could play the urgencies of passion and impulse. Drawing on recent experiments with the sonnet, he invented a new ten-line stanza: a Shakespearian sonnet-quatrain (abab) plus a Petrarchan sestet (cdecde). Just longer than the Spenserian stanza of *The Eve of St. Agnes*, and varied by a three-foot eighth line (e.g., "But here there is no light"), this stanza also mitigated the obtrusive, "pouncing rhymes" that for Keats marred both sonnet forms (*KL* 2.108). The result must have pleased him, for (with minor variations) he used it in all the remaining great odes.

The rich ambiguities of *Nightingale* are apparent in the three characters of its unfolding drama: the bird, the speaker-poet, and the "fancy." The most elusive is the last, which Keats conceives, on the model of *Fancy* (also in the 1820 volume), as a female agent of vision and escape, but also as mischievously disobedient, a "deceiving elf" (74) like Shakespeare's Puck. The nightingale, by contrast, is notable for what it is not: the Philomela of poetic tradition, or indeed any humanizing personification beyond that briefly suggested by "Dryad" (7). Although the nightingale's song, the poet's only immediate connection to the external world, is presumed to be present throughout the ode, it receives the name of "music" only after it ends (80). As *sound* it is left largely to the reader, who must supply (for example) the grammatical object of the verb "listen" (51). As a lodging for the imagination of a "camelion Poet" (*KL* 1.387), the nightingale is equally equivocal. The ode begins *in medias res*, as empathy with the bird's "happiness" that is "too happy" to be endured (6) collapses into the drugged, mortal selfhood of the first quatrain: "as though of hemlock I had drunk, / . . . and Lethewards had sunk" (2–4). Imaginative union with the bird already portends the self-annihilation that becomes temptingly explicit in stanza six. As sensuous imagery "of beechen green, and shadows numberless" (9) arouses the desire to renew that union, it opens yet another cycle of approach and painful withdrawal into the "sole self" (72).

The speaker's desire to escape the self and its human condition drives the first half of his ode. But if he voices some of the deepest urgencies in Keats's work, he also exemplifies the single-minded, unreflective intensity that Keats associated with "poetry" and opposed to "philosophy." In stanza four he brushes aside his reasoning "brain" – no longer "working," as in *Psyche*, but simply "dull" (34) – and bends "the wings of Poesy" (33) to his own escapist ends, which he pursues with the predatory gusto of the eagle that Keats likened to poetry and opposed to "Truth" (*KL* 2.81).[11] Perhaps two weeks before composing this ode, Keats had argued passionately that "troubles" like those catalogued in stanza three are "necessary" to the growth of the human soul (2.102). The ode's speaker responds simply, "Away! Away!" (31). He embodies what Keats called the "Mammon" of his art – its unprincipled but indispensable "self concentration," on behalf of the ends of "Poetry, and dramatic effect" (*KL* 2.322).

His desires are in turn contained and chastened, especially in the last half of the ode, by an array of covert devices: the dissonant implications of particular images, and the defeat of certain expectations raised by the poet's identification of his poem as an "ode." The trance signaled in stanza four by "Already with thee" (35) effectively inverts, for example, the typical "plot" of the sublime ode. Instead of granting vision, imagination blinds, inflicting a paradoxically luxurious mortification of the senses in stanza five, and ushering the speaker, by a precise logic, to the darkened colloquy with death in stanza six. The irony of this outcome remains latent[12] – unnoticed by the speaker, along with the wit with which his Miltonic poeticism for the invisible wings of Poesy, "viewless" (33), can act as a pun that mocks both Poesy and odal form: a comic spirit seems to work just beneath the surface. But as in the sonnet, "Why did I laugh tonight?," which he writes out in the letter that compares poetry to an eagle (*KL* 2.81), the imagery of darkness also suggests a radical loss of existential bearings, with intertextual echoes striking new and critical moral resonances. The luxurious exit offered by "easeful Death" (52), for example, recalls both the language of Spenser's Despair and its context, a stern rejection of suicide as unmanly and "faint-harted" (*Faerie Queene* I.9.52). The adjective that launches stanza six, *Darkling*, evokes the blind Milton's consoling fellowship with the nightingale as he composed *Paradise Lost* (3.37–40), and opens rich analogies between the two poems and their sightless speakers.[13] Such resonant echoes haunt virtually every line in the ode, introducing literary and moral presences that range from

Sophocles, Milton, and Shakespeare to contemporaries such as Wordsworth and Coleridge. Although these need not be heard in order to enjoy the ode, they enhance an understanding of its historical affiliations – of Milton as a poet of inspired darkness and Shakespeare as a "miserable and mighty Poet of the human Heart" (*KL* 2.115), both implicitly reproving the speaker's desire for "easeful" annihilation.

We see Keats's mastery of the stanzaic form in the transition from six to seven, which silently effects such moral discipline: evoking the turn from strophe to antistrophe in the Pindaric ode, Keats uses the stanza break to dramatize the poet's turn from mortal self to "immortal Bird."

> Still wouldst thou sing, and I have ears in vain –
> To thy high requiem become a sod.
>
> 7
> Thou wast not born for death, immortal Bird!   (59–61)

Critics once liked to point out that birds were indeed mortal, missing the dramatic propriety: this speaker now impulsively bestows on the bird what he lacks, displaying a new "disinterestedness of Mind" – a "pure desire of the benefit of others" (*KL* 2.79). In this great penultimate stanza, the chastening of self-interest intensifies, as the speaker tracks the bird's song backward in time, through secular and sacred history, guessing its power on the "sad heart" of Ruth (66), an ancient analogue to the "heart aches" that inspire his ode. Reaching beyond history, the imagination enters the world of "faery," where "magic casements" cannot disguise the anticlimax of a landscape that is only "forlorn" (69–70).

As the last word of stanza seven, *forlorn* concedes that fancy's quest has failed. Resounded at the start of stanza eight – "Forlorn! the very word is like a bell / To toll me back from thee to my sole self!" (71–72) – the word becomes semantically opaque; visionary imagination shuts down. Like the passing bell it echoes, or the song of the nightingale itself, it is mere sound, heard by the one sense that sustains the speaker throughout the ode.[14] *Ode to a Nightingale* offers no final codification of its moral drama. The speaker's own reflection, that elfin fancy has not cheated him as well as it should have, seems deaf to larger moral resonances; and his last bewildered questions – "Was it a vision, or a waking dream? / Fled is that music: – Do I wake or sleep?" (79–80) – conclude nothing but the ode itself and its musical fellowship with a vanished nightingale. But Keats's profoundly contrarian poetry, more successfully than the poem's speaker, has reclaimed one great traditional function of the genre, celebrating the deep longings of the human heart, and subjecting them, with often ineffable tact, to a critique that comprehends their comedy as well as their tragedy.

Like *Nightingale*, *Ode on a Grecian Urn* traces a dramatic arc of imaginative approach and withdrawal. The poet's attention engages with one
scene (stanzas 1–3), then another (4), then rises to general reflections (5), the
sequence joined by repetitions of words and syntax. The questions that
shape four ("Who are these coming to the sacrifice? . . ."), for example, echo
those of one ("What leaf-fring'd legend . . .?"). With such precise inquiry,
the urn seems more explicitly embedded in history than the "immortal"
nightingale. Yet no single original has been identified. It seems Keats's own
invention, a composite of figures and decorations he had seen on vases in
collections and engravings, gathered in a text that works to universalize art
in its relation to history and human life.[15] Celebrated as one of the great
expressions of romantic Hellenism, *Urn* seems to many readers, as it did to
the *Encyclopedia Britannica* in 1857, to breathe the "very spirit of antiquity" (*KCH* 367). It was first published in *Annals of the Fine Arts*, a journal
known for polemics on behalf of the imitation of ancient Greek originals
(Jack, 46 ff.), and its form and style seem shaped by its Hellenic subject-
matter. Keats regularizes the stanza, expanding *Nightingale*'s trimeter eighth
line to the pentameter norm he would use hereafter. The title signals a commentary "on" its subject, and the opening apostrophe is direct and forth-
right in form (if not implication): unlike *Nightingale*, this ode immediately
fulfills generic expectations. Its speaker is poised and syntactically impersonal (there is no "I"), and if a Dionysian scene first attracts his attention,
his chastened imagery offers little to gratify the senses. There is no synaes-
thesia of sensory information, and touch is invoked only sparingly, in the
contrast between the "warm" love of stanza three and the "cold Pastoral"
of five, or in the brief luxury of the heifer's "silken flanks" (34).

As a poetic response to a work of art, *Urn* joins an ekphrastic tradition
that goes back to the odes of Anacreon. In Keats's day, this involved witty
debates over the relative powers of the "sister arts," typically revolving
around Lessing's distinction between the spatial and the temporal arts.[16] As
it celebrates the urn, Keats's ode demonstrates the power of poetry's temporal art to confer what the spatial arts, painting or sculpture, cannot: dura-
tion, comparison, change, music, speech. Wordsworth had praised the
power of the spatial arts to halt time in a sonnet published in *Annals* sixteen
months before *Ode on a Grecian Urn*, but Keats goes much further, trans-
figuring this power by adding what only poetry can give: life, warmth, and
breath to the sculpted figures on the urn.[17] An essay he admired, Hazlitt's *On
Gusto*, had drawn a sharp contrast between the warm, fleshly verisimilitude
of Italian painting and the "ideal, spiritual" forms of Greek statues: "By their
beauty they are raised above the frailties of pain or passion; by their beauty
they are deified." Wielding powers denied the plastic arts, Keats allows *Ode*

on a Grecian Urn to have it both ways. The first three stanzas display "pain and passion" in abundance: a "wild ecstasy" (10), a lover's grief (17–18), a love "for ever warm and still to be enjoy'd" (26). In stanzas four and five, imaginative engagement subsides, and the urn metamorphoses into the "ideal" but inhuman artifice of Hazlitt's essay.

In dramatizing a response to artwork – that "greeting of the Spirit to make them wholly exist" (*KL* 1.243) – *Urn* also dramatizes the epistemological ambiguities inherent in interpretation. The ode, as many have remarked, is continuously self-reflexive, the poet "reading" the urn as we "read" his ode. His reading may even model ours, urging us toward that "deep and innate sensibility to truth and beauty" that Hazlitt attributed to the small, elite audiences of the Italian Renaissance (*Why the Arts Are Not Progressive*), audiences he and Keats found sadly wanting in modern England. In stanza two, for example, the moral and thematic resonance of the speaker's voice varies delicately from word to word, as he notices, empathizes with, and seeks to console his male marble counterpart, the "bold lover" who will "never, never" kiss: "yet, do not grieve; / She cannot fade" (17–19). The verb *grieve* marks a rhetorical and epistemological crux, the point at which the speaker gains imaginative entry into the urn, where Keats lets us see an imagination half-creating the artwork it perceives.

The moral resonance is distinctive: what impels attention is not self-interest, as in *Ode to a Nightingale*, but sympathy. In a delicate irony, it is these disinterested consolations ("she cannot fade") that soon awaken depths of desire to rival those of *Nightingale*: "More happy love! more happy, happy love!" (25). Located at the mid-point of the ode, and often criticized as sentimental, this straining repetition implies the decay of admiration into something like envy, a "fine excess" (*KL* 1.238) emphasizing the contingency of the immortal happiness so contemplated on the warmth of the speaker's mortal imagination. It is as if the trauma that initiates *Nightingale* – an empathy with "happiness" "too happy" to be endured, and so collapsing into killing contrasts – were here moderated, controlled, and transformed into the poised central "turn" of this ode. Yet this poise is precarious, resolving at the stanza's close into increasingly painful contrasts, between the "for ever warm" love depicted on the urn and the "burning," "parching" flux of human passions.

Attention shifts abruptly with a rotation of the urn to show a scene of communal purification and purgation, a sacred ritual and an imminent sacrifice. Like the fancy that in *Nightingale* tracked the enchanting song through history, here imagination ponders the unpictured "little town" that was home to the pictured "folk" (37), and to which they, "for evermore" arrested in the urn's tableau, cannot "return" (38–40). Like the "faery lands forlorn" of *Nightingale*, this image of "desolate" streets signals the end of imaginative engagement. The stanza's last word, *return*, half-rhymes with *morn*, as if *forlorn*, which occurs at precisely this point in *Ode to a Nightingale*, were sounding beneath it. As the stanza's last word, *return* also signals a turn to the final stanza, where abstract diction and clustered puns distance speaker and reader from the urn, and where future readers, "in midst of other woe / Than ours" (47–48), are contemplated in a perspective that has shifted from museum-space to historical time.

This evolving drama could answer the age-old and enduring question, "is ideal art preferred to nature, or vice versa?" Yet any answer would falsify the evolving consciousness Keats has represented, forcing criticism to do to the ode what the urn does to life, still its motions. Yet if so, how do we take the urn's famous aphorism, "Beauty is truth, truth beauty" (49), which seems to offer what the rest of the ode so splendidly frustrates? These five words have provoked a range of interpretation so wide as to elude determinate meaning; what is clear about this knotted chiasmus is its determination to identify two abstract nouns, frequently coupled in contemporaneous artistic and philosophical contexts, both admirable vessels for meanings supplied by the reader, idealist or materialist, aesthete or Marxist.[18] We need to remember that this motto issues from an object that the poet has just said "tease[s] us out of thought" (44); we do not find, and should not expect, the clear imperative that would end another poet's response to this ode a century later: "You must change your life."[19]

Musing on another urn of imagination, *Ode on Indolence* was inspired by a cherished moment of emancipation, conferred by "honied indolence" (37), from the compulsions Keats felt driving his life: Love, Ambition, and Poesy (*KL* 2.79).[20] Keatsian "indolence" was not always so luxurious, however; it could also provoke something close to despair: "I dread as much as a Plague," he wrote Haydon in mid-April, "the idle fever of two months more without any fruit" (2.55). His epigraph cites the lilies of the field – "They toil not, neither do they spin" (Matthew 6.28). As in "O thou whose face hath felt the Winter's wind," a poem Keats wrote out in a letter on "delicious diligent Indolence" (*KL* 1.231–33), the attempt is to reconcile indolence and idleness, to present luxurious passivity as intrinsically creative. Yet as the subject of an ode, the abstraction "Indolence" proves far less successful than an urn or nightingale, and for reasons that illuminate the conditions of their success. Celebrated as *apatheia*, the absence of all affect, "Indolence" blunts the vectored energy of the odal form; when desire threatens to spread its wings, indolence rules against it: "so, ye three ghosts, adieu! Ye cannot raise / My head cool-bedded in the flowery grass" (51–52). *Indolence* depletes anything "to be intense upon" (*KL* 1.192). Keats had not yet devised, as he would in *The Fall of Hyperion*, a successful stylistic equivalent to poetic austerity.[21]

The abstraction that inspires *Ode on Melancholy*, on the other hand, allows him to exploit an abundance of associated images, emblems, and literary sites, from Milton's *L'Allegro* to the physical and mental disease endlessly analyzed by Burton's *Anatomy of Melancholy*. Instead of invoking the goddess Melancholy, the speaker addresses the reader, with an energy of specification we see only here. Identified as a devotee of Melancholy, and forcefully halted, the reader is instructed in the secret rituals, or "mysteries" (8), proper to her cult. The three stanzas follow an order that is logical, not dramatic: (1) abandon the traditional quest for oblivion and death; (2) feed yourself on beauty, however fleeting; (3) this will admit you to Melancholy's "sovran shrine" and make you her trophy. (Keats canceled another, perhaps redundant opening stanza, a grotesque conceit about the wrong way to find Melancholy, with a spectre-bark built of bones and other Gothic properties.) With its striking allegorical personifications of Beauty, Joy, and Pleasure, stanza three verges on the style of the eighteenth-century sublime ode. A sustained imagery of ingestion – "the bee-mouth sips"; "burst Joy's grape"; "taste the sadness" – insists, with increasing intensity, on the simultaneity of pleasure and pain, joy and sadness. In *Ode to Psyche*, Keats applied the oxymoronic cliché of sensibility, "pleasant pain" (52), to poetic composition; here he presses it to a moral verge where masochism and sadism meet. What he gains is an impressively strong, assertive lyric stance, able to welcome "the wakeful anguish of the soul" (10) without bitterness or complaint. Instead of lamenting the indissolubility of pleasure and pain, as in many other poems, he stipulates it, and exemplifies an exuberant egotism that can reduce an angry "mistress" to an aesthetic spectacle. What he gives up is any thought that poetry might speak for the "human friend Philosopher" (*KL* 2.139).

This is the implicit work of *To Autumn*, which Keats composed on 19 September after a walk through the fields outside Winchester, on a day of clear, chaste weather – "Dian skies," as he phrased it to Reynolds two days later, just after he had decided to give up *Hyperion* and its artful Miltonic idiom (*KL* 2.167). As in *Psyche*, he turns (more accurately, returns) from the problematic epic to an odal form he now knew well, in which virtually any technical decision reflects on his "songs of spring" (23). The result is a sustained naturalism, a maturity and equanimity of tone, and masterful craft. *To Autumn* looks not to myth, art, or abstraction for inspiration but to the present English countryside, of the sort itemized in the *Examiner*'s "Calendar of Nature" for September, 1819: "the month of the migration of birds, of the finished harvest, of nut-gathering, of cyder and perry-making"

(29 August 1819, p. 574). Despite its apparently mimetic naturalism, however, the ode participates in a rich georgic tradition (literature about agriculture) that links it to Chatterton, Thomson, and Virgil, among others, but in a diction that, like Chatterton's, is emphatically native: except for one verb, *maturing* (2), Keats banishes the Latinate vocabulary of Milton and Renaissance humanism, in favor of words, many of them agricultural and domestic, that had been naturalized by the time of Chaucer. As in *Lyrical Ballads*, this winnowing of diction affects not only sound and imagery, but also the ode's moral stance, its apparently lucid substantiality.

To *Autumn* is often seen as a reconciling coda to the May odes or even to Keats's career, a final Shakespearian acknowledgment, in the phrase from *King Lear* cited by Middleton Murry and many after him, that "ripeness is all"[22] – the root sense of "maturity." In the centered poise with which it contemplates mingled beauty and sadness, *Autumn* most closely resembles its tonal and philosophic antithesis, *Ode on Melancholy*. The patterns of frustrated desire in *Nightingale* and *Urn* have largely disappeared, and the imagination seems content with what nature offers; the three stanzas represent the "progress" and "setting" of the season and perhaps the day, in Keats's finest realization of his poetic "axiom" (*KL* 1.238). Like the spring odes, it enlists the reader's imagination, but for ends that seem more disinterested and impersonal. Autumn's gender, for example, is left indeterminate, so that it is the reader who imagines it as male or female. The figure whose hair is "lifted by the winnowing wind" (15) is often perceived as female, although iconographic tradition frequently represented the season as male, and long, flowing hair was a familiar feature of Apollo. The point is not that Keats conceives Autumn as neuter or androgynous, but that the pleasure of the image, a pleasure that in its tactile intimacy is incipiently erotic, is not made contingent on gender. Such generosity effectively banishes from the ode the conflicted misogyny Keats displays in contemporary letters.

The ode's "maturity" is often credited to a philosophical acceptance of process. But if we read carefully (no ode better rewards such attention), we find many poetic and linguistic devices that complicate assent to process, inviting but refusing it, as if to deny or mitigate its painful effects. The apparently powerful syntax of stanza one, which enacts Autumn's fecundity, is strung with infinitives (to bend and fill, to swell and plump) which, however muscular, never find completion in a finite verb. The final cameo implies but also seems to postpone the coming of winter, as Autumn conspires

> . . . to set budding more,
> And still more, later flowers for the bees,
> Until they think warm days will never cease,
> For summer has o'er-brimm'd their clammy cells.   (8–11)

The gently ironic perspective of line ten casts the bees as diminutive instances of the point Keats made back in March: "while we are laughing the seed of some trouble" is being planted in "the wide arable land of events" (*KL* 2.79). Although only summer is named, we know that winter is coming, and that in this now-literal "arable field" outside Winchester the illusion that "warm days" are eternal is doomed, as are, perhaps, the bees themselves. A product of inference, not statement, this realism is neither eased nor sentimentalized by moral reflection, as with Aesop's exemplary grasshopper; these are industrious, Virgilian worker-bees (*Georgics* 4.156 ff), whose destiny depends not on vice or virtue but on the same, inexorable, equal-handed power that fills their "clammy cells." The line that exposes the ironic effect of summer's generosity (10) is made to conspire in this generosity, by forming a couplet that prolongs the stanza's closing cadence (cdecDDe). Here, in Keats's one re-adjustment of the May stanza, meter functions as a formal, nonsemantic analogue to the passage of time.

In stanza two, dedicated to the eye and by implication to the sister art of painting, temporal change seems halted altogether by devices similar to those on the Grecian Urn: its four scenes evoke an eternal Autumn, in which sensuous personifications embody the careless leisure of pastoral, but are stationed within a landscape marked by the georgic labor necessary at the season's turn: the granary floor (14) will soon be covered by the grain reaped in the next tableau; the "half-reap'd" furrow will get fully so; gleaners will follow the reapers; the cyder-press will have its "last oozings." Change is deftly and precisely implied, but the text refuses to represent or endorse it.

As the temporal art of music becomes the presiding mode of stanza three, resistance to process relaxes. The speaker rejects nostalgia – "Where are the songs of spring? Ay, where are they? / Think not of them, thou hast thy music too" (23–24) – hinting instead at a pastoral singing-contest between seasons, perhaps between this ode and those of spring. Although spring is briefly remembered by *bloom* (25), a verb added in revision, the catalogue of autumn's creatures and sounds points to coming winter, still unnamed. Sentences shorten, finite verbs multiply. After the magnificent display of stanza two, personification subsides (in *choir* and *mourn* [27]), and vanishes in the last four lines, where an absolutely literal diction enacts acceptance of what is and will be. Twice displaced from its destined victims, verbal forms of "die" (25, 29) are applied harmlessly to immortal things, the day and the wind, in a delicate euphemism we sense as protective, merciful, and unavailing. Here, if anywhere, Keats succeeds in reconciling "poetry" with "philosophy."

The major odes have attracted voluminous commentary, which sometimes seems to tower over their few hundred lines as the "Cliff of Poesy" towered over their author (*KL* 1. 141). By 1980, nearly 900 items had reached print, with hundreds more added since.[23] This reception is distinctive in several respects. Since the time of Browning, the craft of the odes has won the admiration, imitation, and envy of Keats's fellow artists: Van Gogh, Ruskin, Stevens, Clampitt, among many others. The critical record also illuminates nineteenth-century canon-formation: although the odes were praised in passing by several reviewers in 1820, it was their republication by Milnes in 1848, in the rich context of Keats's biography and letters, and an established myth of his martyrdom, that conferred their prestige at a time when the shorter lyric was replacing the long narrative poem as the standard of poetic greatness. A survivor of Keats's generation, Severn could describe him in 1879 as the poet of "only five perfect odes," poignant but inadequate surrogates for the major works he never completed.[24] To younger readers such as Swinburne (writing three years later), however, the odes justified Keats's place among the English poets, and late Victorian critics even sifted this richness: *Nightingale*, *Urn*, and *Autumn* were the favorites, as they are today.

The twentieth century brought new academic, pedagogical, and commercial contexts for the odes, as modern literature was introduced into the university curriculum, and "general education" became a fixture of American higher education. In 1926 H. W. Garrod pronounced the odes "worth *study*, worth, that is, some pains of scholarship," and over the next decades their texts, sources, and composition were investigated in detail.[25] They became exemplary anthology pieces, as well as demonstration-poems for successive critical movements. Cleanth Brooks's New-Critical reading of *Urn* (1947) became an anthology piece in itself, and influential readings followed from such scholars as Earl Wasserman (1953), David Perkins (1959), and W. J. Bate (1963). The odes then encountered a brisker critical climate, in which the formalism and elitism associated with the genre became a liability, and their canonical authority fell under suspicion, the more so, perhaps, because it was celebratory, long-continued, and virtually unanimous. During this, perhaps the most interesting phase of their history, the odes continued to test increasingly diverse ways of reading, ranging from Helen Vendler's dedicated formalist analysis (1983) to studies of intertextuality, historical context, gender, and linguistic play. Whatever their critical allegiances, we hope that readers of the new century will not forget that Keats's odes are, after all, poems, to be known through the open and attentive reading they so forcefully presume and so abundantly reward.

NOTES

1 Some include *Ode on Indolence*. For the minor odes, see Jack Stillinger's list in *The English Romantic Poets*, 4th edn., 706.

2 Tony Harrison, "Laureate's Block"; cited by BBC News, 9 February 1999.

3 John Aikin, *Essays on Song-Writing* (London, n.d.), 20.

4 Stuart Curran, *Poetic Form and British Romanticism*, 71.

5 For more detail, see my "Keats, the Greater Ode, and the Trial of Imagination."

6 Susan J. Wolfson, *The Questioning Presence: Wordsworth, Keats, and the Interrogative Mode in Romantic Poetry*, chapter 13.

7 Even Psyche's "soft-conched" ear (4) can be found, as the *concha*, in contemporary anatomy textbooks (though not in Keats's medical notebook); this was an established term for the external ear by 1683 (*OED*, sv *concha* 4.a). See Charles W. Hagelman, Jr., "Keats's Medical Training and the Last Stanza of the 'Ode to Psyche,'" *KSJ* 11 (1962), 74–82, and Alan Richardson's essay in this volume.

8 *KL* 2.89; see John Barnard, "Keats's Tactile Vision: 'Ode to Psyche' and the Early Poetry," *Keats–Shelley Memorial Bulletin* 3 (1982), 1–24.

9 See Harold Bloom, *The Visionary Company* (New York: Doubleday, 1963), 422.

10 "Dear remembrance" compels the goddess at the opening of Tighe's *Psyche* (8), as grief does the elegist of *Lycidas* (7).

11 "Milton in every instance pursues his imagination to the utmost – he is 'sagacious of his Quarry,' he sees Beauty on the wing, pounces upon it and gorges it to the producing his essential verse," Keats writes in his copy of *Paradise Lost* (Cook, *John Keats*, 344). He may be remembering Hazlitt's essay *On Gusto* (*Examiner*, May 1816), which admired how Milton's comparison of Satan to a vulture "grapples with and exhausts his subject."

12 Some find a premonition in the grammatical ambiguity of "Already with thee! tender is the night": the poet may be claiming unity with the nightingale, or may be recognizing that the tenderness it enjoys is exclusive. See Wasserman, *The Finer Tone*, 198, and Wolfson, *Questioning Presence*, 314–15 (for the significance of this and other grammatical and syntactic ambiguities); both credit Clyde S. Kilby (*Explicator* 5 [1947]).

13 On this intertext, see John Hollander, *The Figure of Echo* (Berkeley: University of California Press, 1981), 90; and Eleanor Cook, "Birds in Paradise," *Studies in Romanticism* 26 (1987), 421–43.

14 For a summary of comments on "forlorn" see James O'Rourke, *Keats's Odes and Contemporary Criticism*, esp. 4–8. See also Garrett Stewart, in this volume.

15 Joseph Severn recalled showing Keats the vase described. On possible originals, see Ian Jack, *Mirror of Art*, 214–24, and William C. McDermott, "Keats and Sosibios," *Classical Journal* 44 (1948), 33–34.

16 See Theresa M. Kelley's essay in this volume, and her "Keats, Ekphrasis, and History," in Roe, *Keats and History*, and Grant F. Scott, *The Sculpted Word*. On the "sister Arts" debate, see John J. Teunissen and Evelyn J. Hinz, "'Ode on a Grecian Urn': Keats's 'Laocoön,'" *English Studies in Canada* 6 (1980), 176–201. German critic and dramatist G. E. Lessing (1729–81) wrote an influential treatise *Laokoön* (1766), in which he contemplated the differences between poetry and the plastic arts.

17 *Upon the Sight of a Beautiful Picture*, first published in 1815, appeared in *Annals*, January 1818. Commenting on its similarity to Keats's ode, Wordsworth claimed he had "priority" (R. P. Graves, cited by Robert Woof, "Haydon, Writer, and the Friend of Writers," in *Benjamin Robert Haydon* [Kendal: Wordsworth Trust, 1996], 47).

18 Keats had paired the terms before: "What the imagination seizes as Beauty must

be truth" (November 1817; *KL* 1.184); "I never can feel certain of any truth but from a clear perception of its Beauty" (December 1818; 2.19). So had Hazlitt's essays *On Gusto* and *Why the Arts Are Not Progressive*, cited above. For critical commentary, see *KCH*, Jack Wright Rhodes's *Annotated Bibliography*, and Harvey T. Lyon, *Keats's Well-Read Urn* (New York: Holt, 1958).

19 German poet Rainer Maria Rilke (1875–1926), *Torso of an Archaic Apollo* ("Du musst dein Leben ändern"). For a lucid synopsis of the controversy over Keats's final thirteen words, see Stillinger, "Who Says What to Whom at the End of *Ode on a Grecian Urn?*," "*Hoodwinking*," 167–73; see also James O'Rourke, *Keats's Odes and Contemporary Criticism*, 46 ff.

20 It is something of the Cinderella of the group; Keats left it out of the 1820 volume, and for a long time critics paid relatively little attention to it. Composed sometime before June 9 (*KL* 2.116), it is unique among the odes in having a specific autobiographical source named by Keats, an allegorical daydream he describes in his journal-letter of 19 March 1819 (2.78–79).

21 See my "Stylistic Discipline in *The Fall of Hyperion*."

22 John Middleton Murry, *Keats and Shakespeare* (London: Oxford University Press, 1925), 189. Its seeming unconcern with contemporary politics has provoked historicist critique. See Jerome J. McGann, "Keats and the Historical Method in Literary Criticism," and among many replies, Paul Fry, "History, Existence, and 'To Autumn,'" and James Chandler, *England in 1819* (Chicago: University of Chicago Press, 1998), 425–32.

23 See Rhodes's bibliography. For the nineteenth century through the 1860s see *KCH*; G. S. Fraser's *John Keats: Odes* (London: Macmillan, 1971) offers a perceptive selection of criticism pre-1960s; for more recent work, see the bibliographical essays by Stillinger and Kucich, and the annual *KSJ* bibliography.

24 William Graham, *Last Links with Byron, Shelley, and Keats* (London: Smithers, 1898), 101.

25 H. W. Garrod, *Keats* (Oxford: Clarendon Press, 1926), 74.

FURTHER READING ON KEATS'S ODES

Bate, W. J. *John Keats*, 486–524, 580–85.

Fry, Paul. *The Poet's Calling in the English Ode*. New Haven: Yale University Press, 1980, chapters 9 and 10.

Gittings, Robert (ed.). *The Odes of Keats and Their Earliest Known Manuscripts*.

Jack, Ian. *Keats and the Mirror of Art*. Oxford: Clarendon Press, 1967.

O'Rourke, James. *Keats's Odes and Contemporary Criticism*. Gainesville: Universty of Florida Press, 1998.

Perkins, David. *The Quest for Permanence*, chapters 7–9.

Rhodes, Jack Wright. *Keats's Major Odes: An Annotated Bibliography of the Criticism*. Westport, Conn.: Greenwood Press, 1984.

Sperry, Stuart. *Keats the Poet*, chapter 10 and Epilogue.

Stillinger, Jack. "Imagination and Reality in the Odes," *Hoodwinking*, 99–119.

Vendler, Helen. *The Odes of John Keats*.

Wasserman, Earl. *The Finer Tone*, chapters 2 and 6.

Wolfson, Susan J. *The Questioning Presence*, chapters 13 and 14.

7

SUSAN J. WOLFSON

Late lyrics

Form and discontent

When T. S. Eliot cited *Ode to a Nightingale* for the "impersonal" art that he esteemed over the Wordsworthian effect of "personality," he was repeating Keats's own favoring of a "poetical Character" that, unlike "the wordsworthian or egotistical sublime," presented "no self [. . .] no Identity" (*KL* 1.386–87). This value would become the New Critical standard of "objective" poetic form, for which Keats's Great Odes provided textbook models.[1] It is thus remarkable to see this hallmark Keatsian effect so starkly subverted by poems he wrote after these odes, from late 1819 to early 1820: "The day is gone," "I cry your mercy," "What can I do?," "Physician Nature," a revision of "Bright Star," and an enigmatic fragment, "This living hand" – all inspired, or haunted, by Fanny Brawne. Desperately in love, despairing of success as a poet, struggling financially and in failing health, with no aim of publication, Keats still turned to poetic form to grapple with a passion, so he told her, that he knew had turned him "selfish," that is, self-occupied (*KL* 2.123; 223).

When these poems were eventually published, readers were embarrassed. From R. M. Milnes's *Life, Letters, and Literary Remains* (1848) on, most biographers, editors, and critics cited them (if at all) only as biographical documents of weakening power. Other than "Bright Star" and "This living hand," they were barely treated, then usually with excuse. "Hardly Keats at his best," laments Robert Gittings; although "of intense moment to the poet and his immediate circle," these "look strangely in the company of his more considered work." H. W. Garrod is blunter and more categorical: "upon whatever page of Keats' poetry there falls the shadow of a living woman, it falls calamitously like an eclipse."[2] E. C. Pettet, the least forgiving, despises "Physician Nature" in particular:

> Never before, either in his letters or his poetry, had he so nakedly and emphatically confessed his "torturing jealousy" [. . .] and it is the entire indulgence in this unlovely, deliquescent emotion, without pride, rebellion, anger, cynicism, or other bracing attitude, that makes this poem so distastefully mawkish. We

are forced to admit its biographical interest, but it is certainly one of Keats's poems that we wish he had seen fit to destroy in the cool light of some morning's afterthought.[3]

What Keats did not destroy, Keatsians did. W. J. Bate's massive, canonical biography is typical in scarcely mentioning these poems, then only as "flaccid" writing. The few who have given them more than cursory or contemptuous attention do not contest this judgment but wield terms other than aesthetic – existential (Paul de Man), or sociohistorical (Jerome McGann).[4]

In this essay I take up aesthetic questions, with an interest in how a poetry driven by crises of self and identity involves its formal resources, how, too, the contingency and instability of such resources press Keatsian aesthetics into critical discoveries. As all readers of these late poems (including Keats) understand, Keats in love vexes Keats the poet. "This moment I have set myself to copy some verses out fair. I cannot proceed with any degree of content. I must write you a line or two and see if that will assist in dismissing you from my Mind," he tells his "dearest Girl" in October 1819 (*KL* 2.223). This arrest, in the midst of even so mundane a business as fair-copying (making a clean draft), reflects the power of archetypal "Girl" to disrupt the enamored poet's self-possession and autonomy. If male poetic tradition is famed for dominating and internalizing the "feminine," Keats's late lyrics betray, even as they may desire, such license.[5] The poet's cry to "Physician Nature" – "let my spirit blood! / O ease my heart of verse and let me rest; / . . . till the flood / Of stifling numbers ebbs" (1–4) – epitomizes the crisis: does a plea *in* verse to be eased *of* verse name a cure, or perpetuate a cause? Is a verse whose numbers don't numb a force of spiritual ease or an aggravation of disease?

Keats wrote "Physician Nature" probably in February 1820, in the wake of his first major haemorrhage. The prescription seemed clearer in September 1818, when he was the physician, nursing his dying brother, seeking relief with *Hyperion* and feeling not unpleasantly "haunted" by "the voice and the shape of a woman": "This morning Poetry has conquered [. . .] I feel escaped from a new strange and threatening sorrow. – And I am thankful for it" (*KL* 1.370). One of the early aspirations of this medical student turned poet was for power to "beguile" Dido of "her grief . . . / Or rob from aged Lear his bitter teen" (*Imitation of Spenser* 21–22). "Beauty [is] not in the absence of the Passions, but on the contrary – it is heightened by the sight of what is conquered," proposed Coleridge in a lecture of 1818. Yet such success, he had argued in *Biographia Literaria* the year before, requires "subjects very remote from the private interests and circumstances of the writer himself," from his "personal sensations and experiences." Shakespeare's power depends on "the alienation [. . .] the utter *aloofness* of the poet's own feelings, from those of which he is at once the painter and the analyst."[6] What happens to poetic form when it is helplessly informed by the poet's own feelings?

One way to forestall the question is to put feelings into a sonnet, a form with a long history and a set of performative patterns precisely tailored for the man in love:

> Should e'er unhappy love my bosom pain,
> From cruel parents, or relentless fair;
> O let me think it is not quite in vain
> To sigh out sonnets to the midnight air! (*To Hope* 25–28)

So Keats himself wrote in 1815. *To Hope* is not itself a sonnet, but it is a close reference: its stanzas of *ababcc* in iambic pentameter are in the pattern of a Shakespearean sonnet sestet. Yet this cherished tradition could also pain individual talent with its demand to sigh it all in 140 syllables, in fourteen lines measured and rhymed more or less by prescription. Such constraints, perhaps too akin to a lover's enthrallment to his relentless fair, were rankling Keats by 1819, as a meta-sonnet (about the form and its traditions) shows. "Incipit altera Sonneta," he introduces it, adding, "I have been endeavouring to discover a better sonnet stanza than we have" (*KL* 2.108).[7] With self-possessed formal innovation, he exercises his skill around the figure of a woman in thrall:

> If by dull rhymes our english must be chaind
> And, like Andromeda, the Sonnet sweet,
> Fetterd in spite of pained Loveliness;
> Let us find out, if we must be constrain'd,
> Sandals more interwoven & complete
> To fit the naked foot of Poesy;
> Let us inspect the Lyre & weigh the stress
> Of every chord & see what may be gained
> By ear industrious & attention meet,
> Misers of sound & syllable no less
> Than Midas of his coinage, let us be
> Jealous of dead leaves in the bay wreath Crown;
> So if we may not let the Muse be free,
> She will be bound with Garlands of her own.   (*KL* 2.108)

It may be, as Karen Swann argues in a sharp reading of Keats's gendering, that everything "must be constrained": our english, Andromeda, the sonnet, the naked foot of Poesy ("already a 'foot,' a measured unit"), poets themselves. Given such "unoriginated, inescapable limits," Keats writes of "happy capitulation"; through "the enthralling power of feminized forms," the poet is seduced into imagining himself as a woman who loves enforced seduction.

Yet Keats is also just as busy interweaving his constraints, staging an escape-artist performance.[8] Take the emblematic play of the first rhyme, *chaind* and *constrain'd*. The hard consonance (strengthened by the intermediary stress on *pained*) frames the quatrain; yet line four breaks out, its syntax running to *Poesy* (6). *Poesy*, moreover, is a feminine foot (the unstressed *-sy* is the syllable to be rhymed) that is only loosely fettered by poetic chains: it is not bound to the *abc* rhyme pattern of 1–10; and if it is set to be caught by *be* and *free* (11 and 13), no other rhyme is so distant, suppressed, asymmetrical. The sentence it ends (moreover still) has already initiated a chord of exhortations – Let us / Let us / let us – that remains more audible than the rhyme-words (including line eleven's *be*) made faint by enjambment (stress / Of; less / Than; be / Jealous). In a poem about writing poetry, we might expect such thematically laden words as "bound" (the principle of rhyme) and "sound" (rhyme itself) to be advertised as key rhymes. But as the merely internal rhyme of these words (10, 14) in the poet's agenda hints, Keats is advertising advertence from the binds of tradition. By letting the syntax of the last two lines mime a Shakespearean couplet, he dramatizes the shaping of his poetic form against any such prescription. Even the sestet: the sonnet closes in a quatrain, of conspicuously muted rhymes whose atonality (*Crown* / *own*) works in favor of a deft sight-rhyme pun: Keats unbinds the dead letters of "*Crown*" to write "her *own*" – the trope of a poet coining his *own* freedom with(in) this form.

These plays of (and on) form are launched from an allusion to Andromeda, the fair girl fettered for destruction by a sea-serpent (a penalty for her mother's boasts of her beauty), then liberated by the avatar of the poet, Perseus riding to rescue on his winged steed Pegasus, the emblem of soaring inspiration. The lore of Perseus has even more to do with this power than Keats's brief mention of chained Andromeda lets on. He is the famed slayer of the demonic female enthraller Medusa, she whose gaze arrests men into mere forms, stony paralyses of themselves. Perseus takes her head as his trophy and assumes control of its spell; winged Pegasus is born from her bloody corpse. This mythology sets an alluring horizon for Keats's intent to have his way with a feminized poetic form, and suggests why he returned to sonnets to write of his psychomythia with Fanny Brawne. Yet this cause and occasion proves the antithesis of self-possession: "I cannot exist without you. [. . .] You have absorb'd me," Keats writes to her in that letter of October 1819. "I have no limit now to my love," he protests; "I could die for you. [. . .] You have ravish'd me away by a Power I cannot resist; and yet I could resist till I saw you." "I cannot breathe without you. / Yours for ever," he signs off (*KL* 2.223–24), his "without you" telling two seemingly contradictory, but damningly related stories: "without possessing you" and "independently of you." The Keatsian ideal of a poet of no self returns as an anguished erotic reality, an embodied negative *in*capability. A few days later, he writes, "I must impose chains upon myself – I shall be able to do nothing – I shold like to cast the die for Love or death [. . .] my mind is in a tremble, I cannot tell what I am writing" (2.224). In this unsweet self-chaining, Keats reverses both the sonnet's gendering and its drama. He is now a trembling Andromeda, his powers of writing slipping away.

"I am almost astonished that any absent one should have that luxurious power over my senses which I feel," Keats had written to his "sweet Girl" in July, "astonished" half-giving her a Medusan power. So, too, a chance misspelling in his next sentence: "Even when I am not thinking of you I receive your influence and a tenderer nature *steeling* upon me" (*KL* 2.126, my emphasis). A few weeks on, these petrifying terms stage an alienating self-division: "I am indeed astonish'd to find myself so careless of all cha[r]ms but yours" (2.133). By August, Keats sets his defenses, not writing to her, then sending a letter calculated to sound "unloverlike and ungallant": "My heart seems now made of iron," he insists, substituting his steely mettle for her power (2.141). This was the claim of an enabling distance: away for the summer with Brown at Shanklin, then Winchester, Keats had not seen his dear girl for weeks, and was beginning to compose himself in independence: "I have had no idle leisure to brood over you," he tells her bluntly, adding, "'t is well perhaps I have not – I could not have endured the throng of Jealousies that used to haunt me" (2.140–41).

In one sonnet, not to but about her, he deftly modulates this distance into hyper-formalized self-possession:

> The day is gone, and all its sweets are gone!
>   Sweet voice, sweet lips, soft hand, and softer breast,
> Warm breath, light whisper, tender semi-tone,
>   Bright eyes, accomplish'd shape, and lang'rous waist!
> Faded the flower and all its budded charms,
>   Faded the sight of beauty from my eyes,
> Faded the shape of beauty from my arms,
>   Faded the voice, warmth, whiteness, paradise,
> Vanish'd unseasonably at shut of eve,   (1–9)

These lines play out the elegiac inspiration. Following the toll of *gone*, the trochee-deadened anaphora of *Faded* dominates (in both sound and insistent sense) the represencing evocations, which take shape in mostly weak rhymes. At the same time, the endwords *paradise* and *eve* (8–9), linking vertically, spell the most famous poetic tale of forlorn male enamoration. This link may even be a rueful echo: gone from Adam for a day, his Eve at least returns "at shut of Ev'ning Flow'rs" (*Paradise Lost* 9.278). Yet on this very stage of mourning, Keats's poetry begins to compose some subtle returns:

> . . . at shut of eve,
> When the dusk Holiday – or Holinight –
> Of fragrant curtain'd Love begins to weave
> The woof of darkness, thick, for hid delight;   (10–12)[9]

As end-rhymes replace the anaphora of absence ("Faded . . . Faded . . . Faded . . . Faded"), Keats's drama of erotic love palpably designs poetic love: *Holinight / delight* makes audible a strain heretofore submerged – *light* (3), *bright* (4), *sight* (6), *white*ness (8) – the terms that hold the beloved in memory, which "hid delight" crowns in sound and sense. Keats worked at his wording to accomplish this poetic shape (see Stillinger's textual notes, 491), and it is no coincidence that Love is figured as a writer of sorts: a weaver (Keats first wrote a more punning "texture" for "woof" – *texere* being Latin for *weave*). The sonnet is aimed at this success, of love becoming a manageable, even salvational text: "But, as I've read Love's missal through to-day, / He'll let me sleep, seeing I fast and pray" (13–14).

Yet this wit does not quite balance the books, for the poet, too, has become a text, a cliché of Love-convention, its latest iteration. Keats's couplet, with its stock figures and stylized sentiment, might have come out of a Renaissance anthology, as the work of any practiced sonneteer. Expressions of love, protesting autonomy, authenticity, and spontaneity, are also, paradoxically, the most prone to formula. Keats's alertness to this ironic effect is evident enough when he asks his "dear Girl" to consider the poverty of "artificial Passion" (*KL* 2.140–41), however gallant; "I have met with women whom I really think would like to be married to a Poem," he wrote to her a little earlier (2.127). Any explanation of feeling, epistolary or poetic, has to treat with artifice, but a lover's casting in with tradition may court with a vengeance Eliot's axiom that "Poetry is not a turning loose of emotion, but an escape from emotion; it is not the expression of personality, but an escape from personality" ("Tradition," 10). One poet's escape route is another poet's imprisonment in artifices of personality.

At the same time, Eliot's stark alternatives (poetry is not "turning loose" but an "escape from" emotion) frames the threat Keats recognized when he wrote to Reynolds of having "escaped from" the pressing sorrow of Tom's illness into "the relief, the feverous relief of Poetry": "I have relapsed into those abstractions which are my only life" (*KL* 1.370). The fragility of the illusion is inescapable: escape is a sympathetic relapse, relief another fever. "I live now in a continual fever," he told Dilke the day before, adding "I really have not self possession" (1.369). By the time Keats realizes his possession by Fanny Brawne, he knows that poetry will be feverous. The sonnet to her that begins "I cry your mercy" is a single-sentence cry, where syntax ruptures, grammar contracts and disjoins, meters halt and fracture, and poetic form is pressed to its limits. It is a high-stakes gamble. To Stuart Curran, "Keats's condensation of uncontrollable passion" by means of "a breathtaking technical mastery" creates "a virtuoso display as an end in itself," yet "such a polished representation of frenzy, in which the polarities of plenitude and emptiness are discovered to be the same, strains the sonnet form to the utmost and bears intimations of decadence."[10] Curran's Keats is a consummate artist at the brink of failure. In this utmost strain, technical virtuosity may expose a too palpable, too momentary stay against confusion:

> I cry your mercy – pity – love! – aye, love,
>> Merciful love that tantalises not,
> One-thoughted, never wand'ring, guileless love,
>> Unmask'd, and being seen – without a blot!
> O, let me have thee whole, – all, – all – be mine!
>> That shape, that fairness, that sweet minor zest
> Of love, your kiss, those hands, those eyes divine,
>> That warm, white, lucent, million-pleasured breast, –
> Yourself – your soul – in pity give me all,
>> Withhold no atom's atom or I die,
> Or living on perhaps, your wretched thrall,
>> Forget, in the mist of idle misery,
> Life's purposes, – the palate of my mind
> Losing its gust, and my ambition blind.

The phrase "I cry your mercy" is part of the crisis. Usually idiomatic ("I beg your pardon"), here it is dramatic desperation, elaborated with a rhetoric of negatives ("never wand'ring, guileless," "without a blot") that can't help but recall Othello's unhinged retort to his beloved's protest of never-wandering love: "I cry your mercy, / I took you for that cunning whore of Venice" (4.2.90–91). Tradition, *pace* Eliot, shows no escape.[11]

The phantom fate of living as the wretched thrall of love, with the rest of life a "mist," is the encompassing tradition, the old Petrarchan fate that a swerve into Shakespearean sonnet-form cannot avoid. The Petrarchan project is to turn the beloved into words and signs, a mode of representation, argues Nancy Vickers, that "safely permits and perpetuates" the poet's fascination and unifies his poetic self ("his text, his 'corpus'") in "the repetition of her dismembered image." Yet the result, Vickers continues, may be only "a collection of imperfect signs, signs that, like fetishes, affirm absence by their presence": the poet "speaks his anxiety in the hope of finding repose through enunciation, of re-membering the lost body, of effecting an inverse incarnation – her flesh made word," but "successes are ephemeral, and failures become a way of life."[12] This is surely Keats's fate. That his sonnet's key term of incarnation, that thrice reiterated *all*, gets absorbed and reversed (as word and idea) into *thrall* is just one of the treacheries of form. Is Keats remembering the voice he had another archetypally bereft lover hear: "death pale were they all / They cried La belle dame sans merci / Thee hath in thrall" (*KL* 2.96)? If, as William Wimsatt argues, rhymes "impose upon the logical pattern of expressed argument a kind of fixative counterpattern of alogical implication," such rhyme-work is intensified when, as here, the argument itself is about being transfixed and fixated. For then rhymes apply a parallel logic.[13]

Another treachery in Keats's sonnet is its formation as an apostrophe. Invested as "a figure of vocation," a performance of poetic power to invoke presences, the sonnet's enactment of such "calling" is turned back by irrevocable absence.[14] The very vocative, "I cry," releases a rhyme of this fated isolation: the echo at the end of the line, "aye," a cry that puns on its utterer ("I") to leave the self only self-answered. "I cry," moreover, reaches a delayed, yet treacherous, rhyme in line ten's terminal "I die." (If, in the rhyme scheme, "I die" is supposed to be partnered with "misery" [12], the weakness of this rhyme, both in sound and stress, releases "I die" to its stronger chime with "I cry.") The rhyming of *love* solely with its repetitions (end-rhymed and internal) is another treacherous echoing. All these ironies of form are the verbal swirl of an interiority in which the mind is both subject and object, blind to all but the circle of desire upon itself. In "my ambition blind," is "blind" adjective or verb?

When Keats confessed to his "dear Girl" in August 1819, "it seems to me that a few more moments thought of you would uncrystallize and dissolve me," he knew the antidote: "I must not give way to it – but turn to my writing again – if I fail I shall die hard" (*KL* 2.142). In thoughts that uncrystallize and dissolve, sonnet-writing may promise self-possession, only to betray such promise. In an ode to her that begins "What can I do to drive away / Remembrance from my eyes?" Keats plays out the question for thirty lines. Then, as if to remember some poetic learning, he turns its last iteration, "Where shall I learn to get my peace again?" (30), into the first line of a sonnet-stanza, fourteen iambic pentameters, twelve in couplets, mapped on a quasi-Shakespearean trajectory to forceful epigramatic summation:[15]

> Where shall I learn to get my peace again?
> To banish thoughts of that most hateful land,
> Dungeoner of my friends, that wicked strand
> Where they were wreck'd and live a wrecked life;

That monstrous region, whose dull rivers pour
Ever from their sordid urns unto the shore,
Unown'd of any weedy-haired gods;
Whose winds, all zephyrless, hold scourging rods,
Iced in the great lakes, to afflict mankind;
Whose rank-grown forests, frosted, black, and blind,
Would fright a Dryad; whose harsh herbaged meads
Make lean and lank the starv'd ox while he feeds;
There flowers have no scent, birds no sweet song,
And great unerring Nature once seems wrong.   (30–43)

Having complained of sonnet-constraint, Keats now motivates it: this sonnet-stanza conceives the whole world as a dungeon. He even risks a tight final couplet ("seldom a pleasing effect" in sonnets, he had said [*KL* 2.108]) in order to amplify a sarcastic echo of the famous close of the first epistle of Pope's *Essay on Man*:[16]

All Nature is but Art, unknown to thee;
All Chance, Direction, which thou canst not see;
All Discord, Harmony, not understood;
All partial Evil, universal Good:
And, spite of Pride, in erring Reason's spite,
One truth is clear, "Whatever IS, is RIGHT."   (1.289–94)

The metrically tortured lines that precede Keats's closing couplet anticipate his summary reversing of the Popean epigram, the whole constituting his latest and most bitter satire of such easy "tallies" of rationalizing tautology (so he complained of Popean poetics in *Sleep and Poetry* 194–99). That Keats ironizes this kind of couplet in the event of a sonnet embedded in an ode extends his critique to the sonnet's famously rounded dramas: "the sonnet swelling loudly / Up to its climax and then dying proudly" (*To Charles Cowden Clarke* 60–61). In this late ode, Keats writes a sonnet-stanza that swells and amplifies the lover's anguish into such a hellishly limitless world-view that the poet is willing to reverse his initial petition to be relieved (merely) of a longing for the "liberty" lost to love (6):

O, the sweetness of the pain!
Give me those lips again!
Enough! Enough! it is enough for me
To dream of thee!   (54–57)

In this revised imagination, pain is at least sweet. The rhyme with *again* half-puns "a gain" in saying that it is "Enough! Enough!" to be just an anguished lover. But the full sentence attenuates even this gain: *me* and *thee* join only in a rhyme played through the (metrically stressed) fantasy bond, *dream*, the restless half-life that produces the poet's initial anguish.

The wish for poetic form to work a dream resolution of worldly anguish is contested again by formal dynamics in *A Dream, After Reading Dante's episode of Paulo and Francesca* (a sonnet Keats transcribed in the letter of 1819 that included "Incipit alter Sonneta"). Not only were these lovers doomed by the hostilities of their own world, but their romance had also received fresh attacks in Keats's world, in the Tory reviews of Hunt's *The Story of Rimini*. Publishing this sonnet in Hunt's journal *The Indicator* (28 June 1820), Keats deliberately sets it in this arena. *A Dream* is a satire on the illusion of dreaming the dungeon dragon-world away with an escape into poetry:

> As Hermes once took to his feathers light,
> When lulled Argus, baffled, swoon'd and slept,
> So on a Delphic reed, my idle spright
> So play'd, so charm'd, so conquer'd, so bereft
> The dragon-world of all its hundred eyes;
> And, seeing it asleep, so fled away –   (*Indicator* text 1–6)

Worldly antagonists may be charmed into fictions (Argus, a dragon), but this is no simple flight into imagination. Keats's language brings in its wake a text in which disciplinary eyes are wakeful, multiple, and intent to drive lovers into the storms of human history: the Cherubim deputized to eject Adam and Eve from Eden, their shapes "Spangl'd with eyes more numerous than those / Of *Argus*, and more wakeful than to drowse, / Charm'd with *Arcadian* Pipe, the Pastoral Reed / Of *Hermes*" (*Paradise Lost* 10.130–33). The shape of Keats's imagination whirls through this portent of radical grief to "that second circle of sad hell" (9), where the fair *form* of imagination is coupled in rhyme to a melancholy *storm*:

> Where 'mid the gust, the world-wind, and the flaw
> Of rain and hailstones, lovers need not tell
> Their sorrows. Pale were the sweet lips I saw,
> Pale were the lips I kiss'd, and fair the form
> I floated with about that melancholy storm.   (10–14)

With tacit allusion to Shakespeare's terse sonnet closures, Keats's couplet deploys a semantically charged enjambment: a desired fair form possessed by the poet even amidst a storm. The poem's dreamiest syntax, the alliterative lilt of "fair the form / I floated with," seems even to soften the "melancholy storm." But *storm* is the last word, and more than a few readers have sensed a coda to *The Eve of St. Agnes*.

As the letter-text shows, a storm of worldly realities was the genesis of this poetic *Dream*. Writing to George and Georgiana in April 1819, Keats was fuming over a practical joke played on Tom (recently deceased): in a "cruel deception," one of Tom's friends had sent him love-letters signed "Amena Bellefila"; he fell for the ruse and was humiliated when it was exposed. Still burning at this "diabolical scheme," Keats means "to be prudently vengeful" with "the villain," and it is from this fantasy that his letter moves into his infernal dream (*KL* 2.90–91):

> I will harm him all I possibly can – I have no doubt I shall be able to do so – Let us leave him to his misery alone except when we can throw in a little more – The fifth canto of Dante pleases me more and more – it is that one in which he meets with Paulo and Franc<h>esca – I had passed many days in rather a low state of mind and in the midst of them I dreamt of being in that region of Hell. The dream was one of the most delightful enjoyments I ever had in my life – I floated about the whirling atmosphere as it is described with a beautiful figure to whose lips mine were joined a[s] it seem'd for an age – and in the midst of all this cold and darkness I was warm.

Keats describes his dream of Dante's Hell as an escape from his own "low state of mind" and his hellish anger over Tom's suffering. Yet this seeming counterworld, however erotic, delightful, and warm (even on the verge of inspiring a rhyme that would move from *harm* to *warm*), is a consciously oppositional desire, a fantasy formed by the pressures of historical existence, but never in isolation from these, even as the romance of Paolo and Francesca never could be.

Keats's last lyrics are always alert to how poetic form may charm and then expose illusion. "Physician Nature," perhaps the last ode he wrote, takes one last risk. It is the only poem in which he writes the name "Fanny" and then puts it in a scheme of rhyme. Inspired by anxiety about their separation and her social life without him, as he was recovering from that haemorrhage of February 1820, Keats's ode tests an impossible dream:

> Let me begin my dream.
> I come – I see Thee, as Thou standest there,
> Beckon me out into the wintry air.   (6–8)[17]

"My dear Fanny," he wrote in a note these same weeks, "When I send this round I shall be in the front parlour watching to see you show yourself for a minute in the garden. How illness stands as a barrier betwixt me and you!" (*KL* 2.263). The ode-poet worries that his "dearest love, sweet home of all my fears / And hopes" (9–10), is attracting other eyes: "Who now, with greedy looks, eats up my feast?" (17); "do not turn / The current of your Heart from me," he pleads (21–22), punning with bleak metaformal wit on the "turn" of the poetic line. He at last introduces the name *Fanny* at the top of the fourth stanza:

> Why this – you'll say – my Fanny! is not true;
>   Put your soft hand upon your snowy side,
> Where the heart beats: confess – 'tis nothing new –
>   Must not a woman be
>   A feather on the Sea,
> Sway'd to and fro by every wind and tide? –
>   Of as uncertain speed
>   As blow ball from the mead? (33–40)

The stanza that names her coerces her confession to a generic fault in "woman."

This is a striking categorical escalation – or, perhaps less so, if we see it propelled by another young, vivacious, heartbreakingly inconstant woman whom Keats loved, also named Fanny. "My seal is mark'd [. . .] with my Mother's initial F for Fanny," he explained to Fanny Brawne, in the only extant letter in which he even mentions his mother (*KL* 2.133). Fanny Keats had a "doting fondness" for all her children, but "particularly John" (so George recalls); she "was extremely fond of him and humoured him in every whim, of which he had not a few" (*KC* 1.314; 288). Why, then, would Keats give Joseph Severn the impression that "his greatest misfortune had been that from his infancy he had no mother"?[18] Perhaps her painfully erratic behavior. A little more than two months after his father died, in 1804, eight-year-old John's mother remarried, but unhappily. She disappeared mysteriously soon afterwards, and returned 1807, ill and consumptive. John took charge, nursing her, reading to her, fixing her meals, and guarding her door as she slept. She never recovered, and died in 1810, when he was fourteen. These extremes of doting fondness and abandonment – the first inexplicable, the second mortal – may have knotted what this favorite son would later call his "gordian complication of feelings" about women (*KL* 1.342): love betrayed to pain and anger at her disappearance; relief and hostility at her return; guilt over her debilitation (as if it answered an angry wish to punish her); grief and anger aggravated by guilt at her death – at once her final punishment and the latest, most radical abandonment. The myth of "no mother" eradicates at its source an insoluble complication. The letter in which Keats mentions her to the other Fanny is full of grievance: "You cannot conceive how I ache to be with you: how I would die for one hour [. . .] The first week I knew you I wrote myself your vassal.[. . .] I am lost. [. . .] You absorb me" (2.132–33). "I have been endeavouring to wean myself from you," he writes two months later, on the verge of recognizing the regression (2.160). Keats's "dearest Girl" Fanny Brawne was fated for already haunted psychic territory, scripted for mythologies that alternately charge her with and defend her from her lover's worst imaginings.

Little wonder that "Physician Nature" casts her doubly, in bitter suspicion and sacred worship, as if Keats were using the language of the latter – "Let none profane my Holy See of Love" (51) – to control the former. This oscillation shapes the stanzas: most open with three pentameter lines (*aba*) that expand an expression of pain, desire, reverence, or suspicion; next is a trimeter couplet (*cc*) that yields a pause or suspense; the verse then returns to a rhyming pentameter (*b*), almost always completing a syntactic unit; then it closes in a second trimeter couplet (*dd*). The form is designed to organize a flux into accomplished pairings and completed patterns. Yet the name *Fanny* proves a problem. In a self-answering to his taunting question to her about the wayward character of "woman," Keats elaborates:

> I know it – and to Know it is despair
>   To one who loves you as I love sweet {~~Girl~~} Fanny,
> Whose heart goes fluttering for you every where,
>   Nor when away you roam,
>   Dare keep its wretched home:
> Love, Love alone, has pains severe and many –
>   Then Loveliest keep me free,
>   From torturing Jealousy.   (41–48)

The stanza-patterning of *Fanny* with *many* is strained by a feminine imperfect rhyme (indeed, *many* seems more prone to a tripling with *free* and *Jealousy*). Yet Keats wanted to retain this effect of dissonance, having tried the lines variously without rhyming *Fanny*, even discarding the name altogether.[19] It is as if he meant to recognize what the resistant rhyme reports: as the feminine measure *Fanny* at once teases at and slips poetic control, so its referent, intensely desired, seems to be slipping out of the poet's life, "this emprisoning of you," as he criticized his desires in February 1820 (*KL* 2.257).

"My dearest Girl," he writes to her that August, "I wish you could invent some means to make me at all happy without you. Every hour I am more and more concentrated in you" (*KL* 2.311). The helpless fascination remains, the letter concluding with desire given over to the fantasy of two equal surrenders: "I wish I was either in your a[r]ms full of faith or that a Thunder bolt would strike me" (313). He was already set to leave for Italy, and this seems to have been the last time he wrote to her. But if Keats is "averse" to the painful seeing of her, his habitual remedy of verse continues to draw his imagination (*KL* 2.312):

If my health would bear it, I could write a Poem which I have in my head, which would be a consolation for people in such a situation as mine. I would show some one in Love as I am, with a person living in such Liberty as you do. Shakspeare always sums up matters in the most sovereign manner. Hamlet's heart was full of such Misery as mine is when he said to Ophelia "Go to a Nunnery, go, go!"

Keats's *with* clause is doubly damning: "in Love with" such a person; "in Love, even as" such a person lives in liberty from (in faithless inconstancy to) the claim of love – hence the bitter echo of Hamlet's self-concentrated misery (*Hamlet* 3.1).

Summoning Shakespeare's "sovereign manner," Keats's revision of "Bright Star," drafted on his voyage to Italy, uses Shakespearean sonnet-form to entreat astrologic transcendence in the deathwards progressing of desire. He begins with an address to a seemingly desirable ideal, yet by the second line is defining this by subtraction:

> Bright Star, would I were stedfast as thou art –
> Not in lone splendor hung aloft the night . . .

But with this subtraction so leisurely, so attractively elaborating the ideal ostensibly rejected, the sestet dramatically synthesizes the apparent contradiction of tone and argument. The steadfast qualities of the stellar ideal are given a vital, sensuous relation to fair human love:

> No – yet still stedfast, still unchangeable
>   Pillow'd upon my fair love's ripening breast,
> To feel for ever its soft swell and fall,
>   Awake for ever in a sweet unrest,
> Still, still to hear her tender-taken breath,
> And so live ever – or else swoon to death –   (9–14)

In this delicate suspense of present participles and infinitive verbs, there is still only a desire of "would." Moreover, it is a problematic romance: a perpetual babyhood interchangeable with death, plotted by incantations of *still* (9 and 13). From the perspective of line fourteen, the sense of "for ever" gathers that of stasis, which as we know from *Ode on a Grecian Urn* ("for ever warm and still to be enjoyed") is also the cold pastoral of death. The final dash is the textual signal that points to this future.

In the nineteenth century, "Bright Star" was called "Keats's Last Sonnet."[20] One of the last pieces of poetry that he may have written shifts its stage of address from the world of the living to the world of the dead:

> This living hand, now wa[r]m and capable
> Of ea[r]nest grasping, would, if it were cold

and in the icy silence of the tomb,
So haunt thy days and chill thy dreaming nights
heat
That thou would wish thine own dry of blood
So in my veins red life might stream again,
and thou be conscience-calm'd – see here it is
I hold it towards you –   (*Facsimile* edition, 258)

These lines manipulate a peculiar revivifying effect against the death so reported, which poetic form abets with a suspense of syntax: the first sentence dilates, displays, and defers the completion of its sense, slowly but relentlessly releasing a subjunctive contingency ("would, if it were . . .") into a daunting consequence ("thou would"). The terse exhortation and declaratives that follow the dash after "conscience-calm'd" sharpen the assault, seeming in their epigrammatic summary almost to parody the close of Shakespearean sonnet. The dilated subjunctive proposition ("would, if it were . . . that thou would") concentrates in a petition of actuality and immediacy; the tone shifts from stagey eloquence to sudden colloquialism; the meters break from an expansive iambic rhythm into a set of spare monosyllables. "Warm is the nerve of a welcoming hand," Keats wrote in some verses of June 1818 that he sent to his brother on the other side of the world (*KL* 1.304). "This living hand" is a macabre parody, conjuring warm life into icy death.

That this conjuration is set both in the present moment of writing and in the future of reading gives it a peculiar shock-*affect* at stark variance to the final *effect* proposed with bitter irony: being "conscience-calm'd." The parting shot, "see here it is / I hold it towards you," issues an invitation, but to what? Does *it* refer to a warm living hand or a cold dead one? The reader has to imagine the present as past, the sensation of earnest grasping as the chilling grip of a nightmare, the actual as spectral, and the spectral as actual. The image of "hand" not only evokes this ghoulishly amputated, somatic animation, but also, by denoting "handwriting," proposes a textual vitality. In this register (as Timothy Bahti has deftly argued), the poem effectively works "for ever": the poet's hand has to be reanimated by the reader, revived as living and capable of writing "This living hand . . . ," and fated, in the sequence described, to write itself back into the silence of the grave, thence to emerge again.[21] The verse breaks off, suspended in mid-line, its last "heated" word, *you*, asking the reader to surrender to the writer in a charged economy of antagonisms – of friendship turned to haunting, of life to death. Has Keats at last made aggressive poetic capital out of the knowledge that anguishes his efforts to give form to his desire for Fanny Brawne?

The canny, even hostile forming of this fragment and the crises of form that affect all of Keats's late lyrics predict the movement of criticism in our own century "beyond formalism" – beyond, that is, the ideal of poetic form once felt to be so capably at work, for both Keats and criticism, in the Great Odes. Yet the Great Odes themselves weirdly point the way "beyond," even in the New Critical climates of reading. In 1953, referring to an understanding of poems as "organic wholes," Earl Wasserman found *Ode to a Nightingale* a "turmoil" of "disintegration," of "patterns flying apart, not coming together," where "forces contend wildly [. . .] not only without resolution, but without possibility of resolution," leaving "no center of reference," merely "bewildering oscillations."[22] Such effects would soon be described as a poetics of indeterminacy. As early as 1959, David Perkins proposed that none of the odes "can be regarded as a settlement or resolution of the central uncertainties"; Stuart Sperry's splendid chapter ("Romantic Irony") on these former icons of New Critical unities described "a state of perpetual *indeterminacy*."[23] The so-called loose, unmasterful verse of Keats's late lyrics now seems the emergence of forces already roiling the Odes, where poetic form is tuned to an investigation of poetic forming as factitious, temporary, and historically situated, thoroughly implicated with systems of experience and processes of language that it cannot transcend. In the poetic forming of his late lyrics, Keats seems, simultaneously, to be working out an anguished but inevitable formalist criticism.

NOTES

1 T. S. Eliot, "Tradition and the Individual Talent" (1917), *Selected Essays: 1917–1932* (New York: Harcourt Brace, 1932), 9–10. For the best New Critical esteem, see Cleanth Brooks on *Ode on a Grecian Urn* ("Keats's Sylvan Historian") and on *Ode to a Nightingale*, "Implications of an Organic Theory of Poetry," *Literature and Belief*, ed. Meyer H. Abrams (New York: Columbia University Press, 1958), 62–63.

2 Robert Gittings, *The Mask of Keats* (Cambridge: Harvard University Press, 1956), 69; H. W. Garrod, *Keats* (Oxford: Clarendon Press, 1926), 59.

3 E. C. Pettet, *On the Poetry of Keats* (Oxford: Clarendon Press, 1957), 246.

4 Walter Jackson Bate, *John Keats*, 620n13; 617–18. John Barnard generously accords an appendix to "The Poems to Fanny Brawne" (*John Keats*, 149–52) yet echoes the familiar judgment "of Keats's loss of control over his conflicting emotions" in a poetry "unresolved in tone and subject, and marred by flaccid writing" (127). To de Man, the "radical change in tone" in these late poems (at once wrapped in intimacies of "self" and anguished by "an acute sense of threatened selfhood") suggests that Keats was about to add more genuine dimension to his poetic development ("Introduction," xxvii–ix). McGann shifts the focus outward, arguing that the "biographical nexus [. . .] reveals the forceful presence of larger, socio-historical frames of reference," within which the poems have to be read ("Keats and the Historical Method in Literary Criticism," *Beauty of Inflections*, 48).

5 For the male writer's vulnerable fantasies of autonomous creativity, see Sonia Hofkosh, "The Writer's Ravishment: Women and the Romantic Author," *Romanticism and Feminism*, ed. Anne K. Mellor (Bloomington: Indiana University Press, 1988), 93–114. For my fuller treatment of issues of form and formalist criticism in Keats's late poetry, see *Formal Charges: The Shaping of Poetry in British Romanticism*, and "What's Wrong with Formalist Criticism?" *Studies in Romanticism* 37 (Spring 1998), 86–93.

6 S. T. Coleridge, *Lectures 1808–1819 On Literature*, ed. R. A. Foakes, 2 vols. (Princeton: Princeton University Press, 1987), 2.224; *Biographia Literaria* (1817), ed. James Engell and W. Jackson Bate, 2 vols. (Princeton: Princeton University Press, 1983), 2.20–23. Hazlitt's lectures at the Surrey Institute, which Keats attended, praised Shakespeare for being "the least of an egotist it was possible to be" (*Complete Works*, ed. P. P. Howe [London: Dent, 1930–34], 5.47), and he typically sharpened the point against Wordsworth's habitual egotism.

7 While *altera* means "another" (it is the sixth he transcribed in this letter), the sentence just after allows a pun on another way to do a sonnet.

8 Karen Swann, "Harassing the Muse," 91. John Hollander traces Keats's "original way of loosening the links of rhyming's chains without actually breaking them or having them slip off," a pattern in which the "distant rhyme words themselves tell intercalated tales in the sonnet's unfolding story"; *Melodious Guile: Fictive Pattern in Poetic Language* (New Haven: Yale University Press, 1988), 94.

9 Here and following, I restore the capitals Stillinger has emended; for Keats's revisions (discussed below), see Stillinger's *The Poems of John Keats*, 491–92.

10 Stuart Curran, *Poetic Form and British Romanticism*, 54.

11 Gittings comments on another related tradition, the echoes, stylistic and thematic, of Chaucer's Troilus in the last lyrics (*The Mask of Keats*, 73–78). Keats knew Shakespeare's Troilus, too: just after met Fanny Brawne, he describes his imaginative identification with one of his love-sick laments, and quotes him to her, June 1820 (*KL* 1.404, 2.294). See Greg Kucich's essay in this volume.

12 Nancy Vickers, "Diana Described: Scattered Woman and Scattered Rhyme," *Writing and Sexual Difference*, ed. Elizabeth Abel (Chicago: University of Chicago Press, 1982), 102–5.

13 William Wimsatt, "One Relation of Rhyme to Reason" (1944); *The Verbal Icon: Studies in the Meaning of Poetry* (Lexington: University of Kentucky Press, 1954), 153.

14 For the rhetorical designs, see Jonathan Culler, "Apostrophe" (1977), *The Pursuit of Signs: Semiotics, Literature, Deconstruction* (Ithaca: Cornell University Press, 1981), 142.

15 For other embedded sonnets in Keats's poetry, see my *Formal Charges*, 282n18.

16 Noted by Miriam Allott, *The Poems of John Keats*, 688.

17 For the verses so preserved, I follow Keats's draft (Stillinger, *Facsimile Edition*, 226–31).

18 Quoted in William Sharp, *The Life and Letters of Joseph Severn* (London: Sampson Low, Marston, 1892), 5n.

19 See Stillinger's *Poems*, 495 and *Facsimile Edition*, 230–31.

20 Milnes first gave it this title in *Life, Letters, and Literary Remains, of John Keats*, 2.306.

21 Timothy Bahti, "Ambiguity and Indeterminacy: The Juncture," *Comparative Literature* 38 (1986), 220–22.

22 Earl R. Wasserman, *The Finer Tone: Keats' Major Poems*, 7, 10, 178, 184, 208.

23 David Perkins, *The Quest for Permanence: The Symbolism of Wordsworth, Shelley, and Keats*, 284; Sperry, *Keats the Poet*, 245, his emphasis.

8

JOHN BARNARD

Keats's letters

"Remembrancing and enchaining"

All letters involve self-representation, even business letters. The elaborate opening and closing salutations adopted in France show the need for an acute awareness of the social positioning of writer and recipient, but also demonstrate that letters, like any literary form, have generic expectations. Most of Keats's letters are personal, written to friends or family, the idiom allowing for a playfulness, intimacy, and directness usually not appropriate for a business letter – though Keats's letter to his new publishers, Taylor and Hessey, 10 June 1817, is a wittily self-conscious performance to offset the awkwardness of immediately requesting an advance. Any letter is a performance addressed to an absent reader (or readers) at some point in the future. As such, it is a potentially dangerous form, since anyone writing a risk-taking letter (whether a request for a loan, an apology, or a declaration of love) must, if it is to succeed, accurately imagine its recipient's response both to the situation itself and to the words and tone chosen.

Keats's marvelously alive letters are always alert to their recipient's interests and their relationship to him. They are also highly conscious of the occasions of their own writing. First published in the mid-nineteenth century, they are widely admired by general readers, and have been extensively used by critics and biographers.[1] For critics, the letters are an invaluable supplement to the poetry, providing variant drafts, comments on the origins and development of certain poems, and eloquent "speculations" (Keats's term) on the nature of poetry or the achievements of predecessors and contemporaries. For biographers, the letters give insight into Keats's mind at work and play, and a record of his experiences, often on a daily basis. Both these enterprises tend to treat the letters as transparent documents of fact. This is the method of Lionel Trilling's fine essay, "The Poet as Hero: Keats in his Letters," which calls on the letters, predominantly, to document Keats's moral and aesthetic self-discovery.[2] But Keats's letters are also performances. The first to focus on the importance of Keats's self-representation in the letters is Christopher Ricks, in his brilliant study, *Keats and Embarrassment*.

Ricks reads the letters as literary texts – ones, moreover, that illuminate the particularities and peculiarities of Keats's poetic language and sensibility. While this fresh and attentive analysis dramatically changed our sense of the letters (and the poems, Ricks's chief concern), it was not particularly interested in the letters as an autonomous body of writing.

Yet it is worth reading Keats's letters in their own right. Setting them as a whole against the corpus of the poetry, there is a case for believing them to be the greater literary achievement. The letters give a remarkably full narrative of Keats's major creative periods, of his swift self-making, and of the development of the intellectual life and mind of a quintessential "Romantic poet." They are a prose analogue to Wordsworth's *Prelude* (later subtitled "Growth of a Poet's Mind"), but unlike that mostly retrospective epic, Keats's letters were written to the minute.[3] Within such a narrative, the poems figure more as works in process than as the completed canonic texts usually discussed. "Our slowness in evolving a poetics of the letter," notes Timothy Webb, has prevented full recognition of the free-standing literary achievement of Keats's letters. Webb, Ricks, and others have begun to develop such an account. Susan Wolfson stresses the self-interrogating character of Keats's "epistolary poetics": "Epistolary composition, for Keats, is an expansive action rather than a closed artefact, one premised on a flux of correspondence where the roles of actor and audience, speculator and spectator continuously and generously interchange." Cedric Watts suggests that the correspondence of Keats's final year can be read as a "collective masterpiece, an epistolary novel consisting of his own letters and those of his friends and acquaintances." Andrew Bennett reads in Keats's letters a parallel analysis of narrative structure in his poetry, while Webb shows how the performative nature of the letters is paradoxically coupled to Keats's sense of the inadequacies of language, in particular of the written word.[4]

Yet notwithstanding this theoretical issue, one of the most striking things about the letters, as opposed to the poetry, is their ability to include the language of everyday life and sociability in Regency London and England, recorded in a variety of linguistic and tonal registers and in a vocabulary ranging from slang (including bawdy puns) to intense but speculative explorations: the holiness of the heart's affections, "Negative Capability," life as a "Mansion of Many Apartments," the march of intellect, "the vale of Soul-making." While Keats's published "Poesy" rarely admits the colloquial or everyday, the letters are full of both, and their nonsense poems for his sister show a talent for light verse that Keats felt unable to exercise in the high calling of "Poesy" for publication. Writing to and for family and his closest friends, he found a space in which to relax, experiment, entertain, memorialize, speculate, pun, and joke, and do so in what is very close to a speaking voice. This, above all, was a space in which he was sure of his audience's interest and support, a space entirely free of the intense anxieties and aggression induced by the expectations of his reading publics (male and female) and their representatives and guides, the periodical reviewers. If Keats's published poems sometimes experiment uneasily with the conventions and decorums of the genre at hand, as a letter-writer he almost always controls the possibilities of this apparently open literary form.

One sign of the remarkable quality of Keats's letters is how many have survived. Their recipients thought them worth keeping, and sharing. The correspondence is virtually coincident with his life as poet. His last letter was written to Charles Brown from Rome on 30 November 1820 (*KL* 2.359–60), when he had given up poetry, less than three months before his death. Almost the first we know of, just five years before, is a verse epistle (Keats dated it "November 1815"; *KL* 1.100–3) to G. F. Mathew, a would-be poet and, briefly, a friend. Keats would place this first in the section of three "Epistles" in his first volume, *Poems* (1817), a section also including *To My Brother George* and *To Charles Cowden Clarke*, dated August and September 1816, respectively.[5] Such epistles, along with poems addressed to women in his circle and to friends and mentors such as Leigh Hunt and B. R. Haydon, show Keats writing for a sympathetic (and encouraging) private audience. *Poems* had an inbuilt coterie audience, and its personal poems were simultaneously public and private.

It is this circle, not coincidentally, which preserved the large majority of Keats's letters or transcribed lost originals, the latter chiefly made by Richard Woodhouse (the lawyer who advised Taylor and Hessey, Keats's publishers) and Keats's brother George in America, who were convinced of Keats's importance as a poet. More letters came to light following Milnes's publication in 1848, and in 1891 Senorita Rosa Llanos Keats presented the British Library with a substantial collection of letters written by Keats to her ancestor and his sister, Fanny. By the early twentieth century most of the known letters had been located and were brought together in H. E. Rollins's magisterial edition (1958).[6]

Rollins includes 320 letters, mostly from Keats, but also some to him. The latter show that Keats's letters are only one side of an ongoing conversation. For example, Keats's apparently slight poem, *Robin Hood* (in the 1820 volume), is best understood through the poetic and intellectual exchanges with his friend and fellow poet J. H. Reynolds early in 1818.[7] And it was a letter from Woodhouse later that year that prompted his memorable speculation about the "camelion Poet" of no fixed identity (*KL* 1.378–82, 386–88). Yet the relative paucity of surviving letters *to* Keats is due partly to Keats himself, who, on at least one occasion (in May 1819) made "a general conflagration of all old Letters and Memorandums, which had become of no interest to me" (2.112). This is an irreplaceable loss of context, for Keats's letters are vitally intertextual. Most obviously, they refer to other letters: ones Keats has received, ones he has written, ones he apologizes for not having written. The letters contain about seventy drafts of poems or excerpts of work in progress. Many of these were sent to Reynolds, whose relationship with Keats from April 1817 to May 1818 helped him work free of Hunt's influence. Other poems were copied for his siblings, most remarkably in the long journal-letters to George and Georgiana in America from 1819. Keats's letters also refer to other writers; he quotes from them, sometimes by name, sometimes not, and on occasion copies out long passages (Shakespeare, Burton, Hazlitt). And he reports jokes, conversations, and stories from his immediate circle. The variety of voices and texts jostling for place alongside one another is a consistent source of the letters' animation and vitality. Relatively few are concerned with business. In numbers of pages, letters to his immediate family account for 36 percent, 44 percent if those to Fanny Brawne are counted. Correspondence with Reynolds accounts for another 9 percent. The rest are mainly, but not exclusively, to men, including long letters to Haydon, Woodhouse, Taylor, Brown, and Bailey.

These facts reveal some of the roles letters played for Keats. One was to keep in active contact with his increasingly separated and vulnerable siblings, and to keep his brothers abreast of the development of his poetry, poetic ideas, and his plans. The sustained correspondence with Reynolds and shorter exchanges with Haydon, Bailey, Taylor, and Woodhouse center on his poetic ambitions and the nature of poetry and the poet (a subject less prominent in his letters to Fanny Brawne except insofar as, in very practical terms, his lack of income impeded their marriage). Writing letters also served Keats as a relief from poetic composition, as a preparation for it, and sometimes as occasions for poems, such as the troubled verse letter he wrote to Reynolds, 24 March 1818, which, unlike other such epistles, Keats did not choose to publish. He seems to have "parcelld out" some days for "Letter Writing" (*KL* 1.219). On 23 January 1818 he reports, "this is my fourth letter this morning" (1.215): these were a brief letter to Haydon, a business letter to his publisher, one to Bailey (containing *Ode* ["Chief of Organic Numbers"]) and one to his brothers, completed the next day (1.207–17). Between 21 and 31 January, in fact, he wrote at least six letters, composed six new poems, began to prepare Book II of *Endymion* for press, and heard Hazlitt lecture on poetry at the Surrey Institution.

This writing (and receiving) of letters was of crucial importance to Keats as a brother, friend, writer, and lover. But writing-paper was expensive, as was postage. There were several ways of sending and paying for postal service.[8] Within London, letters could be exchanged very quickly. Mail from elsewhere in England took rather more time and expense, and mail to and from America was slow and unforecastable. These factors had a direct bearing on the forms of Keats's letters. Take, for example, the letter he wrote to Clarke after the two had stayed up all night, in October 1816, reading a "beautiful copy" of Chapman's folio *Homer* that Clarke had on loan. Keats finally left "at day-spring" for his lodging in Southwark, about two miles away. Just a few hours later, by ten o'clock, Clarke found on his breakfast table "a letter with no other enclosure than Keats's famous sonnet, 'On First Looking into Chapman's Homer.'" Keats had composed it in the early hours and was able to send it straight to Clarke by messenger.[9] While the accompanying letter is no longer known to exist, a similarly excited and swift exchange, also involving a sonnet, has survived. On the evening of 19 November 1817 Haydon made a profile sketch in his studio of Keats. The next day Keats sent him the sonnet beginning "Great Spirits now on Earth are sojourning" by messenger. Spaciously written out, the brief note and poem (praising Wordsworth, Hunt, and Haydon) take up one side of a half sheet. Probably using the same messenger, Haydon replied at once, proposing a change: why not end the climactic question, "hear ye not the hum / Of mighty Workings in a distant Mart?" (12–13), at "Workings," omitting the rest of the line? The next afternoon Keats replied, "My feelings entirely fall in with yours' in regard to the Elipsis and I glory in it," wrote out the sonnet again, and sent it off by the twopenny post, stamped at seven o'clock that evening. Later that night, Haydon showed the sonnet to Reynolds, and overnight Reynolds wrote his own sonnet lauding Haydon, sending it to him the next day, 22 November.[10]

When, however, Keats was staying at Shanklin in the summer of 1819 – a self-imposed exile from Fanny Brawne so that he could concentrate on composing – he warned her that there was no "opportunity of sending letters every day" (even as he urged her to "Write speedily") (*KL* 2.127). This single-sheet letter, written 8 July, was stamped in Newport, Isle of Wight, on 10 July (2.126), as prepaid to cover the one hundred miles by mail coach to London. Keats would have had to walk the nine miles from Shanklin to Newport, or use a messenger or the carrier. The post had to leave Newport in time to catch the four p.m. packet from Cowes, four miles away, to Southampton where the mail would be transferred to the eight p.m. mail coach in order to reach London the following morning. Fanny would have received the letter in Hampstead by the afternoon of 11 July, all at a cost to Keats of nine pence. At best, there was a four or five day gap in their exchange of letters. This kind of letter – written outside London and using the normal mail service – took a standard form and was charged by distance from London.

The whole production of a letter was far more crafted than we are used to today. In addition to paper, it involved quill, penknife (for quill-sharpening), ink and inkwell, blotting sand, sealing wax and on occasion a seal-stamp. Keats wrote in a bold and regular hand, on occasion personalizing his page. In letters to his sister, he frequently used a Tassie gem to impress Shakespeare's head or a lyre on his letters' black wax seal, and he gave her one of Shakespeare for sealing her own letters.[11] In a letter of 10 July 1818 to Tom, he marked off the left-hand side of the first page, in order to write out his mock Scots ballad, "Ah! ken ye what I met the day," starting his letter proper on the right-hand side; in a letter to him the following week he sketched Loch Lomond, to flesh out his description.[12] A single sheet gave him three and half pages for the text of the letter itself (*KL* 1.367). He would fold the sheet in half and, with the fold to the left, write his first page, then open the sheet and fill the next two pages, on either side of the fold. He would then refold the sheet, and with the first page on top, fold the top and bottom to meet at the middle. This left two quarter pages for more letter text. The letter was finally folded from the left and right sides, but slightly unequally, to allow a seal of wax or gum to secure what became the rear blank, leaving the unsealed side blank, ready for the address. Each sheet was charged at a standard mileage rate, with any additional sheets (folded inside the first) costing the same again. Given this expense, double use could be made of a page by "crossing" its script – that is, turning the page 90 degrees and writing more, at right angles. Keats wrote in this way to Bailey, 22 November 1817, and to Taylor, 5 September 1819, when he crossed his letter with a sample from *Lamia*.[13]

For business letters, the matter to hand, not space, dictated length. But for letters to family or friends, Keats, like his contemporaries, usually filled all the space available, leaving narrow margins. Hence on one occasion he felt he had to ask Reynolds's forgiveness "for not filling up the whole sheet" (*KL* 2.147), and this expectation encouraged him to play out his material, particularly at the end of letters. Keats's deliberate use of space is evident in the letter he wrote to Shelley, 16 August 1820, and in the last letter that he wrote to Mrs. Brawne (Fanny's mother). The letter to Shelley (2.322–23), written from Hampstead, replies to Shelley's own (which Keats has "beside" him), generously inviting Keats to stay in Italy, a warmer climate for his failing health. Relations between the two had never been easy, and were probably more difficult for Keats, who felt condescended to by Shelley, the titled and more established poet, still publishing, in fact, with the firm that had been glad to rid themselves of Keats after the commercial failure of the 1817 *Poems*. So it matters that Keats addresses Shelley as a social and intellectual equal, beginning "My dear Shelley." Thanking him for the invitation, Keats deals courageously and openly with his physical state, then thanks Shelley for sending (through Leigh Hunt) a copy of his recently published play, *The Cenci*. After commenting on the domination of contemporary poetry by commercial considerations, Keats, who has said that the only part he can be "judge of" is "the Poetry, and dramatic effect," delivers his judgment on Shelley's poem (and, by implication, Shelley's work as a whole):

> <u>an artist</u> must serve Mammon – he must have "self-concentration" selfishness perhaps. You I am sure will forgive me for sincerely remarking that you might curb your magnanimity and be more of an artist, and "load every rift" of your subject with ore. The thought of such discipline must fall like cold chains upon you, who perhaps never sat with your wings furl'd for six Months together. And is not this extraordina[r]y talk for the writer of Endymion? whose mind was like a pack of scattered cards – I am pick'd up and sorted to a pip.

Keats writes with wit, self-knowledge, and irony. His quotation from Spenser's description of the Cave of Mammon (*Faerie Queene* Book 2, Canto 7.28.5) tells Shelley that he has the potential to create the true gold of poetry ("Embost with massy gold of glorious gift," as Spenser describes the Cave in the previous line). Keats's images of "cold chains" and "wings" are surely and deliberately Shelleyan, while "magnanimity" is a flattering, but accurate, characterization of Shelley's beliefs as a poet and thinker. Keats trades upon this "magnanimity" in his assurance of Shelley's forgiveness for his frank, "sincere" advice, and he gains credit from his self-critical admission of the insufficiency of the disordered poet guilty of writing *Endymion*; "pick'd up and sorted to a pip" balances the confession with a claim of subsequent maturation. Wishing Shelley well with *Prometheus Unbound*, Keats sends a copy of his own most recent volume:

> I remember you advising me not to publish my first-blights [*Poems* (1817)], on Hampstead heath – I am returning advice upon your hands. Most of the Poems in the volume I send you have been written above two years, and would never have been publish'd but from a hope of gain; so you see I am inclined enough to take your advice now.

Keats can give advice to the extent that he can take it himself, an equality demonstrated by the exchange of gift volumes. He closes his letter in a polite gentlemanly manner:

> I must exp[r]ess once more my deep sense of your kindness, adding my sincere thanks and respects for Mrs Shelley. In the hope of soon seeing you {I} remain

> most sincerely {yours,}
> John Keats —

This very carefully composed letter must have been difficult to write, and the sign of its studied nature, despite its easy colloquial movement and syntax, is the extra care Keats took with his handwriting – and the fact that he fills only two and a half (rather than the available three and a half) pages of the sheet (see Motion's *Keats*, 528–29 for a photograph).

Keats's letter to Mrs. Brawne differs in one respect, but is tellingly similar in another. It was written two months later, on 22 or 24 October (after Keats had embarked for Italy, sensing he would never return) on board the *Maria Crowther* while it was lying in quarantine off Naples. Keats could not bring himself to write directly to Fanny Brawne, perhaps because there was no style answerable to his situation, but also because he despised the sentimentality of Rousseau's love letters. "Thank god that you are fair and can love me without being Letter-written and sentimentaliz'd into it," he had told her in February, referring to that example (*KL* 2.267). He tells Mrs. Brawne about the journey, his fellow passengers and the extraordinary helpfulness of his companion Joseph Severn, and his impressions of the Italians. Throughout, he interjects messages for Fanny. Towards the end he reports, "Severn is writing to Haslam, and I have just asked him to request Haslam to send you his account of my health" (2.350; Haslam was one of his oldest and dearest friends, who had made the arrangements for Keats's travel to Italy) – thoughtfully ensuring that the family will receive an outsider's neutral report. The rest of the letter moves from himself to Fanny, to her family, and to Keats's particular friends – a reaching out from Italy to those he has left behind:

> O what an account I could give you of the Bay of Naples if I could once more feel myself a Citizen of this world – I feel a Spirit in my Brain would lay it forth pleasantly – O what a misery it is to have an intellect in splints! My Love again to Fanny – tell Tootts I wish I could pitch her a basket of grapes – and tell Sam the fellows catch here with a line a little fish much like an anchovy, pull them up fast   Remember me to M^{rs} and Mr Dilke – mention to Brown that I wrote him a letter at Port[s]mouth which I did not send and am in doubt if he will ever see it.
>
> my dear Mrs Brawne
yours sincerely and affectionate
John Keats —

This letter obeys the decorum of a family letter, written evenly and clearly and filling the whole sheet.[14] Yet at the last moment Keats gave way to his feelings: at the foot, below his signature, is scrawled in a smaller shaky hand, "Good bye Fanny! god bless you." The difference between the carefully shaped handwriting in the body of the letter and that in the postscript shows how difficult it must have been for Keats, seriously ill on board ship, to maintain mastery of his writing materials (quill, inkpot, and paper) for the length of this letter. The postscript's truthfulness belies the control evident throughout the rest of his letter, and moves towards the wordlessness of grief and despair.

Keats's journal letters, composed over several days, belong to a quite different genre. His first ones, in the summer of 1818, were written to Tom from his Northern walking tour with Brown. But his sense of audience was wider, as the close of his letter from the Lake District, 27 June 1818 (*KL* 1.301), shows:

> Let any of my friends see my letters – they may not be interested in descriptions – descriptions are bad at all times [. . .] I am anxious you should taste a little of our pleasure; it may not be an unpleasant thing, as you have not the fatigue [. . .] Content that probably three or four pair of eyes whose owners I am rather partial to will run over these lines I remain; and moreover that I am your affectionate brother John.

It is clear from this and other references that while Keats wrote with a particular individual in mind, he also expected his letters to be read by his circle of friends. The letters from Scotland not only bound Keats to his brother, but were meant to bring his friends together round Tom, who was on his own in London, ill with consumption (he would die by year's end). A further role of these letters, as a memorial of his tour, appears in Keats's initial intention of copying them into his first long journal-letter to George and Georgiana:

> For want of something better I shall proceed to give you some extracts from my Scotch Letters – Yet now I think on it why not send you the letters themselves – I have three of them at present – I beli[e]ve Haydon has two which I will get in time.
>
> (21 October 1818; *KL* 1.401)

Keats never did recover the letters he had written to Tom on 10–14 July and 3–6 August; instead of returning them, Haydon promptly pasted them into his journal (*KL* 1.327n, 352n). Keats may have sent as many as five letters to Tom, but regarded them in effect as his own property, or perhaps felt that what had been written to one brother in journal form could be quite properly posted off in another larger journal letter to the other.

The ability to send off additional letters to George and Georgiana points to a radical difference between mainland and overseas post. Length was virtually unconstrained, hence the relaxation ("For want of something better"). But getting post to America was an elaborate and slow business. Keats had help in sending off his first such letter (14–31 October 1818; 1.391–405): Haslam took all the sheets, except for the very last which Keats wrote and sent on to him by the twopenny post, to a firm of London stockbrokers (Capper and Hazlewood, 15 Angel Court, Throgmorton Street), where it was put into the Boston post bag to be forwarded by an intermediary to await the next ship bound for Philadelphia, in six weeks' time (1.401, 405). The service was erratic. Keats's letter of 12 November 1819 had gotten only as far as Edgartown, Massachusetts by 23 February 1820 on its way to Kentucky (2.228n), and he had to wait almost a year for George's reply to his first letter (promptly sharing it with Georgiana's mother, then others; 2.109). The family's physical separation and the yawning gaps in communication meant that Keats used the open form of the long journal letter to try to overcome this distance through "remembrance" and "enchaining":

> Tuesday – You see I keep adding a sheet daily till I send the packet off – which I shall not do for a few days as I am inclined to write a good deal: for there can be nothing so remembrancing and enchaining as a good long letter be it composed of what it may – (21 September 1819; 2.208)

By sending news, reports on work in progress, drafts, jokes, gossip, and a sometimes daily account of his own doings (even, occasionally, issues of *The Examiner* [KL 2.213], to keep George and his wife in touch with the world they had left behind), Keats also kept them alive in his consciousness:

> – Suppose Brown or Haslam or any one whom I understand in the n{e}ther degree to what I do you, were in America, they would be so much the farth{er} from me in proportion as their identity was less impressed upon me. Now the reason why I do not feel at the present moment so far from you is that I rememb{er} your Ways and Manners and actions; I [have] known you[r] manner of thinking, you[r] manner of feeling: I know what shape your joy or your sorrow w{ou}ld take, I know the manner of you walking, standing, sauntering, sitting down, laugh{ing,} punning, and eve[r]y action so truly that you seem near to me. You will rem{em}ber me in the same manner – and the more when I shall tell you that I shall read a passage of Shakspeare every Sunday at ten o Clock – you read one {a}t the same time and we shall be as near each other as blind bodies can be in the same room – (16 December 1819; KL 2.5)

Keats's effort to overcome separation through sharply visualized (or through willed revisualized) memories of those who are absent can take an alternative form, that of imagining his writing is a kind of speaking, and that he is in the room with George and Georgiana:

> – I must take an opportunity here to observe that though I am writing <u>to</u> you I am all the while writing <u>at</u> your Wife – This explanation will account for my speaking sometimes <u>hoity-toityishly</u>. Whereas if you were alone I should sport a little more sober sadness. I am like a squinti[n]g gentleman who saying soft things to one Lady ogles another – or what is as bad in arguing with a person

on his left hand appeals with his eyes to one [on] the right. His Vision is elastic he bends it to a certain object but having a patent sp[r]ing it flies off.

(*KL* 2.204–5)

This playfulness, and the way one idea strikes off another, are part of a performance, one meant to amuse as well as engage his readers.

The performative nature of Keats's letter-writing is intimately connected with his sense of the genre's decorum. If letters served his emotional and creative ends, they also had to take account of a recipient's particular needs. Reynolds was in poor health when Keats wrote a letter to him beginning:

My dear Reynolds,

What I complain of is that I have been in so an uneasy a state of Mind as not to be fit to write to an invalid. I cannot write to any length under a dis-guised feeling. I should have loaded you with an addition of gloom, which I am sure you do not want. I am now thank God in a humour to give you a good groats worth – for Tom, after a Night without a Wink of sleep, and overburdened with fever, has got up after a refreshing day sleep and is better than he has been for a long time . . .   (*KL* 1.275–76)

Letters, no less than conversation, are a form of social behavior, in which self-presentation is an essential component. On 17 September 1819 Keats wrote to George, when both were facing severe difficulties:

be not cast down any more than I am. I feel I can bear real ills better than imaginary ones. Whenever I find myself growing vapourish [depressed], I rouse myself, wash and put on a clean shirt brush my hair and clothes, tie my shoe-strings neatly and in fact adonize as I were going out – then all clean and comfortable I sit down to write. This I find the greatest relief –   (*KL* 2.186)

Keats's letter-writing helped him maintain balance as well as contact with his family and friends, giving him a space in which to relax, to speculate, and to escape the solitary pressures of composition. But the passage above (as both Watts and Webb show) is also markedly literary. Tristram Shandy's remedy for writer's block is to shave, change his clothes, "and in a word, dress myself from one end to the other of me, after my best fashion" (IX.xiii).[15]

Keats's letters share Sterne's sense of the inadequacies of language to encompass lived experience. Like Sterne's, his playfulness, his liberal use of dashes, his digressiveness, and his self-mockery constantly make his reader aware of the act of writing, with frequent references to his faulty or gouty "Quill" and "vile old pen" (*KL* 2.5, 31, 35–36, 242, 262). As he told Reynolds (3 May 1818),

If I scribble long letters I must play my vagaries. I must be too heavy, or too light, for whole pages – I must be quaint and free of Tropes and figures – I must

play my draughts as I please [. . .] This crossing a letter is not without its asso-
ciation – for chequer work leads us naturally to a Milkmaid, a Milkmaid to
Hogarth Hogarth to Shakespeare Shakespear to Hazlitt – Hazlitt to
Shakespeare and thus by merely pulling an apron string we set a pretty peal of
Chimes at work – Let them chime on [. . .]   (KL 1.279–80)

However intimate and exposing, letters are a performance. The self presented is a literary construct, but one which attempts through its own self-
awareness to reach, genuinely, across time and space to his correspondents.

We may see this double awareness – of performative self-consciousness
and sincere communication – in Keats's long journal letter, composed from
14 February to 3 May 1819. He regales his brother and sister in law with a
long quotation from Hazlitt's attack on Gifford (KL 2.71–73), widely
thought, though mistakenly, to have been the author of the attack on Keats's
poetry which appeared in the influential *Quarterly Review* in 1818. He then
changes direction abruptly:

This is the sort of feu de joie [Hazlitt] keeps up – there is another extract or
two – one especially which I will copy tomorrow – for the candles are burnt
down and I am using the wax taper – which has a long snuff on it – the fire is
at its last click – I am sitting with my back to it with one foot rather askew
upon the rug and the other with the heel a little elevated from the carpet – I am
writing this on the Maid's tragedy which I have read since tea with Great pleasure – Besides this volume of Beaumont & Fletcher – there are on the tabl[e]
two volumes of chaucer and a new work of Tom Moores call'd "Tom Cribb's
memorial to Congress["] – nothing in it – These are trifles – but I require
nothing so much of you as that you will give me a like description of your-
selves, however it may be when you are writing to me – Could I see the same
thing done of any great Man long since dead it would be a great delight: as to
know in what position Shakspeare sat when he began 'To be or not to be" –
such thing[s] become interesting from distance of time or place. I hope you are
both now in that sweet sleep which no two beings deserve more tha[n] you do
– I must fancy you so – and please myself in the fancy of speaking a prayer and
a blessing over you and your lives – God bless you – I whisper good night in
your ears and you will dream of me –
Saturday 13 March. I have written to Fanny this morning [. . .]
                                                          (KL 2.73–74)[16]

Keats writes himself into his letter half-mockingly, half-seriously: the act of
self-presentation is in part a late night relaxation. Intimately domestic, the
scene is that of the literary man as bachelor, posed for his correspondents
and surrounded by recent books and older ones by writers he admires, one
serving as a writing desk. At the same time, these "trifles" do conjure an
image George and Georgiana might cherish: the aspirant writer quietly

settled in his study. Keats asks for a reciprocal verbal picture in return. The parties need to imagine one another. Keats goes on to do just that, as he blesses their sleep.

Keats not only stages this exchange, but with it, also illustrates his speculation about the way letters "remembrance" and "enchain" the two sides of a correspondence (*KL* 2.208) or function as a "memento" to bring the recipient "back" to the writer (112). On 21 September 1819, he reflected on the fact that bodies change every seven years: "seven years ago it was not this hand that clench'd itself against Hammond" (208, referring to the surgeon to whom he had been apprenticed in 1811). Hence, bosom friends after being separated for many years

> meet coldly, neither of them knowing why – The fact is they are both altered – Men who live together have a silent moulding and influencing power over each other – They interassimulate. 'T is an uneasy thought that in seven years the same hands cannot greet each other again. All this may be obviated by a willful [i.e., willed] and dramatic exercise of our Minds towards each other.
>
> (*KL* 2.208–9)

Keats's verb "assimulate" – whether an unconscious misspelling or canny neologism – brings together "assimilate" and "simulate": the active sympathy of two minds, through a simultaneous imitation and willed identification each of the other, can rekindle, and even recreate, lost friendship.[17] Similarly, the "willful and dramatic exercise of our Minds," working through the marks on the pages of letters, can bring together writer and reader.

This is necessary because words cannot do everything alone, as Keats well knew:

> Writing has this disadvan[ta]ge of speaking. one cannot write a wink, or a nod, or a grin, or a purse of the Lips, or a <u>smile – O law!</u> One can-[not] put ones finger to one's nose, or yerk in the ribs, or lay hold of your button in writing –
>
> (*KL* 2.205)

If writing cannot replace seeing, speaking or gesturing, Keats's letters persistently seek ways to circumvent this disadvantage, often by drawing attention to such limitations and then soliciting the reader's imaginative generosity to overcome physical separation and absence in the illusion of "now": "in all the most lively and titterly parts of my Letter you must not fail to imagine me as the epic poets say – now here, now there, now with one foot pointed at the ceiling, now with another – now with my pen on my ear, now with my elbow in my mouth – O my friends you loose the action – " (2.205). Keats's skepticism goes hand in hand with his determination to make language work for him, hence the fondness for wordplay, punning, conversational reporting, and the recounting of stories. Pulled both ways, Keats is, Webb says, "trapped by the paradoxical nature of representation, recognising the limits of language yet inventively and deliberately resisting them" (168–69). The success of Keats's reaching out to friends and family through his letters' "enchainings," memorializing, playfulness, seriousness, and self-referentiality depends upon that recognition.

The literariness of Keats's letters is revealed by the letter-like quality of a disturbing late poem (or perhaps dramatic fragment):

> This living hand, now warm and capable
> Of earnest grasping, would, if it were cold
> And in the icy silence of the tomb,
> So haunt thy days and chill thy dreaming nights
> That thou would wish thine own heart dry of blood,
> So in my veins red life might stream again,
> And thou be conscience-calm'd. See here it is –
> I hold it towards you.

If this is a poem, the addressee is necessarily the reader. Imagining his death, the poet demands the death of the reader in order to re-animate him. It is appropriate that "living hand" refers both to the live poet's body, and to the handwriting that has the potential to live after him ("hand" is a synonym for handwriting). These lines are a discomfiting breaking of fictional decorum, aggressively directed at the reader's own being, and animated by a self-pity grotesque in its unanswerable rightness.[18] Keats's letters no less intently reach out towards their readers, but imagine these readers as present, their own lives and concerns existing parallel to the writer's own. Unlike "This living hand," Keats's letters depend upon and animate the fiction of a mutual reciprocity between writer and reader.

NOTES

1 In *Lord Byron and Some of His Contemporaries* (1828), Leigh Hunt excerpted a letter (10 May 1817; *KL* 1.136–40); R. M. Milnes published about eighty letters (whole or excerpted) in *Life, Letters, and Literary Remains, of John Keats* (1848).

2 Lionel Trilling, *The Opposing Self*, 3–49.

3 See John Barnard, *John Keats*, 141–44.

4 Timothy Webb, "'Cutting Figures': Rhetorical Strategies in Keats's Letters," *Keats: Bicentenary Readings*, ed. Michael O'Neill (Edinburgh: Edinburgh University Press, 1997), 144–69; Wolfson, "Keats the Letter-Writer: Epistolary Poetics," 59; Cedric Watts, *A Preface to Keats* (London: Longman, 1985), 160–61; Andrew Bennett, *Keats, Narrative and Audience: The Posthumous Life of Writing*.

5 No letters survive from before December? 1814 and very few until the summer of 1816, when (not long before his twenty-first birthday) Keats dedicated himself to poetry.

6 There are also over forty letters from Keats known about, but lost. In 1995, one such, to his brothers, 30 January 1818, was discovered in Altavista, Virginia; see Dearing Lewis, "A John Keats Letter Rediscovered," *KSJ* 47 (1998), 14–18.

7 See Keats's letter to Reynolds 3 February 1818 (*KL* 1.225), and John Barnard's essay, "Keats's 'Robin Hood,' John Hamilton Reynolds, and the 'Old Poets,'" *Proceedings of the British Academy* 75 (1989), 181–200.

8 For details of the postal service, see *Shelley and his Circle* vol. 2, ed. Kenneth Neill Cameron (Cambridge and London: Harvard University Press, 1961), 914–25, and vol. 4, ed. Donald H. Reiman (1973), xxii–iv. Other information used below about Keats's letter of 8 July 1820 to Fanny Brawne is from W. H. Reid and J. Wallis, *The Panorama* (London, [1820]), 54, and *Paterson's Roads* (18th edn.; London, 1826), 27.

9 Charles and Mary Cowden Clarke, *Recollections of Writers* (1878), 128–30; "Recollections of John Keats" first appeared in *Atlantic Monthly*, 1861, then *Gentleman's Magazine*, 1874.

10 For Keats's letter of 20 November, see Andrew Motion's *Keats*, 128, and the plate in *KL* 1, after 114; for the group of letters, see *KL* 1.117–20. Keats put the sonnet in *Poems* (1817), the second of two addressed to Haydon.

11 *KL* 2.238 (British Library Add MS 34019 ff.24^v and 27^v). James Tassie manufactured immensely popular colored paste reproductions of antique gems, as well as signets to use on sealing wax.

12 For the letters' texts, see *KL* 1.327–33 and 333–36. For plates, see Robert Woof and Stephen Hebron, *John Keats* (Grasmere: The Wordsworth Trust, 1995), 111; for the first page of the letter of 10 July, and for a detail of the letter of the 17th, see Carol Kyros Walker, *Walking North With Keats*, illustration 78.

13 For the letter to Bailey, see Motion's *Keats*, 209; for the letter to Taylor, see the plate in *KL* 2, after 208. Keats's reference to this practice, in a letter to Reynolds 3 May 1818 (*KL* 1.280), is quoted below.

14 For a photograph, see Timothy Hilton, *Keats and his World* (London: Thames and Hudson, 1971), 122. Tootts is probably Fanny's ten-year-old sister; Sam is her teenage brother; the Brawnes were residing in Dilke's half of Wentworth Place.

15 Watts, *Preface to Keats*, 162, Webb, "'Cutting Figures,'" 152–53; Webb notes that the unusual verb "adonize" occurs in Smollett's translation of *Gil Blas* as "an exact rendering of Lesage's 'm'adoniser.'" Rollins notes the echo of Sterne's *Tristran Shandy* (2.186n, crediting Maurice Buxton Forman's edition of Keats's letters). For other echoes of Sterne, see *KL* 1.160 and 245.

16 For an interesting comparison between this passage and Severn's painting of Keats reading at Wentworth Place, see Webb, "'Cutting Figures,'" 148–49. For a black and white photograph of the painting (in the National Portrait Gallery in London), see Motion, *Keats*, plate 64, and Woof and Hebron, *John Keats*, 122.

17 For comments on this word, see Wolfson, "Epistolary Poetics," 59; Webb, "'Cutting Figures,'" 165. Christopher Ricks's *Keats and Embarrassment* comments on many of Keats's telling misspellings.

18 For the dynamics of address in these lines, with relevance to the dynamics of a letter, see Susan J. Wolfson, *Formal Charges: The Shaping of Poetry in British Romanticism*, 187–92 and notes.

9

GARRETT STEWART

Keats and language

What kind of topic is this? What else is there? Language in Keats: that wouldn't get us where we need to go, either. Keats in language? Up to his ears in language. Some writers in English, some very few, have written more brilliantly. None has worded more gorgeously. Vowels are for Keats a passion, consonants an ecstasy, syntax a life force. Okay, then: Keats in language. And we respond in kind. There is no way to approach Keats with mere close reading. Proximity breeds immersion. Like his verse, reading operates from the inside out, silent music rippling with inference.

So rapt by the syllables of English verse was Keats that even (or especially) at his most aching, gripped by mortality and stung by frustrated ambition, his words often become his theme. Ideally wielded, they heal. In the process, they become his diagnosed means as well. Trained as a physician, self-schooled as a poet, Keats was an intuitive anatomist of language, its closely articulated skeletal structure, its ligaments and fibers, its muscular tensions and release, its rhythmic corridors of breath – while also a genetic specialist in its origins and mutations. With pen rather than stethoscope, he took the phonetic pulse of his every word through the listening ear of script.

No poet (which is saying something) ever wrote with more preoccupation about the nurturing of verbal gifts. Such resolute self-reflexivity makes the unabashed loveliness, sometimes the strain, of his lines seem less an indulgence than a monitored experiment. Among Keats's most stirring turns are his testings of phrasal intent and limits. Some of his most striking images are less finished products than provisional challenges to the organizing power of words – and all the more indelible as a result. Without being explicitly autobiographical like Wordsworth, he is never anything but. His verse struggles with what it would take to be great: a true healer/philosopher/poet, but poet first, with the words craving their own sense of inevitability within the freest pitch of invention. Even the tribulations of a wearied spirit become transformed into exercises in poetic stamina.

Each reader must have a favorite typifying line. Some likely ones surprise with their persisting cultural capital. On 6 November, 1998, the "Arts and Leisure" section of the *New York Times*, alluding to the poet for whom art was never leisure, announced the opening of the refurbished, and freshly burnished, main reading room of the New York Public Library: "Open for Travel in the Realms of Gold." What is it about the launching metaphor of *On First Looking into Chapman's Homer* that renders it so memorable, even for the mass ear? The answer goes to the quick of Keatsian language, with its tireless internal adhesions. The inverted syntax of "Much have I travell'd in the realms of gold" spreads "h*ave*" and "tr*avell'd*" even as it launches an internal, slant rhyme of *ell'd* (in *travell'd*) into g*old*, a treasured yield that averts a clichéd "realms of old." Keats often plays in this manner between cause and effect, here through metaphor's double "transfer" (the root meaning) from time-travel via books to their glittering rewards. Everywhere he travels, he listens *in* to the shape of words, wringing overtones from contingencies, making accidents happen as lyric events.

This is true of his prose commentary as much as of his verse. In his matchless letters, as well as in his marginalia in his copies of Shakespeare and Milton, Keats is preternaturally alive to verbal wizardry, especially of these two poets. Without using technical terms of phonology, Keats repeatedly takes up the sound of language – scriptive and enunciative at once, its homophonic puns conveying or producing meaning. Appreciative verbal criticism benefits immensely from beginning with Keats's own. The thing half said from within an intention otherwise directed attracts his ear. On lines from Shakespeare's Sonnet 12, Keats calls out an unintended and untenable pun on life-from-death in the image of cut-and-bound wheat carted off like an aged corpse: "Borne on the bier with white and bristly beard." In a punning gloss of his own, he cries to Reynolds (*KL* 1.188–89; Reynolds had given him this volume), "Is this to be borne?" By all means, including (we might add, in the same spirit) the latent anagrammatic anticipation of "bread" in the causal "beard" of harvested wheat. It is Keats's tempered rather than aggressive verbal play that characterizes him and the poetry he reveres; he loves how Shakespeare's sonnets seem "full of fine things said un*inten*tionally – *in* the *inten*sity of working out conceits" (my emphases). As in Keats's letter, these Shakespearean things are often what we might call aural conceits, phonetic rather than semantic byplay. A more integrated lexical indecision flickers in the immediately preceding lines from the sonnet, which Keats also quotes. In what we could call a pre-Keatsian mode of phonetic association, Shakespeare images a sheepfold's leafy "canopy" as "Summer's green" – phrasing whose liaison (sibilant spill-over) tacitly "intensifies" itself on the spot to "screen." Keats introduces these lines with "Hark ye!" and we can't resist, hearing the phrase with his heightened aural sense of tautly unmotivated contingency. The same is true of his pungent stumblings in copying out "which erst from heat did canopy the herd." First writing "not" for "erst" ("lately"), he corrected – but not without first misspelling "herd" as "heard," as if in punning deference to the *erst / erd* chime.

This poet's ear for his predecessors is endlessly vigilant and exquisite. Though he would complain that Milton's poetry corrupts a "northern dialect" with "greek and latin inversions and intonations" (*KL* 2.212), Keats's notes on *Paradise Lost* from the preceding year attest to a deep appreciation for the idiolect of Miltonic diction. Regretting Latinate syntax, Keats warms to Latinate etymologies. God's aura of "reluctant flames, the sign / Of wrath awaked" (*PL* 6.58–59) impresses him with how "reluctant" works "with its original and modern meaning combined and woven together" – the etymological "fighting back" (*re-luctari*) with the more passive sense of "unwilling" or "grudging," perhaps even woven with the overtone of a "relucent" grandeur, "shining back" (*re-lucere*) in retribution against those who turned forever from the light. The lines he likes tend to achieve more than at first meets the ear. When Satan, promoting Pandemonium, struggles for a comparison that would negate a tragic discrepancy – "here, as in the vales of Heaven" (*PL* 1.321) – Keats hears "a cool pleasure in the very sound of vale," the English word being "of the happiest chance." He knows the cool is also chilling because, quite apart from evoking the delusion of "veil," it bears a twofold Latin underlay. The verbal topography draws on a root system that twists *volvere* (to roll, as in undulate) with the plangent *vale* (valediction) of farewell: the lingering, fallen goodbye to a now forever veiled and invisible origin, divine but irretrievable. A comparably dense interplay of referential suggestion would seem to inform the smiting assonance of his most Miltonic *Hyperion*. In its opening line, "Deep in the shády sadness of *a* vále" (my italics), "shady" doesn't impose an unconvincing transferred epithet borrowed, for mood, from the symbolic lay of the land. Rather, the Titans' grief is plausibly penumbral in its own right, a shadowy gloom that will soon eclipse the sun god himself, Hyperion. The futility of resistance or even comprehension in this Titanic decline serves to insinuate, moreover, as if by bitter inaptness, the shadowy "sadness of avail": no action avails, or is available. The line itself makes a homophonic mockery of all meaning as well as of all hope.

Keats is the kind of writer who can't help but pun on "the <u>rogue</u>glyphics in Moor's Almanack" (*KL* 2.247).[1] This tossed-off joke, in part about the fugitive phonetic element in alphabetic characters, often dissonant and mischievous (the fusing *g* sounds), maps directly onto Keats's most considered views of how meanings emerge on both glyphic and phonic levels of signification (in script and sound). He saw this literary instinct at work in the

Shakespearean actor Edmund Kean, whose performance he reviewed in 1817 ("Mr. Kean"). Kean knows the hieroglyphic meaning of his script, textually sanctioned, irrevocable, as if impressed in stone. But there is also an enunciative double, the supplement of *performance*, about which Keats writes:

> A melodious passage in poetry is full of pleasures both sensual and spiritual. The spiritual is felt when the very letters and points of charactered language show like the hieroglyphics of beauty: – the mysterious signs of an immortal freemasonry!

In other words, linguistic open secrets, sublimed signs that need (and reward) deciphering. In contrast to the lettered text, a "sensual life of verse springs warm from the lips of Kean." Keats intuited the way the charge of verse enunciation (on page and on stage) may work against the hieroglyphic grain of the etched letter, to release a surprise from within the stabilized script of normative syntax (recall the phonetic twin "born" delivered stillborn from "borne" in Sonnet 12). Like Kean, he revels in the sonorous splendor of vagrancy and slippage (the glory of rogue enunciation) inspired by Shakespeare's "hieroglyphics of beauty."

Such sonority had been Keats's effort from the start, though never allowed to override his apprenticeship to English verse tradition. From *Imitation of Spenser* forward, his poems mark a disciplined acquisition of mastery. Never more touchingly, in hindsight, than in his sonnet, "Oh Chatterton!" Here was a legendary poet whose life ended (in suicide) at a cruelly early age and whose verse (as Keats explains in tandem with remarks about Milton's un-English inversions) seemed incomparably pure because uninfected by foreign borrowing.[2] In his poignant sonnet, metaphor enfolds a further relay of sound at the fused interface of two characteristically Anglo-Saxon words, a kind of nativist punning in allegiance to his genealogical forebear: "O how nigh / Was night to thy fair morning!" (6–7). In the ear of sympathetic meditation, mortality puts "nigh" back in "nigh(t t)o" in the process of making phonetic nearness into a melodrama all its own.

So it goes, onward, upward, but always *inward*, penetrating the deepest recesses of language in action. In *Sleep and Poetry*, Keats explores – and strategically blurs – the border of art and the unconscious, underpoliced by the dream logic of words themselves. The sideswiping pun in his question, what is "mo(re r)egal" than an "eagle" (21–22) – poetry is the answer – is comparable to the effect more subtly hinted in the preceding self-braided praise of sleep: "Silent *ent*angler of a beauty's tresses" (15), including an undertow (undertone) of metrical self-reference in "beauty'(s s)tresses." At other times, poetry comes "like fearful claps of thunder, / Or the low rumblings earth's regions under" (27–28), with the hint of the earthquake that might "regions sunder" as easily as words rupture. Or, in the delicate byplay of "No one who once the glorious sun has seen" (41), "one" releases "on(ce)" to its kaleidoscopic shuffle as "(s)un" in a kind of phonetic anagram/mar of dreamlike association. Later, an unconscious soundplay figures the serial, escalating poetic devotion that will, like "flowers" (as if standing here for the pure "flowers of rhetoric" – or figures of speech) "entice me *on*, and *on*, / Through alm*on*d bloss*om* and rich cinnam*on*; / Till in the bos*om* of a leafy world / We rest in silence" (118–20). Until such achieved silence, language must sustain the syllabic momentum of felt process. Picking up on the pastoral "leafy" in a subsequent poem about the actual creation of *Sleep and Poetry*, Keats writes as if he had internalized the dated mode in being able to "feel a free, a leafy luxury" (*Dedication. To Leigh Hunt, Esq.* 12–13). Such is the freedom that verbally looses, or hinges, a predicate into its object, the verb "feel" into its phonetic inversion "leaf," the last with its rustling pun on those poetic "leaves" (pages) over which Keats senses a new command.

In another figure that outstrips the pastoral basis of much romantic verse, Endymion, admonished against dreamy frivolity, utters his transcendental aspirations. The effort is to inseminate the unseen with beauty, so that (with again the metrical sense) "the airy stress / Of music's kiss impregnates the free winds" (*Endymion* 1.783–84). Couched in the romantic icon of the eolian harp (an instrument of tuned strings wakened to music by the wind), the dreamed result shows a Keatsian stamp when at last, unbinding the line's closure with visually mimetic enjambment, the winds are kissed by music, and "a sympathetic touch unbinds / Eolian magic from their lucid wombs" (785–86). Lucid? How so? Transparent? Invisible? Clear in tone? Or something else and more, a cause to this effect? Metrical regularity and slippery wordplay have seldom mated more tightly. Long tensed with their own force, the winds are at last delivered of a lyre-like music from their "loosed" wombs. Phonetic leeway figures its own punning release.

In one of Keats's most memorable early poems, "In drear nighted December," where the twin yearnings of sex and literary ambition converge, the inability to speak of fled love, even in poetry, is lamented and overcome at once. "The feel of not to feel it" (21) is the poem's stress, a negativity "never said in rhyme" (24). Never till now – as the flagged term "rhyme" gathers the preceding stanzas' last words, "prime" and "time," into a sweeping compositional symmetry. John Jones has made much of Keats's coining (now standard English) of "feel" into a noun, a marginally more palpable substantive than the standard "feeling."[3] Increasingly in his later work, neologism becomes one of his most resourceful verbal moves, tweaking the lexicon to bring forth unexpected shades of inference. Not far removed in spirit are covert conflations of two words into an inspired third, the call of meaning in process. "In drear nighted December" relieves the appointed dreariness by just such tonic oscillations. If, for instance, one hears the absent or banished "verse" in the crevasse of "ne*ver s*aid," striving for a voice it cannot (supposedly) find, one may also, and more potently, feel the true force of "feel" in the opening line: the slipping away of "love" in the "fee*l ov*" its already lapsed passion.

Words in Keats are the theater of a world interfused with affect and its vanishments, mutable, layered, elusive. When transposed to poetry, these are the effects of which his late poem *Lamia* is a parable. Slightest shifts of wording lever broadest implications. Metaphor and its sliding approximations, syntactic inversion and suspension, internal rhyme, phonetic drift, etymological irony, strategic coinage, metrical eccentricity, run-on line endings, double-pronged grammar: these are only some of the ways Keats, grasping the very poetry of verbal articulation, nerves his verses for their widest work. The seductive eponym of *Lamia* gets vaporized at the end of the poem under the keen eye of the spoiler philosopher, Apollonius (his name and character a parody of Apollo), leaving her lover empty-armed and dead. Straining the conceptual in favor of the emotional limits of poetry, a zeugma (two different senses on the same predication) renders the death not just instantaneous but grammatically *simultaneous* with the loss:

> And Lycius' arms were empty of delight,
> As were his limbs of life, from that same night.   (2.307–8)

In the arms of love, "empty of" means bereft of the object of embrace; applied to limbs, it means drained of life from within. Lack has been internalized as evacuation – in the very moment, and as the very definition, of death. The sense of this fatality as a foregone conclusion is then drawn out in the last triplet. "On the high couch he lay! – his friends came round – " (309), it begins. As they approach, the just slightly posthumous recognition of death registers in the shifting valence of "support" between comforting allegiance and a mere lifting of the body. After they "came round," that is, just this: suspense, then the clench of fatality.

> Supported him – no pulse, or breath they found,
> And, in its marriage robe, the heavy body wound.   (310–11)

Whether they "wound" Lycius in the robe (transitive verb) or found him "wound" (past participle), the doom is sealed – and precisely without the "wound" (external injury, the whole body's spiritual death blow) that is spelled out to the eye and canceled by rhyme and grammar. If (as "woond") "wound" refuses a rare triplet possibility in a poem of couplets, it would seem to promise another couplet: the thrust of a new idea going nowhere, truncated, forever denied a rhyme. Such half-possible, syntactically incorrigible sense is what Christopher Ricks calls an "anti-pun" – an unintended intensity of discharged suggestion of the sort Keats detects in Shakespeare.[4] It is an effect recruited here, summoned and overruled by sense, for another of Keats's split-second shuttles from unsaid cause to phrased effect.

Two prior instances of verbal slippage in *Lamia*, one syntactic, one phonetic, catch the chameleon-like heroine in the throes of an eventually lethal mutation. As the she-snake disappears from the forest, for flight into Lycius's world,

> Still shone her crown; that vanish'd, also she
> Melted and disappear'd as suddenly.   (1.165–66)

Locked in this couplet, a hovering grammar completes her disappearance as a kind of afterthought: "her crown vanish'd / the crown having vanish'd, so did she" is what line 165 suggests, just before full syntax specifies "melted and disappear'd." Metamorphosizing, Lamia is almost too quick for the reading eye as well as for the enamored gaze. Such grammar of vanishment haunts the broken rhyme, just before Lycius's death, between "no sooner said" (Apollonius's searing words) and "vanished" (her violent removal) – as if the rhyme (2.305–6) had withdrawn, under sympathetic duress, from the realm of consonant couplets and other well-matched couplings. In her final disappearance at her wedding (precipitating Lycius's death), Lamia is pierced by cold philosophy, her own sight swallowed up in the confrontation. "Some hungry spell that loveliness absorbs" (259) comes forward as an independent inverted clause (for "absorbs that loveliness"), with the rhyme-word positioned to educe a fuller, cross-lexical match with "There was no recognition in those *orbs*" (260). The word "absorbs" seems on its own phonetic terms to vacuum out all ocular and visionary energy from the scene. Keats is the preeminent poet of just these seductive verbal melds and meltings, as well as those syntactic vanishing acts, that this late poem turns to parable.

Most readers think of the Great Odes when thinking of Keats, each rounded upon its own "questioning presence" while answering to the others.[5] Where, then, is the salient wavering of verse language in this presence? Just where you would expect it with Keats: everywhere. Language is not only shown off as flexed expressive gesture but held out as a register of salvation. At the low ebbs of chilled desire, wording alone (and often only wording) can snap the poet out of his lassitudes while bringing the poem itself to life. Inflected by pun, syntactic ambiguity, buried metaphor, muted phonetic echo – the most overt to the most delicate of effects – the verse line is often a life-line to a keenness of utterance that alone begins to salvage the mind from its death drift. The retrieved consciousness of self in these Odes finds renewed footing in a certain unapologetic self-consciousness of enunciation. Unlike escapist illusionism in *Lamia*, here linguistic immediacy, passionately engaged, becomes a saving grace. Inner listening won from listlessness is a repeated drama: the conversion of form into content as its rescue and redirection.

From *Psyche* forward, the Odes concern that disposition of spirit which is the condition of verse. "O Goddess!" (1), the poet hails Psyche, begging "pardon" for phrasing her secrets even to her own "soft-conched ear" (4) – her "couched" (9) dalliance with Cupid. Keats plays "conched" and "couched" as internal echo, the words of poetry and desire differing only by the mirroring letters *n* and *u*. The words commune across an unexpected hieroglyphic distance, just as a pun has vied for conceptual space in the opening line: "hear these tuneless numbers, w/rung." Wrenched from the heart, "By sweet enforcement and remembrance dear" (2), these numbers are simultaneously sounded out by silent script. Such hearing threads another pattern through the first stanza, a submerged metaphoric refrain on the noun of vision. The poet, soaking up the beauty of the sleeping couple with "awaken'd eyes" (6) – are these Psyche's or his? – espies "cool-rooted flowers, fragrant-eyed" (13). This apparent synesthesia (blending of senses) actually makes "eye" a metaphor for a flower's center. This isn't a naively mixed metaphor, but rather a Keatsian "catechresis": a seemingly extravagant or absurd figure of speech that actually bears a compelling logic. All seems to be seen and seeing at this "tender eye-dawn of aurorean love" (20). With a phonic hint at a clichéd and personifying epithet for morning itself, "tender-eyed dawn," Keats produces the awkwardly fresh and arresting "eye-dawn," implying that sight itself contains a whole diurnal world. Sensuous vision still depends, first and foremost, on the conches of the versed ear.

The "happy, happy dove" (22) that is "winged Psyche" (6) yields to the "light-winged" nightingale in the next and more renowned Ode (7). Now a poet recounts a dream vision, threading familiar paradoxes of melancholic desire from amid the waverings of a death-wish, to end in self-reflection: "Do I wake or sleep?" (80). He begins as "a drowsy numbness / Pains" the sense (1–2) – as if lack of feeling, carrying its own oxymoronic sting, had to seek relief in hemlock-like oblivion. Life is wearying, and poetry needs at times to "forget," in willed transcendence, what the nightingale "hast never known" (21–22):

> The weariness, the fever, and the fret
> Here, where men sit and hear each other groan.   (23–24)

The *Ode*'s aural thematics gather in this closely bounded internal echo – and narrowed breathing room – between the adverb ("here") and the all-consuming verb ("hear") of universally audited pain. The *Ode*'s phonic *ambition*, by contrast, is to transfigure groan into chant, to widen the space for a here-and-now of alleviating melody.

Aurality is one of the defaults, along with smell, in the *Ode*'s twilight forest glade, where nothing can be seen. The poet gives the sound-heavy luxuriance of "verdurous glooms" (40) instead of gloomy verdure (substance subsumed to mood). In this "embalmed darkness," where the primary sense of "balm-laden" courts mortuary overtones, he has to "guess each sweet" scent (43). Confusing sense, synesthesia concentrates it. Yet as alert as the poem is to its emerging verbal energies, and to the victory they must eventually enact over the inertia they name, its most escapist nocturnal evocation also has a verbal penumbra. When, just before this sweet guesswork, the poet was imagining "the Queen-Moon . . . / Cluster'd around by all her starry Fays" (36–37), his line works a supernatural metaphor for moonlight's radiating gleams. Critics have often regretted the image, but close listening catches the "luster" within the fantasized "Cluster" after all.

The refulgence sheds no sustaining light below, however. "Darkling I listen," the poet concedes (51), his death-wishing in play between intransitive and transitive verbal possibilities, the former punning on the latter: "To cease upon the midnight with no pain" (56) is to die away, "easeful" (52) upon the stroke of twelve, but the phrase also sounds "seize upon" the dead of night, the embrace accent(uat)ed by the spondaic downbeat of "with no pain" – the unusual terminal variation "a hallmark of the Keatsian style."[6] As throughout this drama about sounds that save, grammar is again at the mercy (or the behest) of soundplay. "Cease" soon echoes in the "perilous seas" (perilous cease / perilous ease) in "faery lands forlorn" (70). This last syntactic inversion lets its adjective hang there until the next stanza recalls it in recoil:

> Forlorn! the very word is like a bell
> To toll me back from thee to my sole self!   (71–72)

In an unmodulated repetition across the stanza break, this lone two-syllabled word (except for "very") installs a self-resonating, pendulous iteration (*for* / *lor* / *For* / *lor*) from which the belling of *toll . . . sole* seems further precipitated. The "very word" has become a textual *deus ex machina*, a cue and rescue from the heart of utterance, returning the poet from enraptured auditor to self-attuned expressive agent. Such self-conscious iteration rings in the diminished belling of

> *Adieu!* the fancy cannot cheat so well
>   As she is fam'*d to do*, deceiving elf.
> *Adieu! adieu!* . . .   (73–75, my emphases)

Purging the romance of "easeful Death," this personification of delusion as deceiving elf capitalizes on its rhyme-base, "sole self" (72), to which the poet has in this very process been recalled. To say "adieu" to phantasmal, life-denying options (the "soul's elf," the spirit's bewildering alter ego) is an arduous poetic achievement in its own right, and once again the "very word" is the escape from a life-sapping dream.

The world-worn Keatsian speaker turns next to a Grecian Urn and an ode *on* (or upon) it: not "about" or (as in earlier odes) "to" it (though address is the rhetoric) but the ambiguous work of poetic form on the worked surface of the *objet d'art* itself. Does the silent surface express "more sweetly" than the poet's rhyme (4)? Or may verbal energy exert its own "sweeter" (12) aesthetic? In the urn's fostering by "slow time" (2), for instance, another heavily accented spondaic line-ending at once slows down the line (Fussell, 49) and sounds the agency of "slow(ed t)ime." Stilled by precisely this preternatural temporality are the marble lutanists whose "unheard" melodies (11) of amorous dalliance pipe "Not to the sensual ear, but, more endear'd" (13), to the mind's silent audition. Susan Wolfson notes that Keats's sight rhyme with "unh*ear*d" compounds an accidental syllabic dislodging within "end/*ear*ed" to call up the subvocal end (and purpose) of all writing (320). The ear offers itself as the core of all poetic end*ear*ment. No sooner risked than overruled is another truant anti-pun, the "sensual leer" (instead of sensory audition) that might have degraded aesthetic imagining to sheer voyeurism.

In the last stanza, amorous chase has been reduced, by a double punning, to a clear-cut distinction between flesh and artifact. But wordplay still insists on the deathless appeal of art's solace in a world of punishing flux. The urn is bedecked "with brede / Of marble men and maidens overwrought" (41–42). This is not (paraphrasing) a "race of marble-hearted men" content with perpetual pursuit, with "maidens forever wrought to flight." Rather, Keats's phrasing pictures a weaving ("brede" for braid) of sculpted men and maidens equally "wrought" out of the marble urn-surface. As such, the "silent form" (Keats addresses it) "dost tease us out of thought" (44) – a loosening of strictures nowhere better exemplified than in the slackening of lexical boundaries to sound "dost ease." Such peace cannot cheat so well, however, for its transcendence is wholly bracketed from all of life's other necessities and defeats. Its serene finality revolves like the urn itself, in sculpted perfection and foreclosure. The limited scope of that notorious maxim "Beauty is truth, truth beauty" (49) is betrayed from within by a self-enclosed phonetic parallelism, by syntactic chiasmus (*eu u, u eu*), and by the way the elliptical grammar of the second clause puts a keener emphasis on the euphony of the first, where it may seem – may sound – as if "Beauty is truth" were harboring a more narrowly defined "beauty's truth," or a delimited "beauteous truth" of the isolated aesthetic moment. A pretty truth, the notion that truth is beautiful, but a truth applicable only in art.

Melancholy enters the sequence of Odes almost dialectically, as a countering celebration of just that bittersweet transient beauty from which the urn suspends our attention. Like Psyche, Melancholy is a goddess whose temple is to be internalized by the poem, a "sovran shrine, / . . . seen of none save him whose strenuous tongue" (26–27) can, not sing or poetize exactly, but savor. Yet a tacit vocal strain is the light tonguing of sound across "who*se strenuous t*ongue" – precisely as this risked (even if subvocal) tongue-twister anticipates the true melancholic's power to "burst Joy's grape against his palate fine" (28). Here is an enunciative pressure beyond all rough *scraping* (the antiphonal echo in "Joy'*s grape*"). It is frictionless, implosive. In recompense and edification, the poet will "be among her cloudy trophie*s* h*ung*" (30) – almost saying *sung*, almost saying "strophes."[7] The poet hints that he will be hymned into perpetuity by his own expressive devotion, made fabled, his praises sung.

None of this is in *To Autumn*, where the grape of fruition is de-metaphorized and bestowed in the real fruits of a season. The question about praising song – "Where are the songs of spring? Ay, where are they? / Think not of them, thou hast thy music too, – " (23–24) – has already been answered by the verse itself. It includes the intricately punning music of the "wailful choir" of "small gnats" that "mourn / Among the river sallows, borne aloft . . ." (27–28), bleating lambs and singing crickets, and then, at last:

> The red-breast whistles from a garden-croft,
> And gathering swallows twitter in the skies.   (32–33)

Recalling the bridging of earth to sky in the opening stanza, where the curving land is pictured as "close bosom-friend of the maturing sun" (2), the space here is spanned by sound waves rather than solar warmth – and generalized to the "skies" of any autumnal locale. If this final "gathering" bodes the migration at the season's end, the distant twittering permits Keatsian sonar to take the full depth of the season's music. What results is the exquisitely minimal reverberation of "red-brea*st whist*les" with its almost anagrammatic variant in "swallows *twitt*er." Text and context mesh to perfection, with all sounds harmonized in the poet's unexpected cross-lexical chords.

The proof of such effects lies everywhere in Keats, but their test as "poetry," rather than merely gifted verse, Keats knew, would be whether a more ambitious work could mobilize the verbal fathomings of the world and marshall a tragic momentum through them. He gave it two remarkable tries, *Hyperion: A Fragment* and its revision as *The Fall of Hyperion: A Dream*. There is a new density and sculptural splendor in the Miltonic syntax and diction of the first, a monument in its own truncated form to the smashed icon of past grandeur, sun-god Hyperion. The Titans have been overthrown by an unheralded force in the universe, whose beauty is not only its truth but its power: the Olympian hierarchy, whose first-born, Apollo, waits in the wings. For now, the fallen giants writhe in agony. Poetic syllables enter the turmoil through avenues of sound, with "*for* the solid r*oar* / Of thunderous waterfalls and t*or*rents h*o*arse, / P*ou*ring a constant bulk, uncertain where" (*Hyperion* 2.7–9). How well the sound of "torrent's source" that presses to be heard in "torrents *ho*arse" conveys the phantasmal mark of its own "uncertain" origin.

This kind of backdoor enunciation is close cousin to words invented, rather than dislodged, on the spot. Keats is no stranger to such concoctions. In *Ode on Indolence*, as befits the occasion, poetic license slips into a mimesis of poetic laxity. Aching "for an age so shelter'd from annoy, / That I may never . . . / . . . hear the voice of busy common-sense!" (38–40), the poet refuses the commonsensical (busy, buzzing) voice that would say "annoyance" rather than the indolently briefer "annoy," a noun Keats coined. In similar luxury, another coinage, "With jellies soother than the creamy curd" (*Eve of St. Agnes* 266), gets "more soothing" and "smoother" into one sensation. Neither, however, predicts the rampant minting of new words and their intimations in the *Hyperion* ventures, where the governing Apollonian struggle to compass transhistorical loss with understanding, to compose it into words, forces description into a veritable frenzy of neologism. Even (especially) for the unprecedented tragic upheaval, old words won't do. Fallen Saturn's "old right hand lay nerveless, listless, dead, / Unsceptred; and his realmless eyes were closed" (*Hyperion* 1.18–19). The adjectival contortion Keats coins with "nerveless" (availing, too, a redundant ghostly hint of a negative prefix: *ne*) marks a depletion anatomical and spiritual at once, a giant potency not only enervated but potentially cowed. As the turn of the line prolongs "dead" into "dead/un," it hails another neologism, "Unsceptred": the hand bereft of its emblem of authority. So, too, "realmless eyes," disenfranchised not only by grief but also by the fall and erasure of all they used to survey.

The premium on new words for old losses is, if anything, increased in Keats's revisionary sequel. When the downfall of Titanic majesty is symbolized in Moneta's ravaged temple, the poem's very title, *The Fall of Hyperion*, gets echoed and distilled in the capping-off of an epic analogue that makes all historical decay seem, by comparison, "the faulture of decrepit things" (1.70). As with so many of Keats's coinages, several phrasings vie for the semantic space: here, "fault," "failure," and "fissure," each recalling those "rent towers" of earthly cathedrals (67) so entirely eclipsed by this more profound decay of grandeur. By default, then, all visionary grandeur is transferred to the grievous spirit of memory, Mnemosyne or Moneta. In *The Fall*, the torquing force of neologism lends an unexpected but precise stress to the verbal power evoked in her first appearance. In a devastating advance over Porphyro's "soother jellies," it is her "sooth voice" (1.151) – soothsaying, smooth, soothing at once, prophetic and medicinal – that arrests the poetic initiate. Later, too, concerning the enormous burden of this sad voice, Keatsian coinage fuses an ongoing grief (mourning) with the plaintive sound (moan) of its enunciation, setting off "Moneta's mourn" (232) as a unique kind of speech act, for which he conceived "mourn" as a noun. Her resonant syllables derive from all that "the hollow brain / Behind enwombed" (76–77), where the strained transitive verb "enwomb" may call up the more familiar "entomb" as a lexical shadow. For Moneta's more-than-mortal suffering Keats the surgeon of verse converts a medical idiom (mortal sickness) into a coinage that passes over toward oxymoron: Moneta's eloquent brain is the living grave of "an immortal sickness which kills not" (258). Begging to "behold" (289) her deathless knowledge – to contain (grasp) as well as to envision it – the would-be visionary poet responds in kind to her unprecedented expressive license with a further strain of new words. In Keats's image of the supplicant as "adorant at her feet" (283), "adorant" elevates and vectorizes the standard act of "adoring" with such a noun-form as "aspirant."

The knowledge to which this poet aspires is the scene already laid out in *Hyperion*. An almost lugubrious phonetic density, we have seen, channels our approach to the pent-up, penned-in agony of the Titans. The verse moves to inhabit their grief with the ponderous spondees and downbeats of "their big hearts / Heaving in pain, and horribly convuls'd" (2.26–27), only for the perfect iambic cadence of the next line to convey a helpless pulse of life that persists in such pain "With sanguine feverous boiling gurge of pulse" (28), where the rare word "gurge" is related to "gorge" (whirlpool). This is an anguish that phonetically pervades the bloodiness of "*sangui*ne," just as "spoiling" and the negative "urge" of im/pulse seem spun from junctures in the line's phonetic sludge ("feverou*s boiling*," "boilin[*g g*]urge"). As if to release these clogged effects, Oceanus breathes his syntax into new transmutions.

In explaining why such powers as theirs should be eclipsed and leveled like this, it is as if he had learned from the very sea-changes of his own oceanic realm. Just as "we" (the Titans) triumphed over chaos, he says, so out of our doom will come new beauty: "So on our heels a fresh perfection treads" (2.212). The negative suggestion of "treads on us" slips in on the very heels of its more neutral and dispassionate alternative, restated here: "A power more strong in beauty, born of us" yet "fated to excel us, as we pass / In glory that old Darkness" (2.213–15). With "pass" at the enjambment, we might expect "on" or "away" to complete the verb in the march of evolutionary time. But what follows is not the simultaneous "while" of at least glorious extinction, but a transhistorical analogy: all time is spatialized as immortal symmetry, the lingering present tense of Titanic majesty at one with the new Olympian ascendancy, both fated and fulfilled in the mythic long view. As befits such a ratio of escalated beauty, Oceanus's narrative pivots on a chiasmus: ". . . nor are we / Thereby more conquer'd, than by us the rule / Of shapeless Chaos" [was] (215–17). His elliptical grammar leaves out that [was], but only for it to be understood in instantaneous hindsight; the sequence of conquest is more emphatically a mirrored symmetry. Oceanus wields the belatedly stabilized grammar of fate's eye view. Such see-saws of prehistoric justice are even more compressed later in warmonger Enceladus's expectation of "Our brightest brother, still . . . undisgraced – ": "Hyperion, lo! his radiance is here" (2.344–45). If "undisgraced" evokes the impending event, the fate is already told in the syllables that proceed from *Hy* to *lo* (high to low) – "lo!" even calling in Apol*lo*, the new sun god: "For lo! 'tis for the Father of all verse," he is hailed into the poem (3.13).

As this cry makes clear, Apollo's power is less a matter of solar radiance than of glowing music. To this effect, the syntax of goddess Mnemosyne (his patron and Muse) is attuned. Apollo has, she tells him, found a lyre

> Whose strings touch'd by thy fingers, all the vast
> Unwearied ear of the whole universe
> Listen'd.   (3.64–66)

A receptive "ear" is always waiting at the heart of an "unwearied" (that is, responsive) audience, a "universe" ready for "verse" as soon as strings are "touch'd," and in a kind of subgrammar, "touch'd" as if moved, simultaneously. Around the double sense of "touched," then, a function of cause and effect once again is hinged the mystery of poetic song. As if alluding to his own "end/eared" cross-lexical harmonics in the *Ode on a Grecian Urn*, Keats, the poet of sound, praises Apollo, the god of song, for instilling the "ear" into the very core of all things "unwearied" and hence "d/ear." But at first Apollo, too, is sapped by bafflement at the tragedy in which his own ascendancy is implicated. True to form, he finds wonderfully inert words for his own blocked eloquence – at one point, three such in a row with silent letters that seem to spell numbed verbal power: "a melancholy numbs my limbs" (3.89). When this fragment breaks off less than forty lines on, it does so in a typical indeterminacy of syntax for a last description of a transformed Apollo: "and lo! from all his limbs / Celestial * * * " (135–36). Does this final floating adjective describe Apollo's revivified limbs or, rather, a not yet named something about to flow "from" them? Both, as far as we can say, while also – given the unended epic – neither.

Within the year, Keats has launched again upon his story, now without Apollo and with the challenge of poetry located in the person of the narrating poet himself. With new flexibility and assurance of style, *The Fall of Hyperion: A Dream* sets out a parable not of deification but of a poet's own coming-of-age. If "first in beauty should be first in might," as Oceanus proposed in *Hyperion* (2.229), the myth requires a further evolutionary telos that would lead on through the thrilling liberties of the present retelling. The poem needs, that is, to be less about the gestation of an Olympian divinity than about the immediate birth pangs of the poetic sensibility itself in its struggle for legitimation. The ascendant Apollonian spirit is translated from content toward form in a proem about the potential fitness of the narrator's own poetic spirit for the revelation that will befall him. No poem by Keats tells us more about his matured poetic agenda. No poem understands better the extraverbal yearnings of the words it continues to brandish.

In the opening confession, the speaker's days are seen spent in daydreams – and their writing. Writing sets him above the unlettered, yes, but hardly guarantees his status as true visionary poet. There are many avid dreamers who have not "Trac'd upon vellum or wild Indian leaf / The shadows of melodious utterance" (1.5–6) – as if writing were transcription rather than a set of arbitrary or hieroglyphic marks. This implicit mystification of poetry as the index of voice prepares us for the delphic revelations of the goddess Moneta to the straining brain of the speaker, an intricate vision which only the mnemonics (memory effects) of writing could ever, outside of supernatural trance, hope to communicate. (The goddess of Memory herself, Mnemosyne, will appear later in the dream [2.50].) Once the speaker has feasted all his other senses on a lavish meal, he needs to quaff a magic elixir, a potion whose "full draught is parent of my theme" (46). Whatever its thematic investment in "melodious utterance," can it be doubted that every great poem needs a first draught?

The immediate result is the dreamer-poet's sudden visionary panorama of the Titanic palace as mausoleum, its massive range of columns "ending in mist / Of nothing" (1.84–85). Avoiding, but barely, in "midst of nothing," with its sensory evocation of a tragic vanishing point, the phrase figures negation as obscurity, redoubling the ineffable. But why is the Keatsian poet there at all, summoned before mist-enwrapped, veiled Moneta? He cannot guess, since far more worthy mortals labor with their tragic perception and its commitments; they grapple with "the giant agony" of the world "for mortal good" (1.157–59) rather than mythologize, for poetry, the agony of giants for their lost "giant hierarchy" (223). Moneta is quick to agree but explains that such benefactors would never seek her temple. Dream is access, and those who labor are no dreamers. Her present visitor is "a dreaming thing; / A fever of thyself" (168–69), where heated, deluded self-preoccupation insinuates the sense, by sound, that he is "afever" of self.

The fever of words continues. When the poet describes the location of Moneta's shrine as near an "image" of Saturn, "Whose carved features wrinkled as he fell" (1.225), we may catch the sound of "scar," in anticipation of the marble fissures as wrinkles. The sound sustains the ironic spatialization of tragic time: the god's supersession is a forced aging registered as the instantaneous conversion of life into superannuated image, giant being into commemorative icon. As soon as the cracks come, upon impact, they register irreversible wear in the sudden image of his epochal decline. Here is a fantasy of total mimesis, with the contingencies of sculptural form absorbed into content. Art tells the truth in the very accidents of its own medium.

But listening to the visionary devastation of Moneta's lament, the would-be tragic poet, like Apollo (his counterpart in *Hyperion*),

> had no words to answer, for my tongue,
> Useless could find about its roofed home
> No syllables of a fit majesty
> To make rejoinder to Moneta's mourn. (1.228–31)

Yet the foundation is laid, right there, for fit utterance, in the buried metaphor of the phrase's own reverberant "roofed *home*." The phrasing captures the gently strenuous work of tongue upon the arched dome of the very "palate fine" that closed *Ode on Melancholy* with what Herbert Tucker notes as a "monumentalization" of the mouth's own enunciatory space (284). For the inner architecture of utterance in *The Fall*, too, palatal has become palatial – the rounded space of expressivity resonating with Moneta's "globed brain" (1.245) and her "sphered" language (249). Again, the rondure of the tragic "sphere" (or englobing dome) – the new region of Keats's verse – is punctuated by a phonetic irony at the borders of words, releasing the true force of the "immortal's sphered words" (249). Named here at this brink of revelation, between the words as it were, are feared words, the sublime mix of pity and fear that, transferred to the poet, empowers him to new and often subliminal tragic soundings.

Slippages of syntax rush in to augment those of diction. The inspired narrator can now

> take the depth
> Of things as nimbly as the outward eye
> Can size and shape pervade.   (1.303–6)

To "take the depth" is not merely to take the measure or to measure the depth, but to seize and master the heretofore unfathomed. This is the agency of contemplated vision, of an inward (no longer "outward") eye. Once more, Keats's sense is completed in analogy, doubly enhanced. A dawning power of vision not only can "size" (measure) things, but also can pervade sizes and shapes; "size" switches on the instant from verb to a noun form in an inverted objective case. The appointed poet who can "size and shape pervade," who can permeate both the massive volume of tragedy and its clarifying outlines, its vast scale and its true profile: this is the poet of the new tragic sublime, gorgeous in its terror, rounded in its fearsome reverberations. The writer who began his career negotiating, along the hypnotic underside of word-sounds and the undulating tremors of syntax, between the unconscious oscillations of Sleep and Poetry has, just before death, reached through the rigors of a dream vision to the true waking accent of tragedy, again the "beauteous truth" of its bleak realizations.

NOTES

1 Rollins takes some of the fun away with his clarifying bracket: "{hie}*rogue*glyphics."

2 Chatterton "is the purest writer in the English Language. He has no French idiom [. . .] 'tis genuine English Idiom in English Words" (*KL* 2.167; cf. 2.212).

3 John Jones, *John Keats's Dream of Truth*, 8–9.

4 Christopher Ricks, "William Wordsworth: 'A pure organic pleasure from the lines'" (1971); *The Force of Poetry* (Oxford and New York: Oxford University Press, 1987), 101.

5 See Susan J. Wolfson, "The Odes: Reader as Questioner," *The Questioning Presence: Wordsworth, Keats, and the Interrogative Mode in Romantic Poetry*, 301–32.

6 Paul Fussell, Jr., *Poetic Meter and Poetic Form* (New York: Random House, 1966), 49–50.

7 Points made respectively in my *Reading Voices: Literature and the Phonotext* (Berkeley: University of California Press, 1990), 173, and Herbert F. Tucker, "Of Monuments and Moments: Spacetime in Nineteenth-Century Poetry," *Modern Language Quarterly* 58.3 (September 1997), 284.

10

CHRISTOPHER RICKS

Keats's sources, Keats's allusions

At the root of "allusion" is the verb "to play" (from the Latin, "ludere"). A calling into play is not the same as referring to or mentioning, and it need not be covert or indirect. Like other poets, Keats sometimes puts his allusion in direct quotation:

> – Of bad lines a Centaine dose
> Is sure enough – and so "here follows prose."
> ("Dear Reynolds" 112–13; *KL* 1.263)

Keats follows *Twelfth Night. Or, What You Will*. With any allusion, the play's the thing (wherein I'll catch the conscience and the consciousness). The concept of allusion and its application ask to be flexible, as with the due amount of play in any steering wheel.

Keats alludes to mythology, history, topical circumstance, and so on; this essay attends to the calling into play of the words or phrases of a previous writer. An allusion predicates a source (no coincidence); but identifying a source is not the same as postulating an allusion, for a source is not necessarily called into play by its beneficiary. What goes to the making of a poem does not necessarily go to its meaning. Sometimes readers will disagree as to whether a line of Keats had its source in, say, *Hamlet*; sometimes, they may agree that such was a source but disagree as to whether he was alluding; and often readers will disagree as to just what they should make of what Keats made of that which he alluded to. This, not because in criticism anything goes, but because much goes. Poems have a way of being undulating and diverse.

In a consideration of Dryden and Pope ("Allusion: the Poet as Heir"), I took the cue of J. B. Broadbent's words: "Literary allusion can be a lesson in the abuse of authority as well as in the generous spending of an inheritance. We need an essay on 'The poet as heir.'"[1] The inheritor needs to be not only generous but responsible, given that an inheritance is held in trust. Most allusions that are subtle and effective are likely to respect inheritance. For Augustan poets, the essential inheritance had been royal, political, legal, and literary. This art of allusion was fecundated by a parallelism – one that acknowledged dissimilitude within the similitude, as a worthwhile metaphor does – between allusion as a form of inheritance and its preoccupation with particular kinds of inheritance. An exemplary Augustan allusion is this:

> Say from what cause, in vain decry'd and curst,
> Still Dunce the second reigns like Dunce the first?
>
> (Pope, *The Dunciad* [1728–29] 1.5–6)

Alluding to a verse of Mr. Dryden's not in *Mac Fleckno* (as it is said ignorantly in the Key to the *Dunciad, pag.* 1) but in his verses to Mr. *Congreve*:
> And Tom *the Second reigns like* Tom *the First.*
>
> (Pope's parodic note to his poem)

A sense of the central or essential inheritance changes in history, the change both creating and created by changes within literature and its shaping spirit of imagination. For Wordsworth, the essential inheritance had been the power of perception: our most important inheritance is the senses and pre-eminently the eye and the ear. For Keats, the crucial inheritance is that of English poetry itself. This simultaneously simplifies and complicates his art of allusion. Simplifies, because there is no longer the imaginative enterprise of reconciling two things (literary inheritance and something importantly other); complicates, because if there be no tension between the literary and the non-literary, where will this leave literature? Nowhere because everywhere?

Keats's singular art might be seen as fulfilling allusion or as nullifying it. Interplay between art and all that is not art: this pinpoints the crux. Is Keats the great poet of aestheticism, of art for art's sake? Or does he put aestheticism in its place, a place of honor that does not enjoy a monopoly of honor? Not the be-all ye need to know, leave alone the end-all.

What is art, that it should have a sake?

Keats made much of his poetic inheritance. Those who knew him thought of him as an heir who would have heirs. "Though born to be a poet," his friend Charles Brown averred, "he was ignorant of his birthright until he had completed his eighteenth year" (*KC* 2.55). This is to respect Keats along his own lines: "The Genius of Milton, more particularly in respect to its span in immensity, calculated him, by a sort of birthright, for such an 'argument' as the paradise lost."[2] In praising Milton, Keats wields words in a way that both is and is not Milton's: "its span in immensity" is a paradox of the kind with which Milton illuminated the world (the immense is the immeasurable, how then can it have a *span?*); yet Keats's wording does not mimic Milton, whose own paradoxes are differently jointed, compressed into oxymorons: "darkness visible," "pretious bane."

Reviewing *Endymion*, Francis Jeffrey had recourse to the figure of inheritance. Praising Keats's evocation of the richly strewn ocean-floor (3.119–36), he was sure that, though "abundantly extravagant," it "comes of no ignoble lineage, nor shames its high descent."[3] Keats's seascape acknowledges its lineage, its unrepressed memory of Clarence's dream in *Richard III* (1.4.22–33). How deftly, in the words "high descent," Jeffrey catches the paradox of a creativity that owes much to another's creativity: "high," noble, even royal of blood, like Clarence; "descent," to the ocean-bed. It is true of Keats's deepest imaginings that they enjoy a sea-change, for *Endymion* gathers strength of life not only from Shakespeare's imagining but, within that, from Shakespeare's dreamer's imaginings. Imagination within imagination.

Even when down to earth, Keats relishes Shakespeare's flights. Return to those lines that bring his verse-letter to Reynolds to a close, or rather bring to a close the verse part so as to open the prose part: " – Of bad lines a Centaine dose / Is sure enough – and so 'here follows prose.' – " (*KL* 1.263). *Enough?* Not until we comprehend that Keats has Malvolio in play, as had those pranksters in *Twelfth Night* who gulled him with the spoof love-letter from the great lady of the house:

> Soft, here followes prose. – *If this fall into thy hand, revolve. In my stars I am above thee; but be not afraid of greatness: Some are born great, some achieve greatness, and some have greatness thrust upon them.* (2.5.156–60)

Keats was born great, whatever his social class; he achieved greatness; and he did so because greatness was thrust upon him, by courtesy of his predecessors, their greatness. Keats wished well. Benvolio, not Malvolio. The poetry of the past was very seldom social oppression and was very often the means of escape, not only from class but from something else that may oppress, a grievance as to class.

What Keats most valued in the English poets, irrespective of anything with which they could furnish his art, was a sense of brotherhood with his peers. He declines the invitation to figure in the dark melodrama of Harold Bloom's *Anxiety of Influence*.[4] How unmisgivingly Keats speaks of influence, especially while happily under it.

> And many a verse from so strange influence
> That we must ever wonder how, and whence
> It came. Also imaginings will hover
> Round my fire-side . . . (*Sleep and Poetry* 69–72)

This verse knows what it owes to Wordsworth, and playfully is pleased if we know too. Keats finds in *To the Daisy* the gift of which Wordsworth speaks, "A happy genial influence, / Coming one knows not how, or whence." With this proviso only, that this time we do know how and whence the happy genial influence came, and need not ever wonder. The "imaginings" within Keats's lines embody the kindly hovering of which they speak. A mystery remains, but it is mitigated by the simply unmisgiving. For Keats, allusions are debts of honor. He is indebted to Wordsworth's lines about a debt, about what is owing:

> And all day long I number yet,
> All seasons through, another debt,
> Which I, wherever thou art met,
>   To thee am owing;
> An instinct call it, a blind sense;
> A happy genial influence,
> Coming one knows not how, or whence,
>   Nor whither going.   (*To the Daisy* 65–72)

Thither, to Keats, this is one place where these lines – unbeknownst to their creator – were going.

Keats spoke with inspiration of inspiration, its astonishment. His friend Richard Woodhouse set this down vividly in the summer of 1820:

> He has said, that he has often not been aware of the beauty of some thought or expression until after he has composed & written it down – It has then struck him with astonishment – & seemed rather the production of another person than his own – He has wondered how he came to hit upon it. [. . .] – Perhaps every one in the habit of writing verse or prose, may have had a some-what similar feeling, that of the extreme appositeness & happiness (the *curiosa felicitas*) of an idea, of the excellence of which he was unaware until he [. . .] came to read it over. It seems scarcely his own; & he feels that he could never imitate or hit upon it again: & he cannot conceive how it came to him – Such Keats said was his Sensation of astonishment & pleasure when he had pro-duced the lines "His white melodious &c – It seemed to come by chance or magic – to be as it were something given to him. –
> (*KC* 1.129; expanding contractions and eliding canceled readings)

This is itself inspired and astonishing. Much of what Keats says is germane to the local wonders of allusion. Paradoxically it is often by courtesy of another, with the aid of allusion, that a poet becomes himself. Allusion calls into play "the production of another person," "something given to him," something "scarcely his own." "He cannot conceive how it came to him": and this is partly because the conceiving is not his alone, any more than is the conceiving of a baby, a new lease of life.

And, as Woodhouse remarked, Keats's insight is "expressed in these lines so happily that they are an illustration of the very thing itself":

> Apollo then,
> With sudden scrutiny and gloomless eyes,
> Thus answer'd, while his white melodious throat
> Throbb'd with the syllables. – "Mnemosyne!
> Thy name is on my tongue, I know not how." (*Hyperion* 3.79–83)

The cry itself is on Keats's tongue, he knows not how. Yet perhaps one aspect of the how is the grace of Wordsworth, "Coming one knows not how."

Keats's play with allusion animates his great letters. In a letter-journal to George and Georgiana far away in America (12 March 1819), he described not only what but how, physically how, he had been reading, exactly how he stood and sat the while. And then:

> These are trifles – but I require nothing so much of you as that you will give me a like description of yourselves, however it may be when you are writing to me – Could I see the same thing done of any great Man long since dead it would be a great delight: as to know in what position Shakspeare sat when he began "To be or not to be" – such thing[s] become interesting from distance of time or place. I hope you are both now in that sweet sleep which no two beings deserve more that [than] you do – I must fancy you so.   (*KL* 2.73–74)

This takes its origin, as so often in Keats, from the imagining of someone imagining (Shakespeare writing *Hamlet*). Although "To be or not to be" is simply referred to, it hangs in a web of allusion. A happy web withal.

"There's magick in the web of it." To the curse upon Hamlet and death's troubled sleep ("To sleep! perchance to dream; ay, there's the rub"; 3.1.65) is added the curse upon Othello. Iago's imaginings are malign as he exults over Othello:

> Look, where he comes! Not poppy, nor mandragora,
> Nor all the drowsy syrups of the world,
> Shall ever medicine thee to that sweet sleep
> Which thou ow'dst yesterday.   (3.3.331–34)

But what in Iago was sickly sweet is turned by Keats, by magic, into sheer love, not a gloating curse but "a prayer and a blessing":

> I hope you are both now in that sweet sleep which no two beings deserve more that [than] you do – I must fancy you so – and please myself in the fancy of speaking a prayer and a blessing over you and your lives – God bless you – I whisper good night in your ears and you will dream of me –   (*KL* 2.74)

The words "that sweet sleep" are rinsed, restored; their having been so is part of love's point. True, it is a simple run of words, but Keats deepens its simplicity, gracing Iago's disgrace. Iago had assured himself, a few lines earlier: "Trifles, light as air, / Are, to the jealous, confirmations strong / As proofs of holy writ" (3.3.323–25). Keats had doffed his thoughts on posture: "These are trifles."

Keats's imagination can transubstantiate, can convert gall to manna. Not imagining only, but imagining into. This is what he pondered in Milton: "One of the most mysterious of semi-speculations is, one would suppose, that of one Mind's imagining into another" (marginalia to *Paradise Lost* 1.53–75; see Cook, 337). But is this a semi-speculation or a double one? There is imagining, there is *imagining into*, and there is *imagining after*. Keats needed this prepositional extension to express his awe at Pandemonium:

> What creates the intense pleasure of not knowing? A sense of independence, of power, from the fancy's creating a world of its own by the sense of probabilities. We have read the Arabian Nights and hear there are thousands of those sort of Romances lost – we imagine after them – but not their realities if we had them nor our fancies in their strength can go further than this Pandemonium. (on *Paradise Lost* 1.710–30; Cook, 340)

A world of its own, and yet one open to us all. A palace of art, or rather – in this grim case of Milton's Pandemonium – of devilish aestheticism.

In their lightfooted pounce, Keats's marginalia in his copies of Milton and Shakespeare offer no less vivid evidence of how his poetic imagination worked and played than do his letters. In the same spirit he evokes Edmund Kean's Shakespearean acting as continuous with Shakespeare's own imaginative powers: "There is an indescribable gusto in his voice, by which we feel that the utterer is thinking of the past and the future, while speaking of the instant."[5] Gliding from "the past" to "the future," Keats's sentence then swoops, not as you expect, upon "the present" but upon "the instant." He is imagining not only the consummate actor, but the character and the playwright. His insight commands the vistas, at once exhilarating and dizzying, of the imagining of imagining.

Ever alert on allusion's traces, Keats is drawn to such moments when an imagination creates imaginers, actors for instance. Or imaginings that are dreams; Mercutio's imagining of dreams' imaginings in *Romeo and Juliet* is midwife to Keats's lines in *Endymion*:

> Look not so wilder'd; for these things are true,
> And never can be born of atomies
> That buzz about our slumbers, like brain-flies . . . (1.850–52)

These atomies were born of Shakespeare and of Mercutio, a team now joined by Keats in team-work, dream-work:

> Drawn with a team of little atomies
> Athwart men's noses as they lie asleep.
>
> (*Romeo and Juliet* 1.4.57–8)

Dreams are real but do not present realities exactly; the same is true of actors.

Dreams and actors, engaging in feats of imagination, meet in the post-masque moment of *The Tempest*:

> These our actors,
> As I foretold you, were all spirits, and
> Are melted into air, into thin air:
> And, like the baseless fabrick of this vision,
> The clowd-capp'd towers, the gorgeous palaces,
> The solemn temples, the great globe itself,
> Yea, all which it inherit, shall dissolve;
> And, like this insubstantial pageant faded,
> Leave not a rack behind: we are such stuff
> As dreams are made of, and our little life
> Is rounded with a sleep. –   (4.1.148–58)

The actor playing Prospero speaks of the actors of the masque within the play. He intimates to the audience that each of us is an actor. A line-ending ("spirits, and / Are melted") pauses and poises upon *and* for a minuscule moment, to intimate such vistas.

This supreme speech was for Keats a source and a resource, inviting his art of allusion:

> The Morphean fount
> Of that fine element that visions, dreams,
> And fitful whims of sleep are made of, streams
> Into its airy channels with so subtle,
> So thin a breathing, not the spider's shuttle,
> Circled a million times within the space
> Of a swallow's nest-door, could delay a trace,
> A tinting of its quality: how light
> Must dreams themselves be; seeing they're more slight
> Than the mere nothing that engenders them!
>
> (*Endymion* 1.747–56)

The traces are there for all to see and feel, light but not slight, engendered not by a mere nothing but by a great something, Shakespeare's vision (itself of another's vision). "A tinting of its quality" is there, a Shakespearean quality. "That fine element that visions, dreams, / And fitful whims of sleep are made of": Keats is finely in his element, which is Shakespeare's element, for such is what it breathes, what it is made of – *made of*, the reading in Keats's volume of Shakespeare, subsequently established as *made on*.

Prospero prophesies. "The great globe itself, / Yea, all which it inherit, shall dissolve" (4.1.153–54). Keats inherits this, this thought, these very words. Not until all dissolves will Shakespeare's words (he trusts) dissolve. Two points of principle underlie all this. First, that Keats's way with Shakespeare does not insist a reader know Prospero's lines. Irrespective of Shakespeare, Keats's lines are a thing of beauty and a joy for ever. A poet does well to have the courtesy and the prudence not to make the taking of an allusion a precondition of a reader's appreciation. The allusion is a bonus, not an entrance-fee. Furthermore, allusion, like many other resources of art, often effects most when it manages to be self-referential, yet without narcissism. Some impulse that underlies allusion (inheriting, playing, borrowing) may fit happily with the preoccupations and subject-matter of the work itself. For it is characteristic of art to find energy and delight in an enactment of that which it is saying. Keats inherits Shakespeare's evocation, "all which it inherit"; Shakespeare's spirit and spirits inspire him and his breathing; his art is tinted with its quality. Recall Woodhouse on Keats and inspiration, an insight "expressed in these lines so happily that they are an illustration of the very thing itself."

Keats's respect for Milton and Shakespeare is inseparable from, though not indistinguishable from, the allusive achievements that are thanks to them. He is truly grateful, as the allusive poet had better be. Take his excitement at a great speech in *A Midsummer Night's Dream* in which ill will arrives at good will. Titania's speech begins in an evocation of jealousy, but how poor is jealousy in comparison with goodnesses, with the gracious, with love and gratitude:

> These are the forgeries of jealousie,
> And never since the middle Summers spring
> Met we on hil, in dale, forrest, or mead,
> By paved fountaine, or by rushie brooke,
> Or in the beached margent of the sea,
> To dance our ringlets to the whistling Winde,
> But with thy braules thou hast disturb'd our sport. (2.1.77–83)

Keats marvels lucidly:

> There is something exquisitely rich and luxurious in Titania's saying "since the middle summer's spring" as if Bowers were not exuberant and covert enough for fairy sports until their second sprouting – which is surely the most bounteous overwhelming of all Nature's goodnesses. She steps forth benignly in the spring and her conduct is so gracious that by degrees all things are becoming

happy under her wings and nestle against her bosom: she feels this Love & gratitude too much to remain selfsame, and unable to contain herself buds forth the overflowings of her heart about the middle summer. – O Shakespeare thy ways are but just searchable! The thing is a piece of profound verdure.[6]

Keats, like Nature (as Shakespeare has passionately imagined her), steps forth benignly. Nature is grateful for our gratitude, is at one with all imaginative energies, and Shakespeare is a force of nature. In crying "O Shakespeare thy ways are but just searchable," Keats stops "but just" this side idolatry. Wycliffe's translation of Romans 11.33 had praised God "and his ways unsearchable," and Boswell had exclaimed in his life of Johnson (aetat.20): "How wonderful, how unsearchable are the ways of GOD!"

The filament between Keats's gratitude to Shakespeare and his allusions can be glimpsed in the phrases within his commentary that call allusion into play. For allusion too is a "second sprouting," may be gracious, does not "remain self-same" – yet this because of an extension, not a repudiation, of the self and the same. Like a due allusion, "The middle Summers spring" is a renovation, generously two seasons at once, its own and not its own. T. S. Eliot evoked another loveliness of seasonable surprise that may owe something to Shakespeare and to Keats (though probably as no more than source, not as allusion), there in the first line of *Little Gidding*: "Midwinter spring is its own season."

"A piece of profound verdure": such was Keats's tribute to Shakespeare's words, to Titania's words, to the nature of Nature. From a speech later in the same scene there grew a piece of profound verdure in Keats:

> I cannot see what flowers are at my feet,
>   Nor what soft incense hangs upon the boughs,
> But, in embalmed darkness, guess each sweet
>   Wherewith the seasonable month endows
> The grass, the thicket, and the fruit-tree wild;
>   White hawthorn, and the pastoral eglantine;
>   Fast fading violets cover'd up in leaves;
>   And mid-May's eldest child,
>   The coming musk-rose, full of dewy wine,
>   The murmurous haunt of flies on summer eves.
>   (*Ode to a Nightingale* 41–50)

> I know a banke where the wilde thyme blowes,
> Where Oxslips and the nodding Violet growes,
> Quite over-cannoped with luscious woodbine,
> With sweet muske roses, and with Eglantine;
> There sleeps *Tytania*, sometime of the night,
> Lull'd in these flowers, with dances and delight:
>   (*A Midsummer Night's Dream* 2.1.249–54)[7]

The flowers, violets, musk roses, and eglantine; the darkness of the night; the sweet that is not sickly, and the wild that is not dangerous: all these are transplanted from Shakespeare's garden to Keats's. The violets re-double still and multiply. Yet Keats has made the verdure his own. How much is effected by the imaginative simplicity that changes Oberon's couplets to diverse couplings of rhyme that incorporate, mid-way, the shortening, the compacting, of a line ("And mid-May's eldest child"). And how characteristic of Keats's good-will that what in Oberon's scene-setting is to issue only three lines later in ill-will ("And make her full of hateful fantasies"), is in the *Ode* an imagining of love and truth. This too is then a "second sprouting." Though not the kind of allusion that crystallizes overtly (as does "here follows prose"), this is allusion nevertheless, a diffusion of atmosphere that calls tenderly into play (for "tender is the night") the air of an earlier play.

Shakespeare has soaked Keats's heart through. The heart of the passage in the *Ode* is Shakespearean. Or rather, one of the heart's chambers is. It was a needless either/or that led Helen Vendler to insist (in an endnote) that here Keats draws upon poetry alone:

> To deck his bower, Keats turns not to nature but to art: the violets and musk-roses and eglantine are borrowed from Titania's bower [. . .], described by Oberon (as this bower is described by Keats) from memory, not sight.*

> *Robert Pinsky [. . .] cites this passage as an example of the poetry of realist description. It is, in fact, just the opposite (since Keats is "blind"); it is an example of pure imaginative conceiving and literary allusion.[8]

For Vendler, not nature but art. Why not both? Keats's husbandry sees to it that the second sprouting, rooted in poetry, is equally rooted in roots, in nature, in common or garden sproutings.

Art's relations to art are the stronger when art acknowledges the power of what is not art: nature, say. This independent power is happy with interdependency.

> "This is an art
> Which does mend nature, change it rather, but
> The art itself is nature."
> "So it is."
> (*The Winter's Tale* 4.4.95–97)

Keats is deeply touched by Shakespeare, because Shakespeare's words realize the true voice of feeling. His friend Charles Cowden Clarke never forgot this in the young Keats:

> It was a treat to see as well as hear him read a pathetic passage. Once, when reading the "Cymbeline" aloud, I saw his eyes fill with tears, and his voice

faltered when he came to the departure of Posthumus, and Imogen saying she would have watched him –

> 'Till the diminution
> Of space had pointed him sharp as my needle;
> Nay followed him till he had *melted from*
> *The smallness of a gnat to air;* and then
> Have turn'd mine eye and wept.[9]

Keats's eyes fill with tears as he reads aloud of Imogen's tears, or rather, her imagining of tears. In her dear resilience she is not in tears, but is imagining how she would have ended in tears had she suffered (as had the man who tells her of it) the sight of her departing loved one. The speech is among Shakespeare's greatest, with the art in the precision. There is "from" at the line-brink, at a parting, the delicatest lattice. There is the movement from the open sound to the closed conclusion in the sequence "mine eye and wept." There is "my needle," not *a* needle since the speaker is a woman. And how pointed "needle" is, for it pricks, and a needle has an eye, so Imogen's heart and mind move with rueful effortlessness from "my needle" to "mine eye," with a faint touch upon *mine* as against the needle's. Not only the mind's eye, but the heart's eye.[10]

"Nay followed him": and as with "Here follows prose," Keats is happy to follow Shakespeare in imagining a sadness of departure. Shakespeare's passage is a point of departure for Keats:

> "Now adieu!
> Here must we leave thee." – At these words up flew
> The impatient doves, up rose the floating car,
> Up went the hum celestial. High afar
> The Latmian saw them minish into nought;
> And, when all were clear vanish'd, still he caught
> A vivid lightning from that dreadful bow. (*Endymion* 2.578–84)

Keats's lines are buoyed not only by a memory of Shakespeare's Imogen but also by Shakespearean powers. There is the elision (urged by the meter) that catches impatience in "*The imp*atient doves," in the Augustan manner, "Th'impatient." There is the play of one linguistic world against another in the mildly oxymoronic phrase "the hum celestial," as though the humdrum hum might always sit happily next to the celestial. Then the open endings "afar" and "bow" against the closed "caught" and "nought" (owing something to such an effect in Shakespeare's ear and Imogen's mouth). And the philosophical paradox "minish into nought" (is this possible?), along with "minish" as itself a 'minished form of *diminish*, not a diminishing of Shakespeare's "diminution" but an extension of its imagination. With the sound effect of "minish" into "vanish'd," minish does not vanish; it is still echoed, and so has not, at least, vanished from memory, from our hearing.

That Keats owes a debt to Shakespeare, and pays it, is not to be doubted. But are we contemplating a source or an allusion? We might learn from Keats, who never relaxes his intelligence but always has a relaxed intelligence. We might let memory play, let Mnemosyne be our muse, without insisting either/or:

> several things dovetailed in my mind, & at once it struck me, what quality went to form a Man of Achievement especially in Literature & which Shakespeare possessed so enormously – I mean <u>Negative Capability</u>, that is when man is capable of being in uncertainties, Mysteries, doubts, without any irritable reaching after fact & reason –   (*KL* 1.193)

Dovetailing, Keats both does and does not depart from Shakespeare.

It is characteristic of his genius that what informs his art informs his life no less. He wrote to his loved one Fanny Brawne, two years after *Endymion*:

> Yesterday and this morning I have been haunted with a sweet vision – I have seen you the whole time in your shepherdess dress. How my senses have ached at it! How my eyes have been full of Tears at it! [. . .] say what you think – confess if your heart is too much fasten'd on the world. Perhaps then I may see you at a greater distance, I may not be able to appropriate you so closely to myself. Were you to loose a favorite bird from the cage, how would your eyes ache after it as long as it was in sight; when out of sight you would recover a little.   (?May 1820; *KL* 2.290–91)

This, which owes as much to ordinary life as to Shakespeare's art and Keats's own, is not "too consolatory to console" (to apply to Keats a fine formulation by Frank Kermode), and is itself art, as Keats's letters so often are.

Keats has us exercise our imagination upon a poet's imaginings. This always has the danger that we may imagine something that is not there. Keats himself was aware that a poet's intentions cannot be limited to conscious intentions: "One of the three Books I have with me is Shakespear's Poems," he wrote to Reynolds, a brother poet; "I neer found so many beauties in the sonnets – they seem to be full of fine things said unintentionally – in the intensity of working out conceits" (22 November 1817; *KL* 1.188). Said in the sonnets, for sure, but said so as to surprise the sayer, as we have heard Keats himself say of inspiration:

> He has said, that he has often not been aware of the beauty of some thought or expression until after he has composed & written it down – It has then struck him with astonishment –

"Said unintentionally – in the intensity of working out conceits": this immediately conveys that the intensity of poetry may be continuous with its being issued unintentionally, inspired as unpremeditated verse. In his letter to

Reynolds, Keats had to correct himself – not as to Shakespeare's greatness, but as to just where the instance that he loved was to be found:

> He has left nothing to say about nothing or any thing: for look at Snails, you know what he says about Snails, you know where he talks about "cockled snails" – well, in one of these sonnets he says – the chap slips into – no! I lie! this is in the Venus and Adonis: the Simile brought it to my Mind.
>   Audi – As the snail, whose tender horns being hit,
>   Shrinks back into his shelly cave with pain [. . .]
>   So at his bloody view her eyes are fled
>   Into the deep dark Cabins of her head.   (*KL* 1.189)[11]

Yet far from having left nothing to say, Shakespeare helps others – Keats among them – to find what they have to say.

"As the snail . . . So . . .": "The Simile brought it to my Mind." When Keats breathes open a sonnet with the line "To one who has been long in city pent," there can be no doubt of an allusion to *Paradise Lost* (9.445–66): "As one who long in populous City pent . . ."[12] In Milton this had been something imagined within an imagining, in a simile, "As one who . . . Such pleasure took the serpent . . ." In Keats, it has become the fresh air itself, a larger air than the psychic fresh air, the inner weather, that refreshed Satan for a while: "Such pleasure took the Serpent" (9.455). The whole of Keats's sonnet is alive with diverse moments from Milton (the singular "angel's tear" flows from the "tears such as angels weep" that Milton had conceived, *Paradise Lost* 1.620). But Keats is not pent in Milton, nor Milton in him. Both breathe. The breathing-room comes in part from Keats's having been prompted by a simile, already an imagining upon imagining:

> To one who has been long in city pent,
>   'Tis very sweet to look into the fair
>   And open face of heaven – to breathe a prayer
> Full in the smile of the blue firmament.
> Who is more happy, when, with heart's content,
>   Fatigued he sinks into some pleasant lair
>   Of wavy grass, and reads a debonair
> And gentle tale of love and languishment?
> Returning home at evening, with an ear
>   Catching the notes of Philomel, – an eye
> Watching the sailing cloudlet's bright career,
>   He mourns that day so soon has glided by:
> E'en like the passage of an angel's tear
>   That falls through the clear ether silently.

Milton's "sweet recess" becomes the pleasant lair where was bred the "very sweet" of Keats's sonnet. Milton's "heavenly" becomes "heaven"; what was "pleasing" and "pleases more," "Such pleasure," all turn in Keats to the relaxedly "pleasant," rather as the "tedded grass," cut and drying, reverts to the relaxedly uncut, the "wavy grass." But "to breathe" remains exactly, entirely, happily, the same. With a nimble leap, Milton's name "Eve" returns home as "evening." With a dear new creation from Milton's creation, what in *Paradise Lost* had been "the air," and of Eve "her every air," becomes in Keats the "debonair." But then what is debonair but *de bonne aire*? Satan's disposition, though not his nature, is changed for a moment by the good air:

> That space the Evil one abstracted stood
> From his own evil, and for the time remaind
> Stupidly good, of enmitie disarm'd,
> Of guile, of hate, of envie, of revenge.   (9.463–6)

Again and again there is an *As* or a *So* or a *Like* in the passages to which Keats is drawn and upon which he draws, whether as source or as allusion. There is present not only the imagined but the imaginary. It is this act of imagining *within* a work of imagination that from one point of view compounds the store set upon imagination, imagination upon imagination after all. But from another point of view, to distinguish the imaginary from the imagined must be to introduce a crucial distinction that is in its turn germane to the distinction between imagination and all else. "Imaginings will hover / Round my fire-side" (*Sleep and Poetry* 71–72). But in the words of Samuel Beckett – who alludes consummately to *Ode to a Nightingale* in his story *Dante and the Lobster*: "Take into the air my quiet breath" – there are, after all, "Things and imaginings."[13] So there are, although things too have to be imagined, and although imagination is at work in all our seeing and our remembering. There remains a distinction between the imagined and the imaginary. Leave alone the imaginative.

The imaginary within the imagined, this most draws Keats. It may be a simile within description's imagination ("As the snail . . ."), or an imaginary landscape within an imagined world. Dover Cliff in *King Lear* (4.4.12–25) exists differently from all that is in its vicinity in the play, in that no such cliff is there for Gloucester to throw himself from. And if it should be retorted that, this being a play, no Earl of Gloucester and no therapeutic Edgar really exist either, it would still be the case that Dover Cliff has a different order of existlessness. It is fully imagined, yes, but known to be something other than imagined, to be imaginary on this occasion, while existing as a real cliff outside the play in geological time.

Dover Cliff (Shakespeare's, Edgar's) fascinated Keats. It dominates one of his greatest letters, that to the painter Haydon in May 1817, where Keats ponders what it is that might, in the words he quotes from *Love's Labor's Lost* (1.1.7), "make us heirs of all eternity":

> – truth is I have been in such a state of Mind as to read over my Lines and hate them. I am "one that gathers Samphire dreadful trade" the Cliff of Poesy Towers above me – yet when, Tom who meets with some of Pope's Homer in Plutarch's Lives reads some of those to me they seem like Mice to mine.
>
> (*KL* 1.141)

This gazes up the sheer cliff, not down it as Edgar had done with his here-imaginary cliff, but Keats still remembers the fishermen who in Edgar's vertiginous fancy "appear like mice." One kind of awe ("the Cliff of Poesy Towers above me") is blessedly countered by the opposite kind, the heartening, with *yet*: I hate my lines and yet Pope's lines "seem like Mice to mine."

Keats makes new while not making free. Even his misquotations can catch a truth. The exchange in this scene when Edgar's false intimation, "Hark, do you hear the sea?," is met by Gloucester's reply "No, truly," is truly misremembered by Keats, as incorporating the pressure of *not*: "the passage in Lear – 'Do you not hear the Sea?' – has haunted me intensely" (*KL* 2.132). No *not* in Edgar, and yet Gloucester does not hear the sea, truly does not, there being no sea just there except in Edgar's words. Which is not quite the same, given the imaginary within the imagined, as saying Shakespeare's words, since different kinds of imagining are called for, called upon.

The currency that Keats's predecessors enjoy within his work is never small change (as Byron's allusive largesse ringingly is). The characteristic Keatsian wealth of allusiveness is more diffused than a coin of allusion. The distinction between a source and an allusion becomes more than usually elusive once what is in play is a more impalpable allusiveness. Here is saturation, and not crystallization:

> Fade far away, dissolve, and quite forget
>   What thou among the leaves hast never known,
> The weariness, the fever, and the fret
>   Here, where men sit and hear each other groan;
> Where palsy shakes a few, sad, last gray hairs,
>   Where youth grows pale, and spectre-thin, and dies;
>   Where but to think is to be full of sorrow
>   And leaden-eyed despairs,
>   Where Beauty cannot keep her lustrous eyes,
>   Or new Love pine at them beyond to-morrow.
>
> (*Ode to a Nightingale* 21–30)

This never forgets Shakespeare's Sonnet 73 ("That time of year thou mayst in me behold"), a tissue of metaphors throughout, imaginings within an imagined state of mind, with what is beheld being beholden entirely to elaborated metaphors, one after the other: "In me thou seest . . .," "In me thou seest . . .," "This thou perceivst." It is the poem that most dissolves into a poem of Keats. A tabulation may tell the story even though it conveys none of the feeling, the shared mood that is but one of Keats's moods in his poem. Keats's stanza is a second sprouting from Shakespeare's sonnet: *fade, away, thou, leaves, where, shakes, few, sad, youth, dies* (death), and *love*. More, Keats's entire poem, "a piece of profound verdure," is alive with the verdurous glooms of this sonnet. Shakespeare's "hang / Upon those boughs" becomes, with a different suspension, Keats's "hangs upon the boughs." Although no single shared word is unusual, the density achieves a cumulative plausibility: in the order of the sonnet, *time, sweet, birds / Bird, sang / sing, seest / see, twilight / light, such, day / days, fadeth / fading, night, take, Death, self, whereon / wherewith, thy, more, well, long*.

F. R. Leavis, not usually a critic who goes in for the tentativeness of "It is as if . . .," was duly teased by Keats and aestheticism. "It is as if Keats were making major poetry out of minor – as if, that is, the genius of a major poet were working in the material of minor poetry."[14] Aestheticism may be judged both to overvalue art and to undervalue it, as valuing only art and as misrepresenting art's relation to all else. Alluding sardonically to the closing lines of *Ode on a Grecian Urn*, Philip Larkin spoke of

> the two kinds of poem I sometimes think I write: the beautiful and the true. I have always believed that beauty is beauty, truth truth, that is not all ye know on earth nor all ye need to know, and I think a poem usually starts off either from the feeling How beautiful that is or from the feeling How true that is. One of the jobs of the poem is to make the beautiful seem true and the true beautiful, but in fact the disguise can usually be penetrated.[15]

T. S. Eliot, no aesthete, clarified what is at issue:

> It is the function of a literary review to maintain the autonomy and disinterestedness of literature, and at the same time to exhibit the relations of literature – not to "life," as something contrasted to literature, but to all the other activities, which, together with literature, are the components of life.
>
> (*The Criterion* 1 [July 1923], 421)

Keats's greatest poems, and letters, realize the extremity both of heroic submission to art and of resistance to art's inordinacy or hubris.

At the level of explicit asseveration (as against realization in art), this putting of art in its true place is not particularly difficult, whether in prose or in verse. Saying it is one thing, showing is another. So there is something unfelt about the amiable acrostic to Georgiana Keats, with its unimaginative invoking of the imagination, its orotund didacticism:

> Imagine not that greatest mastery
> And kingdom over all the realms of verse
> Nears more to heaven in aught than when we nurse
> And surety give to love and brotherhood.
>
> ("Give me your patience, sister" 6–9)

True love and brotherhood, or rather these qualities truly realized within art, issue from Keats's sense of the brotherhood of poets, calling sometimes upon allusion, a mastery and a surety.

On First Looking into Chapman's Homer achieves its own genius in acknowledging with gratitude the genius of George Chapman. For this, Keats had cause to be grateful to his friend and mentor Clarke:

> One scene I could not fail to introduce to him – the shipwreck of Ulysses, in the fifth book of the "Odysseis," and I had the reward of one of his delighted stares, upon reading the following lines: –
>
>> Then forth he came, his both knees falt'ring, both
>> His strong hands hanging down, and all with froth
>> His cheeks and nostrils flowing, voice and breath
>> Spent to all use, and down he sank to death.
>> *The sea had soak'd his heart through . . .*   (*Recollections*, 130)

We share Clarke's delight at this delighted stare, with yet one more great writer to soak Keats's heart through. Keats was among the most magnanimous, great-hearted, of men and of poets. Of the politics of reviewing and of letters in his defense, he wrote to George and Georgiana: "This is a mere matter of the moment – I think that I shall be among the English Poets after my death" (14 October 1818; *KL* 1.394). "I think" is pure Keats, in its confident freedom from arrogance, as is "among the English poets," since his poems had always been among theirs, enjoying their company and having them live again in the life of his allusive art.

NOTES

1 Christopher Ricks, "Allusion: the Poet as Heir" (1973); *Studies in the Eighteenth Century* 3, ed. R. F. Brissenden and J. C. Eade (Canberra: Australian National University Press, 1976), 209–40; J. B. Broadbent, *Paradise Lost: Introduction* (Cambridge: Cambridge University Press, 1972), 100–2.

2 Keats's marginalia (ca. 1818) in his copy of *Paradise Lost*. See Appendix 4 in *John Keats: The Complete Poems*, ed. John Barnard (2nd edn., 1977), or Elizabeth Cook's edition, 336.

3 Francis Jeffrey, *Edinburgh Review*, August 1820; rpt. *KCH* 207.

4 Harold Bloom, *The Anxiety of Influence* (New York: Oxford University Press, 1973).

5 John Keats, "Mr. Kean," *The Champion*, 21 December 1817; Appendix 5 in Barnard's edition, or Cook, 346.

6 Marginalia in his Folio of Shakespeare. See Caroline F. E. Spurgeon, *Keats's Shakespeare* (London: Oxford University Press, 1928), 52, or Cook, 333–34.

7 Text of the First Folio (1623), of which Keats had a facsimile copy (rpt. 1808); the other edition he owned (text of Johnson and Steevens, 1814) has "whereon" and "lush" for "where" and "luscious."

8 Helen Vendler, *The Odes of John Keats*, 84, 306 n.6, citing Robert Pinsky, *The Situation of Poetry* (Princeton: Princeton University Press, 1976), 51.

9 Charles and Mary Cowden Clarke, *Recollections of Writers* (London, 1878; facsimile rpt. Sussex: Centaur Press, 1969), 126, his italics; see *Cymbeline* 1.3.18–22.

10 Cf. Keats: "When by my solitary hearth I sit, / And hateful thoughts enwrap my soul in gloom; / When no fair dreams before my 'mind's eye' flit" (*To Hope* 1–3), quoting *Hamlet* (1.2.185).

11 Rollins notes that "the tender horns of cockled snails" is from *Love's Labor's Lost* (4.3.338); Keats quotes *Venus and Adonis* 1033–38.

12 There is a further vista whenever an allusion may play with the fact that others have alluded hereabouts. Coleridge calls up Milton's line in "How many bards in city garret pent" (*The Nightingale* 2), and Keats put it into the making of his "How many bards gild the lapses of time!" (*Poems*, 1817). On such incremental allusion, see Michael Whitworth, "'Sweet Thames' and *The Waste Land*'s Allusions," *Essays in Criticism* 48 (1998), 35–58.

13 Samuel Beckett, *More Pricks than Kicks* (London: Chatto & Windus, 1934), 20; "Things and imaginings," *Ill Seen Ill Said* (New York: Grove Press, 1981), 20.

14 F. R. Leavis, *Revaluation* (London: Chatto & Windus, 1936), 251.

15 Philip Larkin, *Let the Poet Choose*, ed. James Gibson (London: Harrap, 1973), 102.

11

THERESA M. KELLEY

Keats and "ekphrasis"

Poetry and the description of art

Ekphrasis] from *ekphrazein*: to speak out, to tell in full;[1] an extended and detailed literary description of any object, real or imaginary.[2]

> One morn before me were three figures seen,
>> With bowed necks, and joined hands, side-faced;
> And one behind the other stepp'd serene,
>> In placid sandals, and in white robes graced:
> They pass'd, like figures on a marble urn,
>> When shifted round to see the other side;
>>> They came again; as when the urn once more
> Is shifted round.

Keats, Ode on Indolence 1–8

To say that Keats was fascinated by art approaches understatement. The poetry of that fascination is unequivocal. From the early sonnet *On Seeing the Elgin Marbles*, to the sculptured figures of the *Hyperion* poems and the odes of 1819, Keats returns to the world of art, haunting its forms in return for the ways in which those forms haunt his poetics. Still other poems include ekphrastic elements: *On a Leander*, his verse-epistle to Reynolds, and *Ode to Psyche*. As readers have long recognized, Keats's poetry often takes the mode of *ekphrasis*, the verbal or rhetorical description of artwork: a funerary urn, the Elgin Marbles, and typically, figures that Keatsian narrators present as though they were art objects – Madeline in *The Eve of St. Agnes*, the goddesses in *Ode to Indolence*, the fallen Titans of the *Hyperion* poems.[3]

In addition to its pictorial signifying, ekphrasis also has a rhetorical character, argues James Heffernan, who notes the self-conscious craft with which ekphrastic poetry moves, steadily or furtively, between imitation of and resistance to the tactile, sensuous persuasiveness of art objects. Derived (according to some accounts) from the Greek roots *ek* (out) and *phrassein* (speak) – literally, to speak out or declare – *ekphrasis* once meant to tell something fully. This sense became allied in classical Greek rhetoric to *phantasia* and *enárgeia*, or "vividness," the capacity to describe something so well that it seems to come alive in the minds of the audience.[4] Ekphrasis is fundamentally linked to the doctrine of "sister arts" – the ancient and putatively familial rivalry between the verbal and the visual arts that its practitioners trace back to the Latin poet Horace's claim that poetry is a speaking picture and that painting is silent poetry.[5] In recent views, ekphrasis has less to do with sisterhood than with sibling rivalry. W. J. T. Mitchell sees a gendered economy in this, whereby the poet, speaking for and from the world of masculinity, action, and narrative, insists (or desires) that the work of art is spatial, female, and mute. Jean Hagstrum identifies an uneasy blend of assistance and superiority in the way ekphrasis "giv[es] voice and language to the otherwise mute art object." Murray Krieger suggests that if this is the advantage of words (they may tell a story that visual art can depict only in a single frame), it is betrayed by the romance of lyric poetry with the "still moment," imitating the very stasis that it is supposed to evade by proceeding incrementally, in time.[6]

The critic who inaugurated modern debates over verbal and visual advantages is Lessing, whose *Laocoön: An Essay on the Limits of Painting and Poetry* (1766) demonstrated the limitations of painting and cautioned poetry against the mimicry of verbal description.[7] Although Keats practices incessantly what Lessing preached against, it is Lessing's *Essay*, whose principles were repeated and debated well into the nineteenth century, that best conveys what is at stake in Keats's sustained poetic commitment to ekphrasis. Put briefly, his poetry enacts the rivalry with painting (as Lessing urged) by deploying poetic resources against the suasions of the visual, even in the midst of describing them. At the same time, however, and often in the same poetic time, Keats discloses the desire hidden in the folds of Lessing's polemic. Lessing's *Essay* opens with a long rant about how English poets in love with ekphrasis have been led astray by classical arguments about poetry and painting – specifically Simonides's praise of poetry as a speaking picture and painting as silent poetry, and Horace's later abbreviation of this analogy as *ut pictura poesis* ("so it is with poetry as with painting").[8] "In poetry," Lessing complains, the "sister-arts analogy" has "engendered a mania for description and in painting a mania for allegory, by attempting to make the former a speaking picture, without actually knowing what it could and ought to paint, and the latter a silent poem, without having considered to what degree it is able to express general ideas" (5). Yet Lessing's title and subtitles betray the problem which this complaint attempts to camouflage. The "Laocoön" is not a painting but a monumental sculpture in relief of Laocoön and his sons as they struggle in the fatal coils of a great serpent. As David Wellbery suggests, Lessing is attracted to the massive, three-dimensional materiality of the sculpture, yet his argument requires that he reduce its bulk, in order that it may illustrate how artwork exists on a single plane.[9] Such flattened works are less likely to be taken for the real thing, for real people or (and this may be what concerns Lessing most) for works whose materiality and texture need to be denied in order to preserve the priority of verbal art.

This hidden complexity and anxiety – call it a double bind – is at the productive core of Keats's poetic ekphrasis. This core involves Lessing's brief for the capacity of words and poems to convey a story; at best, a work of art conveys only (in the phrase of some translators) the "pregnant moment." And because the viewer has to imagine the larger narrative, this moment must neither emphasize a paroxysm of extreme suffering, nor be the climax of the action (19–20).[10] In this core, too, abides Keats's ekphrastic representation of female figures as objects that inspire desire and dread. Finally, here, too, are Keats's sustained recognitions of history and time passing as he makes the story evoked in the visual works of art tell against the grain of their mute forms. This last effect arises, in some measure, because Keats's ekphrastic poems typically concern an artwork or figure from the antique past. Obliged to narrate the temporal distance between the poem and its subject, the speaker's sequence of words slips, almost without notice, into the narration of times past, or even into "history" as the largest concern of narrative structure. Ekphrasis thus makes it possible to stage and narrate a poet's relation to an art work and to the past to which that work does in some sense belong.

Given the range and extent of poetic ekphrasis in Keats's poetry, the unconfident, oddly provisional stance of two of the best known examples – the sonnet *On Seeing the Elgin Marbles* and *Ode on a Grecian Urn* – is surprising. Keats's first known attempt at extended ekphrasis, *On receiving a curious Shell, and a Copy of Verses, from the same Ladies* (1815; published in *Poems* 1817) projects far more confidence in the mode, describing the shell in a series of rhetorical questions about the miniature figures placed inside (1–12). What are we to make of the tonal perplexity with which *Ode on a Grecian Urn*, written four years later, begins – especially since the performance of ekphrasis is supposed to exude a speaker's confidence for the task?

Ode on a Grecian Urn looks stranger still when compared to a classical prototype, Greek poet Theocritus's first *Idyll*, which Keats had probably read in translation.[11] Here, a goatherd describes a carved wooden cup he will give to shepherd Thyrsis if he will sing well. He does not merely describe the different landscapes and the human figures carved on the rim and inside the cup, but also tells Thyrsis what they are doing, saying, even thinking:

My large two-handled cup, rich-wrought and deep;
Around whose brim pale ivy seems to creep,
With helichryse entwin'd: small tendrils hold
Its saffron fruit in many a clasping fold.
Within, high touch'd, a Female Figure shines; –
Her cawl! – her vest – how soft the waving lines!
And near, two Youths (bright ringlets grace their brows)
Breathe in alternate strife their amorous vows!
On each, by turns, the faithless Fair-one smiles,
And views the rival pair with wanton wiles.[12]

Of the next scene, in which an old fisherman lifts and throws his net from a rocky shore, the goatherd remarks, "you'd swear the fisher fished with all his might." In the last scene, a boy sitting in an orchard is so preoccupied with weaving traps to catch insects that he is oblivious to two foxes that have slipped in to steal the fruit. The older fox, the goatherd explains, is plotting a way to outfox the younger one by grabbing the fruit first. In the perspective of Lessing's cautions about what artworks cannot convey and, by implication, the limitations of ekphrasis, Theocritus violates every rule in the book. His ekphrasis presents scenes as though they were in motion, together with a keen omniscience about what human and animal figures are thinking or saying.

Keats's *Ode* begins instead with various personifications of the urn, including a reference to the standard rivalry between pictorial and verbal art, and then asks about the static figures depicted on its surface:

Sylvan historian, who canst thus express
A flowery tale more sweetly than our rhyme:
What leaf-fring'd legend haunts about thy shape
Of deities or mortals, or of both,
In Tempe or the dales of Arcady?
What men or gods are these? What maidens loth?
What mad pursuit? What struggle to escape?
What pipes and timbrels? What wild ecstasy?   (3–10)

It is as if Keats's speaker were deliberately replacing the knowledge possessed by Theocritus's speaker (of scenes on the cup, of the thoughts of its figures) with questions limited to exteriors: the figures and scenes on the urn's surface as tentative signs of possible meaning. There is also a differential complementarity: Theocritus's speaker warns Thyrsis that it would be a shame not to sing, since no one sings in Hades; Keats's urn is, evidently (the speaker is notably silent about this), a funerary urn. In stanza four, Keats's speaker turns away from the scenes depicted to imagine one that is not; Theocritus's ekphrasis is wholly concerned with the wooden cup and the three scenes it depicts. Pope's complaint that his description is too long (it takes up most of the first *Idyll*) misses the point; the task of ekphrasis is to elaborate, as Homer does when he describes the shield of Achilles in *The Iliad*.[13] That Theocritus goes on so long registers, in marked contrast to Keats's *Ode*, a high degree of poetic assurance and a corresponding poetic abundance. Much like the goat that gives prodigious quantities of milk, enough to fill the cup again and again (says Theocritus's goatherd speaker), Theocritus's ancient ekphrasis is convivial, even chatty; it is also prodigious in the details it offers to the reader. Although Keats's poet speaks for fifty lines, he finds few answers to the questions he asks; the urn insists on staying a "silent form" to "tease us out of thought" (44).

Why did Keats in 1819, the year of his greatest poetic achievements, depart from just the kind of ekphrastic self-confidence he had learned and already practiced? Beginning with *On Seeing the Elgin Marbles*, his ekphrastic poems articulate an array of linked concerns that help to answer this question. Keats was fascinated by the Marbles. Their acquisition and transport to England is its own tragicomic story of ruin and loss as well as great art. Rescued, according to Lord Elgin, from imminent destruction by the Turkish army occupying Greece, some of the Marbles, ironically, went down with a ship carrying them back to England; others arrived more or less safely, then were "housed" for several years in an outdoor shed, while Parliament, Lord Elgin, and a slate of witnesses (including B. R. Haydon) debated their value as art and what the nation should pay for them. They were purchased and installed in the British Museum in 1816, where Haydon insisted that Keats see them. Keats's sonnet, as Grant Scott and Noah Heringman have argued, is inflected by the cultural history of the Marbles as artworks separated from their original site and structure.[14] His ekphrasis is involved with evoking this history.

The weight of this history on the poet's consciousness makes him as attentive to the event of "Seeing" as to describing the Marbles. *On Seeing the Elgin Marbles* begins with an admission: "My spirit is too weak – mortality / Weighs heavily on me" (1–2). This state of mind mixes ekphrasis with subjective response: "each imagined pinnacle and steep / Of godlike hardship tells me I must die" (3–4). The imagery is striking. Keats uses topographical features to indicate, rather than precisely to describe, the creative endeavor: the arduous sculpting of the figures on great marble blocks, themselves quarried with difficulty. The "godlike hardship" also belongs to the Marbles. Cut down and shipped in pieces, their quasi-divine material forms are damaged and broken apart beyond even the predations of Turkish artillery. Keats's ekphrastic gesture is to accommodate the Marbles and their relation to time, that "rude / Wasting" which he compares, in a climactic flourish of approximations, to "a billowy main – / A sun – a shadow of a magnitude" (12–14). This is a remarkable early nineteenth-century conjunction of the aesthetic and the material. Like geological formations – those singularities and out-croppings of so many sublime landscapes – Keats's Marbles are figured, in Heringman's resonant phrasing, as "hybrid aesthetic objects" occupying "interstices between formed and unformed matter" (44). They are doubly freighted, with a heavy sense of their history as objects from an earlier culture (the debate about their acquisition partly concerned just how ancient the Marbles were), and as objects that look like material shadows of the geo-logical past. Captured, as it were, sailing by, an image itself captured with the figurative "billowy main" of its passage, the Marbles represent time passing as well as past.

This daring ekphrasis runs sharply against Lessing's objection to the "sister-arts" analogy (that poetry is a speaking picture and painting is silent poetry). Although Keats's subject, and sensation, is ruin, it is ruin so written over with the passage of time that his speaker engages rather than evades the question of how ruin afflicts even art objects. In a willing translation of the sculptural into the verbal, Keats's sonnet relocates the inner conflict that Lessing finds in the sister arts – the conflict between the commanding mate-riality of sculpture and its inability to "speak," as poets can. An "undescrib-able feud" works in the poet's "brain" (9–10) as he tries to imagine, simultaneously, achievement and ruin, materiality and its vanishing point, together with the paradox of a "godlike hardship."

Much closer to the protocol of ekphrastic self-confidence is *Fragment of Castle-builder* (written the same year). Canvassing the visual and specifically architectural features of his room, Castle-builder invents an architectural ekphrasis whose richness of detail forecasts the even more sumptuous feast for the eyes (and other senses) in *The Eve of St. Agnes*. The title and the repeated use of the modal "should" (26, 28, 59, 63, 65) recognize this room as a rich poetic "phantasy" (47), created out of thin air. The features and appointments seem both substantial and yet patently invented. The "golden fishes" in otherwise clear glass panes cast "glassy diamonding on the Turkish floor," where an elaborate scene is visible even to "the dullest spirit" (29–35). Love and death are the theme, complete with a lady's glove, a crum-pled love story, a broken viol, a precious folio volume of Anacreon's verses, a skull, an hour-glass, a looking-glass faintly inscribed with the ancient warning "Mene, Mene, Tekel, Upharsin" (54), and some Greek sculptures. To complete the stage set, Castle-builder adds paintings, mostly by Salvator Rosa, Titian, and one by Keats's friend, Haydon (67–69).[15] As Scott notes (*Sculpted Word*, 69), *Fragment* is the "comic" counter-ekphrasis to *On Seeing the Elgin Marbles*. Unlike the sonnet, where ekphrasis confronts the "undescribable," the poet of *Fragment* creates a room with breezy confidence, furnishes it from tales of romance and myth, and declares it his own. Yet the sonnet's negative poetics tell us more, for Keats's relation to ekphrasis and the sister-arts tradition becomes arresting on precisely those occasions (more frequent after 1817) when description invokes difficulty or even hazard for the speaker or what is being described.

A month after writing the sonnet on seeing the Marbles, Keats began *Endymion*, a romance with obvious affinities to the pictorialism of Spenser's allegorical romance *The Faerie Queene*. The ekphrastic core of Spenserian pictorialism is on full display, much as it was in poems by eighteenth-century Spenserians. Unlike them, however, Keats reiterates Spenser's equally insistent notice that ekphrastic description may hide moral and physical horrors beneath a glamorizing, seductive verbal display. The mediating figure for the hazard and power of such ekphrasis (as is frequently the case for Keats) is a woman, here sorcerer-goddess Circe.[16] Her dire enchantments of mortal man interrupt Endymion, enraptured with the moon-goddess Cynthia, just as he is about "to swear / How [this] goddess was past all things fair" (3.189–90). Endymion encounters one of Circe's victims, the seagod Glaucus, given the gift of prophecy when he magically acquired divinity. Still enchanted even after he is betrayed by Circe, Glaucus wears the magical cloak she had given him. "O'erwrought with symbols by the deepest groans / Of ambitious magic" (198–99), the cloak graphically displays evidence of Circe's mesmerizing power over her victims, and the way ekphrasis can become potent and risky magic. The passive syntax underscores the cloak's control of its gazer, and of ekphrasis itself, all in the guise of responding to the desire to see more:

> every ocean-form
> Was woven in with black distinctness; storm
> And calm, and whispering, and hideous roar,
> Quicksand and whirlpool, and deserted shore
> Were emblem'd in the woof; with every shape
> That skims, or dives, or sleeps, 'twixt cape and cape.
> The gulphing whale was like a dot in the spell,
> Yet look upon it, and 'twould size and swell
> To its huge self; and the minutest fish
> Would pass the very hardest gazer's wish,
> And shew his little eye's anatomy.   (3.199–209)

The zoom lens of this ekphrasis is triggered by those who look at it, but the capacity to swell or shrink its figures is a property of the cloak or its maker, not the speaker/viewer. As it half-performs its own ekphrasis (stages the bewildering dynamics of gazing on art), the cloak disturbs the traditional economy of the mode, in which the gazer confidently manages the descriptive project. This effect may not be good news for the gazer's self-possession, any more than the cloak is for Glaucus himself. "Ample as the largest winding-sheet" (196), the cloak has a deadening effect on the old man, which Keats renders as pseudo-ekphrasis by transforming Glaucus into a statue. His features are "lifeless," he seems "not to see" (219–20), and even after he suddenly wakes from his trance-like state (221), his face still bears the figural contours of a landscape, or a statue:

> his snow-white brows
> Went arching up, and like two magic ploughs
> Furrow'd deep wrinkles in his forehead large,
> Which kept as fixedly as rocky marge,
> Till round his wither'd lips had gone a smile.   (222–25)

Similar transformations or the threat of them occur elsewhere in *Endymion*. In Book I, the lovestruck, lovelorn hero falls into a "fixed trance," "as dead-still as a marble man, / Frozen in that old tale Arabian" (405–6). In the episode with Glaucus, the authority for this ekphrastic hocus-pocus is Circean enchantment, but the poem's recurring figures of "fixed" or transfixed bodies suggest how unstable the rhetorical economy of ekphrasis is, how the describer's powers may succumb to visual enchantment or be undermined by sympathy for the object of his gaze.

  In several later poems, Keats warns more directly of this danger, which he often figures as women or death or both. *The Eve of St. Agnes* (where Spenserian ekphrasis is formally marked by Keats's use of the Spenserian stanza) is shot through with ekphrastic gestures and portraits. Even secondary characters such as the old Beadsman – whose "frosted breath, / Like pious incense from a censer old, / Seem'd taking flight for heaven, without a death, / Past the sweet Virgin's picture" (6–9) – looks like a still-life, deader than the picture of the Virgin. His breath is the only seeming motion, and even so, rises as though leaving the body for good. His sympathy with those whose state is so close to his own (the narrator notes with a twitch of irony) inspires him to think of how the "sculptur'd dead . . . seem to freeze" (14), may even "ache in icy hoods and mails" (18). In the last stanza, Keats first had the Beadsman die "stiffen'd – 'twixt a sigh and laugh" (Stillinger, *Poems*, 318n). In the published version, the Beadsman "slept among his ashes cold" (375–78), the poem's last line.

  These framing stanzas, with human bodies turning into cold sculpture, darken the sensuously ekphrastic descriptions of the lovers and their environment in the heart of the poem. Offering a nicely pointed preamble to the angelic, near seraph-like Madeline are "carved angels, ever eager-eyed," who

"Star'd, where upon their head the cornice rests, / With hair blown back, and wings put cross-wise on their breasts" (34–36). Like the lovers on the Grecian Urn, these architectural features mimic frozen life-forms. In the view of the narrator, and of Madeline's fiery lover-to-be Porphyro, this is the fate of maidens enamored of "enchantments cold" (134), old legends and ethereal visions of future lovers. Warm ekphrasis, by contrast, spills out in multisensory array. Two stanzas rework the architectural ekphrasis of *Fragment of Castle-builder* for Madeline, no mean castle-builder herself:

> A casement high and triple-arch'd there was,
> All garlanded with carven imag'ries
> Of fruits, and flowers, and bunches of knot-grass,
> And diamonded with panes of quaint device,
> Innumerable of stains and splendid dyes,
> As are the tiger-moth's deep-damask'd wings;
> And in the midst, 'mong thousand heraldries,
> And twilight saints, and dim emblazonings,
> A shielded scutcheon blush'd with blood of queens and kings. (208–16)

Illuminated by this casement, Madeline seems a kind of a religious statue:

> Full on this casement shone the wintry moon,
> And threw warm gules on Madeline's fair breast,
> As down she knelt for heaven's grace and boon;
> Rose-bloom fell on her hands, together prest,
> And on her silver cross soft amethyst,
> And on her hair a glory, like a saint:
> She seem'd a splendid angel, newly drest,
> Save wings, for heaven. (217–24)

The poem's penchant for turning artworks into the ekphrastic subjects extends to food and fragrance. On a rich "cloth of woven crimson, gold, and jet" (256), Porphyro piles sweets and "delicates . . . heap'd with glowing hand / On golden dishes and in baskets bright / Of wreathed silver" (271–73). Porphyro arranges exotic and even heavenly treats ("Manna and dates . . . / From Fez") as though for a reader's mouth-watering, though strictly visual, delectation (stanzas 30–31). As tokens of Porphyro's desire, even hunger for Madeline, the descriptions "soother," "creamy," "lucent," "spiced," "sumptuous" fix her, even as the situation does: she asleep, dreaming of a lover; he beside her, planning to become one.

In the register of Keatsian ekphrasis, *The Eve* is self confident, as Porphyro almost always is, about its capacity to describe and fix a scene, a character, a feast array. The flicker of hazard for those so pinioned is indicated by Porphyro's lapse on the verge of success. As he awakens Madeline (he hopes) to erotic life, "Upon his knees he sank, pale as smooth-sculptured stone" (297) – as if he had become Endymion marble-fixed in his love-trance, or one of the sculptured dead about whom the Beadsman worried.

In *Lamia* (written later the same year), a curious half-ekphrasis makes poetic stuff of the body in pain. Keats depicts the first stage in enchantress Lamia's painful transformation into a real woman:

> Left to herself, the serpent now began
> To change; her elfin blood in madness ran,
> Her mouth foam'd, and the grass, therewith besprent,
> Wither'd at dew so sweet and virulent;
> Her eyes in torture fix'd, and anguish drear,
> Hot, glaz'd, and wide, with lid-lashes all sear,
> Flash'd phosphor and sharp sparks, without one cooling tear.
> The colours all inflam'd throughout her train,
> She writh'd about, convuls'd with scarlet pain:
> A deep volcanian yellow took the place
> Of all her milder-mooned body's grace;
> And, as the lava ravishes the mead,
> Spoilt all her silver mail, and golden brede;
> Made gloom of all her frecklings, streaks and bars,
> Eclips'd her crescents, and lick'd up her stars:
> So that, in moments few, she was undrest
> Of all her sapphires, greens, and amethyst,
> And rubious-argent: of all these bereft,
> Nothing but pain and ugliness were left.   (1.146–64)

In the strict sense of ekphrasis that Lessing attempted to regulate, this isn't one. Or is it? I have quoted this passage at length to document the time it takes even to describe this transformation as it keeps moving between change and static features. This movement is part of its particular cruelty, lavishly recording all those cosmetic and jeweled parts that are stripped from the gorgeous serpent until she is reduced to "pain and ugliness," then vanishes to reappear in her next, equally strippable disguise, a gorgeous woman of Corinth. As a kind of side-show ekphrasis in which the tropological turning of metaphor and transformation conjoin, this passage looks like the work of a poet so fully in control of the picture being made and unmade before our eyes that the limits of painting are also made to vanish.

The edge of antagonism and sexual animosity at work in the metamorphosis of Lamia replies definitively to the Circe in *Endymion*. Unlike Lamia in the throes of transformation, Circe is the agent of transformation in others: she turns men into beasts; she devises a cloak for Glaucus whose ekphrastic details half-wrest control from the speaker who sees and describes them. The sexually tinged antagonism of this representation (Mitchell sees this characterizing ekphrastic rivalries in general) is at issue in *Ode on a Grecian Urn*, though initially cloaked as praise. The ode's figural affiliation to *Endymion* and *Lamia* is specified by two figures: the urn as a "still unravish'd bride" (1) is a female implicitly courting ravishment, rather than, as in *Lamia*, threatening it; the urn as a "brede / Of marble men and maidens overwrought" (41–42) recalls Polwhele's translation of Theocritus's first *Idyll*, in which the inside of a "rich-wrought cup" depicts a faithless fair woman who smiles on her rival lovers. When Keats's speaker finally abandons his praise of the urn's art for telling "more sweetly" than rhyme, it is to suggest, punningly, that the unravished bride's brede is "overwrought." The figural return to *Endymion* is completed: if Circe rules over men, and her magical cloak, "o'erwrought with symbols," half-seizes ekphrastic power from the speaker/viewer, the ode-poet presents the urn's artistry, its "brede" (meaning "intricate design," but also punning on what its figures can't do, "breed"), as "overwrought" (42).

At the same time (and contra Mitchell's claims), the *Ode* turns away from the poetic itinerary of male anxiety about predatory females, be they goddesses or urns. The pivot is history, more precisely, the history the urn cannot tell because it is concerned (in the protocol of ekphrasis) with complete forms whose temporal and aural stillness invites the poetic mirroring Horace suggested when he called poems speaking pictures and pictures silent poems. The history the urn cannot tell, but the poet-speaker does, concerns absence and mortal loss. In stanza four the poet describes a procession, headed for some sacrifice, having "emptied" a town that he imagines only by asking questions about it. But now unanswerable questions conduct to a comprehensive realization:

> What little town by river or sea shore,
>   Or mountain-built with peaceful citadel,
>   Is emptied of this folk, this pious morn?
> And, little town, thy streets for evermore
>   Will silent be; and not a soul to tell
>   Why thou art desolate, can e'er return.   (35–40)

The two strains in Keatsian ekphrasis merge here. Its hazards (which the poet has slyly implied in stanzas just previous, with repeated, semi-hysterical notice of how "happy" lovers must be who can never ever touch) are met by a stubborn poetic extension of the logic of ekphrasis beyond the limits Lessing set. As in *On Seeing the Elgin Marbles*, description of a work of art includes plangent notice of time passing and mortality.

In *Hyperion, A Fragment* and *The Fall of Hyperion, A Dream*, Keats pits ekphrastic description against the progressive history of Hyperion's fall to his Olympian successor, a story that neither version could complete. At issue is Keats's mature poetic relation to a model of history as progress. The idiom of ancient fable conveys what he described, a few months before beginning *Hyperion*, as a "grand march of intellect" in modern times (3 May 1818; *KL* 1.282), but in neither attempt could Keats stay with that march long enough to present a concluding, triumphant tableau of Apollo and the Olympian pantheon enthroned after the Titans' fall. In both, a "still [and sad] moment" of ekphrasis (Krieger) freezes the narrative, lingering with the fallen Titans, paralyzed into colossal statuary, or its fragments. While more Egyptian than Greek in cast, these figures (of Greek gods, after all) recall the intersection of ruin and materiality in Keats's sonnet on the Elgin Marbles.

In *Hyperion*, Keats presents Saturn and Thea as sculptures whose heavy materiality reminds us (with an equally heavy poetic hand) that they are gods no more. In their fallen states they are merely and unhappily split off from their former divine beings and bodily selves, cast off by the march of theodicy in transition. Keats describes Saturn not even as a magnificent piece of classical statuary, but rather as a statue fallen into abject fragments: he sits "quiet as a stone," with "bow'd head," his right hand "nerveless, listless, dead, / Unsceptred; and his realmless eyes . . . closed" (1.4, 18–20). Described by lacks, he is cut off from his being and full embodiment; even the negating adjective "unsceptred" is separated from his body by an end-stopped line. The next disembodied hand belongs to Thea, who "with a kindred hand / Touch'd his wide shoulders" (23–24), her magnificent face "as large as that of Memphian sphinx, / Pedestal'd haply in a palace court" (31–32). The narrator compares this tableau to "natural sculpture in cathedral cavern" (86), an ekphrastic analogy that half-crosses geological with sculpted art. In Book II, he extends this mode to their "bruised" and "dungeon'd" peers (4, 23):

> Scarce images of life, one here, one there,
> Lay vast and edgeways; like a dismal cirque
> Of Druid stones, upon a forlorn moor.　　　(2.33–35)

The pun on "scarce" imagines them as scarce, like precious antique sculptured figures, and as beings scarcely alive. As he surveys them all, Saturn cannot explain "why ye, Divinities, / The first-born of all shap'd and palpable Gods, / Should cower beneath" the comparatively "untremendous might" of the Olympian victors (2.152–55). The question is less riveting that its ekphrastic claim about the materiality of the Titans, a claim that haunts Keats's ekphrastic performances just as much as it is denied in Lessing's brief for words over images.

In *The Fall*, Keats more insistently binds ekphrasis to material form. The first to experience this binding is the poet himself, as he describes the onset of his dream: "The cloudy swoon came on, and down I sunk / Like a Silenus on an antique vase" (1.55–56). The old marble monument that harbors the fragments of a statue of Saturn and the eternally living, eternally dying Moneta elaborates the hybrid of nature and art more briefly offered in *Hyperion*. The poet confronts an ekphrastic crisis, the inadequacy of description:

> what I had seen
> Of grey cathedrals, buttress'd walls, rent towers,
> The superannuations of sunk realms,
> Or nature's rocks toil'd hard in waves and winds,
> Seem'd but the faulture of decrepit things
> To that eternal domed monument.   (1.66–71)

Compressed in *Hyperion* in the phrase "cathedral cavern," in *The Fall* this poetic labor is weighed down by a massive, fault-ridden materiality that expands the compound of geological formation and cathedral structure. Saturn is more insistently material. The poet-dreamer asks Moneta, "What image this, whose face I cannot see, / For the broad marble knees" (1.213–14). Her answer gives a formal witness to the old god's self-dispossession: "this old image here, / Whose carved features wrinkled as he fell, / Is Saturn's" (224–26). Saturn is no longer "like" sculpture (*Hyperion* 1.86); he *is* sculpture, its very image deformed by his fall. As Keats reprises the scenes of *Hyperion* in the rest of Canto 1 of *The Fall*, he expands the ekphrastic tags that had insisted on the statue-like materiality of the fallen gods. The tableau of fallen Saturn and Thea is now an image of their mortal history compressed into sculpture:

> Long, long, those two were postured motionless,
> Like sculpture builded up upon the grave
> Of their own power. A long awful time
> I look'd upon them; still they were the same,
> The frozen God still bending to the earth,
> And the sad Goddess weeping at his feet;
> Moneta silent. Without stay or prop
> But my own weak mortality, I bore
> The load of this eternal quietude,
> The unchanging gloom, and the three fixed shapes
> Ponderous upon my senses a whole moon.   (1.382–92)

The poet's sympathetic witness to this history nearly turns him into a statue of a witness, the tragic version of Porphyro before Madeline. Like the sonnet on the Elgin Marbles, the *Hyperion* poems are far less concerned with ekphrastic desire and eroticized combat than with who will control the work of ekphrasis, whether to represent the work of art or the work of the poet who gazes at it. Why is this so?

One answer has to do with materiality and history, which together have palpable designs on how readers and viewers imagine and verbally characterize works of art. It is as though these poems had developed the point implied by Keats's decision to write *The Fall* as a poet's first-person narrative. In this reorientation, the story of the Titans is subjected to the arrest and delay that ekphrasis always makes possible, so that the disruptive content – an understanding of history not as progressive, not as the achievement of victors – can become available to a human speaker struggling in his own time, with the materiality and mortality of being.[17] Whereas Lessing tried to suppress the permeability between works of art frozen in time and the poetic expression of temporality, Keats presents the fallen Saturn (as Chronos, he is time frozen in time) in a narrative that lingers with and thereby expands the god's agonized recognition of time's slow but inexorable passing. In Keats's poetry, then, ekphrasis foregrounds how works of art are, like geological formations, made in time and out of matter. This recognition has, as his speakers often acknowledge, sustained consequences for human poets.

NOTES

1 Jean H. Hagstrum, *The Sister Arts* (Chicago: University of Chicago Press, 1958), 18 note.

2 "Ekphrasis," *Oxford Classical Dictionary*, ed. Simon Hornblower and Antony Spawforth, 3rd edn. (Oxford: Oxford University Press, 1996).

3 Ian Jack studies Keats's formative poetic interest in the visual arts in *Keats and the Mirror of Art* (Oxford: Clarendon Press, 1967). William St. Clair offers a detailed history of the Elgin Marbles debate in *Lord Elgin and the Marbles* (London: Oxford University Press, 1967), 127–43; for Keats's fascination with the Marbles, see Grant Scott, *The Sculpted Word: Keats, Ekphrasis, and the Visual Arts*, 45–67, and Kelley, "Keats, Ekphrasis, and History," Roe, ed., *Keats and History*.

4 For histories of the definition of *ekphrasis*, see *Oxford Classical Dictionary*, 3rd edn.; James A. W. Heffernan, *The Museum of Words: The Poetics of Ekphrasis from Homer to Ashbery* (Chicago: University of Chicago Press, 1993), 191 note; and Scott, *Sculpted Word*, 1.

5 Hagstrum assesses this long tradition in *Sister Arts*.

6 W. J. T. Mitchell, "Ekphrasis and the Other," *South Atlantic Quarterly* 91.3 (Summer 1992), 695–719; Hagstrum, *Sister Arts*, 18, note; Murray Krieger, "The Ekphrastic Principle and the Still Movement of Poetry," *The Play and the Place of Criticism* (Baltimore: Johns Hopkins University Press, 1959), 127, and

Ekphrasis: The Illusion of Natural Sign (Baltimore: Johns Hopkins University Press, 1992), 1–28.

7 I cite the edition of Edward Allen McCormick (1962; Baltimore: Johns Hopkins University Press, 1984). Scott (*Sculpted Word*, 128–29) notes that Lessing's thesis was summarized in an article, "Coalition between Poetry and Painting," *Universal Magazine*, May 1797.

8 Hagstrum, *Sister Arts*, 9–10.

9 David Wellbery, *Lessing's Laocoon: Semiotics and Aesthetics in the Age of Reason* (Cambridge: Cambridge University Press, 1984), 119–22.

10 See W. J. T. Mitchell's assessment of this position in "Space and Time: Lessing's *Laocoon* and the Politics of Genre," *Iconology: Image, Text, and Ideology* (Chicago: University of Chicago Press, 1985), 95–115.

11 In his October 1818 journal-letter to George and Georgiana, he refers to being "with Theocritus in the Vales of Sicily" (*KL* 1.404). Hunt describes Theocritus's own ekphrasis ("an exquisite picture") in an essay published years after Keats's death; *A Jar of Honey from Mount Hybla* (London: Smith, Elder, 1848), 62–63. Among those who note ekphrastic parallels between Keats's ode and Theocritus's first *Idyll*, see Bruce Thornton, "Cold Pastoral: Theocritus's Cup and Keats's Urn," *Classical and Modern Literature* 7 (Winter 1987), 11–18; Leo Spitzer, "The 'Ode on a Grecian Urn,' or Content vs. Metagrammar," *Essays on English and American Literature* (Princeton: Princeton University Press, 1962), 72; and Kenneth S. Calhoon, "The Urn and the Lamp," *Studies in Romanticism* 26 (1987), 8–10.

12 Translation by Rev. Richard Polwhele, *The Idylls, Epigrams, Fragments of Theocritus, Bion and Moschus* (Bath: R. Crattwell, T. Cadell, 1792 [title page for v. 1 1791]), 1.6–7; reprinted six times before 1822, this is the one Keats would most likely have consulted. "Cawl" is the obsolete form of "caul," a close-fitting cap or hood worn by women. Now best known for his diatribe against women writers and artists, *The Unsex'd Females* (1798), Polwhele renders the woman's gaze (faithless, wanton) more harshly than do other translators. Compare Daryl Hine's *Theocritus, Idylls, and Epigrams* (New York: Atheneum, 1982), 3–4: "none of their dialogue touches her deeply, / Rather, she gazes on one of them one moment, absently smiling, / Then in an instant she casts her attention again to the other."

13 Alexander Pope, *Discourse on Pastoral Poetry*, in *Pastoral Poetry and an Essay on Criticism*, ed. E. Audra and A. Williams (New Haven: Yale University Press, 1961), 29. For discussions of Homer's ekphrasis and narrative delay, see Hagstrum, *Sister Arts*, 19–21, and Scott, *Sculpted Word*, 2–4.

14 For the Parliamentary debates, see St. Clair, *Lord Elgin*, 127–43, 911–13; Scott, *Sculpted Word*, 64–67; Heringman, "Stones so wonderous Cheap," in *Ideology and Romantic Aesthetics: A Forum*, ed. Susan J. Wolfson, *Studies in Romanticism* 37 (1998), 43–49.

15 *Fragment*, notes Wendy Steiner, participates in the extensive nineteenth-century recognition of interconnections between the verbal and pictorial arts; *Pictures of Romance* (Chicago: University of Chicago Press, 1988), 59.

16 See my *Reinventing Allegory* (Cambridge: Cambridge University Press, 1997), 161–75.

17 For the anti-progressive historicality of *Hyperion*, see Alan Bewell, "The Political Implications of Keats's Classicist Aesthetics," and Tilottama Rajan, "Keats, Poetry, and 'The Absence of Work,'" *Modern Philology* 95 (February 1998), 334–51.

FURTHER READING ON KEATS AND EKPHRASIS

Brooks, Cleanth. "Keats's Sylvan Historian: History without Footnotes."

Bryson, Norman. "Intertextuality and Visual Poetics," *Style* 22 (1988), 183–93.

Der Neue Pauly Enzylopädie der Antike, ed. Hubert Cancik and Helmuth Schneider. Stuttgart: J. B. Metzler, 1997.

Goslee, Nancy Moore. *Uriel's Eye: Miltonic Stationing and Statuary in Blake, Keats, and Shelley*. Birmingham: University of Alabama Press, 1985.

Hollander, John. "The Gazer's Spirit." *The Romantics and Us*. Ed. Gene Ruoff. New Brunswick: Rutgers University Press, 1990, 130–67.

"The Poetics of Ekphrasis," *Word and Image* 4 (1988), 209–19.

Hurley, Ann and Kate Greenspan, eds., *So Rich a Tapestry: The Sister Arts and Cultural Studies*. Lewisburg, Penn.: Bucknell University Press, 1995.

Scott, Grant F. "Ekphrasis and the Picture Gallery." *Advances in Visual Semiotics*. Ed. Thomas A. Sebeok. New York and Berlin: W. De Gruyter, 1995, 402–21.

"The Fragile Image: Felicia Hemans and Romantic Ekphrasis." *Felicia Hemans: Reimagining Poetry in the Nineteenth Century*, ed. Nanora Sweet and Julie Melnyk. London: Macmillan, 2001. 36–54.

"Shelley, Medusa, and the Perils of Ekphrasis." *The Romantic Imagination: Literature and Art in England and Germany*. Ed. Frederick Burwick and Jürgen Klein. *Studies in Comparative Literature* 6. Amsterdam and Atlanta: Rodopi, 1996, 315–32.

Wolf, Bryan. "Confessions of a Closet Ekphrastic: Literature, Painting, and Other Unnatural Relations," *Yale Journal of Criticism* 3 (1990), 181–204.

12

GREG KUCICH

Keats and English poetry

I long to feast upon old Homer as we have upon Shakespeare, and as I have
lately upon Milton.

Keats to Reynolds, 27 April 1818

Describing himself as "one who passes his life among books and thoughts
on books" (*KL* 1.274), Keats "feasted upon" great poets with extraordinary
relish, an appetitive reading he put in terms of delightful eating, drinking,
imbibing, and inhaling. His copies of mighty poetic forebears teem with
marks and annotations that witness a critical engagement as well as a rapid,
enthusiastic absorption of words and thoughts.[1] This poetic "food" ("How
many bards" 2) could provide creative inspiration when Keats craved it
most, consolation in times of distress, and themes for his own poetry (*On
First Looking into Chapman's Homer*; *On Sitting Down to Read "King
Lear" Once Again*). The "Remembrance of Chaucer," he buoyantly affirmed
during a lull in the writing of *Endymion* in May 1817, "will set me forward
like a Billiard-Ball" (*KL* 1.147). Keats often began writing with a ritual of
welcoming into his mind "throngs" of elder bards whose "pleasing chime"
inspired him ("How many bards"). As he matured, such chimes could be less
pleasing, even sometimes a convulsive din, provoking sensations of insufficiency before such creative amplitude or apprehensions of not finding a voice
of his own among the throng. "Aye, the count / Of mighty Poets is made up;
the scroll / Is folded by the Muses," laments the narrator of *Endymion*; "the
sun of poesy is set" (2.723–25, 729).[2] Yet for all this seeming finish, the play
of predecessor poets in his own voice vitally informed Keats's creative efforts
and his sense of poetic identity. He envisioned these interactions as a "greeting of the Spirit" (*KL*1.243), a partnership in "immortal freemasonry" – as
he described actor Edmund Kean's way with Shakespeare ("Mr. Kean";
Cook, 346).

Keats's ambition to "be among the English Poets" (*KL* 1.394) carries this
conversational sense as well as a canonical one. These conversations were

not discrete compositional moments. With astonishing powers of assimilation, Keats echoes multiple voices in prose passages, individual poems, even in single lines or phrases – sometimes in harmony, sometimes in vexation, and often with significant revision, struggle, or ambivalence. The conversations took place, moreover, within historical, political, and social contexts, ones that affected his choice of readings as well as his interpretive and poetic responses. Contemporary politics of empire and gender inform many of Keats's views of his traditions: his early aspiration to join a "brotherhood in song" (*To George Felton Mathew* 2), his figure of literary discovery as imperial conquest (*On First Looking into Chapman's Homer*). Reading widely in different periods and national traditions (Ovid, Horace, Dante, Petrarch, Tasso, Ariosto, Boiardo, Molière, Boccaccio, Ronsard, Voltaire, Rousseau), Keats was motivated to concentrate on "English Poets" – particularly the "old Poets," of the Renaissance and before (*KL* 1.225) – not just because this was his national foundation but also because of his interest in contemporary debates about the cultural urgency and political significance of reviving England's literary tradition, one generally thought to have peaked in the Renaissance.

Keats was reading Chaucer carefully as early as 1817, when he wrote out his sonnet "This pleasant tale" in Charles Cowden Clarke's copy of Chaucer. It would be one of his first publications.[3] He returned to Chaucer in the coming years, and sharply identified with Chaucer's Troilus in his passion for Fanny Brawne in 1819–20. His interest in the poetry was various and shifting, but it tended to focus on these features: the medieval atmosphere, the skilled verse narrative and complex character portrayal, and, above all (as the bond with Troilus suggests), Chaucer's deep sympathy for broken-hearted love.[4] Influenced by Leigh Hunt's chivalric poem, *The Story of Rimini* (1816), Keats was drawn to the aura of medieval chivalry, finding Chaucer's Gothic splendors particularly compelling. When he acquired his own book of the poet in May 1818, he was eager to enhance its antique physical quality: "What say you to a black Letter Chaucer printed in 1596," he wrote enthusiastically to Reynolds about a Gothic-script edition (actually, 1598); "aye I've got one huzza! I shall have it bound gothique a nice sombre binding – it will go a little way to unmodernize" (*KL* 1.276). The romance of "old Chaucer" (*Endymion* 1.134) suffuses the setting of *The Eve of St. Agnes* (as Hunt noticed) and still more palpably the setting and language of *The Eve of St. Mark*, "an imitation of the Authors in Chaucer's time," Keats described it, adding, "'t is more ancient than Chaucer himself" (*KL* 2.204). In this poem of somber tone, set in winter "anguish" (*KL* 2.201) and infused with superstition (the appearing of the ghosts of those doomed to die soon), Keats's imagination was tuned to Chaucerian gothique.

But it wasn't just this tone. As early as *Endymion*, Keats was asking for Chaucerian inspiration to tell of his own "goodly company," "that I may dare, in wayfaring, / To stammer where old Chaucer used to sing" (1.129, 133–34). As the occasion of *Endymion* might already suggest, his attention to *The Canterbury Tales* and *Troilus and Criseyde* involved Chaucer's narrative powers and, particularly, his evocations of psychic interiority and deep pathos: "In our very souls, we feel amain / The close of Troilus and Cressid sweet" (*Endymion* 2.12–13). Hazlitt, one of Keats's most important guides, had recommended the cultivation of these Chaucerian strengths in a lecture of early 1818. Keats soon took the advice, shaping his first well-condensed narrative and his first successful portrait of pathos in *Isabella; or, The Pot of Basil*. Although the plot outline came from Boccaccio, narrative devices such as the dream vision and descriptive elements (Isabella's collapse in grief) derive from passages in Chaucer's *The Prioress's Tale* and *The Knight's Tale* of the sort that Hazlitt admired. What Hazlitt called Chaucer's "depth of simple pathos" eventually came to stand for Keats as the poetry of the human heart, a kind of writing he increasingly preferred to the poetry of enchantment.[5] "I am more at home amongst Men and women," he told his publisher late in 1819; "I would rather read Chaucer than Ariosto" (*KL* 2.234) – perhaps, too, because it was Chaucer who reflected the turmoils of his own romance with Fanny Brawne.

When Keats first read *Troilus and Criseyde*, some years earlier, he marked descriptions of the lovers' "wo" and "pain" (1.546; 3.1531). He also knew Shakespeare's *Troilus and Cressida* and cited it in October 1818 with similar attention, yet more specifically, to Troilus's anguish: "I throw my whole being into Troilus [. . .] repeating those lines, 'I wander, like a lost soul upon the stygian Banks staying for waftage'" (*KL* 1.404; referring to Troilus's anticipation of lovemaking; 3.2.9–11). In October 1818 Fanny Brawne was a new fascination, and as his passion intensified, so did Keats's identifications with Troilus, both Chaucer's and Shakespeare's. By October 1819, he was writing to her (*KL* 2.222–23):

> My sweet Girl,
>   I am living to day in yesterday: I was in a complete facination all day. I feel myself at your mercy. Write me ever so few lines and tell you [?me] you will never for ever be less kind to me than yesterday – You dazzled me [. . .]
>
> Ever yours
John Keats
>
> A hertè mine!

The postscript is the lament of Chaucer's Troilus over the loss of Criseyde, "Ah hertè mine!" A late lyric to her that begins, "What can I do to drive

away / Remembrance from my eyes?" quotes Troilus again: "How shall I do
...?" (18). This is but one of many instance in the poems to or about her
(see Robert Gittings, *Mask*, 73–78). By February 1820, in fatally weak
health, Keats agonized in fantasies of her turning away: "My greatest
torment since I have known you, has been the fear of you being a little
inclined to the Cressid" (*KL* 2.256). The "old" poet who had inspired his
medieval enchantments now gave him a language for the torments of
modern love.

In the poetics of enchantment, Keats's truest presider was Spenser. It was
Spenser's "gorgeousness of the imagery" – especially in *The Faerie Queene*
– Clarke recalled, that most delighted a young Keats and inspired his desire
to write poetry (*KC* 2.149). Indeed, his first poem (circa 1814) was an
Imitation of Spenser in Spenserian stanzas – the stanza that also shapes some
of his last efforts, *The Jealousies* and "In after time a sage of mickle lore."
Keats's markings in *The Faerie Queene* Book I are consistently drawn to
Spenser's powers of description, worked through both the pacing and the
beauty of his words. Keats loved the verses on the plumage on Arthur's
helmet (7.32) and Una's radiance (3.4), and both he and Hunt marked their
copies, with the caesurae (medial pauses) that interplayed with the terminal
ones – as in the setting of Archimago's hermitage:

> A little lowly hermitage it was //
> Down in a dale, // hard by a forest's side, //
> Far from resort of people // that did pass
> In travel to and fro: // a little wide //
> There was a holy chapel edified, //
> Wherein the hermit duly wont to say
> His holy things // each morn and eventide;
> Thereby a crystal stream did gently play //
> Which from sacred fountain welled forth alway.   (I.I.xxxiv)[6]

He also marked a stanza in which the lulling of poetic sound reinforces the
description:

> And more, to lull him in his slumber soft,
> A trickling Stream from high Rock tumbling down,
> And ever drizling Rain upon the Loft,
> Mixt with a murmuring Wind, much like the sound
> Of swarming Bees, did cast him in a Swoon.   (I.I.xli)

Enraptured with the euphony, rhyme, and cadences, Keats celebrated the
"Spenserian vowels that elope with ease, / And float along like birds o'er
summer seas" (*To Charles Cowden Clarke* 56–57). Reading these sensuous
delights gave one a vivid imagination of them, as if one had actually "fondled

the maidens with the breasts of cream" (34). Spenser fostered Keats's development of mellifluous, sensuously dense language, spectacularly so in the luxurious Spenserian stanzas of *The Eve of St. Agnes*. As a gift for Fanny Brawne near the end of his life, Keats employed himself "in marking the most [beaut]iful passages in Spenser," telling her, "It has lightened my time very much" (4 July 1820; *KL* 2.302).

Keats's "ramp[ing]" through *The Faerie Queene* in search of sites of beauty, as Clarke described this way of reading (*KC* 2.148), is just as significant for the way it ignores the epic's main organizing principle, its moral allegory. This was a common approach to Spenser (as well as to *Paradise Lost*) in the early nineteenth century, but in Hunt's circle it was a passion. An enthusiasm for Spenserian beauties helped solidify the young aspiring poet's sense of belonging in Hunt's supportive literary coterie. Hazlitt (in a lecture Keats knew) declared that "the moving principle of [Spenser's] mind" is the "love of beauty"; if readers of *The Faerie Queene* "do not meddle with the allegory, the allegory will not meddle with them" (*Lectures*, 34, 38). Keats's marking of gorgeous descriptions in *The Faerie Queene* closely matches the pattern in Hunt's copy.[7] Such early poems as *Written on the Day That Mr. Leigh Hunt Left Prison*, *To My Brother George*, and *Specimen of an Induction to a Poem* celebrate a shared love of Spenserian beauty. Hunt also guided, through manuscript corrections, Keats's first poetic effort to fashion a series of lovely Spenserian pictures, *Calidore*, a poem titled after Spenser's heroic knight.

This enthusiasm for Spenser's aesthetics in disregard of the moral allegory also played into the reform politics of the Hunt circle. Spenser's allegory entailed religious conventions and monarchial politics, while Hunt's circle advanced critiques of these very institutions. As if aware of this contradiction, Hunt proposed that Spenser, despite his loyalist politics, had been a victim of court oppression. Keats usually addressed Hunt by his *nom de guerre* in the arena of Regency oppression, "Libertas," when celebrating their joint admiration of Spenser (*To My Brother George* 24). Keats's last known poetic composition, "In after time," consists of a single Spenserian stanza in which the aristocratic values championed by Spenser's Artegall give way to the reformist politics of print culture.

This revisionary reading of Spenser brought Keats back to features of the allegory that, when modified, served important creative, psychological, and existential concerns – chiefly, the conflict between imaginative ideals and harsh reality. His notes on *The Faerie Queene* reflect an attention to the psychological structure of the allegory, of minds torn between enchanting illusions and grim realities. Keats marks Fradubio's account of his fatal enchantment with foul Duessa's illusory beauty (1.2.30–45) and Arthur's account of his dream of Gloriana and the bitter sorrow of its dissolution (1.9.15). In his own versions of such tormenting enchantment, Keats leaves behind the allegorical framework – of virtue tested by temptation, of evil exposed – and foregrounds psychological conflict. Arthur's dream shimmers behind the knight-at-arms's conflicted dream-experience in *La Belle Dame sans Merci*; the Bower of Bliss (*Faerie Queene* 2.2.12) haunts Keatsian bowers of dreaming, from *Calidore* to *Endymion* to *Ode to a Nightingale*. But Keats's way with Spenserian material is to unfold the psychodynamics implicit in the allegory – of imaginative idealism pressured by a sense of reality – and leave the conflict unresolved, or resistant to any clear moral interpretation. So, too, Spenser's chief plot device, a questing knight's passage through a castle's chambers of enchantment, becomes in Keats's hands a psychological exploration: the ambiguities of realism and idealism in *The Eve of St. Agnes*, the language of open-ended growth in the "Mansion of Many Apartments" (*KL* 1.280–82). A revisionary "meddling" with Spenser's allegory proved more productive than Hazlitt's disdain, for it sharpened Keats's sense both of his modern moment and of his independent place "among the English poets."

Such productive assimilation owes a great deal to Keats's central conviction of the easy, welcoming nature of Spenser's influence, an eighteenth-century tradition that Hunt perpetuated. Spenser's reputation for gentleness and malleability, along with the fragmentary character of *The Faerie Queene* (long as it was), invited modern attempts to extend and modify his achievement, even as the poem's eccentric qualities and otherworldly allegory encouraged parody – not sharp, but in a spirit of mirth that his example seemed to sanction. Keats engaged Spenser in all these modes, saluting his "kind" countenance (*Specimen* 49), indulging in short parodies (*KL* 1.145; *Character of C. B.*), and even attempting a parodic romance, *The Jealousies*, updating the play between fairy land and England in *The Faerie Queene*. A sense of Spenser's affable spirit is evident in the examples of generous influence that Keats marked in *The Faerie Queene*: the poet's plea for Cupid with "thy mother mild" to come to "mine ayd" (1.Prologue.3); his invocation of the muses, "gently come into my feeble Breast," as he nerves himself to finish the narrative of Redcrosse's battle with the dragon (1.11.6). As if to ask Spenser himself for his own gentle fortification, Keats placed on the title page of his first volume (see p. 2, above) a motto from Spenser and a profile portrait that the first reviewers, noting the motto, took to be Spenser. Keats declared within:

> Spenser! thy brows are arched, open, kind,
> And come like a clear sun-rise to my mind;

> And always does my heart with pleasure dance,
> When I think on thy noble countenance.
>
> *(Specimen of an Induction to a Poem* 49–52)

The poem that follows this *Induction* in the 1817 volume restages such affection in the figure of "the far-fam'd" Sir Gondibert, "ready to greet / The large-eyed wonder, and ambitious heat / Of the aspiring boy" and induct him into the brotherhood of knights (*Calidore* 109–33).

If Spenser was a figure of kindly greeting (even though his allegories required updating), Shakespeare's genius was more daunting to Keats's aspirations. Was there anything left to say after Shakespeare? Nevertheless, Keats always felt a profound affinity with Shakespeare's genius, imagining him as an encouraging "Presider" (*KL* 1.142), and finding in his art an inexhaustible store of poetic riches – examples, too, of how poetry could convey complexities of psychology, of political power, and a sharpened insight into the suffering and contrariety of human experience. Foremost among the mighty poets, Shakespeare often seemed to Keats "enough for us" (1.143), and to write "a few fine Plays" in his tradition became his "greatest ambition" (*KL* 2.234). While only a fragmentary historical tragedy, *King Stephen*, came forth, Keats was thoroughly Shakespearean in his modes of thought and expression. Steeped in Shakespeare's words, he read, marked, and perpetually reread the plays and poems. Among the few books he took to Italy was his seven-volume 1814 Shakespeare edition: "'There's my Comfort,'" he had written (*KL* 1.128), quoting *The Tempest* (2.2.47, 57), when he unboxed the same set back in April 1817, in preparation for work on *Endymion*. It could have been the motto of his life as a writer.

In their saturation with Shakespearean phrasings, allusions, and puns, Keats's letters and poems nearly constitute a dialogic idiom.[8] A marginal comment on Lear's passion, beginning with a quotation, shows this astonishing alchemy:

> "the seeded pride that hath to this maturity blowne up" Shakespeare doth scatter abroad on the winds of Passion, where the germs take buoyant root in stormy Air, suck lightening sap, and become voiced dragons – self-will and pride and wrath are taken at a rebound by his giant hand and mounted to the Clouds – there to remain and thunder evermore –   (Cook edition, 335)

Shakespeare seeded Keats's genius with such "fine Phrases" (*KL* 2.139). Amazed at the abundance of metaphorical conceits, he was also drawn to compact riches. "I neer found so many beauties in the sonnets," he exclaimed to fellow poet Reynolds, "they seem to be full of fine things said unintentionally – in the intensity of working out conceits [. . .] for look at Snails, you know what he says about Snails, you know where he talks about 'cockled snails' [. . .] He speaks too of 'Time's antique pen' – and 'aprils first born flowers' – and 'deaths eternal cold'" (*KL* 1.188–89) – citing phrases from *Love's Labor's Lost* (4.3.338) and Sonnets 19, 21, and 13. Like Spenser, Shakespeare was a genius of poetic beauties, many of which Keats incorporated into *Endymion*.[9] He liked the condensed compounds and participle-epithets, underlining such phrases as Cleopatra's reference to "Broad-fronted Caesar" (*Antony and Cleopatra* 1.5.29) and Goneril's outcry against Albany, "Milk-liver'd man" (*King Lear* 4.2.50). Hence Keats's own condensed phrasings, such as "light-winged Dryad," "deep-delved earth," and "purple-stained mouth" (*Ode to a Nightingale* 7, 12, 18). "Shakespearean hieroglyphics," as he called this kind of language ("Mr Kean"; Cook, 346), could capture in a single phrase a labyrinth of complexities. "Shakespeare always sums up matters in the most sovereign manner" (*KL* 2.312).

It was the spectacular depth and range of psychological insight that made Shakespeare "sovereign" among the poets. "The Genius of Shakespeare," Keats wrote in his 1808 reprint of the 1623 Folio, "was an inate universality – wherefore he has the utmost atchievement of human intellect prostrate beneath his indolent and kingly gaze – He could do easily Man's utmost" (Cook, 334). Guided by Hazlitt's esteem, Keats cited him to define the "quality" of a "Man of Achievement especially in Literature." This is "Negative Capability," a capacity – "which Shakespeare posessed so enormously" – to efface the self through sympathetic identification with others and yet remain in "uncertainties, Mysteries, doubts without any irritable reaching after fact & reason" (*KL* 1.193). Keats elaborated this capability when, again with Shakespeare in mind, he depicted the ideal "poetical Character" as a "camelion," taking "as much delight in an Iago as an Imogen" (1.386–87). This flexibility is sharpest in its Keatsian enactments in the multiple ironies, conflicting perspectives, and dramatic reversals of such poems as *The Eve of St. Agnes*, *Lamia*, and the "Great Odes" of 1819.

Shakespearean negative capability was significant, too, for its associations with the reform politics that Keats endorsed. Nicholas Roe has shown how the eighteenth-century theories of imaginative sympathy that inform Keats's Shakespearean ideal frequently advanced, by way of Hazlitt's criticism, liberal arguments for communal sympathies and egalitarian politics.[10] This political inflection was acute when Keats was writing about negative capability, in late December 1817. The week before, Hunt's *Examiner* had featured several articles contrasting the "selfish," "narrow," and "irritable" principles of government ministers and greedy theater managers with the expansive social sympathies of the reform movement in general, and with Shakespeare's equanimity in particular (Roe, 238–39). Keats's use of such language about Shakespeare's negative capability suggests that he saw it at work in the liberal sympathies of reform politics, and saw it, too, as a resource for his own efforts "to put a Mite of help to the Liberal side of the Question before I die" (*KL* 2.180). This political sense of negative capability informs *To Autumn*, often considered Keats's most purely detached poem.[11]

But it was not just political imperatives that sharpened Keats's view of Shakespearean capability. It was, more generally, Shakespeare's profound sympathy with human suffering. He was, above all, "a miserable and mighty Poet of the human Heart" (*KL* 2.115), one who probed "the fierce dispute / Betwixt Hell torment & impassion'd Clay," so Keats described *King Lear* in a sonnet he wrote in January 1818 as "prologue" to rereading it (*KL* 1.215). His first poem, *Imitation of Spenser*, referred to Lear's "bitter teen" (22), and his markings of the plays overwhelmingly focus on suffering: Duke Vincentio's visit to "the afflicted spirits / Here in the prison" (*Measure for Measure* 2.3.4), Ariel's "heart sorrow" (*Tempest* 3.3.81), Lear's "full cause of weeping" and Kent on "the rack of this tough world" (*Lear* 2.4.282; 5.3.314). So deeply did Keats identify with Shakespeare's language of suffering that he called on it to convey his own greatest sorrows: "Hamlet's heart was full of such Misery as mine is when he said to Ophelia 'Go to a Nunnery, go, go!'" he wrote bitterly to Fanny Brawne (*KL* 2.312), and he underscored and dated Edgar's plea for "poore Tom" (*Lear* 3.4.51) as he watched his brother Tom's deathbed; "poor Tom," he says repeatedly in his letters of those months.[12]

Shakespeare's voices of grief shape Keats's poetry, too. His description of "poor Ambition" "spring[ing] / From a man's little heart's short fever-fit" (*Ode on Indolence* 33–34), for instance, echoes Macbeth's thoughts on ambition and "life's fitful fever" (*Macbeth* 3.2.23). His imagination of how a nightingale's song – "The voice I hear this passing night" – could be "the self-same song that found a path / Through the sad heart of Ruth" (*Ode to a Nightingale* 63–66) recalls Bassanio's speech (which he underlined) on the sorrows of ancient lovers experienced "In such a night as this" (*Merchant of Venice* 5.1.1). The anguish of Lear, the old king stripped bewilderingly of his authority, permeates the confused grief of Saturn, the old, dethroned king of the Titans in *Hyperion* and *The Fall of Hyperion*. The "bitter sweet" contrasts Keats located at the heart of Shakespearean suffering ("On sitting down to King Lear once Again"; *KL* 1.215), and marked in such lines as "The web of our life is of a mingled yarn, good and ill together" (*All's Well That Ends Well* 4.3.67), inform the 1819 odes and become personified in the summary figures of *Ode on Melancholy*: "Beauty that must die; / And Joy, whose hand is ever at his lips / Bidding adieu; and aching Pleasure nigh, /

Turning to poison while the bee-mouth sips," and chiefly "Veil'd Melancholy," whose "sovran shrine" is in "the very temple of Delight" (21–26).

Even as Keats was finding in Shakespeare a language for the sorrowful nature of human experience, he also drew from Shakespeare his most sophisticated response to that condition: a poised acceptance of the inevitability, and even the benefits, of suffering. Against the escapist impulses of his earlier poetry, he felt the necessity of "sharpening one's vision into the heart and nature of Man – of convincing ones nerves that the World is full of Misery and He[art]break, Pain, Sickness and oppression," as he said to Reynolds in May 1818, just as Tom's health was beginning to collapse (*KL* 1.281). Descending clear-eyed into that crucible of pain was no easy task, however, as Keats knew. His attempt to look "into the core / Of an eternal fierce destruction," he admitted in a verse-letter to Reynolds some weeks before, produced "horrid moods" from which only a "new Romance" seemed to promise "refuge" (25 March 1818; 1.262–63). How unlike *Lear*, which embraced the "fierce dispute" of the human soul struggling in torment. To "burn through" this play might be transformative:

> Let me not wander in a barren dream
> But when I am consumed with the Fire
> Give me new Phoenix-wings to fly at my desire   (*KL* 1.215)

Such a rejuvenation began to emerge in May 1819, when Keats echoed Lear's nightmare realization on a barren heath that "Man is originally 'a poor forked creature' subject to the same mischances as the beasts of the forest." This insight moved him to redeem such knowledge by imagining the world as a "vale of Soul-making" in which suffering is necessary to shape identity, "to school an Intelligence and make it a soul" (*KL* 2.101–2). Shakespeare's presence in Keats's articulation of this "system of salvation" (102) may be further seen in the echo of Edgar, "Ripeness is all" (*King Lear* 5.2.11) – perhaps Shakespeare's most memorable phrase on the acceptance of suffering – in Oceanus's willingness to accept pain and loss for "wondrous ends": "ripening . . . The ripe hour came" (*Hyperion* 2.193–94). Correspondingly, Autumn need not be a harbinger of death, but may be celebrated as a moment of "ripeness to the core" (*To Autumn* 6).

Keats's statement that he is only "very near agreeing" that Shakespeare is "enough for us" (*KL* 1.143) suggests that other writers had a call on his attention too, even ones that seem so opposite to the Shakespearean values with which Keats identified his efforts. In other words, Milton. Keats did not read *Paradise Lost* in depth until the autumn of 1817, when he studied it with his friend, theology student Benjamin Bailey. Once he took the plunge, he quickly elevated Milton to a principal position among his literary models and conducted a running engagement with his achievement throughout the next two years. "Shakspeare and the paradise lost," he wrote to Bailey in August 1819, "every day become greater wonders to me – I look upon fine Phrases like a Lover" (*KL* 2.139). Yet Keats always felt a significant difference in his relationship to Milton: Milton loomed as an intimidating master who threatened his very existence as a poet. About no other poet would Keats say, "Life to him would be death to me" (24 September 1819; *KL* 2.212). It was not the shorter works – *On the Morning of Christ's Nativity*, *Lycidas*, *L'Allegro*, and *Il Penseroso* – that were a problem: these were happy storehouses of phrase and tropes.[13] It was *Paradise Lost* that cast the long shadow, the epic accomplishment toward which Keats always aspired, but never achieved.

Keats found figures of benevolent guidance in *The Faerie Queene*, but he felt a force of oppression in *Paradise Lost*. He was pained by Satan's horrific nighttime confinement in the serpent in Book 9 (having invaded Eden, hidden thus from angelic discovery, awaiting the morning): "Whose spirit does not ache at the smothering and confinement," he wrote in his copy (p. 153); "no passage of poetry ever can give a greater pain of suffocation" (Cook, 345). Commenting on Milton, Keats almost instinctively slides into a language of conflict and predatory domination. "Milton in every instance pursues his imagination to the utmost – he is 'sagacious of his Quarry' [*PL* 10.281], he sees Beauty on the wing, pounces upon it and gorges it to the producing his essential verse" (p. 142; Cook, 344). No wonder that as he abandoned his attempt at Miltonic epic, his *Hyperion* project, Keats felt at last on "guard against Milton. Life to him would be death to me" (*KL* 2.212). With its fable of impotent Titan gods, its magnificently ponderous language, and its overwhelming aura of oppressive constriction, *Hyperion* itself seems in some aspects a monumental fragment of Keats's tortuous, life-and-death confrontation with Milton.

Keats's agon with Milton (as Harold Bloom makes clear) was not his alone; every epic-aspiring poet (and some novelists, too) had to confront and engage him, whether by imitation, supplement, parody, or revision. "Milton" was a domineering, inaccessible presence at the height of England's poetic tradition, and Keats compounded the problem by centering his response on the formidable challenge of rewriting, by secularizing, the cosmology of *Paradise Lost*. His earliest reference to Milton is to the heaven-ravishing force of his "lofty strain" and "tuneful thunders" (*Ode to Apollo* 21–23). As he read into *Paradise Lost*, he greeted Milton as the "Chief of organic numbers! / Old scholar of the spheres!" (*Lines on Seeing a Lock of Milton's Hair* 1–2), but he was soon mapping the trajectory of modern poetry in terms of a radical secularization of Milton's Christian vision. Like Wordsworth and other contemporary poets, he viewed the epic cosmology of *Paradise Lost* as the benchmark of late-Renaissance literary achievement, but felt it was an historically bound vision from which all modern poetry had to proceed in a new, humanized way. Keats's most sustained articulation of the problem unfolds in his description of human life to Reynolds in May 1818 as a movement through a "Mansion of Many Apartments" – an inevitable progress from "the infant or thoughtless Chamber," to "the Chamber of Maiden-Thought," thence into a labyrinth of "dark Passages." In this last emergence, Wordsworth is the modern genius and guide (*KL* 1.280–82). Milton's Christianity, "his Philosophy human and divine" (Keats suggests) was nested in the Chamber of Maiden-Thought: with its "certain points and resting places in reasoning" about good and evil, it could be "tolerably understood by one not much advanced in years." Such poems as *Tintern Abbey*, by contrast, conveyed a more mature struggle, a powerful feel for the "burden of the Mystery" in dark passages and "a Mist" where "We see not the ballance of good and evil" (281). For such a world, Wordsworth defined a different mode of epic, namely "epic passion," where the challenge was not discerning a grand Providential design, but his "martyr[ing] himself to the human heart, the main region of his song" (278–80). Reworking these themes a year later, Keats's other great allegory of creative process, life as a "vale of Soul-making" through suffering, is one he explicitly describes as "a grander system of salvation than the chrystain religion" (*KL* 2.102).

In between his fashioning of those two extended metaphors, Keats put them into practice as he attempted to rework *Paradise Lost* in *Hyperion*. The enormous labor such a project required is reflected in the astonishing detail of Keats's refiguration of Milton's narrative, linguistic, and theological structures. He patterned his formal structure on the first three books of *Paradise Lost*: Saturn's bewildering fall into a dark vale evokes Satan's experience in the hell of Milton's opening book; the Titan council in Book II (about how to respond to this fall) is an extended allusion to the colloquy in hell of Milton's second book, even down to specific arguments; Milton's Book III moves up to Heaven, Keats's to Apollo's island paradise. Keats does all this in a grand imitation of Milton's blank-verse style: Latinate inversions, such as "Rumbles reluctant" (61), a muscular verse syntax of trochees, past participles, catalogues, and strong stops early in verse lines. In the arena of these Miltonic effects, Keats defines his central project, a transformation of the "Philosophy" of *Paradise Lost*: Oceanus's speech presents the Titans' fall not as the wages of sin, but as a consequence of inevitable change. The vale of sadness into which they fall is a vale of Soul-making on an epic scale. This is a humanized revision of Milton's Protestant outlook on sin and eventual redemption through providential salvation. Notwithstanding the remarkable force of this revisionary descent into the human heart, Keats felt the strain of competing with Milton and tried to reduce his presence in a reworked version of *Hyperion*. *The Fall of Hyperion* adapts a dream-vision structure from Dante, and employs far less Latinate phrasing.

Yet if contesting Milton's epic "Philosophy" was the most powerful, most threatening aspect of Keats's engagement, it was not the only mode. He enthusiastically embraced, for instance, Milton's inveterate hatred of kings. Reading a passage in *Paradise Lost* in which Milton imagines how a lunar eclipse "with fear of change / Perplexes Monarchs" (1.599), Keats exclaims,

> How noble and collected an indignation against Kings [. . .] His very wishing should have had power to pull that feeble animal Charles from his bloody throne. "The evil days" had come to him – he hit the new System of things a mighty mental blow – the exertion must have had or is yet to have some sequences – (p. 85; Cook, 339)

One sequence is Keats's own scenes, in *Hyperion*, of erstwhile king-gods perplexed by astrological mysteries. As this local transfusion suggests, Milton also provided the inventory for imagery and phrasing that Keats loved in all the poets he read. As with Shakespeare, he relished Milton's language, feasting on what he called the "poetical Luxury" of his phrases as if they were so many delicious "cups of old wine" (Cook, 336). But it was Milton's feel for pathos, sometimes independent of and sometimes in contradiction to the imperatives of moral judgment, that arrested Keats's attention.[14] As with Shakespeare, he located this pathos in the play of contraries. He comments on Milton's rendition of the angels in Hell:

> The light and shade – the sort of black brightness – the ebon diamonding – the ethiop Immortality, the sorrow, the pain. the sad-sweet Melody – the Phalanges of Spirits so depressed as to be "uplifted beyond hope" – the short mitigation of Misery – the thousand Melancholies and magnificences [. . .] (Cook, 339)

Keats could feel these contrasts and conflicts quite intensely. He heavily marked Satan's comment on "the hateful siege / Of contraries" (9.121–22) – his simultaneous pleasure in Eden and his mission to destroy it – and summoned this phrase to explain to a friend in September 1818 what it was like trying to write *Hyperion* while tending to his dying brother:

> His identity presses upon me so all day that I am obliged to go out – and although I intended to have given some time to study alone I am obliged to write, and plunge into abstract images to ease myself of his countenance his voice and feebleness – [. . .] Imagine "the hateful siege of contraries" – if I think of fame of poetry it seems a crime to me, and yet I must do so or suffer [. . .]
> (KL 1.369)

It is one of the strengths of Keatsian contraries that he could put this same scene in *Paradise Lost*, Satan's stealing into Eden to seduce Eve, into a lighter, more ironic treatment. Planning the seduction of Madeline, "Stol'n to this paradise, and so entranced, / Porphyro gazed . . . / . . . crept, / Noiseless as fear in a wide wilderness" (*Eve of St. Agnes* 244–50).

Milton's pathos informs both these Satanic affiliations, and it is this capacity that Keats tended to admire most. He regarded the fallen angels' melancholy retreat "in a silent Valley" (*PL* 2.546–47) as "one of the most pathetic" moments "in the whole range of Poetry" (Cook, 338), and he attempted to reproduce it in the opening of *Hyperion*. Keats's markings in *Paradise Lost* consistently highlight such evocations of sorrow as Michael's grim lesson to Adam on the ravages of "Old Age . . . thou must outlive / Thy youth, thy strength, thy beauty; which will change / To withered, weak, and grey" (*PL* 11.538–40), which echoes plangently in *Ode to a Nightingale* in some of Keats's most haunting lines on human suffering:

> The weariness, the fever, and the fret
>   Here, where men sit and hear each other groan;
> Where palsy shakes a few sad, last, gray hairs,
>   Where youth grows pale, and spectre-thin, and dies;
>   Where but to think is to be full of sorrow
>   And leaden-eyed despairs,
>   Where Beauty cannot keep her lustrous eyes . . .   (23–29)

The lines are richer yet for interweaving Wordsworth ("While Man grows old, and dwindles, and decays" [1814 *Excursion* 4.778]), and Wordsworth's hearing of Milton and Shakespeare: "the fretful stir / Unprofitable, and the fever of the world" (*Tintern Abbey* 52–53, sounding along with Milton Hamlet's "How weary, stale, flat, and unprofitable / Seem to me all the uses of this world" [1.2.133–34]).[15]

Does Keats have any affection for fine phrasing in the long century between Milton and Wordsworth? His reactions to eighteenth-century literary culture are notoriously negative: a sharp critique of Pope's Augustan legacy in *Sleep and Poetry* (181–206), scornful marginalia in his 1814 Shakespeare edition on Johnson's criticism. Yet Dryden's vigorous couplet style modeled the verse of *Lamia* (KL 2.165), and even Pope could inspire. If lines of his Homer seemed like "Mice" to Keats once he discovered Chapman (KL 1.141), Pope's translations and original poetry remained important to him. Keats's letters sound phrases from *Essay on Man*, *Eloisa to Abelard*, and even Pope's Homer (KL 1.280, 2.133, 1.354), and he drew on *The Rape of the Lock* for the fairy machinery and the worldly satire of *The Jealousies*. Later eighteenth-century poets such as James Beattie and

Mary Tighe were early delights (*KL* 2.18), and Tighe's *Psyche* stayed with Keats longer than he cared to admit, its imprint clear enough in the lush descriptions of *Ode to Psyche* and *Lamia*.

Lamia, however, reveals Keats's uneasiness about this influence (an uneasiness, Anne Mellor's essay shows, that extends to other women writers). To structure the mortal Lycius's conflicted passion for Lamia, Keats adapted the revision of Spenserian allegory that Tighe developed for her sustained psychodrama between idealism and worldliness in the mortal Psyche's love for Cupid. Keats's sympathetic portrait of Lamia's "frail-strung heart" (1.309) shows the further influence of Tighe's deeply sympathetic representation of Psyche's "frantic sorrow," of her "sorrowing" and "wounded heart" (1.310, 523; 3.119). But if Keats's habitual attention to the language of pathos in his literary models merges, in the case of Tighe, with a sympathy for female subject positions, this sympathy does not extend to Tighe's figures of female empowerment. Tighe's Psyche is an activist questor for experience and identity; Keats's Lamia, after her initial dealings with Hermes and seduction of Lycius, is a passive lover, withdrawing from public life, tyrannized over by Lycius, and ultimately annihilated by Apollonius. The influence of Tighe was a gendered struggle, with Keats welcoming her aesthetics of pathos but resisting her intervention of "feminine" capabilities. He was immersed in Tighe's *Psyche* well into 1819, but insisted as early as December 1818 that she no longer "delighted" him: "now I see through [her] and can find nothing [but] weakness" (*KL* 2.18).

Burns and Chatterton were also important influences and, like Shakespeare and Milton, subjects for poetic reflection. Both presented moving, disturbing histories of personal hardship and great creative potential cut short. Chatterton's suicidal despair haunted Keats. He dedicated his first major endeavor, *Endymion*, a poem he pre-emptively thought a failure, "To the Memory of Thomas Chatterton"; "it is just that this youngster die away," he said of it in the Preface. But it wasn't just Chatterton's death but also his lively language that impressed Keats. He honored Chatterton as "The most english of Poets except Shakspeare" in a draft of the Preface that his publishers rejected (Stillinger, *Poems*, 738), and it was Chatterton's English to which he turned as the literary artifices of Miltonic language became unbearable (*KL* 2.167). Chatterton's most direct poetic influence may be on the medieval language of *The Eve of St. Mark*, and it was Chatterton's idea of a native idiom that stayed with Keats. "I somehow always associate Chatterton with autumn," he wrote to Reynolds in September 1821, just after composing his ode on the season; "He is the purest writer in the English language. He has no French idiom, or particles like Chaucer – 'tis genuine English idiom in English words" (*KL* 2.167). As the link with Autumn and *To Autumn* suggests, Keats also turned to Chatterton because he spoke, above all, of the mortal condition of mutability and suffering that Keats, aided by the English poets, had finally learned to embrace.[16]

Many issues shape Keats's conversations with the poets – his love of luxurious, complex language; his fascination with contrasts; his political investments; his intense concern about membership among the poets. But his chief and recurring emphasis on the power of poetry to convey the pathos of experience reveals a great deal about Keats's outlook on life, his habits of reading and writing, and even his sense of the fragility of his quest, like Chatterton's, to "be among the English Poets." One of Keats's most poignant expressions of such pathos also presents an exceptional instance of the transformative process that enabled him to speak among the poets, in the end, by modulating their own voices. Unable, during the final months of his life, to compose a poetry of his own, he could still feast on fine phrases and mark beautiful passages in *The Faerie Queene* for Fanny Brawne. He highlighted several descriptions of lovers pining in discontent, including this stanza on heartbroken Marinell, in a self-enervating decay, one that bears a startling relation to what Keats would call his own "posthumous existence" (*KL* 2.359) as he lay consumed by disease, thwarted ambition, and unfulfilled love:

> That in short space his wonted chearefull hew
> Gan fade, and lively spirits deaded quight;
> His cheeke-bones raw, and eie-pits hollow grew,
> And brawny armes had lost their knowen might.
> That nothing like himselfe he seem'd in sight.
> Ere long so weake of limbe, and sick of love,
> He woxe, that lenger he note stad upright,
> But to his bed was brought, and layd above,
> Like ruefull ghost, unable once to stir or move. (4.12.10)

Dropping the moral frame of Spenser's allegory and claiming this voice for his own mortal existence, Keats articulates the language of his heart in one of the most remarkable exertions of the dialogic process by which he spoke with, through, and, ultimately, "among the English poets."

NOTES

1 I use the text of Keats's personal editions when quoting passages of poetry that he marked; for their locations, see Frank N. Owings, Jr., *The Keats Library: A Descriptive Catalogue* (Hampstead, n.d.). For convenience I provide corresponding page numbers to Elizabeth Cook's edition. Milnes was the first to print the notes on *Paradise Lost*. For transcriptions, see Caroline Spurgeon, *Keats's Shakespeare* (Oxford: Oxford University Press, 1928); Cook for the annotations

to and markings of Shakespeare and Milton; Amy Lowell, *John Keats* (Boston: Houghton Mifflin, 1925), vol. 2, for Keats's markings of the first volume of *The Works of Mr. Edmund Spenser* (6 vols.; London: Jacob Tonson, 1715); Beth Lau, *Keats's "Paradise Lost"* (Gainesville: University Press of Florida, 1998). For commentary, see Lau, ibid., "Further Corrections to Amy Lowell's Transcriptions of Keats's Marginalia," *KSJ* 35 (1986), 30–39, and "Keats's Markings in Chaucer's *Troilus and Criseyde*," *KSJ* 43 (1994), 39–55; Greg Kucich, "'A Lamentable Lay': Keats and the Marking of Charles Brown's Spenser Volumes," *Keats–Shelley Review* 3 (1988), 1–22; R. S. White, *Keats as a Reader of Shakespeare* (Norman: University of Oklahoma Press, 1987).

2 For Keats's struggles with literary predecessors and tradition itself, see Harold Bloom, *The Anxiety of Influence* (Oxford: Oxford University Press, 1973) and *Poetry and Repression: Revisionism from Blake to Stevens* (New Haven: Yale University Press, 1976), 112–42.

3 *Written on a Blank Space at the End of Chaucer's Tale of "The floure and the Lefe,"* *Examiner*, 16 March 1817 (then in *Morning Chronicle* 17 March). (This tale is now no longer thought to be Chaucer's.) The sonnet on reading Chapman's Homer had been published in *The Examiner*, 1 December 1816.

4 For discussions of these responses, see Robert Gittings, *The Mask of Keats*, ch. 5, and Ronald Primeau, "Chaucer's *Troilus and Criseyde* and the Rhythm of Experience in Keats's 'What can I do to drive away,'" *KSJ* 23 (1974), 106–18.

5 William Hazlitt, *Lectures on the English Poets; The Spirit of the Age*, ed. Catherine MacDonald MacLean (London: Everyman, 1910), 29.

6 The markings are Hunt's; Keats made similar notations; see Greg Kucich, *Keats, Shelley, and Romantic Spenserianism*, 149–50. Keats's attention to this and the next stanza (xli) is noted in Amy Lowell, *John Keats*, 2 vols. (Boston: Houghton Mifflin, 1925), 2.548–49.

7 Now in the Victoria and Albert Museum Library.

8 For Shakespearean echoes and allusions, Miriam Allott's notes in her edition of Keats's poems are a rich resource.

9 For Shakespearean echoes in *Endymion*, see Spurgeon, *Keats's Shakespeare*, 56–65, and Allott's notes.

10 Nicholas Roe, *John Keats and the Culture of Dissent*, 230–67.

11 See Roe, *ibid*, 253–57, and Andrew Bennett, "Agrarian Politics and the Economics of Writing: Keats's 'To Autumn,'" *Criticism* 33 (1991), 333–51.

12 *KL* 1.365, 370, 375, 377, 386, 391, 400, 406, 408; 2.4, 40.

13 Again, Allott is a valuable resource.

14 See Stuart Ende, *Keats and the Sublime*.

15 For a detailed comparison of Keats's interactions with Shakespeare, Milton, and Wordsworth, see Susan J. Wolfson, *The Questioning Presence: Wordsworth, Keats, and the Interrogative Mode in Romantic Poetry*, ch. 8.

16 For commentary on Keats's echoes of Chatterton in *To Autumn*, see Gittings, "Keats and Chatterton," *Mask*, ch. 7; Nai-Tung Ting, "Chatterton and Keats: A Reexamination," *KSJ* 30 (1981), 117, and Vincent Newey's essay in this volume.

13

WILLIAM C. KEACH

Byron reads Keats

Among Keats's contemporaries Byron has a distinctive place. His astonishing public success, his close connections with Leigh Hunt, his recurrently negative and snobbishly sarcastic or condescending judgments of Keats's writing – these and other related factors make Byron's dismissiveness of Keats a painful thing to contemplate. We should be wary, though, of dismissing Byron's dismissiveness. The reasons for, and terms of, his animus against Keats's verse reveal much that is important about Keats's career and his talent – and much about Byron as well. Even the relatively sympathetic and praising remarks he made soon after Keats's death are worth more curious-minded attention than they have received, not least because, in the end, Byron returns to a mainly negative stance. His latest known comment is in a letter to John Murray, 10 October 1822. As usual, and tellingly, the immediate context is Hunt and the Cockney-Suburban School: "I do not know what world [Hunt] has lived in – but I have lived in three or four – and none of them like his Keats and Kangaroo terra incognita – ."[1] The Hampstead world of Keats and Hunt may as well have been a penal colony down under, populated by transported Cockneys, for all Byron cares to know of it. Or so he says to his old Tory publisher.

The class biases and antagonistic literary allegiances critical to understanding Byron's response to Keats return us to other basic questions. How much Keats did Byron actually read? I think he read a great deal of the poetry, more than his private letters would suggest. But when we speak of Byron's reading of "Keats" we need to understand "Keats" to signify more than the metonym for Keats's writing. Byron was also reading Keats the person, the socially and historically situated subject. Sometimes, as in the letter to Murray above, Keats's authorial and personal identities are violently entangled. "No more <u>Keats</u> I entreat – flay him alive – if some of you don't I must skin him myself there is no bearing the drivelling idiotism of the Mankin," Byron cries to Murray after receiving Keats's 1820 volume from him (*BLJ* 7.202), casting Keats the man (or "Mankin") as a miniature

Marsyas, the talented satyr who, for daring to challenge the supremacy of the god of poetry, was flayed alive. The mixture of literary and personal, almost physical, aggression is striking. Even when Byron would have Murray think he can't recall Keats's name – "The Edinburgh praises Jack Keats or Ketch or whatever his names are; – why his is the <u>Onanism</u> of Poetry" (7.217) – the gesture is invested with physical and sexual, as well as social violence. "Jack Ketch" is the proverbial London hangman, and as Byron goes on in this letter to recall "an Italian fiddler" who accidentally hanged himself in a moment of miscarried erotic self-stimulation (scarfing), an intense projective and self-protective engagement belies the lordly dismissiveness and distance.[2]

Recent scholarship has done much to reconstruct the literary-historical context within which Byron's attitude towards Keats can be accurately understood. A major advance came in 1980 with Paul Dawson's "Byron, Shelley, and the 'New School,'" a standard against which to measure the validity and force of subsequent critical commentary on Byron's relation to Keats (by Christopher Ricks, Marjorie Levinson, and Nicholas Roe). More recently, Jeffrey Cox has provided an extended and detailed look at how Keats's reception by his immediate contemporaries was affected by the adversarial literary grouping of Hunt, Keats, and Shelley. Cox's study has an important bearing on understanding Byron's reading of Keats, not least because it shows Byron himself – surprisingly, but not without basis – as a Cockney writer.[3]

In contrast to the perspective of Keats's enemies at *Blackwood's* and *The Quarterly Review*, Byron, Dawson emphasizes, saw the "Cockney School" to which Keats was said to belong as an *"under-Sect"* of the "Lake School" (97, citing Byron's phrase).[4] In *Some Observations Upon An Article in "Blackwood's Magazine"* (1820), Byron calls Keats "a tadpole of the lakes, a young disciple of the six or seven new Schools" (*CMP* 116).[5] Whereas the Tory reviewers sarcastically contrasted the imaginative and social integrity of Wordsworth, Coleridge, and Southey (their loyalty to the permanent values of rural English life and nature) to the upstart urban origins and suburban tastes of Hunt and Keats, Byron believed that the Cockneys, the Lakers, indeed all the "new Schools" were at one in wrong-headedly trying to reform English poetry by following a "system" – an anti-Augustan "system." Their deliberate, explicit rejection of Pope's cultural and aesthetic environment mattered more to Byron than the differences between Oxbridge-educated poets committed to life in in the English countryside and petty bourgeois Londoners whose poetry openly celebrated the pleasures of an outing on Hampstead Heath.

The extravagant and unstable experimentalism of Keats's Cockney style,

Dawson shows, was fundamental to what bothered Byron – and Shelley as well.[6] Shelley shared at least part of Byron's view of Keats as a "tadpole of the lakes" and criticized everything except *Hyperion* on grounds that follow Byron's curious subordination of what to most readers today are striking stylistic differences. "Keats's new volume has arrived," Shelley wrote to Marianne Hunt on 29 October 1820; "the fragment called Hyperion promises for him that he is destined to become one of the first writers of the age. – His other things are imperfect enough, & what is worse written in the bad sort of style which is becoming fashionable among those who fancy that they are imitating Hunt & Wordsworth."[7] Shelley had written to Keats himself, 27 July 1820, "In poetry I have sought to avoid system & mannerism" (2.220–22), and Byron would praise Shelley's poetry for being of "no school," as he complained to him of Keats's "second-hand school of poetry" (26 April 1821; *BLJ* 8.103). That Byron and Shelley could see this school as inculcating a style in which the influences of Hunt and Wordsworth were equally and indistinguishably damaging suggests, argues Dawson, that they "both viewed Keats, not as he was, but as it suited their purposes to see him" (97).

What were Byron's purposes, in particular? One immediate source of his irritable snobbishness towards Cockney Keats was *Blackwood's* insistence on placing Byron himself in the Cockney School. Such inclusion is not always the preferred tactic; there are moments when the Tory reviewers go out of their way to detach Byron and Shelley, as aristocrats, from the perceived vulgar, plebeian aspirations of Hunt, Keats, Hazlitt, and their friends. But Byron could also be seen as having been contaminated by poetical and political ties to these inferiors. Assessing *Don Juan VI-VIII* (1823) – cantos no longer published by Tory Murray but by "Cockney" Leigh Hunt's brother, John – the reviewer for *Blackwood's* is certain "that his lordship must have taken the Examiner, the Liberal, the Rimini, the Round Table, as his model, and endeavoured to write himself down to the level of the capacities and the swinish tastes of those with whom he has the misfortune, originally, I believe, from charitable motives, to associate." He fears that Byron will soon take to rhyming "like Barry Cornwall, [. . .], like John Keats – or [. . .] like the immortal LEIGH REX himself."[8] There are, I shall argue, good reasons for the *Blackwood's* reviewer to be reminded of Keats's rhymes as he was reading *Don Juan*, but the effect of this public linking of Byron to a school he had gone out of his way to denounce was to put him – even Lord Byron – on the defensive.

Such immediate occasions play across broader contexts and directions. All of Byron's intensely negative pronouncements about Keats appear in letters to Murray when Byron was embroiled in "the Pope and Bowles Controversy"[9]

(Keats's recent attack on Popian poetics in *Sleep and Poetry* was one of the things that provoked Byron's ire) and when his relation to his old publisher was coming under increasing strain because of the shock and agitation caused by the early cantos of *Don Juan*. His most notorious pronouncements – "Johnny Keats's p-ss a bed poetry"; "the drivelling idiotism of the Mankin"; "the Onanism of Poetry"; "a sort of mental masturbation – he is always f–gg–g his Imagination" – are in letters of October and November 1820 (*BLJ* 7.200, 202, 217, 225), and elaborate the cartoon of Keats as "a tadpole of the lakes" in his first (unpublished) defense of Pope that March. The next cluster is in March 1821, in Byron's pamphlets on the Pope Controversy. The second of these, *Observations upon "Observations." A Second Letter to John Murray, Esq., on the Rev. W. L. Bowles's Strictures on the Life and Writings of Pope* (dated 25 March 1821, but not published until 1832), has a fresh attack on "Mr. John Ketch" (*CMP* 157), then a compelling paragraph that opens, "The grand distinction of the Under forms of the New School of poets – is their Vulgarity. – By this I do not mean that they are Coarse – but shabby-genteel – as it is termed" (159). This a key text in the evolving sequence. Keats had died on 23 February, but Byron did not learn of this until April, from Shelley; then he writes to Murray, to Shelley, and to Thomas Moore to express sadness but also astonishment at Keats's having "died at Rome of the Quarterly Review" (to Murray, 26 April 1821; *BLJ* 8.102). He never wavers in his opposition to Keats's "Cockneyfying and Suburbing," as he phrases it to Murray (8.102), or to Shelley, "that second hand school of poetry" (also 26 April; 8.103), but he eventually acknowledges Keats's talent: "His Hyperion is a fine monument & will keep his name" (to Murray, 30 July 1821; 8.163). Twice in early August, when he was reading proof on his pamphlet for the Pope Controversy, Byron asks Murray to "omit the whole of the observations against the Suburban School – they are meant against Keats and I cannot war with the dead – particularly those already killed by Criticism" (4 August 1821, *BLJ* 8.166; cf. 7 August, 8.172). The only other references in his letters – apart from "Keats and Kangaroo terra incognita" in October 1822 – come just after Shelley's drowning, late summer of 1822, when he tells Douglas Kinnaird and Thomas Moore that "Shelley's body has been found identified [. . .] chiefly by a book in his Jacket pocket," namely, the leather binding of Keats's 1820 volume (*BLJ* 9.185). Byron pointedly says nothing to them about what he thinks of this book, though it did contain the fragment of *Hyperion* that he said he admired.

Byron's denunciations of Keats combine specific stylistic objections with an undisguised sense of class superiority and a sexual anger that, as we have seen, seems at times obsessive. To explore these links further, more needs to be said about the relation of class superiority to broader matters of cultural and party politics. The pamphlet on the Pope Controversy that Byron published, *Letter to John Murray Esqre*, is addressed to the Tory publisher whose offices in Albemarle Street were a center of literary activity featuring Sir Walter Scott and William Gifford, editor of *The Quarterly Review*, and where Byron had met John Hookham Frere and William Stewart Rose, Tory poets and translators who helped him find his way to the *ottava rima* of *Beppo* and *Don Juan*. Liberal Whig, defender of frame-breakers and enemy of Wellington and Castlereagh though he was, Byron had extensive literary ties with the Tory establishment. He could trade sneers at Keats with the Murray circle while holding political positions totally opposed to those of Gifford, Canning, and Croker. It was the shared class-based repudiation of a rising tide of untitled and unentitled urban poets that made the contradictory situation possible.

In the public *Letter*, Byron refuses any suggestion that he finds the poetry of Keats and Hunt "vulgar" merely because they are Cockneys. He pointedly detaches the word *vulgar* from any exclusive reference to particular classes, to common people, as Shelley had done when he wrote to Hunt himself in August 1819 about *Julian and Maddalo* (*Letters*, 2.108). The vulgar are "shabby genteel," a term in circulation since the mid-eighteenth century, and this is not, Byron insists, the same as "<u>Coarse</u>": "A man may be <u>coarse</u> & yet not <u>vulgar</u> – and the reverse" (*CMP* 159). As Byron goes on, however, it becomes clear that it is precisely the *uncoarse* vulgarity of petty bourgeois and working-class Londoners that animates his dislike of their poetry. He makes the privileges of his own class position clear with a nonchalance that performs the prerogatives it names:

> It is in their <u>finery</u> that the New-under School – are <u>most</u> vulgar; – and they may be known by this at once – as what we called at Harrow – "a Sunday blood" might be easily distinguished from a Gentleman – although his cloathes might be the better-cut – and his boots the best-blackened, of the two – probably because he made the one – or cleaned the other, with his own hands. –
>
> (*CMP* 591)

How amusingly disgusting for Byron and those of his readers who share in his elite Harrovian "we," that a man claiming to be a poet might actually shine his own shoes! Underlying his explicit offhanded gesture is contempt – and also, perhaps, some nervousness – about having to work to fashion one's own public image and, by extension, to entitle oneself to operate in the realm of polite letters. Byron must have been especially put off by Keats's characteristic willingness to figure writing as manual labor – as grasping, holding, harvesting, garnering. That Keats understood all this is evident from his satirical portrait of Byron as the petulant and self-indulgent Lord

Elfinan in *The Jealousies* (*The Cap and Bells*, its alternative title), which he began but left unfinished and unpublished in late 1819.

Keats casts *The Jealousies* in Spenserian stanzas, the verse form Byron had returned to popular acclaim with *Childe Harold's Pilgrimage*, its four cantos just published for the first time together in 1819. This is a late reference to Byron. The distinctive features of Keats's early poetry are also strikingly connected to Byron's own writing, especially to the new idiomatic and colloquial *ottava rima* style Byron began developing in 1818–19, and even more especially to the erotic moments in this writing. Keats and Byron are not doing anything like the same thing, but their differently evolving verse idioms converge in ways that may well have made them both, Byron especially, anxious. Of greatest insight and help here is Christopher Ricks's chapter in *Keats and Embarrassment*, "Keats, Byron, and 'Slippery Blisses,'" which asks many of the questions pertinent to Byron's thinking about Keats: about erotic intensity, excitement, and confusion. Part of what is at stake for Byron, Ricks shows, is precisely erotic affect in and through the work and play of language – especially of rhyme. Though Ricks emphasizes the differences between Byron and Keats in affect, he still leaves us with a sense that what Byron found in Keats's early poetry were not just the vulgar experiments of a disciple of the Cockney-Suburban School, but activities, effects, and potentialities of language that were very close, at times, to those in which he himself was invested.

Ricks gets to the nub of the issue in his comments on Byron's now infamous remark to Murray about "Johnny Keats's p-ss a bed poetry" (*BLJ* 7.200). "Byron's violence of embarrassed disgust is a false reaction to something truly in Keats," he says (86). "False reaction" may not do justice "to something truly in" Byron as well – in the passage from *Don Juan*, for instance, that Ricks compares to a piece of Cockney erotic indulgence in Keats's ottava-rima *Isabella*. "So said, his erewhile timid lips grew bold, / And poesied with hers in dewy rhyme," Keats writes of his lovers (69–70). Here is the passage from Byron, which Ricks quotes (98) in defense of Keats's imaging a kiss as rhyming lips:

> When amatory poets sing their loves
>   In liquid lines mellifluously bland,
> And pair their rhymes as Venus yokes her doves,
>   They little think what mischief is in hand.   (V.1)[10]

Saying nothing directly about kissing, Byron appears to be debunking the very erotic coupling Keats produces, or tries to produce. Even so, his "liquid lines" are a testimony to Keats's sublimation of saliva in "dewy rhyme"; he wrote these lines October–November 1820, having received in early October a copy of Keats's 1820 volume, with *Isabella*. Byron's point, different but related to Keats's, is that the language of "amatory" poets *does* produce real erotic effects, even when what they are most concerned with is the formal, technical seduction of the reader: "The greater their success the worse it proves, / As Ovid's verse may give to understand." Extending the satirical paradox of "the greater . . . the worse" through the internal rhyme of "worse" / "Ovid's verse" is part of Byron's own art of rhetorical seduction on this occasion. He may be reflexively outside or above rather than affectingly within the erotic effects he names (Ricks argues). But then Keats too steps back and away in the stanza following the one quoted above:

> Parting they seem'd to tread upon the air,
> Twin roses by the zephyr blown apart
> Only to meet again more close, and share
> The inward fragrance of each other's heart.   (73–76)

These lines, surely, were a provocation for Byron's comparing a rhyming pair to the dove-pair that pull Venus's car through the air. The poet of *Don Juan* looked closely at what the young Cockney poet was doing with *ottava rima* in *Isabella*.

"[It] will not quite do," Ricks writes in another suggestive generalization, "to claim that Byron was unembarrassable except by Keats. What is true, nevertheless, is that he was moved by Keats to an intensity and violence of embarrassment quite unlike anything else he ever expressed" (85). In his projected public pronouncements, Byron disguises the intensity of stylistic embarrassment in suave skepticism of the this-will-not-do kind. "Now what does this mean?" he asks (*Some Observations*; CMP 114), having quoted nine lines from *Sleep and Poetry* that begin:

> The hearty grasp that sends a pleasant Sonnet –
> Into the brain ere one can think upon it,
> The Silence when some rhymes are coming out,
> And when they're come, the *very pleasant rout.*[11]

Byron knows very well what "this" means. A related self-gratifying pleasure in watching rhymes come out is a hallmark of *Don Juan*:

> Prose poets like blank-verse, I'm fond of rhyme,
>   Good workmen never quarrel with their tools;
> I've got new mythological machinery,
> And very handsome supernatural scenery.   (I.201)

> But tugging on his petticoat he tripp'd,
>   Which – as we say – or, as the Scotch say, *whilk*,
> (The rhyme obliges me to this; sometimes
> Monarchs are less imperative than rhymes) –   (V.77)

> Besides Platonic love, besides the love
>   Of God, the love of Sentiment, the loving
> Of faithful pairs – (I needs must rhyme with dove,
>   That good old steam-boat which keeps verses moving
> 'Gainst Reason – Reason ne'er was hand-and-glove
>   With rhyme, but always leant less to improving
> The sound than sense) – besides all these pretences
> To Love, there are those things which Words name Senses; – (IX.74)

Like Keats, Byron affirms the pleasures of rhyming as a standard by which to record and measure other pleasure. Like Keats too, he is willing to let the chances of rhyme lead him into unexpected turns of thought and feeling: "love" and "dove" are embarrassingly predictable – but "hand-in-glove"?[12] Byron does guard himself with an aristocratic nonchalance unavailable and alien to Keats. But what is being guarded are often similarly conjoined sexual and textual gratifications. Behind many of Byron's denunciations of Keats are slant recognitions of a common writerly impulse, of poetic fellow feeling.

Self-protection and self-defense become prominent issues in Byron's reading of Keats's death, notoriously in the oft-quoted epitaph, "snuff'd out by an article," from *Don Juan* XI (1823).[13] The whole stanza is worth looking at from this perspective:

> John Keats, who was killed off by one critique,
>   Just as he really promised something great,
> If not intelligible, – without Greek
>   Contrived to talk about the Gods of late,
> Much as they might have been supposed to speak.
>   Poor fellow! His was an untoward fate: –
> 'Tis strange the mind, that very fiery particle,
> Should let itself be snuffed out by an Article. (XI. 60)

That Byron credited Shelley's account of *The Quarterly Review*'s devastation of Keats's health testifies to an indirect empathic vulnerability: Byron wincingly remembers what *The Edinburgh Review* "critique" of *Hours of Idleness* felt like. Yet even as he recalls this pain to Murray, he cannot accept that Keats allowed himself to be thus done in:

> I know by experience that a savage review is Hemlock to a sucking author – and the one on me – (which produced the English Bards &c.) knocked me down – but I got up again. – Instead of bursting a blood-vessel – I drank three bottles of Claret – and began an answer – (26 April 1821; *BLJ* 8.102)

A momentary sympathizing produces an antipathetic counter-reaction, with Byron immediately transforming appeals to bodily strength and determination into compositional aggression. The transformations depend, all the same, on a dynamic of identification, on a turning of things associated with Keats – a poisonous review, "bursting a blood-vessel," even the draught of vintage – into gestures that can be accommodated within the Byronic persona. Byron represents Keats's death as something to do with his own bodily and writerly life in ways that find an echo in Byron's exacerbated and overdetermined reactions to Keats's poetry.

Writing to Shelley the same day, Byron is more considerate – of the dead Keats and of Shelley's having to live through his share of journalistic hemlock:

> I recollect the effect on me of the Edinburgh on my first poem; it was rage, and resistance, and redress – but not despondency nor despair. I grant that these are not amicable feelings; but, in this world of bustle and broil, and especially in the career of writing, a man should calculate upon his powers of <u>resistance</u> before he goes into the arena. (*BLJ* 8.103)

As in the letter to Murray, Byron makes himself comfortable by thinking of what "a man" should do when he enters "the arena," the field of battle. This generalization allows him to avoid thinking about the ways in which "rage, and resistance, and redress" are social resources more easily available to him and Shelley than to Keats. Regency literary culture was hardly a level playing field. It is paradoxically an averted identification with Keats, operating across the vast difference in class positions, that inures Byron to the relevance of class difference at the very moment when it should be part of his understanding what it meant for Keats to have been attacked by the two leading Tory magazines of the day.

What, from this perspective, should we make of Byron's singling out *Hyperion* for praise among the poems of the 1820 volume? "His fragment of 'Hyperion' seems actually inspired by the Titans, and is as sublime as Æschylus," Byron writes in a note added to his first projected public attack on Keats in *Some Observations*; "He is a loss to our literature, and the more so – as he himself before his death is said to have been persuaded that he had not taken the right line, and was reforming his style upon the more Classical models of the language" (*CMP* 113; the note is dated 12 November 1821). One thing about the style of *Hyperion* that Byron may well have liked is that it showed Keats moving further away from Byron's own verse – in contrast to the ottava rima of *Isabella*, the Spenserian stanzas of *The Eve of St. Agnes*, and the Dryden-inspired couplets of *Lamia*. There is no reason to believe that Byron would have identified with or embraced the "new" art of Keats's Apollo, with its "blissful golden melody" (*Hyperion* 2.280) and its

> family of rapturous hurried notes,
> That fell, one after one, yet all at once,
> Like pearl beads dropping sudden from their string. (2.282–84)

But Byron would have remembered that Leigh Hunt's *Young Poets* article in *The Examiner* (1 December 1816) had explained the aspirations of these poets as "being to restore the same love of Nature, and of *thinking* instead of mere *talking*, which formerly rendered us real poets, and not merely versifying wits, and bead-rollers of couplets" (*KCH* 42). Keats's extraordinary simile of "pearl beads dropping sudden from their string" at once undoes and redeems or reclaims Hunt's image, in a way that Byron must have appreciated.

Beyond this, Byron would have been intrigued by the thematic configuration of Keats's experiment in Miltonic epic: an older generation of rulers replaced by a new, more vital generation; a still-defiant older sun-god about to be supplanted by a "new" son/sun, and this "by course of Nature's law," as Oceanus says, "not force / Of thunder, or of Jove" (2.181–82). Keats takes the epic mythological materials of Shelley's *Prometheus Unbound* at an earlier and more circumscribed stage of their narrative and political unfolding and uses them to explore an ideal of inexorable artistic progress and power, set against an implicit recognition that the entire process may yield nothing in any given moment but fleeting intensity. How would Byron in 1820–21 have read himself into this allegory? How would he have read Keats into it? We cannot know with any certainty, but my speculation is that Byron's belief that Keats "was reforming his style upon the more Classical models of the language" is more than just a claim of victory in the Regency culture wars – a victory in the battle over Keats's writing that he would have had to share not just with Shelley but also with John Gibson Lockhart and John Wilson Croker. No: Byron's admiration for *Hyperion* suggests the opening up of a deeper sense of connection made possible by, but not limited to, Keats's excursion into Miltonic blank verse, an idiom Byron conspicuously avoided. This deeper sense of connection, along with the distancing demurral, is there in the stanza of *Don Juan* in which Byron wonders how Keats

> without Greek
> Contrived to talk about the Gods of late,
> Much as they might have been supposed to speak. (XI.60)

Contriving to talk in verse much as gods – or people – are supposed to speak (in English, not Greek): as a general characterization, what could more effectively evoke Byron's own greatest writing?

NOTES

1 George Gordon, Lord Byron, *Byron's Letters and Journals*, ed. Leslie A. Marchand, 12 vols. (Cambridge: Harvard University Press, 1973–82), 10.69; hereafter cited *BLJ*.

2 See Marjorie Levinson's commentary, *Keats's Life of Allegory: The Origins of a Style*, 22–25.

3 See Paul Dawson, "Byron, Shelley, and the 'New School,'" *Shelley Revalued: Essays from the Gregynog Conference*, ed. Kelvin Everest (Totowa, N.J.: Barnes & Noble, 1983); Christopher Ricks, *Keats and Embarrassment* (1976); Levinson, *Keats's Life of Allegory* (1988); Nicholas Roe, *John Keats and the Culture of Dissent* (1997); Jeffrey Cox, *Poetry and Politics in the Cockney School: Keats, Shelley, Hunt and their Circle* (1998).

4 Dawson 97. Byron's phrase is from *Letter to John Murray Esqre* (1821); *Lord Byron: The Complete Miscellaneous Prose*, ed. Andrew Nicholson (Oxford: Clarendon Press, 1991), 156. This edition is subsequently cited *CMP*.

5 On Shelley's urging, this letter wasn't published. It first appeared in Thomas Moore's edition of Byron's *Works* (1833, after both Byron and Keats were dead). Byron was provoked by Keats's attack in *Sleep and Poetry* (181–206) on neoclassical poets, including Pope, as a "school / Of dolts" (196–97); see *CMP* 113–16.

6 For my more positive evaluation of this experimentalism, see "Cockney Couplets: Keats and the Politics of Style."

7 *Letters of Percy Bysshe Shelley*, ed. Frederick L. Jones, 2 vols. (Oxford: Clarendon Press, 1964), 2.239; hereafter cited parenthetically.

8 The review appeared as a postscript to a letter signed "Timothy Tickler" (a "tickler" was the rod used on unruly schoolboys), *Blackwood's Edinburgh Magazine* 14 (July 1823), 88–92; quotations are from 88 and 91. Cox discusses this review (*Poetry and Politics*, 20).

9 Byron's phrase (*CMP* 120); Revd. W. L. Bowles's *Works of Alexander Pope* (1806) had a prefatory essay deprecating Pope's poetical and moral character. The "controversy" erupted in 1819 when poet Thomas Campbell attacked Bowles in *Specimens of the British Poets: With Biographical and Critical Notices*. Bowles then defended himself in *Invariable Principles of Poetry: In a Letter to Thomas Campbell*, and over the next two years the battle waged, with Byron joining the fray in 1821 with his public *Letter to John Murray Esqre* (*CMP* 120–60).

10 *Don Juan* is cited by Canto and stanza, following vol. 5 of *Lord Byron: The Complete Poetic Works*, ed. Jerome J. McGann (Oxford: Clarendon Press, 1986).

11 319–22; Byron's transcription (*CMP* 114). He may have been influenced by the reviewer of the 1817 *Poems* for *The Eclectic* (2nd ser. 7; September 1817), who quotes the last couplet and, calling it "precious nonsense [. . .] decked out in rhyme," italicizes these same words (272).

12 See Susan J. Wolfson's discussion of Byron's metaformal fun with the rhymes of these stanzas in *Formal Charges: The Shaping of Poetry in British Romanticism*, 140–41 and notes 10 and 11.

13 For the afterlife of this phrase and its impact on Keats's fame, see Susan J. Wolfson, "Keats Enters History: Autopsy, *Adonais*, and the Fame of Keats," in Roe, ed., *Keats and History*, 29–30.

14

ANNE K. MELLOR

Keats and the complexities of gender

From his own day to ours, Keats – as a poet and as a person – has provoked questions about gender, about what it means to be a male or a female poet, about the nature of masculinity and femininity. Hazlitt first raised this issue in 1822, in his essay "On Effeminacy of Character." Defining "effeminacy" as "a prevalence of the sensibility over the will," "a want of fortitude," a desire for "ease and indolence," and an obsession with the sensations of the moment – as opposed to a "manly firmness and decision of character" – Hazlitt then suggested that there was a corresponding literary style, citing Keats's poetry as a primary example: "all florid, all fine; that cloys by its sweetness." He concluded,

> I cannot help thinking that the fault of Mr. Keats's poems was a deficiency in masculine energy of style. He had beauty, tenderness, delicacy, in an uncommon degree, but there was a want of strength and substance. His Endymion is a very delightful description of the illusions of a youthful imagination, given up to airy dreams – we have flowers, clouds, rainbows, moonlight, all sweet sounds and smells, and Oreads and Dryads flitting by – but there is nothing tangible in it, nothing marked or palpable – we have none of the hardy spirit or rigid forms of antiquity.[. . .] We see in him the youth, without the manhood of poetry.[1]

Numerous contemporary reviewers agreed that Keats's poetry was effeminate, juvenile, or puerile. Writing for *Blackwood's Edinburgh Magazine* in August 1818, "Z." first defined Keats as a "Cockney" poet (vol. 3, 519), slang for an inferior, lower-class Londoner, with connotations of immaturity and effeminacy. It became his theme. In *Blackwood's* January 1826 he was still describing Keats as an "infatuated bardling" who wrote "a species of emasculated pruriency that [. . .] looks as if it were the product of some imaginative Eunuch's muse" (vol. 19, xvi, xxvi).

Exactly what was it about Keats's character and writings that called his masculinity into question? Z. and others, whatever we think of their tone or their politics, alert us to the extremely subtle and complex ways in which Keats challenged the existence of fixed, stable boundaries between the sexes. He did so in two ways: by occupying the position of a "woman" in his life and in his writings, and by blurring the distinction between masculinity and femininity.

Let us look first at a few aspects of Keats's life and death. Orphaned at age fourteen, the eldest of the four siblings, Keats took on the role of mother to the youngest, Tom and Fanny. When Fanny was removed to a bleak situation with her legal guardians, Keats corresponded faithfully, comforting and advising her. When his brother Tom contracted tuberculosis, he nursed him until his early death. His first choice of a profession, to become an apothecary (a combination of a lower-level general practitioner and pharmacist), was one closely associated with nursing, a feminine occupation. Moreover, Keats appeared, even to his own eyes, "girlish." He was small – five feet two inches tall – and fine-boned. The most widely distributed portrait in the nineteenth century was Joseph Severn's of Keats on his deathbed: a wan, delicate face with flowing curls that could be either male or female. This feminization was intensified throughout the Victorian period, as Susan Wolfson has argued, by the fabling of Shelley's *Adonais* (his elegy on the death of Keats) that the sensitive poet had been driven to death by negative reviews, "snuff'd out by an article," as Byron later put it in *Don Juan* (XI.60).[2]

With the publication of Keats's letters, first in 1848, the "feminine" evidence increased. Keats consciously identified his concept of the poet and the poetic process with the feminine gender. In the nineteenth century, the masculine self was thought to have a strong sense of its autonomy and ego boundaries: that "firmness and decision of character" Hazlitt had celebrated. The feminine self was thought to be more pliable and yielding, to possess more permeable ego boundaries.[3] In his descriptions both of his own sense of identity and of the "poetical Character," Keats reversed these stereotypes:

> As to the poetical Character itself, (I mean that sort of which, if I am any thing, I am a Member; that sort distinguished from the wordsworthian or egotistical sublime; which is a thing per se and stands alone) it is not itself – it has no self – it is every thing and nothing [. . .] It has as much delight in conceiving an Iago as an Imogen. What shocks the virtuous philosop[h]er delights the camelion Poet.
> (*KL* 1.386–87)

Keats deliberately resists what he (perhaps unfairly) sees as Wordsworth's masculinist construction of the self: bounded, unitary, stable, complete, and instrumental, an empowered agent. As his echo of *Troilus and Cressida* suggests, he mockingly identifies the Wordsworthian poetical character, or masculinist ego, with Shakespeare's bull-headed, vainglorious, boasting Greek warrior Ajax: "he is a very man per se, / And stands alone" (1.2.15–16). Keats conceives the self as fluid, unbounded, decentered, inconsistent – a self described by Nancy Chodorow and the Winnicott school of psychology as a self-in-relation, or by the French psychoanalytic theories of Jacques Lacan and Julia Kristeva as a self entirely formed within a constantly shifting linguistic universe. Keats's "camelion" self is not "a" self at all: it "has no Identity"; it is "continually in for – and filling some other Body" (1.387).

A self that is permeable, continually overflowing its boundaries, melting into another, and being filled by another has historically been associated with the female, and especially with the pregnant woman who experiences herself and her fetus as one. By erasing the distinction between two and one, such a self denies Aristotelian logical and mathematical differentiations, and so seems to many such "virtuous" philosophers to embrace irrationality and confusion. Keats celebrates this "confusion" (and provocatively identifies it with the male sex) when he defines the quality that forms "a Man of Achievement especially in Literature & which Shakespeare pos[s]essed so enormously," namely, "Negative Capability, that is when man is capable of being in uncertainties, Mysteries, doubts, without any irritable reaching after fact & reason" (KL 1.193). Keats identifies the true poet above all with the capacity for *empathy* or sympathy, a quality everywhere associated with women in his day. Throughout the eighteenth century, a new literature of sensibility had developed, one that advanced the writer as a "man of feeling" but at the same time identified this "man of feeling" with traditionally "feminine" qualities: tears, heightened emotions, excessive passion or love, extreme irrationality, wasting diseases, suicidal impulses, and madness.[4]

If Keats's true poet is, in effect, "feminine," so, too, is poetic creation. Keats's letters identify poetic process with pregnancy or, in another metaphor of female production, with spinning and weaving.[5] First, a humorous example, his report of his friend Charles Brown in the throes of poetic composition: "Brown has been walking up and down the room a breeding – now at this moment he is being delivered of a couplet – and I dare say will be as well as can be expected – Gracious – he has twins!" (KL 2.66). Keats's identification of poetic creation with pregnancy and birth is most fully articulated in his conception of "Soul-making," or becoming a self (KL 2.102–3). He defines soul as "Intelligence destined to possess the sense of Identity" through the agency of the heart, the human capacity for empathy and relationship. This heart-knowledge is "the teat from which the Mind or intelligence sucks its identity." It is thus female, a nursing mother. Keats's entire "system of Spirit-creation," of personal and poetic self-development, grows out of this primal mother-infant bond. For Keats, the mother is the source of life itself, and poetry can at best only replicate the primary dependence of both infant and adult upon this female origin.

Keats underscores this identification of both poetic creation and the acquisition of knowledge with feminine work in a letter to fellow poet Reynolds, in which he compares the gaining of wisdom to the spinning of a spider's web (19 February 1818; *KL* 1.231–32). As he is praising "delicious diligent Indolence" (the very realm of "ease and indolence" Hazlitt would condemn as effeminate), he suggests "that almost any Man may like the Spider spin from his own inwards his own airy Citadel – the points of leaves and twigs on which the Spider begins her work are few and she fills the Air with a beautiful circuiting." Gendering this spider female, Keats aligns himself not with the busy bee of the masculine or Protestant work ethic or with the neoclassical aesthetic theory put forth in Swift's *Battle of the Books* but also with the traditionally feminine occupations of spinning, weaving, and tale-telling. Keats's spiderweb of spiritual and practical knowledge is created by empathically reaching out to and connecting widely disparate points: "Minds would leave each other in contrary directions, traverse each other in Numberless points, and [at] last greet each other at the Journey's end." The insights and information gathered in such wanderings – an "old Man and a child would talk together and the old Man be led on his Path, and the child left thinking" – would not be proclaimed, analyzed, or disputed but "whisper[ed] [. . .] to his neighbor." Keats invokes the village gossip, whispering stories to her friends and neighbors, as his image of shared wisdom. He then moves from epistemology (how we come to know what we know) to politics: such empathically gained and shared experience would create a community based on equality and mutual respect. "Humanity instead of being a wide heath of Furse and Briars with here and there a remote Oak or Pine, would become a grand democracy of Forest Trees" (1.232).

This alignment of the gaining of wisdom and the creation of genuine human community with the work of women is underlined by the reversed mating ritual that immediately follows in this letter. Keats first places himself in the position of a courted female:

> It has been an old comparison for our urging on – the Bee hive – however it seems to me that we should rather be the flower than the Bee – for it is a false notion that more is gained by receiving than giving – no the receiver and the giver are equal in their benefits – The f[l]ower I doubt not receives a fair guerdon from the Bee – its leaves blush deeper in the next spring – and who shall say between Man and Woman which is the most delighted? Now it is more noble to sit like Jove [than] to fly like Mercury – let us not therefore go hurrying about and collecting honey-bee like, buzzing here and there impatiently from a knowledge of what is to be arrived at: but let us open our leaves

like a flower and be passive and receptive – budding patiently under the eye of
Apollo and taking hints from every noble insect that favours us with a visit –
sap will be given us for Meat and dew for drink.   (1.232)

In this remarkable speculation, Keats spells out a theory of knowing that
anticipates the major tenets of what we now call stand-point theory. Keats's
"hints" and "whispers" and "passive and receptive" patience all suggest
ways of knowing distinct from those produced by the scientific or analytical
method that presupposes both a detached, neutral observer and an objective
body of facts that can be known.

Drawing on this Romantic critique of scientific observation and rational
analysis, recent feminist philosophers have re-emphasized the questionable
methodological assumptions: most notably, how the faith in genuinely
impartial observation involves the inability to conceive of "a fact" as "a con-
testable component of a theoretically constituted order of things." Feminist
philosophers suggest that because every act of knowing requires an emotional engagement of the knower with the known, "objectivity" is a psychological and perceptual impossibility. As Mary E. Hawkesworth summarizes,
every act of cognition is "a human practice" that includes the full "complexity of the interaction between traditional assumptions, social norms, theoretical conceptions, disciplinary strictures, linguistic possibilities, emotional
dispositions, and creative impositions."[6] One cannot perceive without experiencing some sort of connection, without bringing to that act of perception
the full range of one's personal, ideologically biased experiences, without
locating the perceived object within a pre-existing framework of coherent
meaning.

Anticipating these epistemologists, Keats implies that knowledge is gained
not from "objective observation" but from many different kinds of activities:
intuiting, imagining, giving, suggesting, receiving. This is the theme of his
remarks on the nature of reality to his divinity-student friend, Benjamin
Bailey, 13 March 1818:

> As Tradesman say every thing is worth what it will fetch, so probably every
> mental pursuit takes its reality and worth from the ardour of the pursuer –
> being in itself a nothing Etherial thing[s] may at least be thus real, divided
> under three heads – Things real – things semireal – and no things – Things real
> – such as existences of Sun Moon & Stars and passages of Shakspeare – Things
> semireal such as Love, the Clouds &c which require a greeting of the Spirit to
> make them wholly exist – and Nothings which are made Great and dignified
> by an ardent pursuit.   (KL 1.242–43)

For Keats, truth or reality cannot exist apart from the perceiving and con-
structing mind: if "passages of Shakspeare" are among those things which

are undeniably "real," then reality is a human production. Although Keats acknowledges the capacity of desire and fantasy to produce "Nothings," he insists that the only knowledge to which the human mind can lay claim is that produced by a "greeting of the Spirit," a reaching out of imagination toward a perceived other. Keats's realm of the "semireal," the realm of value and wisdom, is a connected knowledge, of what we know as a result of a relationship with someone or something else.

Identifying the creative process, the character of the poet, and the acquisition of knowledge with women's work and women's ways of knowing was, however, a source of anxiety as well as of affirmation for Keats.[7] By the early nineteenth century, women poets were strongly associated with certain forms of poetry: the sonnet, the ode, the romance. Ambitious male poets tended to regard these forms as less important, less prestigious, than the more "elevated" genres of epic, heroic tragedy, even satire.[8] Remember that Wordsworth called the sonnet, in his own feminine-figured sonnet ("Nuns fret not . . ."), a "scanty plot of ground" that provides but "brief solace." Keats, like many male poets before him (Virgil, Spenser, Milton, etc.), began his career with these less prestigious forms, aligning himself with a feminine literary culture marked by such sonneteers and lyricists as Charlotte Smith, Anna Seward, Mary Robinson, Anna Matilda (Hannah Cowley), and Mary Tighe. But unlike his male predecessors, Keats found these "lesser" forms exceptionally attractive, a little too hard to bid farewell to, so much so that he felt unable – or lacking in the desire – to stay with his sporadic attempts at epic.

That Keats was not entirely comfortable in this association with "female" poetry can be seen in the letter to Reynolds (above) in which he exhorts, "let us open our leaves like a flower" (1.232). As Margaret Homans acutely notes, he ultimately forces both flower and "Woman" into a surprising identification with a supremely self-possessed Jove, the most powerful of the male Olympian gods – and so reclaims a masculine identity that can prevail over the feminine.[9] This defense against feminine identifications erupts in an earlier letter to Reynolds (21 September 1817), in which Keats bitterly attacks the leading women poets of his day:

> The world, and especially our England, has within the last thirty year's been vexed and teased by a set of Devils, whom I detest so much that I almost [Keats first wrote "always"] hunger after an acherontic promotion to a Torturer, purposely for their accomodation; These Devils are a set of Women, who having taken a snack or Luncheon of Literary scraps, set themselves up for towers of Babel in Languages Sapphos in Poetry – Euclids in Geometry – and everything in nothing. Among such the Name of Montague has been preeminent. The thing has made a very uncomfortable impression on me. – I had longed for

some real feminine Modesty in these things, and was therefore gladdened in the extreme on opening the other day [. . .] a Book of Poetry written by one beautiful Mrs. Philips, a friend of Jeremy Taylor's, and called "the matchless Orinda."   (*KL* 1.163)

He then writes out the entire text of Katherine Philips's *Ode to Mrs. M. A. at Parting* (*Poems*, 1710), a celebration of the delights and glory of an immortal female (even lesbian) friendship. Here are some excerpts from Keats's transcription, lines that show a female instance of self-dissolving empathy: "To part with thee I needs must die / Could parting sep'rate thee and I"; "We have each other so engrost / That each is in the union lost"; "Thus our twin souls in one shall grow, / And teach the world new Love" (*KL* 1.163–65). Perhaps Keats applauded this passionate female friendship because it was a world from which he was necessarily excluded, a world that could not seduce or unman him. The "matchless Orinda" was widely revered, moreover, for idealizing woman as spiritual, emotional, self-sacrificing, hence nonrational. In contrast, Elizabeth Montagu, "the Queen of the Blues" (bluestockings, or female intellectuals), advocated a more assertive, intellectual, and political role for women: she wrote a widely praised *Essay on the Writings and Genius of Shakespeare* (1769) and hosted a famous literary salon where the young novelist Frances Burney described her as reigning forth, "brilliant in diamonds, solid in judgment, and critical in talk."[10]

Keats's hostility to Bluestockings did not grow less as he grew older. In 1818 he confessed to his brother and sister-in-law that his early admiration for the poetry of Mary Tighe and James Beattie had waned as his desire to write an epic increased, a development that he genders as a rejection of "feminine" taste:

> Mrs. Tighe and Beattie once delighted me – now I see through them and can find nothing in them – or weakness – and yet how many they still delight! [. . .] This same inadequacy is discovered (forgive me little George [Georgiana] you know I don't mean to put you in the mess) in Women with few exceptions – the Dress Maker, the blue Stocking and the most charming sentimentalist differ but in a Slight degree, and are equally smokeable.   (*KL* 2.18–9)

Keats later announced that one of his literary goals was to conquer the women writers in their chosen poetic forms: "One of my Ambitions is to make as great a revolution in modern dramatic writing as Kean has done in acting – another to upset the drawling of the blue stocking literary world" (14 August 1819; *KL* 2.139).

Keats's ambivalence about gender infiltrates his poetry as well. He repeatedly assigns the possession of beauty, power and knowledge – everything the male poet desires – to the feminine gender. At the same time, he labors to establish a distance between the male poet and the female object of desire, a space where the poet can preserve a recognizable masculinity.

In *Ode to Psyche*, Keats explicitly engenders his own imagination, his soul or psyche, as feminine, following the classical convention that personifies both the soul and the muse as female. At the same time, he portrays his claim to such imagination or soul as a kind of rape: his "tuneless numbers" are "wrung / By sweet enforcement" (1–2), and his inspired chorus-song will "make a moan / Upon the midnight hours" (44–45). The poems Keats will write as a result of this ravishment of, or by, his own imagination (*Ode to Psyche* calculatedly obscures who is ravishing whom) are figured as "the wreath'd trellis of a working brain" (60). This spatially radiating, interwoven trellis resembles a spiderweb, Keats's image of feminine production. Yet even as Keats figures himself as both a male and a female creator, he hints at his dependence on a primarily female reading audience. The "rosy sanctuary" (temple or "fane") Keats hopes to build for and out of his own imagination (50, 59) evokes the numerous "temples" being built in Keats's day, such as Lackington and Allen's "Temple of the Muses" or Fuller's "Temple of Fancy," to cater to the desires of women shoppers.[11] The ode ends with a final affirmation of female sexuality, of a vaginal "casement ope at night / To let the warm Love in!" (66–67). Keats triumphantly and climactically occupies the positions of *both* the female and the male lover: he has made love to, penetrated, received, and possessed his own Fancy, his own "shadowy thought" (65).

Such cross-gendering is represented in a more troubled way in *Ode on Indolence*, as Grant Scott has compellingly argued (*Sculpted Word*, chapter 4). Keats's very title invokes Hazlitt's contemptuous dismissal of "ease and indolence" as the chief desire of those "who cannot lift up a little finger to save themselves from ruin, nor give up the smallest indulgence for the sake of any other person" ("Effeminacy," 248). Keats first places the (male) poet in the traditionally feminine pose of passivity, indolence, waiting, while three white-robed figures actively move past him, two of which, Love and Poesy, are female, and perhaps the third, too, a pale-cheeked weary-eyed Ambition. Uncomfortable in the sway of this female realm, this poet tries to distance himself from the sentimental odes of such women writers as Tighe and Robinson – "Upon your skirts had fallen no tears of mine" (50) – and to insist on his more virile version of indolence: "I would not be dieted with praise, / A pet-lamb in a sentimental farce!" (54–55). But his emphatic summary adieus to his three ghosts seem less a confident turn to the alternative kind of poetry that he proclaims ("I yet have visions for the night, / And for the day faint visions there is store" [57–58]) than a confession of remarkable anxiety about the strong hold of feminine poetic subjects and practices upon his imagination. If Keats derisively dismisses both heroic masculine Ambition, whose pale cheek and "fatigued eye" here "springs / From a man's little heart's short fever-fit" (33–34), and also his favorite poetic subjects of love and poetic creativity, here identified with a bluestocking "maiden most unmeek" (30), where can he turn? *Ode on Indolence* ends in an aporia, a void: "Vanish, ye phantoms, from my idle spright, / Into the clouds, and never more return!" (59–60). Having separated himself both from virile masculine action and from feminine production, Keats's poet is left without a gender identity and without a poetic subject. Unlike the lilies of the field, which in the ode's epigraph from Matthew, "toil not, neither do they spin," Keats cannot do the work of poetic creation organically, unselfconsciously.

Nor could he turn confidently to those forms of poetic production that his culture defined as masculine: Miltonic epic, classical tragedy, Shakespearean comedy.[12] Keats continued to be attracted to poetic forms and subjects primarily associated with women poets: sonnet, ode, and romance; the emotions, the beauty of nature and of art, the creative process.[13] His Great Odes focus again and again on female power. The Grecian Urn is female, a "still unravish'd bride of quietness" (1) who temptingly, if perhaps delusively, holds out the promise that "Beauty is truth, truth beauty" (49). The Nightingale whose song lifts the poet into a moment of perfect happiness is female, a "light-winged Dryad of the trees" (7), a "deceiving" elf-like fancy (73–74). Both "Veil'd Melancholy," who teaches us to appreciate more intensely the joys and beauties of life by remembering how transient they are, and "Autumn," whom Keats in the letter about the inspiration for this ode described as "chaste weather – Dian skies" (*KL* 2.167), are female. In each of these odes, a male poet seeks to penetrate and possess the power and wisdom of the female object – whether the imaginative creativity of Psyche, the beauty and truth of the Grecian Urn, the appreciation of mutability or melancholy, or the acceptance of death, with the understanding that ripeness is all, which Keats personifies as Autumn. In each, a male poet attempts to establish a perfect fusion with a female symbol, only to acknowledge the impossibility. Having defined his object of desire as female, he is forced to recognize a distance. The nightingale has fled; the Urn's message applies only to those who have escaped history and become works of art; Melancholy can be seen only by the man who "can burst Joy's grape against his palate fine" (28); while Autumn finally sinks as "gathering swallows twitter in the skies." In these poems Keats momentarily succeeds in cross-dressing, in occupying the position of a female, but he is not a transsexual: he cannot become female.

And yet Keats returned obsessively to feminine forms of poetic production. The title poems of the 1820 volume – *Lamia*, *Isabella*, *The Eve of St.*

Agnes – are written in that form Keats identified with female authorship, the romance. "I shall send you the Pot of Basil, Sʳ Agnes eve, and [. . .] a little thing call'd the 'eve of St. Mark,'" he tells George and Georgiana in February 1819, adding, "you see what fine mother Radcliff names I have – it is not my fault – I did not search for them – I have not gone on with Hyperion" (*KL* 2.62). Keats's anxiety concerning his predilection for romance is clear in his defensive "it is not my fault," as well as in the self-demeaning reference to Ann Radcliffe's Gothic romances, whose style he had parodied a year before to Reynolds: "I am going among Scenery whence I intend to tip you the Damosel Radcliffe – I'll cavern you, and grotto you, and waterfall you, and wood you, and water you, and immense-rock you, and tremendous sound you, and solitude you" (14 March 1818; 1.245).

In these romances, Keats tries to develop a more virile version of this feminine form, one less mockable or "smokeable," avoiding the "inexperience of li[f]e" and "simplicity of knowledge" (*KL* 2.174) that he associated with Radcliffe and her female imitators. In *La belle dame sans Merci*, as Karen Swann has shown, he achieved this aim by allying himself with the male knight against the female belle dame.[14] The knight has loved her, then lost her; but why? The explanation offered by the poem is his dream, in which he hears the voices of other men:

> I saw pale kings and Princes too
>   Pale warriors death pale were they all
> They cried La belle dame sans merci
>   Thee hath in thrall.   (*KL* 2.295–96)

This dream implies that it is the woman's fault, that La belle dame has seduced and then abandoned the innocent knight. But why should the knight believe this dream? What does he (and the kings, princes, and warriors of his dream) gain by defining the belle dame as "sans merci," cold, cruel, lacking in compassion? The gain is clear: even though the knight is left "Alone and palely loitering" in a wasteland where the "sedge has withered" and "no birds sing," even though his harsh dream has become his reality and he remains unloved, unloving, even dying, he gets to tell the story. Male voices and this male's story appropriate and silence the female. We never hear la belle dame's side of the story, what she thought or felt. This poem thus becomes, in Swann's memorable phrase, a case of "harassing the muse," a sexual and verbal assault upon a female whose response is neither listened to nor recorded. This short romance underlines the angst Keats felt toward his favorite feminine subject-matter, his psychological need to ally himself with his male peers.

Keats's growing anxiety, even hostility, to the feminine subject of romance is most clearly articulated in *Lamia*, the one romance to which, he was sure, there could be "no objection" about its being "smokeable" (*KL* 2.174). Keats insistently, if reluctantly, turns his readers' sympathies away from the female lover. As Debbie Lee has observed, Lamia is presented from the start as both a nonhuman figure and a racial other. Her name immediately identifies her with lamiae or afrits, mythological creatures described in Lemprière's *Dictionary of Mythology* (a source Keats frequently consulted) as "certain monsters of Africa, who had the face and breast of a woman, and the rest of their body like that of a serpent." Keats might also have encountered lamiae in William Beckford's phantasmal Gothic tale, *Vathek* (1786), where afrits or lamiae serve the diabolical desires of Carathis, Vathek's mother, desires sexually consummated in her union with the Devil.[15]

For Lycius to fall in love with Lamia, a serpent-woman, is to commit himself to a demonic, Circean power. Possessing supernatural knowledge, Lamia can see the comings and goings of the gods, she can make a nymph visible or invisible, she can "unperplex bliss from its neighbour pain" (1.192), a capacity that Keats had earlier identified in his poem "There is a joy in footing slow across a silent plain" with madness, half-idiocy, and mortal incapability (*KL* 1.344–45). In all this and more, Lamia is associated with creative imagination: she has the power to transform the invisible into the visible, to satisfy the desires of the gods, to create the conventions of romance (passionate love, lulling music, a fairy-palace). As such, many readers have found her sympathetic.[16] But by identifying love, the imagination, and the poetic form of romance with an African serpent/woman, Keats calls into question both the truth and the value of female creative power and of romance.

Unlike the passionate, even transcendent love of Madeline and Porphyro in *The Eve of St. Agnes*, Lycius's love for Lamia is doomed from the start. A serpent-woman cannot sustain the delusions of love in the face of cold reason and everyday reality: Apollonius has only to see Lamia once to unmask the serpent. If romance cannot survive the piercing gaze of reason, neither can Lycius live without its comforting illusions. Keats makes this point with the grimly jaunty couplets that open Part II:

> Love in a hut, with water and a crust,
> Is – Love, forgive us! – cinders, ashes, dust;
> Love in a palace is perhaps at last
> More grievous torment than a hermit's fast: –
> That is a doubtful tale from faery land,
> Hard for the non-elect to understand.
> Had Lycius liv'd to hand this story down,
> He might have given the moral a fresh frown.   (2.1–8)

Romance – and with it, the creative power of the feminine imagination – does not, cannot last; and the price exacted for a willing suspension of disbelief on this score is death, the death of Lycius and the disappearance of Lamia. Keats annihilates everything he had earlier associated with the female: the powers of creation, transformation, communion, sympathy, love. All that survives is the rigor of masculine logic and objective truth, embodied in thistle-crowned Apollonius.

But Keats could not rest comfortably within the masculinist constructions of Apollonius or of Hazlitt. For him, the process of poetic creation was inextricably associated with female biology and feminine production: if Apollonius unweaves the rainbow, Lamia continues to weave it. Even when he turned to poetic epic, in *Hyperion: A Fragment* and *The Fall of Hyperion: A Dream*, he continued to assign to the female the possession both of tragic beauty and of sublime wisdom. It is in these incomplete, forever fragmentary swerves from romance that Keats finally succeeded in carving out a space for the male poet, one in which he preserves his sexual independence as the translator of feminine consciousness into an adequate poetic language.

In *Hyperion* Keats tried to assume the mantle of the virile epic poet, adopting Milton's blank verse, verbal intonations, and syntactic inversions in his effort to create an alternative justification of the ways of god to man: a "system of Salvation which does not affront our reason and humanity" but which is founded on the knowledge of suffering (*KL* 2.103). The (problematic) voice of Oceanus asserts, with Miltonic confidence, the existence of a teleological universe founded on progress, a belief that the beauty and greater wisdom to come justify the downfall and sufferings of the old order of gods, the Titans: "for 'tis the eternal law / That first in beauty should be first in might" (2.228–9). But the fragment breaks off abruptly at just the moment when the first in beauty (and Hyperion's successor), Apollo, who has died into life and thus transmuted suffering into a redemptive beauty, must appear. Marlon Ross has suggested that the poem remains a fragment because Keats has knowingly exhausted the limits of patrilineal discourse.[17] I would put the issue differently. Keats has told us that Apollo is a greater god than Hyperion, because his agonies of knowledge have made him more beautiful. But Keats stops writing before he has shown what this new kind of beauty looks like. Why? First, Keats himself had not yet been able to see fully into the "mystery," to comprehend how one could fuse the antithetical realms of life and death, pain and beauty. Second, Keats was increasingly uncomfortable with the Miltonic style he had adopted: it was too assertive and too distanced to enable Keats's more self-conscious questionings and open-ended debates.[18]

When Keats returned to this project in August 1819, eager to complete a mature epic statement of his beliefs, he transformed it into a first-person "dream"-vision, a mode situated, once again, in the realm of feminized fantasy and poetic imagination, here explicitly identified with a "mother tongue." The dreamer-poet is now a direct participant in the poem, acutely aware of his own body, his own anxieties, as he writes:

> Since every man whose soul is not a clod
> Hath visions, and would speak, if he had lov'd
> And been well nurtured in his mother tongue,
> Whether the dream now purposed to rehearse
> Be poet's or fanatic's will be known
> When this warm scribe my hand is in the grave.   (1.13–18)

The answer to the poet's questions – can suffering lead to wisdom and beauty? – now comes in the form of a realized visual image, the female face of Moneta/Athena, the icon of wisdom itself.[19] But this face is also a terrifying image of endless suffering:

> Then saw I a wan face,
> Not pin'd by human sorrows, but bright-blanch'd
> By an immortal sickness which kills not;
> It works a constant change, which happy death
> Can put no end to; deathwards progressing
> To no death was that visage.   (1.256–60)

Gazing on this face and finding beauty in its sublime horror, the male poet finally achieves a stable and culturally productive relationship to female power. He gradually learns to read his mother's tongue, to interpret and understand the source of human life and death, thereby achieving an enduring relationship of equality *and* difference with the female origin of life and wisdom.

Recall that in *The Fall of Hyperion*, the poet-dreamer approaches the goddess as a child does its mother, reaching only up to her "broad marble knees" (1.214) and hearing her "immortal's sphered words" softened "to a mother's" (249–50). He then gazes upon her terrifying face and beautiful eyes, aching "to see what things the hollow brain / Behind enwombed" (276–77). Gradually absorbing Moneta's pregnant tragic consciousness, he acquires "power . . . of enormous ken, / To see as a God sees, and take the depth / Of things" (303–5), a vision he is able to "humanize" (as she has) for mortal comprehension (2.2). The consciousness of the goddess, of sublime wisdom, and the discourse of the poet finally fuse, as Keats modestly implies at the end of Canto I:

– And she spake on,
As ye may read who can unwearied pass
Onward from the antichamber of this dream,
Where even at the open doors awhile
I must delay, and glean my memory
Of her high phrase: perhaps no further dare.   (1.463–68)

Through masculine daring and the feminine courage to suffer "Without stay or prop . . . / The load of this eternal quietude" (1.388–90), the poet discovers what is ultimately for Keats the appropriate relationship between female and male in poetic discourse: that of goddess-mother-muse to human-son-poet. Even as it sustains the role of humble submission and dependency that Keats had earlier adopted in relation to feminine creative power, such reverence no longer engenders the anxiety that some have read in his earlier representations of women: those symbolizings of the imagination that, in Karla Alwes's formulation, "represent both the joy of creativity and the fear that Keats felt over its possible loss."[20] The poet is now able to speak for the next generation, for posterity. For Keats, female reproductive biology continues to take precedence over male poetic creation. Yet poetic language sustains this reproductive process both by acknowledging the sacred priority of the female and by articulating its cultural meaning, the meaning of life itself. Far from the woman-excluding "male preserve" that Homans condemned (368), Keats's poetics rest on a reverent engagement with a sublime power that Keats located first and foremost in the mother.

NOTES

1 William Hazlitt, "On Effeminacy of Character," *Table Talk* (1822); ed. Catherine Macdonald Maclean (London: J. M. Dent / New York: E. P. Dutton, 1959), 248, 249, 255.

2 On the nineteenth-century construction of Keats as effeminate, see Susan J. Wolfson's thoroughly documented essay, "Feminizing Keats."

3 On Romantic-era constructions of gender, see Alan Richardson, "Romanticism and the Colonization of the Feminine," in *Romanticism and Feminism*, ed. Anne K. Mellor (Bloomington, Indiana: Indiana University Press, 1988), 13–25; and my *Romanticism & Gender*.

4 On the new "Man of Feeling," see Janet Todd, *Sensibility, An Introduction* (London: Methuen, 1986) and G. J. Barker-Benfield, *The Culture of Sensibility: Sex and Society in Eighteenth-Century Britain* (Chicago and London: University of Chicago Press, 1992).

5 For a fuller discussion of these images, see Grant F. Scott, *The Sculpted Word: Keats, Ekphrasis, and the Visual Arts*, 105–11.

6 Mary E. Hawkesworth, "Knowers, Knowing, Known: Feminist Theory and Claims of Truth," *Signs* 14 (Spring, 1989), 550, 551. Major contributions to the

field of feminist epistemology include Genevieve Lloyd, *The Man of Reason* (Minneapolis: University of Minnesota Press, 1984), Nancy C. M. Hartsock, *Money, Sex and Power* (Boston: Northeastern University Press, 1985) and *Feminist Epistemologies*, ed. Linda Alcott and Elizabeth Potter (New York: Routledge, 1992).

7 For Keats's anxiety, "angst" and even hostility toward his poetic femininity, toward his alliance with women poets and with a feminized literary culture, see Sonia Hofkosh, "The Writer's Ravishment – Women and the Romantic Author: The Example of Byron," in *Romanticism and Feminism*, 106–9; Margaret Homans, "Keats Reading Women, Women Reading Keats"; Scott, *Sculpted Word*, 104–11; and Susan J. Wolfson, "Keats and the Manhood of the Poet," *European Romantic Review* 6/1 (1995), 1–37. In contrast, I suggested in *Romanticism & Gender* (171–86) that Keats finally overcame this anxiety, to adopt instead a position of reverence toward female creative power.

8 On the poetic and prose romance as a feminine genre in the nineteenth century, see Irene Tayler and Gina Luria, "Gender and Genre: Women in British Romantic Literature," *What Manner of Woman: Essays in English and American Life and Literature*, ed. Marlene Springer (New York: New York University Press, 1977), 98–123; and Laurie Langbauer, *Women and Romance: The Consolations of Genre in the English Novel* (Ithaca: Cornell University Press, 1990).

9 Homans, "Keats Reading," 345.

10 Quoted in *The Oxford Companion to English Literature*, ed. Margaret Drabble (Oxford: Oxford University Press, 1985), 662.

11 Both shops were on the Strand, selling art supplies, water-color paintings, china, books, etc. The word "temple" was used so often by London tradesmen that by 1815 it had become almost a synonym for a shop that sold luxury goods to discriminating, usually female, consumers. Simon During and Ann Bermingham independently pointed out the prevalence of "Temples" in early nineteenth-century London (During noted the relevance to Keats's poetry) in papers delivered at the Huntington Library, January 29–30, 1999, forthcoming in *The Romantic Metropolis*, ed. James Chandler and Kevin Gilmartin (Cambridge: Cambridge University Press).

12 Keats's one, co-authored attempt at a dramatic tragedy, *Otho the Great*, was never staged. On Keats's wrestling with issues of gender in *Otho*, see Philip Cox, "Keats and the Performance of Gender," *KSJ* 44 (1995), 40–65.

13 While male poets could be famed for romances (Scott), sonnets and odes (Wordsworth), in the culturally prevailing Neoclassical hierarchy of the arts, these forms continued to be placed below the "highest" (hence most "masculine") forms, epic and classical tragedy.

14 Karen Swann, "Harassing the Muse," 81–92. I use the letter-text, from the same journal-letter in which Keats mocks his "fine mother Radcliff names."

15 Debbie Lee, "Certain Monsters of Africa: Poetic Voodoo in Keats's *Lamia*," *Times Literary Supplement* 27 October 1995, 13–14; William Beckford, *Vathek, An Arabian Tale* (1786), ed. Malcolm Jack (London: Penguin, 1995), 58. Beckford cites Baron d'Herbelot de Molainville's *Bibliotheque Orientale* (1697), which defines afrits as "a kind of Medusae, or Lamiae, supposed to be the most terrible and cruel of all the orders of the dives."

16 For more positive readings of Lamia, which attribute the ending of their romance

to Lycius's love of dominance or to Apollonius's devouring skepticism, see Susan J. Wolfson, "Keats's 'Gordian Complication' of Women," *Approaches to Teaching Keats's Poetry*, ed. Walter H. Evert and Jack W. Rhodes (New York: Modern Language Association, 1991), 77–85; Greg Kucich, "Gender Crossings: Keats and Tighe," *KSJ* 44 (1995): 29–39; and Maneck H. Daruwala, "Strange Bedfellows: Keats and Wollstonecraft, Lamia and Berwick," *Keats–Shelley Review* 11 (1997), 83–132.

17 Marlon Ross, "Beyond the Fragmented Word: Keats at the Limit of Patrilineal Language," *Out of Bounds: Male Writers and Gender(ed) Criticism*, ed. Laura Claridge and Elizabeth Langland (Amherst: University of Massachusetts Press, 1990), 110–31.

18 The passage in the letter of 3 May 1818, in which Keats praises Wordsworth's power to "feel the 'burden of the Mystery'" (quoting *Tintern Abbey*), is also the site of his most sustained critique of this masculine Miltonic mode (*KL* 1.281–82).

19 On the face of Moneta as the icon of wisdom, see my "Keats's Face of Moneta: Source and Meaning," *KSJ* 25 (1976), 65–80, and my *English Romantic Irony* (Cambridge: Harvard University Press, 1980), 75–108.

20 Karla Alwes, *Imagination Transformed: The Evolution of the Female Character in Keats's Poetry* (Carbondale: Southern Illinois University Press, 1993), 2.

15

ALAN RICHARDSON

Keats and Romantic science

Writing the body

It is richly ironic that Keats's medical training, once cited as a sign of his low cultural standing, has been credited in recent scholarship for the precision and intellectual sophistication of Keats's response to the momentous scientific and medical developments of his era. "So back to the shop Mr John," *Blackwood's* "Z." sarcastically concluded a notorious attack on Keats as a "Cockney" poet, mocking him as an "uneducated and flimsy stripling" in the grip of "mania" and "malady," who would do better as a "starving apothecary than a starved poet."[1] "Z." knew that Keats had been an apprentice to an apothecary-surgeon – the standard way for those without university educations to enter medical practice – and his review evoked the dated stereotype of the quackish, low-status apothecary, dispensing "plasters, pills, and ointment boxes" (524) with knowledge gained mainly from haphazard, hands-on experience. What "Z." ignored (and recent scholarship has painstakingly established) is that Keats became a licensed apothecary at a time when medical education was undergoing significant reform, completing his training at Guy's, one of the most advanced teaching hospitals. Having earned a reputation at Enfield Academy for a brilliant, probing, and retentive mind, Keats found himself at Guy's, an institution that was helping to reshape the profession of medicine with the latest currents in scientific thought. How did this experience mark Keats's thinking and writing?

The misguided (and implicitly condescending) tradition of minimizing Keats's education and intellectual breadth is not the only obstacle to understanding the links between his poetics and his knowledge of contemporary science. There is an equally misleading tradition of casting the relation between science and Romanticism as hostile, a view for which, ironically, Keats is partly responsible. "Philosophy will clip an Angel's wings," worries the narrator of *Lamia*:

> There was an awful rainbow once in heaven:
> We know her woof, her texture; she is given
> In the dull catalogue of common things.   (2.231–33)

Editions of Keats often footnote the "immortal dinner" that Haydon hosted in late 1817 when, in a company that included Wordsworth, Keats is said to have joined Charles Lamb in drinking "Newton's health, and confusion to Mathematics," agreeing that Newton had "destroyed all the poetry of the rainbow by reducing it to the prismatic colours."[2] These sentiments are common in Romantic writing, reflecting the changing status – not least, the professionalization – of both poetry and science during the period. But there was a good deal more commerce between Romantic literature and scientific inquiry than passages such as these, taken out of context, might suggest – especially at a time when the arts and the sciences had yet to harden into two distinct cultures. The career of Erasmus Darwin (during the 1790s one of Britain's most celebrated British poets and most notable scientists) indicates how extensive and productive such commerce might become.[3] With the mechanistic scientific paradigm associated with Newton giving way to a biological emphasis typified by Darwin, science and medicine took on a "Romantic" character, featuring a naturalistic ethos, an attention to "organic form," and developmental and ecological models that show more than superficial resemblance to analogous impulses in the arts.[4]

Keats's scientific education and medical training also bear significantly on the question of his political sympathies and his relation to contemporary radical thought. During the period, medical science, materialistic doctrine, and radical politics were all seen as closely intertwined, and in the reactionary climate of the early nineteenth century, reputations such as Darwin's suffered. Nicholas Roe has established a number of significant connections between Keats and the radical scientific circles of the era – professional, social, and political alliances that brought his medical instructors at Guy's into association with Darwin, Joseph Priestley, and other progressive and iconoclastic scientists and doctors.[5] From an Establishment perspective, speculation on the material basis of thought, on the unity of mind and body, and on the continuities between humans and other animals was especially dangerous, threatening to undermine orthodox notions of immortality and the soul and casting doubt on the special creation of humanity. Although it would be misleading to think of Keats as a simple materialist, the antidualistic accounts of mind associated with Priestley and Darwin have important repercussions, from his chemical metaphors for the poetic imagination to his pervasive description of glowing skin and other manifestations of embodied, impassioned thought. Many incidental features of his poetry, such as his use of particular flowers and herbs with pharmacological associations, take on new meaning in relation to his medical education, as well as aspects that have been regarded as "Keatsian" poetic hallmarks, such as his description of a "material sublime" or the flush of embarrassment.

Keats's scientific education began at Enfield, one of the progressive private academies that profited from the intellectual dynamism of the period's Dissenting culture. The great Dissenting Academies – schools such as Warrington (where Priestley had taught), founded for dissenting Protestants effectively shut out of the "public" schools and the two universities (Oxford and Cambridge) – were at the leading edge of scientific knowledge and were uniquely hospitable to theories with materialistic or otherwise radical implications. Although designed for a less ambitious clientele, Enfield was in touch with the main currents of Dissenting culture; Keats's schoolmaster, John Clarke, was personally connected with Priestley and other leading radical Dissenters (Roe, 27–50). Keats, as "Z." delighted to point out, lacked the elaborate grounding in the Classics offered by the elitist public schools; even so, Keats was an adept Latinist (winning a prize for his translation of the whole of *The Aeneid*) and overall received a remarkably solid education, with a much better introduction to the sciences than he would likely have gained at Shelley's Eton or Byron's Harrow.

Keats left Enfield the summer of 1810, nearing his fifteenth year, to begin a five-year apprenticeship with Thomas Hammond, a successful apothecary-surgeon (analogous to a general practitioner today) who had trained at Guy's Hospital and, as a member of the Corporation of Surgeons, kept up with medical advances. While little is directly known about this period of his life, he would have accompanied Hammond on visits to patients, learned basic medical procedures such as bleeding, plastering, and dressing wounds, helped compound drugs and interpret symptoms, performed post-mortems and assisted in childbirths. The apprenticeship was not without tensions – Keats once "clench'd [his hand] against Hammond" (*KL* 2.208) – but it must have been successful: Keats went on to Hammond's former medical school, undoubtedly with his support, and advanced rapidly. The medical reform act of 1815 required study and practice at a teaching hospital for aspiring apothecaries; following Hammond's lead, Keats seems initially to have begun the more ambitious path of training for the Royal College of Surgeons. Guy's, then joined with its neighbor St. Thomas in the "United Hospitals," has been described as the "most well-rounded medical school in London," with a faculty abreast of the "most advanced scientific and philosophical lines of inquiry."[6] Keats's teachers included celebrities such as Astley Cooper, a leading surgeon and anatomist, and Joseph Henry Green, later to become a close friend and intellectual collaborator of Coleridge. Cooper was only one among a number of Guy's lecturers with close ties to the radical scientific circles of the time (though he had learned like many of his generation to keep his politics under wraps).

In October 1815 Keats registered for a program of medical studies at

Guy's that included courses in anatomy and physiology, chemistry, theory and practice of medicine, "materia medica" (forerunner of pharmacology), medical botany, and surgery and dissection. He began his studies auspiciously, finding rooms with two senior students under Cooper's protection, and was tapped after only four months for the coveted position of surgeon's dresser. This year-long post, which took effect in March 1816, placed him in the top group of medical students, but it also entailed a good deal of demanding and sometimes dispiriting work. Keats attended the surgeon on his rounds, made notes on cases, assisted in operations, bandaged and changed surgical wounds, and took his turn as House Surgeon on call to deal with hemorrhages and other emergencies. In the badly overcrowded surgical theater of the time, with scores of students jostling for a view of the operation, Keats took his place at the front, ready to perform minor surgery, to clamp arteries, or to open veins. Unfortunately, he was appointed dresser not to the deft and masterful Cooper, but to a well-connected bungler known as Billy Lucas (son of Hammond's old master). At a time before anaeseptic procedures and modern anesthesia (rum was it), even skillful surgery was a dangerous and exquisitely painful affair. Attending Lucas (and cleaning up after him) involved intimate exposure to a surgeon that a horrified Cooper himself labeled "rash in the extreme, cutting amongst most important parts as though they were only skin," and causing all within view to "shudder from the apprehension" of some cruel and needless error.[7]

Perhaps it was the dismal example of "Billy" Lucas, along with his growing conviction that he could succeed as a poet, that led Keats to give up on a medical career by the time his dressership ended in March 1817. He had come to feel temperamentally "unfit" to perform surgery, according to Charles Brown: "'My last operation,' he told me, 'was the opening of a man's temporal artery. I did it with the utmost nicety; but, reflecting upon what passed through my mind at the time, my dexterity seemed a miracle, and I never took up the lancet again'" (*KC* 2.56). Yet in most ways Keats seems to have been a remarkably successful student. He passed the tough new apothecary's Licentiate examination on July 1816 at age twenty, a significant achievement that speaks for the strength of his training and the seriousness with which he pursued it. He held on to his medical books (*KL* 1.277) and occasionally considered taking up the profession after all, though never for very long (2.70, 114). Key aspects of his medical knowledge and scientific habits of thought remained with him, leaving their marks on his mature poetry in a number of ways.

Nearly everyone who has looked into the subject agrees on the most fundamental lessons that Keats absorbed from his years of medical training: an "objective exactness" marking his finest poetry (Gittings, 85) along with the related "high consciousness of the body" found throughout his writing (de Almeida, 26). These tendencies come together in the physiological idiom of some of Keats's most memorable pronouncements: his desire for a "Life of Sensations" (*KL* 1.185), his sense that "axioms in philosophy are not axioms until they are proved upon our pulses" (1.279). Although Keats can write as fancifully as any poet and at times voices the desire to transcend the limitations of earthly existence, such moments are typically followed by the recognition – at once chastening and unexpectedly heartening – that the end of sense experience would mean an end to imaginative life. In *Endymion* this is called the "journey homeward to habitual self" (2.276). It is powerfully accelerated in *Ode to a Nightingale* by the swift juxtaposition of a hyper-fantastic heavenly vision ("And haply the Queen-Moon is on her throne") with the sobering admission that "here there is no light" (36–38) – a prelude to one of Romantic poetry's most sensuous and compelling stanzas:

> I cannot see what flowers are at my feet,
>   Nor what soft incense hangs upon the boughs,
> But, in embalmed darkness, guess each sweet
>   Wherewith the seasonable month endows
> The grass, the thicket, and the fruit-tree wild;
>   White hawthorn, and the pastoral eglantine;
>   Fast fading violets cover'd up in leaves;
>   And mid-May's eldest child,
>   The coming musk-rose, full of dewy wine,
>   The murmurous haunt of flies on summer eves. (stanza 5)

"Sensations" – scents of flowers and tree-blossoms carried by light breezes through the "embalmed darkness" – ground a vision that ennobles rather than transcends everyday experience. "Poetic creativity," comments Donald Goellnicht on Keats's general practice, "is ultimately rooted in material existence, in sensations perceived from concrete objects" (64–65), an esthetic he and others have traced directly to the empirical ethos of Guy's hospital, and of Astley Cooper in particular.

Keats's lecture notes report Cooper defining "sensation" in decidedly embodied (if not altogether materialist) terms:

> Sensation – it is an impression made on the Extremities of the Nerves conveyed to the Brain. This is proved by the effects of dividing a Nerve. After a time the sensation of a Nerve will return as it unites [. . .] Volition is the contrary of Sensation it proceeds from the internal to external parts.[8]

If these definitions seem bland or self-evident, in Keats's day they were highly controversial, evincing a brain-based, physiological approach to understanding mind and behavior at odds with the orthodox notions. Especially after the publication of Priestley's *Disquisitions Relating to Matter and Spirit* (1777), any claim that thought was a "property of the *nervous system*, or rather of the *brain*" courted suspicion outside medical and radical scientific circles.[9] In 1815, some months before Keats attended Cooper's lecture (above) on the nervous system, an article appeared in *Edinburgh Review* arguing that the "brain is not at all concerned in the changes which precede Sensation" nor required for the "phenomena of Thought and Volition."[10] Keats's lecture notes tell quite a different story, more in keeping with the progressive, skeptical, and experimentalist character of the London medical schools.

His notes to a subsequent lecture on the glands show how it became natural – once sensation, thought, and volition were located in the brain – to view mind and body as aspects of a single holistic system rather than as distinct, much less dichotomous entities. Again, a simple experiment is cited to help prove that the glands and the nerves that "contribute" to them form part of a network of interlocking functions, in turn connected with the brain and its cognitive and emotive activities. "Nerves are supposed to contribute to this operation, which is proved by the secretion being stopped in those Glands the Nerves going to which have been divided.[. . .] The Passions of [the] Mind have great influence on the Secretions, Fear produces increase <of> Bile and Urine, Sorrow increases Tears" (*Note Book*, 64). Christopher Ricks has helped us see how pervasively and centrally bodily fluids and their dynamics function in Keats's writing: the rush of blood to the skin in blushing or sexual arousal, the welling up of tears, even the operation of sweat glands. Ricks's provocative study is interested in the "moral and social" meaning of these actions, yet such mind-body phenomena also played a large role in the medical and scientific thinking of Keats's time.[11] The flush of embarrassment or the trembling of sexual excitement revealed how richly and inextricably thought and feeling, body and imagination were intertwined – an interaction that interested such influential contemporary medical figures as Darwin, Charles Bell (whose 1807 lectures on physiology and artistic expression were attended by Haydon), and William Lawrence (whose openly materialist lectures on anatomy, physiology, and human nature launched a sensational controversy during Keats's period at Guy's).

And, of course, interested Keats. How complex such interaction can become in his poetry is to be seen in *Isabella*, where Keats does not simply illustrate a conception of mind-body commerce borrowed from contemporary medical science, but enriches and extends it. When Lorenzo determines to reveal his love,

> all day
> His heart beat awfully against his side;
> And to his heart he inwardly did pray
> For power to speak; but still the ruddy tide
> Stifled his voice, and puls'd resolve away –
> Fever'd his high conceit . . .   (41–46)

The heart that conventionally harbors love also, quite inconveniently, registers fear of rejection by speeding up as anxiety quickens the pulse. Because of extensive interconnections among the heart, blood, and lungs (emphasized in Bell's lectures on the *Anatomy and Philosophy of Expression*), the "ruddy tide" of blood chokes up the throat and, in an eminently Keatsian semantic flourish, "pulses" his resolve away.[12] Ironically, Lorenzo finds himself in the odd position of beseeching his own heart to slow down and let him speak the love that hearts traditionally symbolize. Volition ("power to speak") is anything but the prerogative of a conscious, disembodied subject. It arises from a complex system of mental intentions and physiological operations, physical sensations and unconscious as well as conscious fears and desires. Building on conventional associations, Keats features heart and blood to highlight the complications as well as the transports of embodied passion. At the same time, poor Lorenzo's love for wealthy Isabella is rendered more genuine for the reader by its physiological signs. It is literally proved upon Lorenzo's pulses.

Keats draws on a scientific lexicon not only for portraying such imaginative acts, but also for describing the "silent Working" of imagination itself (*KL* 1.185). A number of his terms and metaphors for the imagination, as Stuart Sperry first pointed out, can be traced to the chemistry he studied at Guy's.[13] The links are sometimes surprisingly direct. Writing to Haydon in 1818, Keats wonders at the "innumerable compositions and decompositions which take place between the intellect and its thousand materials before it arrives at that trembling delicate and snail-horn perception of Beauty" (*KL* 1.265); the first page of the course syllabus used at Guy's defines chemistry as the "*The Science of the Composition and Decomposition of the heterogeneous particles of Matter*" (Sperry, 36). A number of related terms that earlier interpreters of Keats took to be transcendentalizing or Platonizing – *sublimation, essence, intensity, ethereal,* even *spiritual* – also described chemical processes, and it is with a sense of this concrete scientific meaning that Keats sometimes used these words. When in late 1817 he said that the "excellence of every Art is its intensity, capable of making all disagreeables evaporate, from their being in close relationship with Beauty & Truth" (*KL* 1.192), he is thinking of the chemical process of evaporation, playing on the technical sense of "intensity" as degree of heat or "caloric," refining out impurities or "disagreeables" to produce a purified "essence." Special cases of evaporation, according to the same syllabus, include the "processes of *Distillation,* and *Sublimation,*" terms that resonate throughout Keats's poetry and letters. Characterizing the effect of astonishing landscapes on poetic creation (in a letter of 1818 to Tom), Keats draws his terminology, Goellnicht shows with italics (58–60), from refining processes in chemistry: "I shall learn poetry here and shall henceforth write more than ever, for the *abstract* endeavor of being able to add a mite to that mass of beauty which is harvested from these grand *materials,* by the *finest spirits,* and put into *etherial* existence for the relish of one's fellows" (*KL* 1.301). These terms reflect no casual Platonizing but rather the habitual precision of a scientifically trained mind.

Chemistry, Sperry demonstrates, gave Keats a "set of analogies useful in explaining the origin and operation of poetry as an immaterial or 'spiritual' power active throughout the universe" (40–41). M. H. Abrams makes an even stronger claim: these metaphors, freighted with scientific meaning, conceive of "the poet's imagination as a process of refining, purifying, etherealizing, spiritualizing, and essentializing the actual into the ideal without transcending the limits and conditions of the material world."[14] The passage in *Endymion* (1.777–807) whose organizing image Keats termed a "Pleasure Thermometer" (*KL* 1.218) may allegorize Platonic ascent, but it more directly represents a process of chemical distillation, driven by steadily increasing caloric "intensity" and resulting in a superfine yet still material essence. Notions of etherealized or supersensible matter played a crucial role in the dynamic materialism of Priestley and the "corporeal" accounts of mind inspired by Romantic-era brain science. With such intuition, Keats has Endymion describe "happiness" as the pursuit of "fellowship with essence; till we shine, / Full alchemiz'd" (777–80). This process, at once social and aesthetic, is a progressive heightening and distillation of pleasurable experience, "leading, by degrees, / To the chief intensity" (799–800):

> at the tip-top,
> There hangs by unseen film, an orbed drop
> Of light, and that is love.   (1.805–7)

As "full alchemiz'd" suggests, Keats's metaphor is a chemical alembic or beaker, with the "orbed drop" an "exact description of a drop of pure distillate as it condenses" on the beaker's lip (Goellnicht, 79).

The chemistry of the Romantic era – virtually a "new science" thanks to the innovative work of Priestley, Humphry Davy, and other experimentalists – implied a constantly changing physical environment, a world of process and transformation in contrast to the fixed and mechanical universe of

Newtonian physics (Goellnicht, 51). So common a phenomenon as the shrinking and expanding of doors and floorboards with the passage of the seasons implied that matter was porous and in motion, defined by fields of energy rather than minuscule building-blocks. It was this fluid and dynamic conception of matter that led Priestley to reject the traditional dichotomy of matter and spirit. Keats's poetry is analogously dynamic, describing a world of change in terms that draw subtly but revealingly on his education in chemistry. Lamia's transformation from a serpent to a "woman's shape" is an especially striking example:

> Her eyes in torture fix'd, and anguish drear,
> Hot, glaz'd, and wide, with lid-lashes all sear,
> Flash'd phosphor and sharp sparks, without one cooling tear.
> The colours all inflam'd throughout her train,
> She writh'd about, convuls'd with scarlet pain:
> A deep volcanian yellow took the place
> Of all her milder-mooned body's grace.   (*Lamia* 1.150–56)

"This description resembles nothing so much as the effects of a violent chemical reaction," comments Sperry (302). Lamia does not change instantly with the touch of Hermes' magic wand; this is merely a catalyst for a slow, convulsive process that, predictably, involves heat rising to an agonizing degree of "intensity." Such passages show Keats casting the romance convention of marvelous transformations into the language of contemporary science and, by the same gesture, implying that chemistry has lent a distinctly magical quality to "ordinary" physical transformations in a fluid and constantly changing material universe.

Keats also drew on his medical training for natural images, ones that gain resonance from connotations in the medical botany. One of the fundamental paradoxes in his poetry – that "there is richest juice in poison-flowers" (*Isabella* 104) – was a commonplace of Romantic pharmacology. According to Cooper, "there is no substance considered as poisonous which in very small doses is not capable of producing a beneficial effect" (quoted in de Almeida, 150). Goellnicht has shown that terms whose meaning have eluded editors and critics, such as "luxuries" and "simple flowers," make sense only in the context of contemporary botany (92–93).[15] *Ode to Melancholy* opens with a stance against the pharmacological substances that would now be called neurotoxins: "Wolf's-bane," "nightshade" and "yew-berries"; even the "globed peonies" subsequently recommended, which seem to belong to a different tonal register altogether, are a folk-medicine prescription (de Almeida, 168–72). The most celebrated – and common – Romantic neurotoxin was opium, the stock "anodyne" and recreational drug of the era: powerful to alleviate pain, routinely prescribed for a huge range of bodily and mental ills, used as a sedative, yet highly addictive (will-eroding) and fatal in overdose. The "drowsy numbness" that so hauntingly opens *Ode to a Nightingale*, making the poet feel as though he had "emptied some dull opiate to the drains / One minute past, and Lethe-wards had sunk" (1–4), captures the ambivalence of a pain-killer that could either suspend consciousness or end it. This numbness has been related to a passage from Cooper's lectures on surgery, concerning an "extraordinary case" of head injury in which the "functions of the mind were suspended from an interruption of the circulation in the brain," the patient "having, as it were, drunk from the cup of Lethe" for more than thirteen months and suffered a complete mental "death" throughout the ordeal (Goellnicht, 226–27). The parallel is probably incidental; Keats had already compared a drink spiked with "some drug" to "Lethe's wave" in his early lyric "Fill for me a brimming bowl," written in August 1814, prior to his studies with Cooper at Guy's. Nevertheless, the verbal connection underscores how opiates, like certain cases of head injury, played a surprisingly controversial role in the philosophical debates of the time, suggesting that material substances and corporeal injuries alike could alter or suspend what many claimed was an immaterial and disembodied mind. The poet's image of numbed consciousness implies in advance that should he succeed in overcoming the limitations of his material body – "I will fly to thee, / . . . / Though the dull brain perplexes and retards," he exclaims to the nightingale (31–34) – his consciousness will be extinguished along with his pain. He will, as he soon intuits, "become a sod," with no living ear to hear the nightingale's song and no brain, dull or otherwise, with which to process it.

Evolution did not figure explicitly in the Guy's teaching curriculum, but de Almeida has persuasively delineated Keats's response to the innovative and controversial evolutionary theories of Erasmus Darwin, J. F. Blumenbach, J.-B. de Lamarck, and William Lawrence, very much part of the intellectual atmosphere of the London medical world. Evolutionary thinking had been stimulated both by the rise of comparative anatomy (integral to the thought and teaching of Cooper and his school) and by discoveries, beginning in the latter part of the eighteenth century, of fossils of extinct species. Contrary to biblical accounts of a single Creation antedating history, fossil species (what Byron, in *Cain*, called the relics of a "pre-Adamite world" and Shelley, in *Prometheus Unbound*, the "ruins / Of cancelled cycles") suggested that creation was a perpetual, constantly unfolding process. Life forms, rather than being fixed from the beginning by divine fiat, continued to evolve, and entire species could die out by failing to adapt to a changing world. Keats gives

Endymion a harrowing glimpse of catastrophic change, recorded by the fossils preserved in the ocean's depths:

> skeletons of man,
> Of beast, behemoth, and leviathan,
> And elephant, and eagle, and huge jaw
> Of nameless monster. A cold leaden awe
> These secrets struck into him.   (*Endymion* 3.133–37)

Endymion is stunned by the knowledge that nature and history destroy in order to create, that progression can entail extinction. Living nature is marked by striving and a struggle to survive, "an eternal fierce destruction" (as Keats puts it in a verse-letter to Reynolds) "where every maw / The greater on the less feeds evermore" (*KL* 1.262).

Such awful knowledge is central to the *Hyperion* poems, which portray the Titans in the process of being superseded by the Olympians. Trembling on the verge of extinction, Hyperion and his titanic race are "fossils," "resonant skeletal remains of an earlier history and generation" (de Almeida, 221). Oceanus, the Titan sea god whose domain is associated both with the evolutionary beginnings of life and with flux, recognizes that the Titans are caught in an inexorable movement from one phase of necessarily provisional "perfection" to the next.

> As Heaven and Earth are fairer, fairer far
> Than Chaos and blank Darkness, though once chiefs;
> And as we show beyond that Heaven and Earth
> In form and shape compact and beautiful,
> In will, in action free, companionship,
> And thousand other signs of purer life;
> So on our heels a fresh perfection treads,
> A power more strong in beauty, born of us
> And fated to excel us.   (*Hyperion* 2.206–14)

If consciousness is shaped by the organic structures that support it – as suggested by Hyperion's "horrors, portion'd to a giant nerve" (1.175) – then superior beauty of form entails greater "perfection" of mind. Hence the "eternal law" Oceanus proffers: "first in beauty should be first in might" (2.228–29). A notion of psychic life evolving and adapting in a pursuit of a "fresh perfection" that advances at the price of periodically catastrophic transitions also helps underwrite Keats's faith, political and aesthetic, in "the general and gregarious advance of intellect" (*KL* 1.281). A progressive view of history, however, does not render him complacent (change moves in a jagged pattern of fits and starts rather than smoothly forward) and his sympathies (particularly in the *Hyperion* poems) extend to the losers in the struggle for perfection no less than to those destined to prevail.

Cooper had helped make Guy's Hospital into "one of the best anatomy schools in Europe," and Keats's anatomical training informs his poetry in a number of ways, from the subtle to the grotesquely overt.[16] The head severed from the corpse of Lorenzo and lovingly cleaned, tended, and preserved by a bereft Isabella (in *Isabella*) reads on one level like a medical student's nightmare, while the uncanny hand of one of Keats's last lyrics ("This living hand"), at once "warm and capable" and yet weirdly detached – as if amputated – gains some of its haunting power from the poet's distinctly clinical tone. The most intricate and extended image draws on Keats's knowledge of brain anatomy, transformed into topographical and architectural images: the internalized landscape and "fane" in the final stanza of *Ode to Psyche*. Some of the most spectacular advances in the history of neuroanatomy were made in the decade preceding Keats's stint at Guy's, and Cooper was certainly familiar with them. The "organologist" F. J. Gall and his assistant J. G. von Spurzheim (who went on to popularize the pseudoscience of phrenology) had recently developed a radically new brain dissection technique that gained the respect even of their critics. Hazlitt, despite his series of attacks on phrenology, attested to the revelatory power of the "transverse section of the brain, divided on the new Spurzheim principles": "It is here, then, the number of the parts, their distinctions, connections, structures, uses: in short, an entire new set of ideas, which occupies the mind of the student."[17] Working, like Gall, from a background in comparative anatomy and a Romantic sense of the dynamic unity of structure, function, and environmental adaptation (though in many ways opposed to Gall), Charles Bell traced out a series of basic neural pathways, made a crucial distinction between sensory and motor nerves, and helped disseminate the controversial new model of nerves as bundles of fibers rather than hollow tubes or solid cords. Along with Luigi Galvani's hypothesis of "electric" neural transmission, duly recorded by Keats in his medical notes (*Note Book*, 58), such fundamental advances in neuroanatomy and physiology helped inspire a series of sophisticated biological accounts of mind, most notably those of Darwin, Gall, Bell, Lawrence, and the French Revolutionary doctor, P. J. G. Cabanis. As Keats's *Anatomical and Physiological Note Book* makes clear, he could not have left Guy's without a fairly extensive exposure to these radical new ideas.

Ode to Psyche, celebrating the "latest born" Olympian goddess (24) and the human mind she represents, draws inventively on the new brain anatomy to gesture toward an embodied psychology of its own. In the last stanza, imagining the "fane" he will build for Psyche within "some untrodden region" of his "mind," the poet describes this newly approachable region in terms that continually broach an identification of mind with brain.[18] The "wild-ridged mountains" suggest the cerebrum with its convolutions (given fresh definition and emphasis by Gall) and its fissures; the "dark-cluster'd trees" with "branched thoughts" suggest that the brain's branching nerves (axons) cannot be entirely separated from the thoughts they channel. "Convolutions," "ventricles" and "other Cavaties," and the nerves that "arise by numerous branches" from the brain's "Substance" all appear in Keats's lecture notes, interspersed with speculative remarks that an evidently fascinated Keats took down from Cooper (*Note Book*, 53–54). The "streams" the poet projects for his mind-region evoke the brain's network of blood vessels, as does Psyche's "rosy sanctuary." This sanctuary will be dressed (recall Keats's position as surgical "dresser") with the "wreath'd trellis of a working brain," an especially rich image evoking both what Keats called the "serpentine" branchings of the nerves and their fibrous structure, only recently established and still controversial. Using the contemporary term for the brain's axonal or "white" matter, student Keats noted, "The Medullary substance seems to be composed of fibres" (*Note Book*, 53–54). Some of the ode's images are less obviously related to neuroanatomy but, in context, resonate with key features of the new biological psychologies. The unusual phrase "shadowy thought," for example, suggests the importance placed on unconscious cognition throughout Romantic brain science.[19] The "casement ope at night" has been specifically, and rather ingeniously, related to the "fenestra rotundum" (literally, "round window") of the inner ear, part of its channel to the brain (Goellnicht, 259). The image has a wider resonance, however, touching on the importance of the brain's permeability to the world (through the ear, eye, and other sensory openings) and its integration with the rest of the body (through the spinal column with its series of "large hole[s] for the passage of the Spinal Marrow" [*Note Book*, 14]), evoking the holistic and ecological character of Romantic accounts of embodied thought.

As "pale-mouth'd prophet" of the most modern Olympian (Psyche was added to the pantheon quite late in the Classical era),[20] the poet of her ode takes on a modern psychological task: exploring the mind's "dark Passages" (the task of Wordsworth's genius; *KL* 1.281). The "untrodden" psychic region imaged in the ode evokes the complex brain made newly evident by Gall, Bell, and other pioneering neuroanatomists, along with the innovative biological psychologies emerging through their efforts, building on Darwin and made notorious by Lawrence's controversial lectures and the phrenology debates. Such science gave Keats a fresh canvas on which to exercise the imaginative powers of an embodied psyche. Birds and bees, Dryads and unearthly flowers populate the "wide quietness" of a mental space built from the subtly naturalized images of a "working brain"; "the gardener Fancy" has a place along with anatomy in a stanza that deftly shuttles between myth and science, conventional poetic topoi (the psychologized landscape, the fanciful bower) and novel images of the mind. The climactic stanza also gives primacy to the passionate, affective aspects of mind (the "casement" remains open to "let the warm Love in") that play a crucial role throughout the embodied psychologies of the Romantic era, opposing the traditional opposition of cognition and emotion no less than the closely related one of mind and body. Keats is one of the first English poets to make "brain" a preferred term for "mind" or "thought," giving his poetry an uncannily modern feel while underscoring its links to the scientific discourses of his own era.

Evoking an embodied, emotive, ingeniously inventive mind, *Ode to Psyche* sums up those aspects of Keats's poetic career that owe most tellingly to his formative years as a student of medicine. His antidualistic approach to mind and body, most spectacularly developed in the brainscape that concludes the ode, recurs throughout his poetry: in the flushed brows and throbbing pulses of his impassioned lovers, in the chemical analogies that give a material edge to his depictions of imaginative creation, even in the psychoactive substances – wine, opium, hemlock – that underscore the fragile, provisional nature of a human consciousness grounded in a mortal and often morbid body. A great part of Keats's unmistakably Keatsian lines – "Sudden a thought came like a full-blown rose, / Flushing his brow, and in his pained heart / Made purple riot" (*Eve of St. Agnes* 136–38) – resides in his unique ability to convey the feel of an embodied sensibility with a finely balanced combination of lexical daring and prosodic tact.

Keats's medical training provided him with a model for his self-conception as a poet. His apprenticeship and then medical residence at Guy's left him with an "extensive knowledge needful to thinking people" (he said in May 1818; *KL* 1.277), especially a knowledge of human suffering at its physical extreme and an ethical ideal of healing – as a poet, if not as a physician. Inclined to see the world as a "gigantic hospital" (Roe, 192) – "Here, where men sit and hear each other groan" (*Ode to a Nightingale* 24) – Keats describes the "great end" of poetry as being "a friend / To sooth the cares, and lift the thoughts of man" (*Sleep and Poetry* 246–47). Apollo – the beautiful and powerful Olympian, patron god both of poetry and medicine, who arrives to displace poisoned, sick Hyperion – provided Keats with a ready image of the poet as healer. But much as there was no guarantee, despite the climate of medical progress and reform, that the Romantic-era physician would be more likely to cure than to kill, Keats's ethical conception of poetry remains an anxious and tentative one, fraught with the possibility that the poet will forget or mistake his proper aim. Moneta, the visionary guide of *The Fall of Hyperion*, harshly warns that the aspiring poet may prove to be his "sheer opposite," the dreamer: "The one pours out a balm upon the world, / The other vexes it" (1.201–2). Keats assumes the mantle of the physician-poet in full awareness of this dilemma; his aura of self-doubt only adds to the humanizing effect of his respect for the limitations of embodied existence. "Tell me," the poet asks Moneta, "sure a poet is a sage; / A humanist, physician to all men" (1.187–90). The question, like so many in Keats's poetry, remains teasingly open.

NOTES

1 Z., "On the Cockney School of Poetry, No. 4," *Blackwood's Edinburgh Magazine* 3 (1818), 519–20, 524.

2 *The Autobiography and Memoirs of Benjamin Robert Haydon* (1853), ed. Tom Taylor (New York: Harcourt Brace, 1926), 1.269.

3 See Desmond King-Hele, *Doctor of Revolution: The Life and Genius of Erasmus Darwin* (London: Faber & Faber, 1977).

4 See G. S. Rousseau, "On Romanticism, Science, and Medicine," *History of European Ideas* 17 (1993), 659–63. The distinction between "organic" and "mechanic" form in literary work was popularized by Coleridge's lectures on Shakespeare, 1812 and after.

5 Nicholas Roe, *John Keats and the Culture of Dissent*, 169–81.

6 Donald C. Goellnicht, *The Poet-Physician: Keats and Medical Science* (Pittsburgh: University of Pittsburgh Press, 1984), 24; Hermione de Almeida, *Romantic Medicine and John Keats* (New York: Oxford University Press, 1991), 7.

7 Quoted in Robert Gittings, *John Keats*, 103.

8 *John Keats's Anatomical and Physiological Note Book*, ed. Maurice Buxton Forman (Oxford: Oxford University Press, 1934), 55–56.

9 John W. Yolton, *Thinking Matter: Materialism in Eighteenth-Century Britain* (Minneapolis: University of Minnesota Press, 1983), 113.

10 Review of Sir Everard Home, "Observations on the Functions of the Brain," *Edinburgh Review* 24 (1815), 440, 448.

11 Christopher Ricks, *Keats and Embarrassment*, 20.

12 Charles Bell, *Essays on the Anatomy of Expression in Painting* (London: Longman &c., 1806), 161–67.

13 Stuart M. Sperry, *Keats the Poet*, 30–71.

14 M. H. Abrams, "Keats's Poems: The Material Dimensions," *The Persistence of Poetry: Bicentennial Essays on Keats*, ed. R. M. Ryan and R. A. Sharp, 43.

15 He quotes Darwin's definitions for "luxuries" ("LUXURIOUS FLOWERS [. . .] several heads of flowers, each growing out of that immediately below it") and for "simple" flowers ("*simple* when no part of the *fructification* is common to many flowers or florets, but is confined to one only").

16 See R. S. White, "'Like Esculapius of Old': Keats's Medical Training," *Keats–Shelley Review* 12 (1998), 30.

17 *The Complete Works of William Hazlitt*, ed. P. P. Howe (London, Dent: 1930–34), 4.73.
18 For the relation of this ode to Keats's medical training, see Goellnicht, *The Poet–Physician*, 135–39, and the essays by Hagelman and Pettit in "Further Reading."
19 On the links between literary and neuroscientific notions of the unconscious in the Romantic era, see Alan Richardson, "Coleridge and the Dream of an Embodied Mind," *Romanticism* 5 (1999), 1–25.
20 "The word signifies the *soul*, and this personification of Psyche first mentioned by Apuleius, is posterior to the Augustan age, though still it is connected with ancient mythology." "Psyche," J. Lemprière, *A Classical Dictionary*, 6th edn. (London: Cadell and Davies, 1806).

FURTHER READING

De Almeida, Hermione. *Romantic Medicine and John Keats.* New York: Oxford University Press, 1991.

Goellnicht, Donald C. *The Poet-Physician: Keats and Medical Science.* Pittsburgh: University of Pittsburgh Press, 1984.

Hale-White, William, Sir. *Keats as Doctor and Patient.* London: Oxford, 1938.

Hagelman, Charles, Jr. "Keats's Medical Training and the Last Stanza of the 'Ode to Psyche,'" *KSJ* 11 (1962), 73–82.

Keats, John. *John Keats's Anatomical and Physiological Note Book.* Ed. Maurice Buxton Forman. Oxford: Oxford University Press, 1934.

Pettit, Henry. "Scientific Correlatives of Keats' *Ode to Psyche*," *Studies in Philology* 40 (1943), 560–66.

Roe, Nicholas. *John Keats and the Culture of Dissent.*

Smith, Hillas. *Keats and Medicine.* Newport, Isle of Wight: Cross, 1995.

Sperry, Stuart M. *Keats the Poet.*

White, R. S. "'Like Esculapius of Old': Keats's Medical Training," *Keats–Shelley Review* 12 (1998), 15–49.

16

JACK STILLINGER

The "story" of Keats

The "story" of Keats – how a young man of no apparent distinction in family or social origins, education, or early accomplishments, grew up to become one of the ten or twelve most admired poets in all of English literature – is really several stories, some of them not entirely consistent or compatible with some of the others.[1] This chapter focuses on two. The first is the story of Keats the young genius whose life and career were cut short – some said by the hostility of reviewers – just as he was about to produce the major works that his friends thought him capable of. This is the Keats of Shelley's *Adonais*; of Byron's famous quip in Canto 11 of *Don Juan* that Keats's "mind, that very fiery particle," was "snuffed out by an article"; and of the inscriptions on his gravestone in the Protestant Cemetery in Rome: the broken lyre symbolizing unfulfilled aspirations; the words that the poet himself requested, "Here lies one whose name was writ in water"; and his friends' well-meant embellishments mentioning the poet's "bitterness [. . .] of heart, at the malicious power of his enemies." The product of this first "story" is the Keats whom the British public thought of, if they remembered him at all, during the first three decades following his death on 23 February 1821.

The second story, more a critical construct than imagined facts of biography, tells how Keats rapidly rose to canonicity, beginning in the middle of the nineteenth century, as his poems became increasingly published, read, quoted, and talked and written about. This is a story about readers' changing interests and values, and how Keats, once he got some readers, has appealed to each separate one of those interests and values ever since. The two stories are connected in that the first, along with some noteworthy attempts by the poet's friends to correct its principal details, became the means of providing the audience and the accompanying attention that enabled the second. The first story is, in effect, the history of Keats getting into the canon by way of biographical interest. The second is, in effect, the history of Keats staying in the canon by virtue of the complexity and open-endedness of his writings. Whether or not these stories are true, it is a fact that Keats has been, just as he predicted he would be, "among the English Poets" (*KL* 1.394) for the last 150 years. What was lacking in the thirty years preceding that period – the 1820s through the 1840s – was a sufficient readership.

I

Some of the first story is biographically accurate. Keats did die young, at twenty-five, and his active writing career amounted to little more than three and a half years, from the earliest sentimental effusions in his first published volume, *Poems* (1817), through the late ode, *To Autumn*, the last attempts at *The Fall of Hyperion* in the fall of 1819, and some private odes and sonnets to Fanny Brawne (1819 to early 1820). Certainly he would have written more had he lived longer, though we have very little idea where his interests would have taken him. But it is clearly erroneous to think that the brevity of his life and career prevented him from achieving anything of significance. On the contrary, even if cut off just as he was getting under way, this "poet of promise" had nevertheless left a body of mature work in narrative and lyric forms sufficient to make him a "major" writer by anybody's standards. The imagined poet of promise was in fact a poet of enormous accomplishments.

The traditional notions of Keats's low origins and patchy education also have required adjustment. His father was head innkeeper, livery-stabler, and principal manager at the Swan and Hoop, a prosperous London lodging owned by his father-in-law (Keats's grandfather), John Jennings. Notwithstanding the reports of hostile reviewers and the fables of literary history, the poet's "low" origins were actually soundly middle class, as we reckon these things today. As for education, from 1803 to 1811 Keats attended an excellent boarding school, John Clarke's at Enfield, north of London, and proved an insatiable reader and remarkable learner. He then served a four-year apprenticeship to an apothecary-surgeon (1811–15), followed by a first year of courses as a medical student at Guy's Hospital in London. He passed the apothecaries' exam and received his certificate to practice as apothecary and surgeon in July 1816, at which point he abandoned medicine for a full-time career in poetry. The literary part of his education was as comprehensive as that of many another famous writer, and the scientific (and human) aspects of his medical training, as Alan Richardson's essay in this volume shows, were a further enrichment.

What has most needed correcting is the idea that Keats was killed by the reviewers. Of all the elements of the story, this is the most often repeated and perforce the most firmly established, extending even into some of the Shelley scholarship of the twentieth century.[2] The assassins in the story are the two most notorious pronouncers on Keats's second volume, the long poem *Endymion* (1818): John Gibson Lockhart, writing in *Blackwood's Edinburgh Magazine* for August 1818, and John Wilson Croker, in the *Quarterly Review* for April (both reviews actually appeared in September, just after a nagging sore throat had forced Keats's early return from an impressive but physically demanding walking tour of northern England, Ireland, and Scotland with his robust friend Charles Brown). Lockhart, in the fourth of his series of articles on the "Cockney School of Poetry," calls *Endymion* "imperturbable drivel- ling idiocy," quotes passages of "very pretty raving" and "loose, nerveless versification, and Cockney rhymes," and concludes by urging Keats to abandon poetry and return to his apothecary's shop (*KCH* 98, 100, 104, 109–10). Croker, declaring that he could not get past the first book of *Endymion* and could make no sense even of that, goes on at length about faulty diction and versification. He too relegates Keats's poetry to the "Cockney School," characterized by "the most incongruous ideas in the most uncouth language" (*KCH* 111). Denouncing the liberalism implied by Keats's connections with his anti-Tory mentor Leigh Hunt, both reviewers make clear that their criticism has a political bias.[3]

Keats's admirers – some scores of his acquaintances at the time and many hundreds of thousands of readers subsequently over the past 180 years – have hated Lockhart and Croker for their contemptuous treatment. But the poet himself seems to have been very little affected. With Shakespeare as his "presider," he had higher standards than his assailants did. "Praise or blame," he told his publisher J. A. Hessey on 8 October 1818, "has but a momentary effect on the man whose love of beauty in the abstract makes him a severe critic on his own Works. My own domestic criticism has given me pain without comparison beyond what Blackwood or the Quarterly could possibly inflict" (*KL* 1.373–74). To his brother and sister-in-law in America he commented a week later, "This is a mere matter of the moment – I think I shall be among the English Poets after my death. Even as a Matter of present interest the attempt to crush me in the Quarterly has only brought me more into notice" (1.394).

It was consumption – what we now call tuberculosis – that killed Keats. But the sentimental fable of fatally harsh reviews quickly arose during the final stage of his illness, and it got into print soon after his death. Here is an example from Shelley's (admittedly self-serving) Preface to *Adonais* (1821):

The genius of the lamented person to whose memory I have dedicated these unworthy verses, was not less delicate and fragile than it was beautiful; and where cankerworms abound, what wonder if its young flower was blighted in the bud? The savage criticism on his *Endymion*, which appeared in the *Quarterly Review*, produced the most violent effect on his susceptible mind; the agitation thus originated ended in the rupture of a blood-vessel in the lungs; a rapid consumption ensued, and the succeeding acknowledgements from more candid critics, of the true greatness of his powers, were ineffectual to heal the wound thus wantonly inflicted.

"Delicate," "fragile," "blighted in the bud" set the tone, and Shelley's descriptions of Keats in the poem – for example, as "a pale flower by some sad maiden cherished . . . The bloom, whose petals nipt before they blew / Died on the promise of the fruit" (48, 52–53) – further emphasize the poet's pitiful weakness.

Shelley did not know Keats very well. Those who did, a group of fiercely loyal surviving friends, almost immediately conceived the idea of writing a memoir to tell the truth about the poet's "beautiful character,"[4] a character that did not include delicacy and fragility. Hessey's publishing partner John Taylor sent announcements to both the *New Times* and the *Morning Chronicle* (29 March, 9 April, and 4 June 1821) to the effect that "speedily will be published, a biographical memoir of the late John Keats" (*Letters of Brown*, 89). Then followed a prolonged squabble among the surviving friends over which was best qualified to do the job and who had the rights to his unpublished poems, letters, and other papers. Charles Brown, Keats's housemate during 1819–20 and the friend closest to him while he was writing *The Eve of St. Agnes*, the odes, and the rest of his most important poems, was a frontrunner, but it was more than a decade before he could begin serious work on the project.

The first memoir in print was Leigh Hunt's chapter, "Mr. Keats, with a Criticism on His Writings," in his *Lord Byron and Some of His Contemporaries* (1828), a lively account that opens with a lengthy paragraph on Keats's physical appearance and contains ten pages of excellently chosen quotations (with *Ode to a Nightingale* entire) to illustrate his descriptive genius, as well as most of his letter of 10 May 1817 on his aspiration "to be in the Mouth of Fame" (*KL* 1.136–40). Hunt draws on and supports elements of the "story" that had been taking shape, with details of the poet's "origin" ("of the humblest description"), his schooling ("the rudiments of a classical education"), and the bad effects of the reviews (a "system of calumny" that injured "a young and sensitive nature").[5] Hunt presents Keats as a sickly person all his life, and concludes with details of the poet's final illness and death in Rome supplied by Joseph Severn. Hunt's memoir is one of a small cluster of events of the late 1820s marking the beginning of Keats's emergence from obscurity. The first English edition of Shelley's *Adonais* appeared in the following year (1829), a publication sponsored by the so-called "Cambridge Apostles"–Richard Monckton Milnes, Alfred Tennyson, and Arthur Hallam – and printed from a copy of the original 1821 Pisa edition that Hallam had brought back from Italy. Also in 1829 appeared a pirated *Poetical Works of Coleridge, Shelley, and Keats*, constituting the first collected edition of Keats's poems, with a memoir of Keats based on Hunt's *Lord Byron*, from the Paris publishers Anthony and William Galignani. Because of copyright laws, this Paris edition could not be sold in England, but it was freely available in the United States, where the Keats section was several times reprinted. It was a principal cause of the rapid growth of Keats's reputation among American readers.[6]

Brown thought Hunt's account of Keats, as he told Fanny Brawne on 17 December 1829, "worse than disappointing; I cannot bear it." But in combination with Galignani's edition, just then being printed, it had the effect of spurring Brown to action: "I am resolved to write his life, persuaded that no one, except yourself [Fanny Brawne], knew him better" (*Letters of Brown*, 295). He read through the letters in his possession, wrote to friends seeking information and papers, but also entered into a prolonged and increasingly bitter controversy with his old schoolfellow Charles Dilke concerning the honesty of George Keats in his financial dealings with the poet. One result was George's injunction against the printing of any of his brother's unpublished poems in Brown's possession, a considerable obstacle to Brown's plans. Brown, who had been living in Italy, returned to England and settled at Plymouth in the spring of 1835 and soon afterward became a member and an officer of the Plymouth Institution, the local organization for the promotion of literature, science, and the fine arts. It was for a lecture at the Institution, on 29 December 1836, that Brown finally wrote his "Life of John Keats." Though not published for another hundred years, in 1937, it is a work of considerable importance in the history of Keats's reputation.[7] After several unsuccessful attempts to get it published on his own, Brown, about to emigrate to New Zealand in the spring of 1841, gave the manuscript along with his copies of Keats's unpublished poems to Richard Monckton Milnes, whom he had met in Italy and considered a good choice: a person who had not known Keats at first hand and therefore could rise above the conflicting interests of the surviving friends. Seven years later, Brown's work became the basis of the first full-scale biography, Milnes's *Life, Letters, and Literary Remains, of John Keats* (1848).

In the history of his reputation, 1848 is the year after which Keats has always been "among the English Poets." With the help of Brown's manuscript "Life," as well as information from several others who had known

Keats intimately and contributed their letters and reminiscences, Milnes gave Keats more respectable origins, a richer education, a healthier constitution, and a much fuller and more vital character. He included sixty-six poems (forty hitherto unpublished) from Brown's and others' manuscripts, as well as some eighty of the poet's letters, most of them published for the first time. In much of the two-volume compilation he let Keats speak for himself through his letters, and the result – just as readers of the poet's letters have been discovering ever since – is a portrait of an interesting and thoroughly attractive personality, one that at the time was guaranteed to stimulate interest in the poetry. Milnes's work was widely reviewed, and Keats's reputation soared dramatically. Most important among the consequences was the new demand for Keats's works in print. The three lifetime volumes (the print-runs no more than 500 copies) were no longer available, and a cheap collected edition published by William Smith in 1840 had not been a commercial success. But some fifty editions or "quasi-editions" – reprints presented as new editions – of the complete poems were published in the four decades between the year of Milnes's work and that of the next two biographies, by Sidney Colvin and William Michael Rossetti (brother of Dante Gabriel and Christina), both published in 1887.[8] With Milnes and fresh biographical interest facilitating the development, Keats at last got the requisite readership, and he has been "with Shakespeare," which is where Matthew Arnold placed him in an introductory essay of 1880, ever since.

II

In the second story that I am presenting, "poor Keats" (the subject of the first) gives way to smart Keats, accomplished Keats, and lucky Keats – this last, among other reasons, because it was just by chance that Brown, preparing to sail to New Zealand, gave his "Life" and the unpublished poems to Milnes. In the first story, Keats is "with" Thomas Chatterton (to whom Keats dedicated *Endymion*), Henry Kirke White, and a few other permanently young poets famous for dying before they fulfilled their promise. In the second story, Keats is with Shakespeare – and Chaucer, Spenser, Milton, and a handful of others – at the top of all lists of the most esteemed writers in English poetry. Regardless of the critical standards in use at a particular time, Keats regularly comes through with flying colors.

Keats has been likened to Shakespeare for some central stylistic similarities: richness of language, concreteness and particularity of descriptions, and an almost magical dexterity in harmonizing and varying the sounds and rhythms of his lines. For many decades now, while readers have grumbled at Milton's high seriousness, Pope's mechanically constructed couplets, Wordsworth's excessive plainness, Coleridge's shaky theology, Tennyson's wasteful musicality, and so on, commentators on Shakespeare and Keats have unstintingly praised their command of language and technique. Both writers have been the subjects of an immense quantity of critical writing. Along with their art, their lives and times have been exhaustively researched for clues to increased understanding, and their texts have been analyzed and interpreted endlessly, lending themselves to every kind of critical and theoretical approach.

This openness to interpretation shared by the two poets may result from their self-division. Their authorial character (as we infer from their writings) and the works themselves are full of ambiguities and contradictions; or, to put it in terms of Keats's definition of *Negative Capability* ("which Shakespeare posessed so enormously"), are full of "uncertainties, Mysteries, doubts, without any irritable reaching after fact & reason" (*KL* 1.193). These two qualities – the durable attractiveness of the works and the kinds of ambiguity that the contradictions produce in those works – are causally related: the writings of Shakespeare and Keats are attractive *because of* these uncertainties, doubts, ambiguities, and contradictions.[9]

One of the wisest and most comprehensive short definitions of canonicity recently in print is by the intellectual historian David Harlan:

> Canonical works are those texts that have gradually revealed themselves to be multi-dimensional and omni-significant, those works that have produced a plenitude of meanings and interpretations, only a small percentage of which make themselves available at any single reading. Canonical texts [. . .] generate new ways of seeing old things and new things we have never seen before. No matter how subtly or radically we change our approach to them, they always respond with something new; no matter how many times we reinterpret them, they always have something illuminating to tell us. Their very indeterminacy means that they can never be exhausted [. . .] Canonical works are multi-dimensional, omni-significant, inexhaustible, perpetually new, and, for all these reasons, "permanently valuable."[10]

This emphasis on multiplicity of meanings, indeterminacy, and interpretive inexhaustibility applies admirably to Keats, both as a person and as a poet.

In 1995, when exhibitions celebrating the bicentennial of Keats's birth were staged at Harvard, the Grolier Club in New York, the Clark Library in Los Angeles, the Dove Cottage Museum in Grasmere, and elsewhere, several Keatses were on display: the Keats of the poetry drafts, produced, as he told his friend Richard Woodhouse, as if by magic (*KC* 1.129); the Keats of the boldly inscribed fair copies; the Keats first known to the public in the magazines and the three original volumes; posthumous Keats, in his character as creator of the one hundred poems first published after his death; the personal Keats seen in the privacy of his surviving letters; Keats as the beloved friend at the center of what we now call "the Keats Circle"; Keats of the various portraits that were made of him; and Keats the artistic collaborator, providing materials for subsequent nineteenth- and twentieth-century book designers, printers, and binders.

Many more Keatses can be extracted from criticism and scholarship over the years (including the several hundred papers delivered at the bicentennial celebrations): Aesthetic Keats, the champion of art for art's sake; Sensuous Keats, the burster of Joy's grape, with or without cayenne pepper on his tongue, and the creator of some of the most palpable imagery in all of English poetry; Philosophic Keats, the describer of the Vale of Soul-making and life as a Mansion of Many Apartments; Theoretical Keats, the formulator of "Negative Capability" and of the idea of the "camelion Poet"; Topographical Keats, the well-traveled tourist through the Lakes and Scotland; Theatrical Keats, the theater reviewer and unproduced playwright; Intertextual Keats, including Spenserian Keats, Leigh Huntian Keats, Shakespearean Keats, Miltonic Keats, and many others; Political Keats, especially in the early poems and letters; a more sharply focused Radical Keats; Vulgar Keats, the only canonical male Romantic poet besides Blake who did not attend a university; Cockney Keats, a reference both to the 1818 Cockney School articles in *Blackwood's* and to the poet's supposed "lowly" upbringing, described in the earliest biographical accounts after his death; Suburban Keats, referring to Keats's politically tinged connections with Hampstead and Leigh Hunt on the outskirts of London; Effeminate Keats, the fainting flower of Shelley's *Adonais*; Masculine Keats, his friends' defense against the notion of the fainting flower; Heroic Keats, the one who suffers and matures from the trials of existence; Consumptive Keats, the one who dies so movingly every time we make our way to the end of the letters.

These different manifestations of the ever-changing chameleon Keats, selected from a large array of possibilities, are interesting in themselves but do not add up to the more concentrated canonical complexity – which I shall call Multiple Keats – that I think is at the heart of Keats's widespread and longstanding appeal to readers. "Multiple Keats" stands for an internal complexity in the poet constituted primarily by self-division – a sort of unresolved imaginative dividedness between the serious and the humorous, the straight and the ironic, the fanciful and the real, the high-flying and the down-to-earth, the sentimental and the satiric, the puffed up and the deflated. It shows itself in many places, both in biographical anecdote and in Keats's writings – and in the poetry, both in the frivolous pieces tossed off for immediate amusement and in the most serious efforts that Keats hoped would one day earn him a place among the English poets. One way of representing this self-division is by referring to various kinds of comedy: the antic, the zany, the farcical, the ridiculous, all of which have a basis in some kind of incongruity or misfittingness. Something doesn't fit with something else.

There are hundreds of passages in Keats's letters involving puns, practical jokes, self-mockery, and comic description – many of them in incongruous juxtaposition with serious matter such as a friend's or his own illness, lack of money, disappointment in love, anxiety about the future, an unfavorable review. Likewise, a sizable number of Keats's poems and passages in the poems are openly funny: the early lines about his trinity of women, wine, and snuff; the sonnet celebrating the grand climacteric of Mrs. Reynolds's cat; the whimsical self-description beginning "There was a naughty boy"; the lines about the cursed gadfly; the lines about the cursed bagpipe; the silly dialogue between Ben Nevis and Mrs. Cameron; the Spenserian stanzas making fun of his friend Charles Brown; the extended self-parody in *The Jealousies*. The comedy in these pieces, just as with the jokes in the letters, regularly depends on juxtaposition of incongruities, as in the overthrow of expectations with a punch line.

Keats often juxtaposes the comic and the serious in poems that are not primarily funny. Consider, for a handful of quick examples, Endymion pausing to rest on his extended travels and, when he casually stretches "his indolent arms" into the air, unintentionally clasping "O bliss! / A naked waist" (*Endymion* 2.711–13); Isabella and Lorenzo's myopic lovesickness in the opening stanzas of *Isabella*; the "monstrous" mice, birds, and Angora cat on Bertha's fire screen in *The Eve of St. Mark* (78–82); Porphyro's cartoon-like tiptoeing across Madeline's bedroom to check whether she is asleep in *The Eve of St. Agnes* (244–52); the redness of Hermes's blushing ears in the first paragraph of *Lamia* (1.22–26). There are larger, more serious mismatches – comic misfitting without the comedy, as it were – everywhere one turns in the major poems. Porphyro is the hero of *The Eve of St. Agnes*, an ardent lover, a Prince Charming to the rescue, Madeline's future husband, and at the same time is associated with images of sorcery, peeping Tomism, cruel seduction, and rape; while Madeline is the beautiful heroine, the belle of the ball, Sleeping Beauty, a pious Christian, Porphyro's bride, and at the same time is a foolish victim of both his stratagem and her own self-deception. In stanza six of *Ode to a Nightingale*, the speaker first thinks it would be "rich to die, / To cease upon the midnight with no pain," then the richness of his thought is immediately nullified by the realism of mortal extinction: "Still wouldst thou sing, and I have ears in vain – / To thy high requiem become a sod," he laments to the nightingale (55–60). In *To Autumn* we read a series of statements about the season's beauties, then we are made to realize that all this beauty is dying, and finally (perhaps), if we put these two contrary notions together, we understand that death is somehow beautiful. In *Ode on a Grecian Urn*, which I shall use as a single extended example of the way Keats's characteristic self-dividedness shows up in the juxtaposed opposites of his poetry, the hypothetical romance world of "Tempe or the dales of Arcady" in ancient Greece (7) stands in obvious and pointed contrast to the speaker's own modern world of process and mortality. On the painted surface of one side of the urn (the subject of stanzas 2–3), the piper's melodies are imagined to be "unheard" and therefore "sweeter"; the piper never tires; the lovers, pursuing and pursued, never age or lose their beauty ("She cannot fade, though thou hast not thy bliss, / For ever wilt thou love, and she be fair!"); the "happy" trees never shed their leaves (it is eternal "spring"). Everything is "far above" the "breathing . . . passion" of living humans, who are subject to "a heart high-sorrowful and cloy'd, / A burning forehead, and a parching tongue." On the other side of the urn (stanza 4), a sacrificial procession of "mysterious priest," lowing heifer, and townsfolk is stopped forever on the way to some "green altar"; they will neither reach their destination nor go back to their "little town" (though the heifer will never reach the altar, and the people, like the lovers, will not age or die). This is different from the process of life in the real (the poet's) world.

There is a greater density of opposites in this poem than in perhaps any other of comparable length in all of English literature. The first image of the urn, as a "still unravish'd bride of quietness," evokes the unstated counternotions of violence and sexual fulfillment in "ravished" bride; "quietness" implies a contrary noisiness. The allied image, of the urn as "foster-child of silence and slow time," makes one think of natural child. Pairings of this sort are a principal element of the ode's structure, and very shortly are made explicit in the first two stanzas in such phrases as "deities or mortals, or . . . both," "men or gods," "mad pursuit . . . struggle to escape," "Heard melodies . . . those unheard," "sensual . . . spirit," and so on. This pairing of opposites turns, in the ode's final two lines, into a pairing of abstractions brought together in the urn's message: "Beauty is truth, truth beauty. . . ." What is important, for present purposes, is the near balance of pluses and minuses accorded to both sides of these pairs. Throughout the poem, in the phrases I have quoted and in the larger oppositions connected with time and timelessness, the two contrasted sides tend to get approval and disapproval almost equally.

Earlier critics – for example, the American New Humanists of the 1920s – tended to read the poem as unequivocal celebration of the timeless world of art, and they censured Keats for the supposed Romantic escapism that such celebration implied. Then in the close attention of New Criticism to ironies, ambiguities, and paradoxes, readers began to notice (just as the speaker in the ode, being a clever reader, had noticed all along in perhaps half the lines of the poem) that the art-world has its drawbacks as a hypo-thetical alternative to the human world: the piper cannot stop playing ("thou canst not leave / Thy song"); the lovers can never finally kiss or make love ("never, never canst thou kiss, / Though winning near the goal"); the trees are confined to a single season ("nor ever bid the spring adieu"); the perma-nent halting of the sacrificial procession leaves an unseen "little town" forever "silent" and "desolate." Some critics took these misgivings, espe-cially the last image (38–40), to signify the poet's rejection of the ideal: the urn in the final stanza, now a "Cold Pastoral," is only a work of art after all, a "tease" just like eternity itself, somehow "a friend to man," but not of much practical help, since the concluding aphorism ("Beauty is truth, truth beauty"), as compelling as its terms are, really makes very little sense.

Both kinds of critical rendering – pro-ideal (therefore escapist) and pro-reality (therefore skeptical of the ideal) – are necessarily one-sided. The poem itself is actually on both sides at once, because the urn, like the ideal that it represents, is both admired and gently pitied throughout the speaker's musings. Readers do not keep returning to the ode to learn that life in the real world is preferable to life on an urn (or vice versa). Rather, they are repeatedly drawn to the spectacle of the speaker's full feeling for uncertain-ties, mysteries, doubts in the face of these oppositions. At any point, a reso-lution could go either way, and they read and reread, I think, to see how the conflict will conclude each time anew.

Ode on a Grecian Urn is an exemplary illustration of Keats's canonical complexity, as the accumulated critical literature on it attests.[11] The poem abounds in multiple and conflicting possibilities for interpretation – in the terms of David Harlan's definition (quoted above), it is "multi-dimensional, omni-significant, inexhaustible, perpetually new" – and it also, in very prac-tical terms, gets the highest ratings (in anthology publishers' surveys) from teachers in graduate and undergraduate literature classes. It seems to be the nature of canonical works to have, or to provide the basis for, more mean-ings than any reader can process at a single reading and therefore to be, in a manner of speaking, infinitely readable. In literature courses having a seminar or lecture-discussion format, canonical works elicit more discussion because of their greater density, ambiguity, and self-contradiction. They are, above all, the works that are more interesting to read, teach, talk about.

III

My second "story" of Keats, therefore, is quite simply (also quite remark-ably) the story of Keats writing a reckonable number of poems of this sort of complexity – among them, *The Eve of St. Agnes*, *La Belle Dame sans*

Merci, Ode on a Grecian Urn, Ode to a Nightingale, To Autumn, Lamia, the *Hyperion* fragments, and several sonnets – and of large numbers of readers from the 1850s to the present day finding them interesting, moving, and delightful. I do not mean to suggest that readers admire indeterminacy and the component qualities – uncertainty, ambiguity, contradiction, and so on – in the abstract. My point is that a poem's indeterminacy, uncertainty, and the rest make every individual reader's reading possible: in effect, the text of a complex poem validates what the reader wants to read in it. Thus for some readers, *The Eve of St. Agnes* has been (and still is) a poem about love, even specifically Keats's love for Fanny Brawne, while for others it is a poem about the authenticity of dreams, about stratagems, about wish-fulfillment, about artistic creativity, about Gothic literature, about family politics, about the crisis of feudalism, about escape, about critical interpretation, and so on and on.[12] As one can see even in the briefest sampling of the critical literature, there have been (and presumably will continue to be) many different explanations of what ails the knight-at-arms in *La Belle Dame.* There are multiple possibilities for interpreting each of the odes and the rest of the poems in the canonical list. The key to understanding the universality of Keats's appeal is the fact that in every case the text may be seen to support the interpretation, even when the interpretation stands in direct conflict with another interpretation based on exactly the same text.

What was absolutely necessary, then, was Keats's attainment of a large readership to make all this multiple interpreting possible; and he did this post-humously, chameleon-like, by being all things to all people who sought out his texts. In the middle of the nineteenth century, when biographical interest in writers was at an all-time high, Keats's fame got an enormous boost from the publication of Milnes's *Life, Letters, and Literary Remains,* in which many readers learned for the first time about the liveliness of the poet's personality, the heroism of his struggle to achieve something lasting in literature, the cruelty of the reviewers, and the tragic shortness of his life. Not long afterward, when first the Pre-Raphaelites and then the art-for-art's-sake enthusiasts made much of him, Keats represented their ideals on two counts: he filled poems such as *Isabella* and *The Eve of St. Agnes* with gorgeous, exquisitely detailed pictures that could be transferred, as it were, directly onto the painters' canvases, and he seemed to act as a theorist as well as a practitioner of aestheticism – in the famous exclamation to Benjamin Bailey, "O for a Life of Sensations rather than of Thoughts!" for example, and his numerous affirmations of the importance of beauty over all other things.[13]

In the early decades of the twentieth century, when the philosophical and moral ideas of a writer were considered of prime importance (an era marked in Keats studies by Clarence Thorpe's *The Mind of John Keats,* 1926), the poet could again provide what was wanted, this time in the thematic seriousness of the *Hyperion* fragments and especially, again, in statements in his letters concerning such concepts as Negative Capability, life as a Mansion of Many Apartments, and the world as a Vale of Soul-making. In the mid-century heyday of New Criticism, Keats supplied poem after poem for "close readings" in the classrooms and the critical journals.[14] More recently, evidences of political and social concerns are among the prime critical desiderata, and again Keats has come through, in a Modern Language Association symposium on "Keats and Politics" (1984) and a spate of fresh books and articles on the topic by Daniel Watkins, Nicholas Roe, and others.[15]

Most important is the fact that all through these decades, as one set of values and emphases succeeded another, Keats has continued to be the author of *The Eve of St. Agnes, Hyperion, La Belle Dame, Lamia,* and the Great Odes – poems that seem open to every possible interpretation and therefore are eminently adaptable to whatever special interest or approach seeks them out. For biographical matter, there is the spectacle of Keats speaking personally to the Urn or the Nightingale, or figuring in love situations in the guise of Porphyro, the knight-at-arms, or Lycius in *Lamia.* For the art interests of the later nineteenth century, no writer created so many pictures in poetry since Spenser and Shakespeare, and nobody so fervently expressed the love of beauty – beauty was truth itself at the end of *Ode on a Grecian Urn.* For Matthew Arnold and all subsequent Arnoldians, the poems have been full of moral situations, and therefore moral ideas – especially in the numerous contrasts of human life with some hypothetical alternative. For the New Critics – and for generations of teachers and readers influenced by them – Keats's complexity of language has provoked repeated investigation, analysis, and interpretive response. For the current concern with politics, consider just the tiny example of "peaceful citadel" in one of the emptied towns imagined in stanza four of *Ode on a Grecian Urn*: the image joins the contrary notions of peace and war (a citadel is a military fortress) and has faint nonpastoral implications both for the religious activity of the townsfolk away on their sacrificial procession and, more generally, for the pastoral tranquility of Tempe and the Vales of Arcady (where, we already have heard, maidens "struggle to escape" the "mad pursuit" of men or gods). Just two words from the poem, "peaceful citadel" could be the starting point for an essay on (say) "The Ominous Politics of *Ode on a Grecian Urn.*" This kind of interpretive plenitude – allowing the possibility of a critical essay for every two words of text, as it were – can illustrate what Keats has been for readers since the middle of the nineteenth century: a figure whose life, letters, and poems taken together are rich and varied enough to satisfy every idea of what a poet and poetry should be.

NOTES

1 For an overview of materials on the development of Keats's reputation, see my "John Keats," *The English Romantic Poets*, 711–16. The most useful collections of early reviews and other nineteenth-century comments are Donald H. Reiman, *The Romantics Reviewed*; Lewis M. Schwartz, *Keats Reviewed by His Contemporaries: A Collection of Notices for the Years 1816–1821* (Metuchen, N.J.: Scarecrow Press, 1973); *KCH*, with a useful introduction by editor G. M. Matthews; and J. R. MacGillivray, "On the Development of Keats' Reputation," in *Keats: A Bibliography and Reference Guide with an Essay on Keats' Reputation* (Toronto: University of Toronto Press, 1949). For early editions and commentary on Keats in the US, see Hyder E. Rollins, *Keats' Reputation in America to 1848* (Cambridge: Harvard University Press, 1946); for his influence on Victorian poetry, George H. Ford, *Keats and the Victorians: A Study of His Influence and Rise to Fame 1821–1895*; and for early biographies, William H. Marquess, *Lives of the Poet: The First Century of Keats Biography*.

2 See the comprehensive account by Susan J. Wolfson, "Keats Enters History: Autopsy, *Adonais*, and the Fame of Keats."

3 See John Kandl's chapter in this volume.

4 Joseph Severn's phrase, in a letter to Brown, 17 July 1821; *The Letters of Charles Armitage Brown*, ed. Jack Stillinger (Cambridge: Harvard University Press, 1966), 78.

5 Quotations are from the 2nd edition, 2 vols. (London: Henry Colburn, 1828), 1.407–43.

6 "The Galignani volume was [. . .] pirated in America, where various composite editions of Keats, reprinted or imitated from it [. . .] show clearly that in the decade from 1830 to 1840 he was much better known and more highly esteemed by the general reading public of the [American] East than by that of Great Britain" (Rollins, *Keats' Reputation*, 29). On its significance in the history of Keats's British reputation, see Joseph Grigely, *Textualterity: Art, Theory, and Textual Criticism* (Ann Arbor: University of Michigan Press, 1995), 31–32.

7 Charles Armitage Brown, *Life of John Keats*, ed. Dorothy Hyde Bodurtha and Willard Bissell Pope (London: Oxford University Press, 1937). A slightly more accurate text from the same ms. is in *KC* 2.52–97.

8 MacGillivray, *Bibliography*, liv–lv.

9 My explanation of Keats's "canonical complexity" draws on my more detailed discussions: "Multiple Readers, Multiple Texts, Multiple Keats," and the last two chapters of *Reading "The Eve of St. Agnes": The Multiples of Complex Literary Transaction*.

10 David Harlan, "Intellectual History and the Return of Literature," *American Historical Review* 94 (1989), 598. Harlan draws on, among others, Frank Kermode and Wolfgang Iser, but his own definition is clearer and more comprehensive than what he quotes from them.

11 For the first 125 years of criticism, see Harvey T. Lyon, *Keats' Well-Read Urn: An Introduction to Literary Method* (New York: Henry Holt, 1958), and for 1820–1980, see Jack W. Rhodes, *Keats's Major Odes: An Annotated Bibliography of the Criticism* (Westport, Conn.: Greenwood Press, 1984).

12 In *Reading "The Eve of St. Agnes,"* chapter 3, I expound fifty-nine different ways of interpreting the poem, a token of a theoretically infinite number of possible readings.

13 See his letters to Bailey, 22 November 1817 (*KL* 1.185); to his brothers, late December 1817 (1.194); to Reynolds, 9 April 1818 (1.266); to Woodhouse, 27 October 1818 (1.388); to George and Georgiana, 24 October 1818 (1.403, 404) and 31 December 1818 (2.19); to Fanny Brawne, February (?)1820 (2.263).

14 As Stuart Sperry remarks, the Great Odes seem "by nature ideally suited to the kind of close analysis that was the radical innovation of the New Criticism" (*Keats the Poet*, 242).

15 The papers of the MLA session were collected by its chair, Susan J. Wolfson, for a forum in *Studies in Romanticism* (1986). See Daniel Watkins, *Keats's Poetry and the Politics of the Imagination* (1989), Nicholas Roe, *John Keats and the Culture of Dissent* (1997), and the essays Roe edited in *Keats and History* (1994).

17

SUSAN J. WOLFSON

Bibliography and further reading

Editions

The Poems of John Keats, ed. Jack Stillinger, Cambridge: Harvard University Press, 1978. Scrupulously assembled; complete textual notes.

The Poems of Keats, ed. Miriam Allott. London: Longman, 1970. Very useful notes, including sources and allusions, and generous references to relevant letters.

John Keats: The Complete Poems, ed. John Barnard. Harmondsworth, Penguin, 1973. Reliable texts, extensive notes, Keats's marginalia to *Paradise Lost*, his review of Edmund Kean's *Richard III*.

John Keats, ed. Elizabeth Cook. New York and Oxford: Oxford University Press, 1990. Includes most of the letters, marginalia to Shakespeare Folio and *Paradise Lost*, and his review of Kean.

The Letters of John Keats, 1814–1821, ed. Hyder E. Rollins, 2 vols. Cambridge: Harvard University Press, 1958. The standard edition.

The Letters of John Keats, ed. Robert Gittings. Oxford: Oxford University Press, 1970, 1979. The best paperback selection, with some corrections of Rollins.

Facsimiles

Poems (1817), *Endymion* (1818), and *Lamia, Isabella, The Eve of St. Agnes & c* (1819). Oxford: Woodstock Press, 1989–91, with introductions by the editor, Jonathan Wordsworth.

John Keats: Poetry Manuscripts at Harvard: A Facsimile Edition, ed. Jack Stillinger. Cambridge: Harvard University Press, 1990. Photographs, elegantly interpreted; an introduction by Helen Vendler.

Jack Stillinger presents a wealth of material across the seven volumes of *The Manuscripts of the Younger Romantics: A Facsimile Edition, with Scholarly Introductions, Bibliographical Descriptions, and Annotations*, ed. Donald H. Reiman. New York: Garland Press, 1985–89.

The Odes of Keats & Their Earliest Known Manuscripts in Facsimile, ed. Robert Gittings. Ohio: Kent State University Press, 1970. Some dispute about "earliest," but the photographs are worthy.

Chief biographies (chronological)

Milnes, Richard Monckton. *Life, Letters, and Literary Remains, of John Keats.* 2 vols. London: Edward Moxon, 1848; rpt. one-volume Everyman. London: Dent; New York: Dutton, 1969.

Colvin, Sidney. *John Keats: His Life and Poetry His Friends Critics and After-Fame.* London: Macmillan, 1917.

Lowell, Amy. *John Keats.* 2 vols. Boston: Houghton Mifflin, 1925.

Bate, Walter Jackson. *John Keats.* Cambridge: Harvard University Press, 1963.

Ward, Aileen. *John Keats: The Making of a Poet.* New York: Viking, 1963.

Bush, Douglas. *John Keats: His Life and Writings.* New York: Collier, 1966.

Gittings, Robert. *John Keats.* London: Heinemann, 1968.

Marquess, William Henry. *Lives of the Poet: The First Century of Keats Biography.* University Park: Pennsylvania State University Press, 1985.

Clark, Tom. *Junkets on a Sad Planet.* Santa Rosa, Calif.: Black Sparrow Press, 1994. A poetic biography.

Coote, Stephen. *John Keats, A Life.* London: Hodder, 1995.

Motion, Andrew. *Keats.* New York: Farrar, Straus and Giroux, 1997.

Lifetime reviews, early reception, rise to fame

Keats: The Critical Heritage (KCH), ed. G. M. Matthews. New York: Barnes and Noble, 1971.

Blackwood's Edinburgh Magazine 3 (August 1818), 519–24. "On the Cockney School of Poetry. No IV." Signed "Z."; *KCH* 97–110.

[Conder, Josiah]. On *Poems* (1817). *Eclectic Review*, 2nd ser. 8 (September 1817), 267–75; *KCH* 63–70.

[Croker, John Wilson]. On *Endymion. Quarterly Review* 19 (April 1818, pub. Sept.), 204–8; *KCH* 110–16.

The Romantics Reviewed: Contemporary Reviews of British Romantic Writers, ed. Donald Reiman. Part C: *Shelley, Keats, and London Radical Writers.* New York and London: Garland Press, 1972.

Ford, George H. *Keats and the Victorians: A Study of His Influence and Rise to Fame 1821–1895.* New Haven: Yale University Press, 1944.

References and bibliographies (chronological)

The Keats Circle, ed. Hyder E. Rollins. 2nd edn. 2 vols. Cambridge: Harvard University Press, 1965.

Stillinger, Jack. "John Keats," *The English Romantic Poets: A Review of Research and Criticism*, 4th edn, ed. Frank Jordan; New York: Modern Language Association, 1985, 665–718. See also Clarence D. Thorpe and David Perkins, "Keats," 3rd edn. (1972), 379–448.

Pollard, David, ed. *A KWIC Concordance to the Letters of John Keats.* East Sussex: Geraldson Imprints, 1989. "Key Words in Context" coordinated to Rollins.

Evert, Walter H. and Jack W. Rhodes. *Approaches to Teaching Keats's Poetry.* New York: Modern Language Association, 1991. Essays, bibliography, and other resources.

Kucich, Greg. "John Keats," in *Literature of the Romantic Period: A Bibliographic Guide*, ed. Michael O'Neill. Oxford: Clarendon Press, 1998. 143–66.

Critical studies

Barnard, John. *John Keats*. Cambridge: Cambridge University Press, 1987.

Bennett, Andrew. *Keats, Narrative and Audience: The Posthumous Life of Writing*. Cambridge: Cambridge University Press, 1994.

Bewell, Alan. "The Political Implication of Keats's Classicist Aesthetics," *Studies in Romanticism* 25 (1986), 221–30.

Bloom, Harold, "Keats and the Embarrassments of Poetic Tradition," *The Ringers in the Tower: Studies in Romantic Tradition*. Chicago: University of Chicago Press, 1971, 71–98.

Bostetter, Edward E. "Keats," *The Romantic Ventriloquists*. 1963; Seattle: University of Washington Press, 1975, 136–80.

Brooks, Cleanth. "Keats's Sylvan Historian: History Without Footnotes" (1944); *The Well Wrought Urn: Studies in the Structure of Poetry* (1947). New York: Harcourt Brace Jovanovich, 1975, 151–66. Exemplary, nuanced New-Critical reading.

Bromwich, David. "Keats," *Hazlitt: The Mind of a Critic*. New York: Oxford University Press, 1983, 362–401.

"Keats's Radicalism," *Studies in Romanticism* 25 (1986), 197–210.

Cox, Jeffrey. *Poetry and Politics in the Cockney School: Keats, Shelley, Hunt and their Circle*. Cambridge: Cambridge University Press, 1998.

Curran, Stuart. *Poetic Form and British Romanticism*. New York: Oxford University Press, 1986.

de Almeida, Hermione. *Romantic Medicine and John Keats*. New York: Oxford University Press, 1991.

ed. *Critical Essays on John Keats*. Boston: G. K. Hall, 1990.

de Man, Paul. Introduction. *John Keats: Selected Poetry*. New York: New American Library, 1966.

Dickstein, Morris. *Keats and His Poetry: A Study in Development*. Chicago: University of Chicago Press, 1971.

"Keats and Politics," *Studies in Romanticism* 25 (1986), 175–181.

Ende, Stuart. *Keats and the Sublime*. New Haven: Yale University Press, 1976.

Fry, P. "History, Existence and 'To Autumn,'" *Studies in Romanticism* 25 (1986), 211–19.

Gittings, Robert. *The Mask of Keats*. Cambridge: Harvard University Press, 1956.

Hartman, Geoffrey. "Poem and Ideology: A Study of Keats's 'To Autumn'" (1973); *The Fate of Reading*. Chicago: University of Chicago Press, 1975, 57–73.

"Spectral Symbolism and Authorial Self in Keats's *Hyperion*" (1974), rpt. *Fate*, 124–46.

Hirst, Wolf Z. *John Keats* Boston: Twayne, 1981.

Homans, Margaret. "Keats Reading Women, Women Reading Keats," *Studies in Romanticism* 29 (1990), 341–70.

Jones, John. *John Keats's Dream of Truth*. London: Chatto and Windus, 1969.

Kandl, John. "Private Lyrics in the Public Sphere: Leigh Hunt's *Examiner* and the Construction of a Public 'John Keats,'" *KSJ* 44 (1995), 84–101.

Keach, William. "Cockney Couplets: Keats and the Politics of Style," *Studies in Romanticism* 24 (1986), 182–96.

Kelley, Theresa M. "Keats, Ekphrasis, and History," Roe, ed., 212–37.

"Poetics and the Politics of Reception: Keats's 'La Belle Dame sans Merci,'" *ELH* 54 (1987), 333–62.

Kern, Robert. "Keats and the Problem of Romance," *Philological Quarterly* 58 (1979), 171–91.

Kucich, Greg. *Keats, Shelley, and Romantic Spenserianism.* University Park: Pennsylvania State University Press, 1991.

"Keats's Literary Tradition and the Politics of Historiographic Invention," Roe, ed., 238–61.

Lau, Beth. *Keats's Reading of the Romantic Poets.* Ann Arbor: University of Michigan Press, 1991.

Levinson, Marjorie. "The Dependent Fragment: 'Hyperion' and 'The Fall of Hyperion,' *The Romantic Fragment Poem: A Critique of a Form.* Chapel Hill: University of North Carolina Press, 1986, 167–87.

Keats's Life of Allegory: The Origins of a Style. New York: Basil Blackwell, 1988.

Luke, David, "Keats's Letters: Fragments of an Aesthetic of Fragments," *Genre* 2 (1978), 209–26.

McGann, Jerome J. "Keats and the Historical Method in Literary Criticism" (1979); *The Beauty of Inflections: Literary Investigations in Historical Method & Theory* (1985). Oxford: Clarendon Press, 1988, 9–65.

Mellor, Anne. "Keats and the Vale of Soul-Making," in *English Romantic Irony.* Cambridge: Harvard University Press, 1980, 77–108.

Romanticism & Gender. New York: Routledge, 1992, 171–86.

Newey, Vincent. "Keats, History, and the Poets," Roe, ed., 165–93.

Perkins, David. *The Quest for Permanence: The Symbolism of Wordsworth, Shelley, and Keats.* Cambridge: Harvard University Press, 1959. Chapters 7–9, 190–301.

Rajan, Tilottama. *Dark Interpreter: The Discourse of Romanticism.* Ithaca: Cornell University Press, 1980. Chapters on the late romances and the *Hyperion* poems.

Ricks, Christopher. *Keats and Embarrassment.* London: Oxford University Press, 1976.

Roe, Nicholas. *John Keats and the Culture of Dissent.* Oxford: Clarendon Press, 1997.

ed. *Keats and History.* Cambridge: Cambridge University Press, 1994. Essays by S. Wolfson, M. Aske, J. Barnard, D. Watkins, K. Everest, T. Hoagwood, M. O'Neill, V. Newey, N. Roe, T. Kelley, G. Kucich, N. Trott, J. Kerrigan.

Ryan, Robert. *Keats, the Religious Sense.* Princeton: Princeton University Press, 1976.

and Ronald Sharp, eds. *The Persistence of Poetry: Bicentennial Essays on Keats.* Amherst: University of Massachusetts Press, 1998. Essays by J. Stillinger, M. H. Abrams, W. J. Bate, A. Ward, R. Sharp, E. Boland, S. Wolfson, D. H. Reiman, E. Jones, D. Lee, T. Hoagwood, H. de Almeida, D. Bromwich, G. Steiner, P. Levine.

Rzepka, Charles J. "Keats: Watcher and Witness," *The Self as Mind: Vision and Identity in Wordsworth, Coleridge, Keats.* Cambridge: Harvard University Press, 1986, 165–242.

Scott, Grant F. *The Sculpted Word: Keats, Ekphrasis, and the Visual Arts*. Hanover: University Press of New Hampshire, 1994.

Sharp, Ronald. *Keats, Skepticism, and the Religion of Beauty*. Athens: University of Georgia Press, 1979.

Sheats, Paul. "Keats, the Greater Ode, and the Trial of Imagination," *Coleridge, Keats, and the Imagination: Romanticism and Adam's Dream*. Columbia: University of Missouri Press, 1990, 174–200.

"Stylistic Discipline in *The Fall of Hyperion*," *KSJ* 17 (1968), 75–88.

Sperry, Stuart M. *Keats the Poet*. Princeton: Princeton University Press, 1973.

Stewart, Garrett. "*Lamia* and the Language of Metamorphosis," *Studies in Romanticism* 15 (1976), 3–41.

Stillinger, Jack. "*The Hoodwinking of Madeline*" *and Other Essays on Keats's Poems*. Urbana: University of Illinois Press, 1971. The title essay, controversial at the time, is now canonical.

"Keats and Coleridge," *Coleridge, Keats, and the Imagination: Romanticism and Adam's Dream*. Columbia: University of Missouri Press, 1990, 7–28.

"Keats and His Helpers: The Multiple Authorship of *Isabella*," *Multiple Authorship and the Myth of Solitary Genius*. New York: Oxford University Press, 1991, 25–49.

"Multiple Readers, Multiple Texts, Multiple Keats," *Journal of English and Germanic Philology* 96 (1997), 545–66.

Reading "The Eve of St. Agnes": The Multiples of Complex Literary Transaction. New York: Oxford University Press, 1999.

"Reading Keats's Plots," de Almeida, ed., 88–102.

"Wordsworth and Keats," *The Age of William Wordsworth*, ed. Kenneth R. Johnston and Gene W. Ruoff. New Brunswick: Rutgers University Press, 1987, 173–95.

Swann, Karen. "Harassing the Muse," *Romanticism and Feminism*, ed. Anne K. Mellor. Bloomington: Indiana University Press, 1988, 81–92. On *La Belle Dame*.

"The Strange Time of Reading," *European Romantic Review* 9 (1998), 275–82.

Trilling, Lionel. Introduction to *The Selected Letters* (1951); rpt. "The Poet as Hero: Keats in His Letters," *The Opposing Self*. New York: Viking Press, 1955, 3–49.

Trott, Nicola. "Keats and the Prison House of History," Roe, ed., 262–79.

Vendler, Helen. *The Odes of John Keats*. Cambridge: Harvard University Press, 1983.

Vogler, Thomas, *Preludes to Vision: The Epic Venture*. Berkeley: University of California Press, 1971. On the *Hyperion* poems.

Waldoff, Leon. *Keats and the Silent Work of Imagination*. Urbana: University of Illinois Press, 1985.

Walker, Carol Kyros. *Walking North With Keats*. New Haven: Yale University Press, 1992. The tour with Brown; beautiful photographs, letters rewardingly annotated, includes the poems composed.

Wasserman, Earl R. *The Finer Tone: Keats' Major Poems*. Baltimore: Johns Hopkins University Press, 1953.

Watkins, Daniel P., *Keats's Poetry and the Politics of the Imagination*. Madison: Farleigh Dickinson University Press, 1989.

Wolfson, Susan J. "Feminizing Keats," de Almeida, ed., 317–56.

Formal Charges: The Shaping of Poetry in British Romanticism. Stanford: Stanford University Press, 1997.

"Keats and the Manhood of the Poet," *European Romantic Review* 6 (1995), 1–37.

"Keats Enters History: Autopsy, *Adonais*, and the Fame of Keats," Roe, ed., 17–45.

"Keats the Letter-Writer: Epistolary Poetics," *Romanticism Past and Present* 6 (1982), 43–61.

The Questioning Presence: Wordsworth, Keats, and the Interrogative Mode in Romantic Poetry. Ithaca: Cornell University Press, 1986.

ed. *Keats and Politics: A Forum. Studies in Romanticism* 25 (1986).

INDEX

Notes: general topics, Keats's poems, volumes, and ideas are listed alphabetically. Other works are listed under author. Not indexed: chronology, bibliography, "Further reading" lists, merely passing references to proper names and places.